Fields of the Lord

Fields of the Lord

Animism, Christian Minorities, and
State Development in Indonesia

LORRAINE V. ARAGON

University of Hawai'i Press
Honolulu

©2000 University of Hawai'i Press
All rights reserved
Printed in the United States of America
05 04 03 02 01 00 5 4 3 2 1

Library of Congress Cataloging-in-Publication Data

Aragon, Lorraine V., 1954–
  Fields of the Lord: animism, Christian minorities, and state
  development in Indonesia / Lorraine V. Aragon
    p. cm.
  Includes bibliographical references and index.
  ISBN 0–8248–2171–8 (cloth: alk. paper).—
  ISBN 0–8248–2303–6 (pbk. alk. paper)
  1. Sulawesi Tengah (Indonesia)—Church history. 2. Sulawesi
  Tengah (Indonesia)—Religion—20th century. 3. Christianity
  and culture—Indonesia—Sulawesi Tengah—History—20th century.
  I. Title.
    BR1221.S84 A73 2000
    275.98'4082—dc21
                                              99–058189
                                                   CIP

University of Hawai'i Press books are printed on acid-free
paper and meet the guidelines for permanence and
durability of the Council on Library Resources.

Printed by The Maple-Vail Book Manufacturing Group

Contents

Acknowledgments

As others such as Keeler (1987) have noted, our Western custom of saying "thank you" is somewhat jejune and inimical to Indonesian perspectives. Debts of significance cannot be released with a few fluffy words floated for a moment in the air. Gifts require continuation of the exchange process, not its cessation through attempted compensation. Obligations are a state of being and a means to create relations anew. So my thanks to thousands of acquaintances in Central Sulawesi are both due in the greatest measure and yet also inevitably trivial, especially because our relationships are not based in written communications. I hope someday the words of this book will have more meaning in Central Sulawesi, but for now I just say, *Lentora rahi kai ompi' ompi' omea dipo tahi'*, "I greatly miss all my siblings across the sea."

In Sulawesi I was moved by the personal sacrifices, and in the best cases friendship, of dozens of missionaries, especially Klazien Ter Veen, Pieter Ter Veen, and Cynthia White Dalziel. That many names of contemporary individuals in this book are pseudonyms is not intended to deprive individuals of credit for their actions or views, but rather to guard their confidentiality and protect sensitive materials from misinterpretations, including my own. I hope some of these courageous missionaries and local Christians will write their own versions of this history. Real names are used only for historical figures and in a few cases where I refer to prominent Sulawesi citizens.

Beginning in 1984, my research in Indonesia has been sponsored by the University of Illinois, the National Science Foundation, the Fulbright-Hays Foundation, the Indonesian Institute of Science (Lembaga Ilmu Penelitian Indonesia), Tadulako University, the Association for Asian Studies and the Luce Foundation, the Wenner-Gren Foundation for Anthropological Research, and the University of Michigan Center for South and Southeast Asian Studies. In the Netherlands I received assistance from the late J. Noorduyn at the Royal Institute for Linguistics and Ethnology (Koninklijk Instituut voor Taal-, Land- en Volkenkunde) and from the Henrik Kraemer Institute. To all these institutions, committees, and individuals I am most indebted.

Earlier versions of some or all of this book were read by two anonymous reviewers, Ken George, Angelia Graf, Calvin Mercer, Richard O'Connor, and James C. Scott. I owe thanks to them as well as to Pamela Kelley of University of Hawai'i Press and Susan Biggs Corrado for pushing me to a stronger and shorter text. I also would like to thank Pat Guyette at East Carolina University's interlibrary loan service as well as Annette Uhlenberg and Elizabeth E. Grant for their efforts in locating unusual sources.

For many years the following people have been significant mentors, colleagues, and friends as well as voices on a page: Greg Acciaioli, Kathleen Adams, John Bort, Bob Bunger, Clark Cunningham, Bill Davenport, Nancy Eberhardt, Cindy Ferré, Lindsay French, Barbara Garrity-Blake, Ken George, Chris Golus, Angelia Graf, David Griffith, Maarten van de Guchte, Nina Kammerer, Rita Kipp, Stuart Kirsch, F. K. Lehman, Masyhuda Masyhuddin, Holly Mathews, Jennifer Nourse, Richard O'Connor, Eliza Reilly, Anna Rice, Susan Rodgers, Sue Russell, Mahir Saul, Pat Symonds, Nikki Tannenbaum, Keith Taylor, Paul M. Taylor, Isabel Terry, Jim Watson, G. G. Weix, Lucy Whalley, Miko Yamamoto, and Tom Zuidema. Without these persons' friendship or commentaries, my work would be poorer than it is.

I also would like to acknowledge the importance of Dr. Maarten W. Elink Schuurman to the 1986–1989 fieldwork on which this book is largely based. Although Maarten's time with me in the highlands was relatively brief, he gave unselfishly of his medical services and held a position among male elders that I could never assume.

Finally, I offer thanks to my husband, Dale Hutchinson, and our son, William Hutchinson. For years Dale encouraged me (goaded me, really) to finish this book when, as far as I could tell, few cared. By contrast, Will made everything else in life all right because he didn't care if I finished my work or not—as long as I played with him. Reflections of their love, poetry, and intelligent questions find their way into my writing's better moments.

Some brief segments of this book have been published previously. I thank the editors and publishers of the articles listed below (of which I am the sole author) for permission to include sections from:

Twisting the gift: Translating precolonial into colonial exchanges in Central Sulawesi, Indonesia. *American Ethnologist* (1996) 23(1):43–60.

Reorganizing the cosmology: The reinterpretation of deities and religious practice by Protestants in Central Sulawesi. *Journal of Southeast Asian Studies* (1996) 27(2):350–373.

Suppressed and revised performances: *Raego'* songs of Central Sulawesi, Indonesia. *Ethnomusicology* (1996) 40(3):413–439.

All photographs in this book are by the author unless otherwise noted.

Note on Language and Orthography

The Tobaku people of Central Sulawesi speak a dialect of an Austronesian language called Uma, which is also referred to as Koro or Pipikoro. Uma was first transcribed by S. J. Esser (1964), with colonial Dutch spelling, and more recently by Summer Institute of Linguistics missionaries, with contemporary Indonesian orthography. Although some Malay (now Indonesian) borrowings occur, Uma is in most respects more similar to ergative Philippine languages, as indeed Sulawesi's proximity to those islands might suggest.

The initial Uma terms in a series are followed by the designation "Uma," while Indonesian terms are followed by "Ind." when clarification is needed. Unless otherwise specified, the Uma language terms presented are in the Tobaku dialect. My transcription of Uma also follows the orthographic conventions of modern Indonesian. As in Indonesian, the Uma "r" is a dental trill and most vowels approximate Italian. "Ng" is always as in English "singer," and "c" is as in English "ch." Peculiar to Uma, the "w" is a bilabial fricative (closer to an English "v" or "b" than a "w"), and within certain morphemes "h" and certain stops are pre-nasalized. Sequential vowels are enunciated individually, not as diphthongs. All syllables end in vowels or glottal stops, which are represented by an apostrophe ('). Word stress occurs on the penultimate syllable of the root, but, unlike in Indonesian, this is not affected by affixations. Martens (1988a) discusses Uma phonology in greater detail. Martens (1988b, 1988c, 1988d), as well as Martens and

Martens (1988), describes Uma morphology and syntax. As in Indonesian, Uma nouns usually are not marked for plural forms. Hence nouns such as *pue'* can be translated as "owner" or "owners."

Introduction

In the Indonesian capital of Jakarta on November 22, 1998, twenty-two churches and five Protestant and Catholic schools were burned and looted following a bloody clash between Christian Ambonese security guards from an amusement park and local Muslim residents of the Ketapang neighborhood. What seemingly began as a routine dispute over gambling escalated into ethnically and religiously motivated attacks spurred by rumors of the vandalization of a nearby mosque. Fourteen people were killed, some burned to death in the buildings set on fire by Muslim mobs, others brutally stabbed with kitchen knives, bamboo sticks, and metal spikes. The Muslim rioters targeted Christian churches of various denominations, including the Salvation Army (Bala Keselamatan, Ind.), a subject of this book. Jakarta, like Indonesia as a whole, is predominantly Muslim and is also mainly Javanese or Sundanese, the ethnic groups native to the island of Java.

In explicit retaliation for the Ketapang incident, six mosques and twenty-three Muslim homes were burned or vandalized on November 30, 1998, in Kupang, the provincial capital of the Christian-majority province of West Timor. These reciprocal acts of violence, which occurred over a thousand miles apart, were linked by media reports, common social tensions, and the incidents' oppositional demographic contexts: attacks on Christians in a primarily Muslim area were redressed by attacks on Muslims in a primarily Christian area. In both cases, the members of the different religious groups also were members of different ethnic groups originating from distant islands of the Indonesian archipelago.

Within a week of the West Timor incident, a Catholic church was burned down in Ujung Pandang, a Muslim stronghold and the largest city in the province of South Sulawesi. In the days following Christmas 1998, more Muslim-Christian street fights, arson, and church vandalism broke out in Poso, the largest Christian city in the province of Central Sulawesi, the setting for the research project described here. The events were described by local observers in Internet reports as a horrifying "flood of blood" (*banjir darah*, Ind.). Further incidents of religious violence between Christians and Muslims ensued during the following months in predominantly Christian Ambon, West Kalimantan, and elsewhere in the archipelago.

Indonesia is a nation of entangled tensions. Long-sublimated economic, political, ethnic, and religious frictions have escalated enormously following the general Asian financial crisis of 1997. Indonesia's economic turmoil and the related political outbursts and riots of May 1998 culminated in the resignation of President Suharto on May 21, after thirty-two years of authoritarian rule known as the "New Order." Incidents of social unrest continued, and religio-ethnic violence escalated distinctly after rule was turned over to President Suharto's confidante, B. J. Habibie. Many of the sporadic, anti-Christian, neighborhood attacks in Java and elsewhere were aimed at ethnic Chinese in a generalized anger over their superior financial position. People of Chinese descent comprise only 3 percent of the population but are said to control 80 percent of the private-sector commerce. Not all Chinese merchants are wealthy, but some are immensely so. Attacks on people of Chinese ancestry in the 1990s echoed the mid-1960s "anti-Communist" rampages that killed between half a million and two million Indonesian citizens.

Although many Chinese in Indonesia are Christians, the Ketapang and Ujung Pandang incidents revealed a public anger not only against wealthy Chinese, but also against all Christians and

Map of Indonesian archipelago. Drawn by Susan Brannock-Gaul.

minority ethnic groups. The West Timor, Poso, Ambon, and West Kalimantan incidents exposed the reciprocal nature of Muslim-Christian resentment. Such rancor was held in check by the military and social policies of President Suharto and his predecessor, President Sukarno, yet their development programs erstwhile kindled the continuing friction.

While this book does not focus specifically on Muslim-Christian tensions in Indonesia, its analysis of twentieth-century mission fields in Central Sulawesi reconstructs certain foundations for those tensions. The colonial and postcolonial events described here fostered social conditions underlying many of the ethnic and religious problems that now must be addressed by Indonesia's future leaders and the international community. "Religion" in Indonesia long has been defined by state authorities in terms of economic development. Simultaneously, national development in Indonesia has been presented through the rhetoric of religion, from the Dutch colonial era up until the present, thereby inserting a moral and religious charge to programs of "modernization" that have unevenly affected different ethnic populations.

The main focus of this book is religious change among the highland communities of western Central Sulawesi. These groups dwell far from roads, electricity, and other urban amenities of the "modernizing" and densely populated nation that is Indonesia. Their mobile, dry-rice farming communities are atypical in one other respect: they are

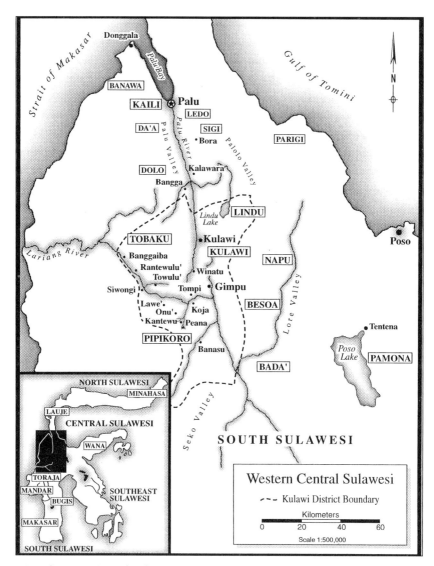

Map of western Central Sulawesi. Drawn by Susan Brannock-Gaul

fiercely Protestant in a nation that is 87 percent Muslim. Their religion, a legacy of Dutch colonial rule, represents for them a set of spiritual and cultural ties to the modern, global world. Yet their local version of Protestantism often places them at odds not only with the

Muslim majority, but also with the Western missionaries who work uneasily with the Indonesian government to perpetuate their "modernization."

My research examines the century-long dialogue concerning religion and appropriate behavior that began in western Central Sulawesi when foreign states demanded adherence to "religion" from interior communities who had their own spiritual ideas and practices but no formalized concept of religion apart from the remainder of their social and moral life. This case of Christian conversion, what I call reconciled religions, elucidates certain dialectical processes of social stratification involved in the cross-cultural transfers commonly classified under the term "globalization." A basic point about religion made here is that, at least among contemporary groups, religions—as ideas, practices, and identities—must be studied and explained in relation to one another. The theoretical aim of this book is to delineate the set of social processes introduced by missionaries, intentionally or unintentionally, that transformed Central Sulawesi religion. Conversely, I trace the social processes of response that have allowed Central Sulawesi people to appropriate and divert certain missionary messages and practices. While pursuing these goals, I define and address features of religious life in ways not covered in most texts on religion.

In the United States, we now take the official separation of church and state for granted and hardly notice the "free market" in religious enthusiasm that it creates. Yet the American separation of church and state began only in the nineteenth century, and official state religions have a longer history in Europe and Asia. In contemporary Indonesia, a particular religion is neither nationally mandated, as it is in Muslim states such as Malaysia or Catholic states such as Spain, nor is it free of state interference. Rather, beginning with independent Indonesia's Constitution of 1945, citizens have been expected to have a world religion (*agama*) and choose from a government-created list of official religions. The result, in a nation of hundreds of different ethnic groups with backgrounds in hundreds of different spiritual traditions, is anxiety over conforming to state regulations, conflict among religious groups vying for government and popular favor, and creative interpretation of local spiritual practices to align them with government classifications (Geertz 1973b [1964]; Kipp and Rodgers 1987).

Even earnest interpretations of local ideologies to suit world religions bring on inevitable failures to resolve the requirements of both local and foreign systems—as a tale from my fieldwork in Central Sulawesi can illustrate. A local Salvation Army officer, Major Isa', reported that many guests from a wedding we had just attended were stricken with violent attacks of vomiting and diarrhea. I suspected rancid pork meat, but Major Isa' said most villagers thought the epidemic was triggered by ancestral anger. The bridal couple, he explained, had not asked their parents' permission to depart the village where the last wedding rite was held. Knowing the importance of such ritual politeness to parents and hosts, I wondered aloud why the couple had been so lax in their manners. "Because their parents are dead!" Major Isa' exclaimed, expressing both exasperation with his congregation and solace in our mutual understanding of the congregation's theological predicament. According to the Christian doctrine introduced by European missionaries, ritual obligations between children and parents end with death. For Tobaku individuals, however, such relationships continue with consequences in perpetuity. Misfortune struck an entire community because the bridal couple failed to make a small ritual gesture of respect that had been obliterated by the Protestant ceremony.

Such local interpretations of events have led outsiders to question the depth and legitimacy of Christian practice in Southeast Asian regions such as Central Sulawesi. Yet the foreign missionaries' own extraordinary efforts, along with almost a century of incentives by both colonial and postcolonial states, have fostered an adamant local devotion to Protestantism in conjunction with such seeming anomalies of theological interpretation and practice. Tobaku highlanders do not think that their veneration of the Protestant God and Jesus absolves them of their moral obligations to the dead. The Bible, moreover, does not specify that it should. Herein lies a predicament that exposes the fault lines between religion, politics, and culture, entities that necessarily overlap, although many believers do not think they do or should.

Protestantism, like many world religions, tends to erect nearly impossible standards of perfection before its followers. Yet recent converts are confronted with additional hurdles. If Tobaku highlanders view themselves as faithful Christians and the Bible does not contradict their religious views, why do outsiders require further behavioral conversion? Where do Asians have room to negotiate between their ancestral cosmologies and the Christian religion that many first adopted under colonial pressures? Why has the Indonesian state depended so heavily on church programs to advance its program of economic development, yet also defied church policies through the elevation of precolonial "animist" performances? What are the regional origins of the Muslim-Christian tensions that erupt now as a seemingly national phenomenon? And finally, where in these contrapuntal processes of church- and state-driven cultural change do the intrinsically spiritual concerns of individuals and communities exist apart from their political context?

Some of the answers I propose for these questions concern contradictions that haunt the association of missionization and colonialism throughout the world. While colonialists use religious and moral training to bring converts closer to their own moral universe, they simultaneously must maintain or even create a more isolated economic, ethnic, and political universe for the converted. Moreover, the physical and social landscape to which any "world" religion is introduced can never accommodate it unscathed. No introduced and parochial vision of religious orthodoxy can ever surmount the cultural pragmatism of local interpretation and ritual practice. Tenets of ancestral or "animistic" religions entail environmental relationships and local concepts of personhood, not just epistemological mistakes.

This book presents an ecological and social landscape through which world religion was spread from a European center to a colonized periphery of the world. It scrutinizes the religious facet of transnationalism that has occurred for millennia, although it now often is overshadowed by concerns with the expansion of market economies and electronic technologies. Indeed, religious proselytization, often accompanied by the expansion of trade and state polities, was among the earliest elements of what we now call globalization.

The popular concept of globalization presumes an overflow or spread of ideas, objects, and practices from one political entity to another. Yet the frequent use of the term as if it were a kind of expansive cloning often obscures concentrations of wealth, social marginalization processes, and the permeable nature of cultural layering, where ideas or other technologies do not move neatly as intact units from one community to another. Much contemporary talk of globalization, in common with other vulgar discourses about hegemonic power, also tends to skip lightly over the institutional strata and processes that mediate between international pressures and individuals' experiences. This book concentrates on those layers and processes.

When discussing my research on Sulawesi Christianity over the years with those who would listen, I have been struck by two simplifying patterns of response. Social scientists or secular humanists often express the view that, as emissaries of colonial or imperialist states, missionaries have irreparably violated or degraded indigenous peoples' cultures. This thought follows an "acculturation" perspective that formerly was more prevalent in social science thought. A grant I applied for some years ago was denied when a reviewer concluded that I proposed to study the rituals of "a dead culture." All too often, missionized groups have been conceived as having lost their "authentic" culture.

The second response I encounter, sometimes but not always from devout Christians, suggests that the Indonesian individuals I describe are "not really Christians," or just "nominal Christians." Central Sulawesi people are viewed as basically still animists altered only by a patina of conversion rhetoric. Often the same people argue for a combination of these seemingly incompatible views. They first suggest that Central Sulawesi people have "lost their culture" under Western influence (acculturation) but then further argue that such people remain animists—as if it were impossible for them to likewise "lose their religion." Thus religion often is viewed as essentialistic in nature even when the cultures that support it are not. Yet religions, as facets of learned culture, are not impermeable.

Tannenbaum (1995) argues that Western scholars often unquestioningly assume Buddhism as the foundation of mainland Southeast Asian values. Analogously, I suspect that many too easily rebuff the idea that Christianity has become a significant foundation of values in Asian societies. Part of the problem again lies with the common assumption that there is some core or essential form of Christianity (or any religion for that matter) that stands apart from all realizations of religion through particular communities and their changing interactions with other groups (Bowen 1993, 330; Saunders 1988). I argue that Central Sulawesi highlanders, who converted generations ago, are not deficient Christians but simply distinctive ones, somewhat comparable to my independent Baptist neighbors in North Carolina.

The research presented here is an anthropological contribution to theories of religious change in "modernizing" states, colonial and postcolonial history, Indonesian or Southeast Asian ethnography, and comparative religion. While I hope that these several areas of scholarship will create an interested audience for the volume, my teaching experience suggests that individuals are most drawn to readings that directly touch their own lives. Therefore, a book exploring an alternate realization of what, for most readers of English, is a familiar religion— no matter whether personally sacred or rejected—may hold a compelling significance. Perhaps immediate personal responses concerning the nature of Christianity will help surmount the distance of reading about a faraway group of people living without roads, electricity, or television in a tropical island rainforest.

Presentation of Chapters

Chapter 1 introduces the research and sets out my approach to Central Sulawesi Christianity and its relationship with state programs for "modernization." I consider definitions and theories of religion in light of changing group relationships, the boundaries between "religion" and other aspects of culture, the mediation of institutions, and the fluctuation of meanings through cross-cultural transmission. I examine the relationship of Central Sulawesi Christianity to uneven economic development and various perspectives on paganism, modernity, and primitivism.

Chapter 2 is an ethnographic sketch of the Tobaku and other Kulawi District highlanders in Central Sulawesi. My discussions of settlement patterns and land use connect the localization of pre-Christian deities with the ecology and practicalities of survival in the highlands. I also examine some ways the Protestant missions, Dutch colonial regime, and Indonesian governments endeavored to subsume and alter villages, farming techniques, gender roles, and family patterns as they incited a combination of religious and economic changes.

Chapter 3 presents a regional view of precolonial Tobaku history, describing early migrations and "founders' cults" as a method of political leadership formation among shifting horticulturists. I discuss the mobility of highland peoples and their extensive trade and tribute relations with lowland polities. I then focus on the prickly alliance between A. C. Kruyt's Protestant mission and the colonial government that advanced their sometimes common, sometimes separate aims. This relationship began Indonesia's attempted homogenization of religion and regional development in Central Sulawesi.

Chapter 4 concerns the history of the Salvation Army—how they pursued their mission goals in western Central Sulawesi through gifts, education, and medical outreach programs. Narratives by early European missionaries reveal both mixed results and some misunderstandings of indigenous spiritual concepts. I argue that Europeans subverted the reciprocity of established highland-lowland trade relation-ships as a means to catalyze the process of missionization and colonial submission. I also describe how the Japanese occupation, postwar rebellions, and early postcolonial government fostered the appropria-tion of Protestantism in highland Central Sulawesi.

Chapter 5 examines how Europeans apprehended and manipu-lated what they could observe of western Central Sulawesi cosmology. This section includes a close scrutiny of precolonial notions of "tradi-tion" (*adat*), deities, ancestors, soul elements, and divine justice or theodicy. Throughout, I focus on how early European comprehension of local theology affected subsequent formulations of Sulawesi Christianity. Ending with diverse local narratives that explain responsi-bility for a disastrous village fire, I illustrate the shifting process of debate that forges an indigenized world religion.

Chapter 6 moves from abstract cosmology to the social engage-ments of rituals that fulfill obligations to living and dead while solving the practical problems of a unified natural world. Here the dialogue between highlanders and church leaders was, and still is, based upon animal sacrifices. I outline precolonial calendrical and life-cycle ritu-als, weaving in their abolishments, curtailments, and cooptations as seen in the 1980s and 1990s. Then I examine how the performative force of ancestral sacrifices and vows has been inserted into generic forms of Protestant services without a loss in efficacy of sacrificial acts. Three specific cases document how atonement for transgressions resulting in misfortunes such as illness is managed through Salvation Army "statement of thanks" services.

Chapter 7 is an examination of how Central Sulawesi high-landers seek to persuade the unseen forces through ritual speech and song genres such as vows, prayers, church testimonials, indigenous songs, and Protestant hymns. I particularly explore a genre of ritual songs called *raego'* that accompanied most precolonial ceremonial events. Although Christian missionaries have sought to eliminate the *raego'* song genre, the New Order government's political interests in "regional arts" created a panoply of *raego'* song types and new usages for religious and cultural presentations. As in the Dutch colonial period, the development aims of church and postcolonial state collide as well as cooperate.

Chapter 8 returns to an analysis of the interaction of contemporary Central Sulawesi Christianity—in its ever more heterogeneous forms—and New Order economic development in Indonesia. Village "leadership" programs, health care, family planning, women's religious organizations, and transmigration all have propelled religious groups to compete for status as they implemented government goals. This proposed transformation of domestic life, moreover, has been spread through the rhetoric of religious authority. I conclude by examining local interpretations of the national philosophy of *Pancasila*, (five principles) and the fragile relationships of Indonesia's Christian and Muslim neighbors who compete to define valid "religion."

Chapter 9 presents the conclusions of this study about the interactive nature of religions, the ability of groups to define differentially the nature and acts of religion, and the means by which religion and development have mutually defined each other in Central Sulawesi throughout the past century. I summarize the specific processes employed by foreigners to achieve religious conversion in Central Sulawesi, and conversely the social responses that allowed highlanders to make a foreign religion theirs to keep.

Before and After Religion

Nine years ago The [Salvation] Army was unknown in Celebes [now called Sulawesi]—an island of the Dutch East Indies—but now, amid the native grandeur of wild and rugged scenery, the music of flute Bands re-echoes the old Salvation tunes which are so familiar to most persons in the British Isles.

The Salvation of Jesus Christ has been received with open hearts by the semi-barbaric people who inhabit the island, and numerous Outposts have been established, where the needs of soul and body are supplied by loving, patient, sacrificing European Officers.

Salvation Army, "Salvation amid Semi-Barbarism"

I n 1909 the Netherlands Indies government awarded the Kulawi District of Central Sulawesi as a mission "field" to the Salvation Army Church (Gereja Bala Keselamatan, Ind., or BK), an offshoot of Methodism created in London during the 1860s. This transfer of authority, and similar parceling of Indies geographical units containing potential Christian souls, was motivated by European ambitions of an integrated religious and behavioral metamorphosis that would legiti-mate colonial rule. Pagan Asians could and should be altered into modern Christian citizens of the Dutch Empire. This book examines these efforts at human metamorphosis and the complicated aftermath of this Procrustean endeavor.

My research, begun in 1984, is based on the words and actions of Central Sulawesi people and the foreign missionaries who have bid highlanders to alter their spiritual ideas and everyday behaviors. I carry out this work as a U.S. anthropologist of European Protestant heritage with irresolute faith in the human institutions of religion. My interest is in how the spirit-"owned" rice fields (*bonea*, Uma) of Central Sulawesi montagnards became the mission fields of expatriate Europeans (*zendingsveld*, Dutch) and the targeted fields of develop-ment (*lapangan pembangunan*, Ind.) for consecutive ruling states.

13

One aim of this book is to explore the distinctive theology and
"culture of Protestantism" in Central Sulawesi as it developed in counterpoint to colonial teachings and subsequent historical and political
contexts. The self-proclaimed "fanatic" Christianity of western Central
Sulawesi is based on philosophical premises and ecological realities that
are unfamiliar to most Western Protestants. Although by any fair-handed
analysis Central Sulawesi Protestantism is equally "Christian" as contemporary Western sects, it is distinguished by several ritual and ideological features. The religion's conceptual union of deity and humanity
within the order of a greater natural world, and its ritual emphasis on
efficacious sacrifices and bargains with God, are aspects that disengage it
from much contemporary Western Protestant practice.

Religions do not exist apart from shifting social and political contexts, so this research examines the cultural patterns that fell by the
wayside or were transmuted during and after the initial missionization
process. Central Sulawesi settlement designs, founders' cults, territorial horizons, domestic relations, health care, gender roles, and
appraisals of familiar and foreign material goods were transformed radically during the twentieth century. These efforts at "modernization"
began during the Dutch era but continued during the succeeding
regimes as states aimed to make the "unorganized" peoples of the interior more sedentary and "legible" (Scott 1998, 2); that is, more comprehensible and more easily managed. This study thus also concerns
Protestantism in its role as a tool of state intervention, but a tool that
could not be fully controlled.

Before the century's end, the Protestant missions and Dutch
colonial government were replaced by an independent Indonesian
state that worked, still in the name of God, to alter the domestic
households and economies of Central Sulawesi highlanders. To borrow Indonesian words employed commonly in the rhetoric of
President Suharto's New Order regime (1965–1998), the topic of my
research is the shift from "before religion" (*sebelum agama*) to "after
religion" (*sesudah agama*) in the western Central Sulawesi high-

lands. These Indonesian images of the historical replacement of "no religion" (Europe's paganism) with a "true religion" (one of five world religions designated by the Indonesian government) originate from colonial definitions of "religion" and the fantasized disjunction between an ancient microcosmic past and the modern macrocosmic present. Indonesia's postcolonial governments, like the colonial Dutch, locate Central Sulawesi highlanders barely at the doorstep of modern citizenship yet plan to carry them over the threshold as quickly as possible, with religion as the handmaiden of social change.

Late nineteenth century Spencerian ideas about social evolution and the march of human progress have been refuted by more recent perspectives in evolutionary biology (Diamond 1999; Mayr 1982, 1991) as well as social science (Comaroff 1994). Yet crude visions of evolution were introduced forcefully into Indonesia by European officials and missionaries, including A. C. Kruyt, the Protestant pioneer to Central Sulawesi (K. J. Brouwer 1951, 26–27; Gouda 1995). Kruyt maintained that by teaching Central Sulawesi highlanders Protestant religion and improved agricultural methods, he was taking them "out of the Stone Age" (A. C. Kruyt 1924, 40). Kruyt argued that their conservative pre-Christian beliefs blocked social progress, which only could be introduced effectively following conversion (A. C. Kruyt 1935/1936). Such teachings about religion and modernity were absorbed into both Indonesian church and state dialogues, where they continue to play themselves out in missionary rationales, state policies, and popular culture.

Despite their many common views and aims, the modernizing projects of Protestant churches and Dutch or Indonesian states periodically have clashed over resource priorities and permissible behaviors, such as the Indonesian ritual performances now termed "regional art" (*kesenian daerah*, Ind.). With data on ancestral ritual performances in Central Sulawesi, I examine the troubled Indonesian boundaries between what have come to be considered "religious traditions" (*adat agama*) and "ordinary (secular) traditions" (*adat biasa*). I also explore how the oral and monistic nature of precolonial Sulawesi cosmology has become reconciled with the written and dualistic aspects of state-based Protestantism. These demarcations interosculate with conflicting twentieth-century images of modernity and state development that have perfused the Indonesian archipelago.

My study of Christianity in western Central Sulawesi is little concerned with asking why highlanders converted. There were numerous compelling reasons to adopt Protestantism. I focus more on their conversion as a long-term relationship whose dynamic began not with the state and missionary messages, but instead with the local listeners' interpretations and responses (Gadamer 1975; Burghart 1996). Christian conversion was essentially the major bridge of an interethnic colonial relationship. Yet the actions of Western missionaries and those of Central Sulawesi highlanders often were piloted by different spiritual and political forces whose invisibility to the other was inexplicable as well as frustrating.

In light of missionaries' reactions to the discrepancies between Western and Sulawesi Protestant practice, I have been drawn to explore certain missionaries' attempted protection of a gift—a religion of salvation—and the impossibility of fully controlling such an ideological gift while giving it. Victorian Europeans and even more recent visitors have considered Protestantism as a kind of "inalienable wealth" (Weiner 1985) over which they could retain authority. In fact, even foreign missionaries' personal visions of orthodoxy have been subject to unanticipated comprehension and creative interpretations of new normative forms. In some situations indigenous spiritual content has been inserted into Protestant ritual forms. In others Christian theology has meshed neatly with local cosmology or existing ritual practice. A major concern of this book is the relationship of Sulawesi and missionary messages, their recurrent mismatch of categorical references, and the uneasy resolutions of practice that often uphold an untenable notion of "pure" Christian orthodoxy.

Theorizing Reconciled Religions

> If we have learned anything about the study of religion in the past century, it is that questions of truth and fiction are largely irrelevant. Every person holds his or her religion to be true.
>
> *Mark R. Woodward*, Islam in Java

Theories of comparative religion, as opposed to descriptions or valorizations of particular religions, are barely over a hundred years old. The late nineteenth century works of F. Max Müller (1872) and E. B. Tylor (1903 [1871]) are credited with initiating European efforts to develop a "science of religion" as a human phenomenon (Pals 1996, 3). Numerous scholars since then have endeavored to define religion either substantively—what it includes and means—or functionally— what it does socially. Yet definitions by their very nature can be only more or less useful, never true (Berger 1969, 176). Moreover, English is a difficult language with which to define religion because our words—supernatural, spiritual, sacred, magic, and belief—tend to lock us into assumptions that we need to avoid in order to do good comparative analyses. Even the general concept of religion as a particular set of doctrines upheld by a bounded community, which originated from the earlier *religio* (Latin), meaning "piety" or "religiousness," is a recent European notion that dates only to the seventeenth century (Hick, in Smith 1978, vii). Some keen observers (Asad 1983; Hick 1989; Smith 1978) of the traps in which conventional definitions of religion and magic have caught us (e.g., Wallace 1967) rebel against the potentiality of definitions altogether, but my efforts here are to keep definitions broad enough to encompass very dissimilar religious experiences worldwide.

For breadth and parsimony I appreciate Frazer's early characterization of religion as peoples' "conciliation of the superhuman powers" (Frazer 1924 [1890], 51). His phrase requires expansion to mention peoples' cosmologies and the institutionalization of morally binding ideals and ritual practices (Bell 1997; Geertz 1983). Yet it is useful to begin defining religion broadly as *a socially organized system of ideas, morally inflected relationships, and ritualized actions that concern powerful unseen entities.* Such a general definition can accommodate diverse practices associated with small-scale and world religions, as well as the recent phenomena of "civil religions" in authoritarian states (Bellah 1970; Coleman 1970; Purdy 1982; Reynolds 1977; here, chapter 8).

Frazer's work on the origins of religion now is thoroughly discredited for its intellectualist and social evolutionary perspectives (e.g., Tambiah 1991). Yet Frazer's cursory definition advances the encompassing terms "conciliation," which implies both interaction and respect, and "powers," which leaves spiritual entities undefined beyond the matter of potency. His definition thus avoids problematic terms used in studies of religion such as "supernatural," "sacred," "belief," and "god," which incline scholars to impose conventional categories from familiar religions, such as European Protestantism, to less familiar religions such as that of precolonial Central Sulawesi.

Following Aristotle, most people of European heritage conceive a clear distinction between natural and supernatural phenomena. The Tobaku people of Central Sulawesi, like many other people of the world, do not (Durkheim 1915; Evans-Pritchard 1937, 80–83). For them, everything is equally "natural," but differences in the knowledge and potency of different entities at different times account for what we might consider "supernatural" beings or events. Moreover, Westerners tend to see humans as apart from and above the remainder of nature while Central Sulawesi people envision their status and well-being as a piece with the other elements of the natural world.

Geertz's focus on shared symbols and meaning (1968, 1973a) drew broader dimensions of culture and ritual into the study of religion. Although his programmatic essays were criticized as inattentive to political factors (Asad 1983), the entire corpus of his work is not (Kipp and Rodgers 1987, 29). Recent theorists have argued for a more systematic focus on political stratification and the performative features of ritual practices (Asad 1996; Bell 1997; Comaroff 1985; Ortner

1989). Yet there is still some theoretical work to be done, especially with regard to broadly comparative definitions and processes of religious change that occur in both ideology and institutions. As social scientists, we need to shed preconceptions of religious life based on the most familiar world religions of state societies and reformulate our concepts to encompass worldwide phenomena of piety that are grounded in distinctive ecological and social environments.

Evolutionary narratives continue to haunt analysts as they debate whether the forces of modernity have brought religion to its death (Gauchet 1997), its resurrection (Lawrence 1989), or both. Such studies tread near the dangerous path of teleology, as recent religious movements become cast as evolutionary endpoints rather than moments in still-flowing time. Moreover, as Comaroff (1994) has argued, the widespread concept of religion as a personal, intellectually based faith itself developed through the political process of modernization.

I suggest that religions be considered as human information systems that apprise members about three domains of knowledge and related practice. The first domain is the nature of deity or invisible forces, including their character, manifestations, and behaviors toward each other and the living. The second domain is the channels of ritual communication between the unseen powers and the human community. These acts of communication may include prayer, song, poetry, choreographed movements, oaths, offerings, blood sacrifices, rising smoke, meditation, fasting, pilgrimages, trances, and so forth. The third domain of religion concerns how humans should behave among themselves to keep the deities satisfied or the forces of the universe in balance. This domain includes what we term "morality," but it also may include social hierarchies, legal codes, calendrical taboos, gender roles, dress codes, and even ideological values of conservatism or progress. One advantage of viewing religious life according to this model is that no specific behavior is precategorized as outside religion. Rather, those boundaries become an empirical question.

This basic three-dimensional substantive definition of religion allows for heuristic comparisons between practices that are elaborated differently or truncated in particular domains; in this case, between European Protestantism, Central Sulawesi precolonial religion, and contemporary Central Sulawesi Protestantism. The European Protestantism introduced in Central Sulawesi was elaborate in its descriptions of deities' characters, whereas the indigenous religion was less specific in that regard. The precolonial religion, by contrast, was more elaborate than Protestantism in its ritual methods to contact and communicate with deity. Both were elaborate in their prescriptions for proper human behavior, but differentially so. These facets of the two religions craved resolution in Central Sulawesi Christianity.

My more specific contribution to religious theory is to define the distinctive social and ideological processes by which the religion of one group has been constructed or modified through relationships with other population groups. As Sperber (1996, 25–26) notes, cultural "representations are transformed almost every time they are transmitted, and remain stable only in certain limiting cases." This book concerns the transformations of the transmissions, what has become the communicative reconciliation of European Protestantism and indigenous Central Sulawesi religions. This transformation unsettles synchronic views of religious orthodoxy and diachronic views of "natural" religious evolution or "conversion" by demonstrating religious polysemy, the process whereby groups with common religious identities make diverse interpretations of identical events or texts.

Some recent studies of missionization have taken a linguistic focus, linking the process of Christianization with European "print-capitalism" (Anderson 1991 [1983], 40; Rafael 1993); Steedly 1996; Thune 1990). Such works demonstrate that within the communicative process of missionization the religious "signifiers" (words and other symbols) often do not encode common meanings or "signifieds" (Saussure 1974). My approach to shifting religions acknowledges another linguistic concept termed "duality of patterning" (Hockett 1958, 1977), whereby elements that comprise structure at one level—

say, a unit of sound or a Protestant ritual format—can be combined variously and carry multiple meanings at another level—say, that of meaningful words or theological interpretations. These principles allow us to better account for religious meanings that shift from one group and time to another.

The contemporary study of religions warrants a return to Weber's comparative historicism, a method to pit inherited ideas against pressing cultural circumstances (Bourdieu 1977; Sahlins 1981, 1985). It also requires Weber and Durkheim's focus on institutions as key intermediaries between vaguely specified hegemonic powers such as the global economy or the state, and individual agents. Thus the following chapters explore highland farming methods and leadership institutions, the relations between Protestant missions and Dutch colonial representatives, the economics of Salvation Army officership, and women's religious organizations of the New Order. Considering such institutions and their relationships allows us to connect the perspectives and actions of individuals to broader social constraints. It allows us to recognize religion's important role in providing "worldly benefits" (Reader and Tanabe 1998) and "magical experiences" (Glucklich 1997), as well as sometimes providing a hope for salvation in another life.

At the book's conclusion, the fundamental processes of religious reconciliations in Central Sulawesi will be set forth. Missionaries redefined the criteria for valid religion while introducing European cultural management and modernization policies as religious doctrines. Missionaries intervened in regional trade patterns and routinely designated Sulawesi highlanders' spiritual concerns as a matter of antiquated technology. These events occurred as state and mission authorities reclassified deities, introduced surrogate rituals, rerouted communications with transformed deities, conflated the rhetoric of spiritual practice and economic development, and placed religious doctrines under the authority of political ones. Central Sulawesi communities responded by interpreting the recorded motives of a Mediterranean God as a defense of local morality. Highlanders maintained vows and animal sacrifices as critical to the effectiveness of Protestant prayers, and Salvation Army officers assumed comparable economic and ritual roles to the precolonial shamans. Negotiations continue regarding what precolonial behaviors are acceptable either as local Christian practice or as ancestral custom. World religions involve inherited traditions and institutions, yet communities' wishes to have them address the practical human problems found in particular ecological and social environments, or "fields," require their reality to remain in potential flux.

Missionization in the Framework of Uneven Development

Minority religious practices such as Christianity are related to ethnic pluralism and uneven national development in post-independence Indonesia. Christian churches are "minority" religions both because ethnic minority populations follow them and because they are minor religions in a Muslim-majority state. Local versions of Christianity are attuned to the spiritual and political interests of interior minority groups as they confront government aims of monotheism and escalated economic development in the peripheral islands of Indonesia.

Most families living in Central Sulawesi's Kulawi District attend church regularly, sponsor church-supervised rites, wear Western-style clothes, send their children to government-approved schools, pay taxes, and purchase clinic medicines. In 1994 the Indonesian government, which rules the largest population of Muslims in the world, stamped a terminal exit visa for the last foreign Salvation Army missionary who was assigned to duty in the archipelago. This much-loved "angel of the forest" (*malaikat hutan*, Ind.) departed for her home in England amid both stifled tears and warm words of encouragement for the Salvation Army's future in Central Sulawesi.

With the complete indigenization of Salvation Army staff in Indonesia, one century's cycle of foreign "civilizing" influence was

This government billboard, erected in the lowland province capital of Palu, features a waving highland couple in ritual dress. It reads, "Become, City of Palu. Aspire to be beautiful, peaceful, safe, and comfortable," 1986.

completed, yet new cycles of missionization spearheaded by other churches in different Central Sulawesi locations were just beginning. Missionization began a twentieth-century process of sedentarization, "deterritorialization" (Appadurai 1990; 1992, 192–194), and "hierarchic inclusion" (Kuipers 1998) where Europeans rearranged the political and physical layout of Central Sulawesi territories, spurring both permanent agricultural settlements and the migration of locals throughout expanded regional horizons. Missionaries implemented the rearrangement of the domestic household to suit both European cultural mores and national development aims.

The Indonesian government still admits some foreign missionaries to Central Sulawesi and other outer-island peripheries, but they are channeled to "more backward" (*terbelakang*, Ind.), more "tribal" places where similar dreams of behavioral transformation and modernization can be initiated anew. Gradually, a mosaic of missionized ethnic minorities in the Indonesian hinterlands resolves itself in relation to what government officials term "more advanced" (*lebih maju*, Ind.), usually Muslim, societies in proximity to urban markets and coastal ports such as Palu. This has been a government policy of economic expansion and enforced nationalism as much as a policy of selective religious intervention.

Like the Dutch administration that preceded it, President Suharto's post-1965 New Order government found Christian missionaries invaluable to its efforts to implement national development programs among outer-island minorities. Western missionaries have facilitated government aims such as creating nuclear family households, defining individual economic responsibilities, increasing ties to the national and global economies, introducing biomedicine, and expanding school attendance. Missionaries also promote the acceptance of national regulations, the use of money, government rhetoric concerning the benefits of progress, and regional record keeping. In turn, missionization often has protected Christian groups from threatening forms of government intrusion such as direct military supervision or relocation out of their ancestral homelands.

Christianity in the western Central Sulawesi highlands—indeed, in the Indonesian nation—has been akin to a weighted pole carried skillfully by tightrope walkers. Minority groups carried their Christianity as a sign of modernity and compliance with government religious codes, yet they carried it modestly so as not to impugn the Muslim majority. The Indonesian government utilized Christian missions as a tool to implement basic economic development programs in its most intransigent peripheries. The government also used the weight of non-Muslim minorities to balance itself against reformist Muslim groups who periodically threatened New Order power by agitating for a Muslim state.

It is doubtful that the New Order government wanted further to empower or enlarge Christian minorities with their ties to foreign, for-

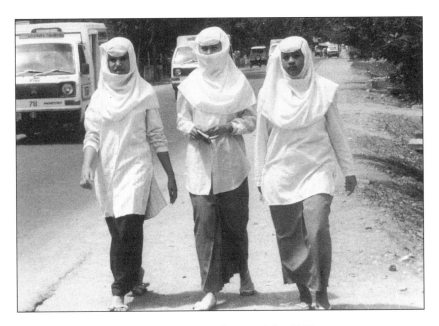

Muslim girls wearing parochial school uniforms in Palu, 1987.

merly colonialist, nations overseas. Rather, it needed help in opening the remaining frontiers. Once security, airfields, roads, schools, domesticated villages, and clinics were established, the foreigners' task was done and government officials assumed charge. As George (1996, 27) notes, the homelands of highland minorities often appear as blank spaces on Indonesian government ethnic maps. Foreign missionaries (and perhaps ethnologists) have been received to pave new roads (sometimes physical roads, but also local "information highways") into these obscure human places in preparation for further government assessment and capitalist expansion.

Highlanders also use Christianity as a means to consolidate their historically fragmented political ties. Protestantism provides them with distant connections to foreign development agencies, allowing them to preclude many disruptive Indonesian government programs aimed at "isolated ethnic minorities." Christianity provides a focus of difference around which to consolidate their regional alliances apart from the

Muslim Malay majority of the nation. Like any good tightrope walker, highland Christians balance their religious rhetoric carefully to keep themselves from falling into the extremes of isolated religious marginality or national ethnic absorption. In this respect, the practices of Central Sulawesi Protestants stand as an interesting comparison to fundamentalist sects in other parts of the world, including the United States, where world religion texts are interpreted selectively and vociferously to lend support to minority sociopolitical concerns (Ammerman 1991; Aragon n.d.; D. Martin 1994; Peacock and Tyson 1989).

It is not surprising perhaps that Central Sulawesi Christians have maintained a measure of cultural and spiritual diversity despite the homogenizing aims of the states and missions that oversee them. It is more interesting that they manage to assert their absolute conformity while simultaneously creating a new set of localized norms. The case I present thus contrasts in both political and doctrinal outcome with the South African case of missionization described by the Comaroffs (1986, 1991), where Protestant theology lends weight to conscious acts of protest and rebellion. Central Sulawesi highlanders do not use Christian teachings to challenge their overseers. Rather, they defend their overseers' orthodoxy, even when it is being ineffably transformed. This makes the Central Sulawesi case differ substantively from many "new religious movements" or fundamentalist revivals worldwide where groups adopt new religions that aid them with unprecedented social pressures (Ackerman and Lee 1988; Antoun and Hegland 1987; Poewe 1994).

The communities of Tobaku people with whom I work converted their religious affiliation in the 1920s and 1930s. Therefore, most early converts were members of a generation prior to the one with which I am most concerned. Moreover, as others including Kipp (1995) and Hefner (1993a) have noted well, conversion may be less significant for its proximate psychological or political motivations than for its ideological and social consequences in the long run. Relative to many other newly converted populations in Central Sulawesi such as

A Tobaku Salvation Army minister blesses his congregation during Sunday services in Lawe', 1989.

certain communities of Wana, Da'a, and Lauje, the Tobaku and other Kulawi District groups I describe are "old" Christians. Although Christianity's central orthodoxies are steeped in Mediterranean and European origins, its more recent congregations—especially in Asia— now represent likely directions and major growth areas for Protestantism in the twenty-first century. The theology and practices described in this book therefore represent a living Christianity not only of the European and Asian past, but also of their present and future.

Fanatic Christians

"We are fanatic Christians (*Kristen fanatik*, Ind.)." Many Tobaku highlanders zealously uttered those words in 1986 when I entered their rainforest homeland ensconced in a horseback caravan of Protestant missionaries and medical personnel. Given the context of our introduction, however, I initially questioned the autonomy and earnestness of the claim. Yet I heard the phrase repeatedly through three and a half years of fieldwork in Central Sulawesi. By the time of my departure in 1989, I came to understand that this expression of fanaticism embraced not only a heartfelt commitment to Salvation Army Protestantism, but also a distinctive body of local theology and practice set amid the shifting ethnic and national allegiances of New Order Indonesia.

Some Tobaku people talk about their practices in the period "before religion" (*sebelum agama,* Ind.) with apparent shame, reinforcing the missionary view that the pre-Christian era was a "dark" (*gelap*) period, marred by evil actions such as headhunting, polygamy, and human sacrifices. This self-denigrating stance, however, often coexists with a rosy view of precolonial history that recalls a golden age when dry rice harvests were plentiful, game was abundant, theft never occurred, and shamans could cure all illnesses (cf. Keane 1995). Some highlanders meld these contrasting views by suggesting that their ancestors flourished because they were "really" Protestant all along; they just awaited the arrival of the missionaries to enlighten them on some additional theological matters. Such shifting visions suggest a dissonance between their current identification with Christianity and their assessment of its worldly blessings.

Precolonial religion in the Central Sulawesi highlands could be characterized as a form of animism, "the belief that natural beings possess their own spiritual principles and that it is therefore possible for humans to establish with these entities personal relations of a certain kind—relations of protection, seduction, hostility, alliance, or exchange of services" (Descola 1992, 114; Bird-David 1999). In Central Sulawesi, these relationships concerned spirits tied to natural phenomena and ancestors who usually were conceived generically as a group rather than as emanations of specific deceased individuals.

In Sulawesi, animistic deities and the souls of dead relatives are not "supernatural," but fully within a unified matrix of the cosmos. Thus shamans or their contemporary manifestations as Salvation Army ministers are not priests of the "supernatural," but rather mediators among different natural realms who help keep the world in a balance favorable to their human community (Abram 1996, 8–15). Additionally, the spiritual entities of animists are not simply perceptual or scientific mistakes (Guthrie 1993), but representations of differing perspectives on the social boundaries of personhood and relationships (Bird-David 1999). Understanding these fundamental differences in philosophical perspective and their realization through clerical institutions is critical to an accurate assessment of Central Sulawesi Protestantism.

Dramatic twentieth-century political upheavals transferred Central Sulawesi highland groups from regional sovereignty to Dutch colonial subjects to Japanese hostages to fugitives from rebel Muslims to their present status as peripheral ethnic minorities in the Java-centered nation of Indonesia. Anthropological writings on religious transitions in Indonesia occurring since the 1960s have described minority peoples' reassessments of their own cosmologies in response to the political promotion of foreign religions. These discussions demonstrate that Indonesian ethnic minorities facing such external confrontations evaluate the extent to which aspects of their ancestral religions parallel features of foreign religions such as Christianity or Islam, and then draw on rhetoric from the world religions to justify and expand their own cosmological ideas (Atkinson 1983; Hoskins 1987a; Keane 1995; Schiller 1997; Tsing 1987; Weinstock 1987). By contrast, Tobaku people often assume that their religious practices are identical, at least ideally, to the practices of Western Protestants.

The extent of Tobaku identification with Western Protestantism was first illustrated to me when Major and Mrs. Isa' asked with curiosity, and some evidence of slighted feelings, why they had not been invited to the three-day and seven-day mortuary rites of an American missionary who died in their area. The Central Sulawesi minister and his wife were bewildered when they heard from me that Americans do not hold three-day, seven-day, or any other extended series of mortuary ceremonies. Although many Tobaku customs have been altered to become acceptable to missionary doctrines, Western Christian concepts and practices also are envisioned to match, or in some cases justify, Tobaku ancestral customs. Such theological negotiations invariably are presented as debates with misguided individuals or ambiguous particulars of normative practice, never as contests with the churches, much less "their" Protestant God.

Central Sulawesi highlanders have transposed and relabeled their pre-Christian deities to conform to missionary-supplied categories such as God, Jesus, the Holy Spirit, and Satan. Precolonial rules associated with the spiritual "owner(s) of the land" (*pue' tana'*, Uma) and important ancestor spirits are now conceived as the will of God. Violators of the ancestral rules and their Protestant reformulations are threatened with the punishments of Satan. Yet "hell" (*neraka*, Ind.; no Uma gloss exists) for most Central Sulawesi highlanders generally is not conceived as distant in space or time. Rather, retribution for one's bad behavior is anticipated at any moment: in the death of a loved one, the failure of a harvest, a dreaded illness. To borrow the vocabulary of Indian religions, karma is expected to appear in this life, soon, rather than in some future incarnation. The present and the afterlife, like both the precolonial deities and God, are part and parcel of a seamless, natural world. That this world is now Christian, blessed and enlightened by the gospel of Jesus Christ and his disciples, does not alter the fundamental principles of the universe.

A Christmas ritual in the Kulawi District, said to be of European origin, illustrates how the elaboration of indigenous founder concepts has transfigured concepts of physical territory into claims of Christian spiritual jurisdiction. All Salvation Army services held just prior to Christmas include a "tree-lighting rite" (*acara pohon terang*, Ind.), where an Indonesian translation of the hymn "Silent Night" (*Malam Kudus*, Ind.) is sung over and over again at a very slow tempo by the entire congregation. During the hymn, the minister in charge hands lighted candles to high-ranking individuals who then proceed in sequence to light candles on the Christmas tree at the church altar. Everyone knows that the order in which people are asked to participate represents their current status in the community. The first person asked, most likely the village headman, lights the highest candle on the tree, the second person asked lights the next candle, and so forth downward, symbolizing the hierarchy.

When I first participated in this ceremony in 1986, I was struck by its implications in a relatively egalitarian religious community and inquired about the ritual's history. I was told it was created by the pioneering missionaries but then was assumed so wholeheartedly by local villagers that a recent attempt to displace the service was met with hostile reactions. Reportedly, a visiting minister came to preach at this same village near Christmas day in the late 1970s. He found the repetition of "Silent Night" at every service very monotonous and the hierarchical display of candle lighting "unchristian." He designed a Christmas service without these two elements and afterward found himself the recipient of angry protests and a request that he never again return to that community.

The way the candle-lighting ceremony is structured and the intense response to its attempted ouster suggest an analysis that can be associated with ancestor spirit or founder cult phenomena. Like the first Uma-speaking wanderers into the highlands who opened the first swidden fields, European missionaries "opened" the first Protestant services and thereby established an initial spiritual connection to the Christian God. These venerated missionary pioneers are now akin to the ancestor spirits insofar as their orally transmitted ritual contracts are sacrosanct, and each annual repetition replays and reconstructs the initial bargain between villagers and the Divine.

The sequential candle lighting may be seen as continuous with village and regional hierarchies established by Dutch colonial officers and missionaries (Kuipers 1998). Such blatant presentations of rigid hierarchy also have become naturalized by New Order government bureaucratization (Brenner 1998, 235; Pemberton 1994). The effort to excise the candle-lighting rites, therefore, was both blasphemous and politically treacherous. This European rite, transferred through missionary communication, was maintained in format yet transformed in substance through the union of its representations with indigenous priorities concerning community founders and New Order flow charts of power—of which the missionaries themselves unwittingly became a part.

The early European missionaries thus introduced biblical doctrines and their own cultural practices as a package, and the two often became indistinguishable within the new religion known as Christianity. Tobaku parents now take names for newborn babies from the Bible or adopt Javanese or European names with which they have become familiar. They also have created patrilineal last names, or "family names," a practice of political control decreed by Europeans. When my friend, Tina Abi', a teacher's wife, explained that the new naming practices were part of Christian religion (*agama Kristen*, Ind), I suggested that they might rather be a matter of European culture (*kebudayaan orang Belanda*). She did not see my point at all. For her, as for so many other Central Sulawesi highlanders, the behaviors introduced by Westerners were by definition Christian. Western religion and Western cultural practices never have been separable for the missionized. Indeed, only our recent restrictive European concept of religion as a delimited set of theological doctrines and practices implies some obvious and natural solution to the question of what behaviors are or are not elements of piety or religious identity.

This unification of ethnic and religious identities parallels the Southeast Asian view where conversion to Islam is identified with "entering Malay-ness" (*masuk Melayu*, Ind.). People who converted to Islam took on a host of foreign ethnic habits, such as new dress and dietary codes. Similarly, I examine how Europeans' politically related cultural habits were introduced in a package of words, ritual performances, and material objects often perceived by Central Sulawesi highlanders as inherently "Christian."

Visions of Primitives Awaiting Conversion

The whole island [Sulawesi] is noted for its mythical stories, legends and quaint customs, but to visit the middle part of the island is to step into a decade long past, where the unique and the antique are crudely combined. Here man is almost primitive, showing a certain wild innocence; God is unknown, and civilization, with all its advantages and curses, has scarcely cast its shadow.

Salvation Army Captain William Harris

The first time I set foot through the gates of the New Tribes Mission school compound near the Central Sulawesi capital of Palu, I was greeted by a hearty young American man who said, "Hi, I'm John Smith of the New Tribes Mission. We work with primitive people who have no religion." This outsider's judgment on highland Central Sulawesi peoples, expressed in the late 1980s, is centuries old but still pervasive among Western missionaries working abroad.

The usually optimistic Major Elizabeth Carron of the Salvation Army once said to me with evident despair, "These people are not very far from animism. They are still ruled by fear." A Dutch Reformed missionary, Mathilde van der Kers, claimed that Central Sulawesi villagers simply are practicing their "tribal beliefs" (*kepercayaan suku*, Ind.) under the guise of Protestantism. Indonesian clergy hailing from the more cosmopolitan areas of the archipelago such as Java, Bali, or Manado echoed similarly critical views of Central Sulawesi religion.

These pronouncements conform to Indonesian government policy which, according to Dutch colonial precedent, registers only certain "world religions" (*agama*) as legitimate. These state-authorized religions, which presently include Islam, Protestantism, Catholicism, Hinduism, and Buddhism, are distinguished sharply from the precontact "beliefs" or "superstitions" (*kepercayaan*) of Indonesian ethnic minorities. Although a few successful attempts have been made to register precolonial religions under the rubric of Hinduism (Schiller 1997; Volkman 1990; Weinstock 1981, 1987), most ancestral community religions and their adherents are at a political disadvantage in the Indonesian state.

Tobaku highlanders, however, converted to Protestant Christianity during the first half of the twentieth century. Thus their communities are not open to New Tribes missionaries whose programs and contracts with the Indonesian government are premised on such derogatory views of indigenous religions. Nor are most Tobaku communities presently slated for compulsory "local transmigration" or removal to the lowlands like some other highland populations who are defined by government officials as "isolated or estranged ethnic groups" (*suku terasing*) "who do not yet have a religion" (*yang belum beragama*).[1]

Nevertheless, Central Sulawesi highlanders still hear disparaging remarks about their "primitivism" and "tribalism" from outside visitors, including church and regional government officials. Like the Meratus of Kalimantan described by Tsing (1996), they are scolded for being "not yet organized" (*belum diatur*). That their Protestantism does not free the Tobaku from such criticisms indicates that their Christianity is not taken as seriously by others as it is by the Tobaku themselves. The denigrating calls for more rapid development in the region also imply that religious devotion is secondary to economic productivity in the eyes of government officials. They seek highlanders' complete sedentarization and incorporation into the maze of modern citizenry, of which world religion is just one notable element.

More than one civil servant working in the provincial capital of Palu marveled aloud at my willingness to enter the highland forests and live with the "headhunters" of the interior.[2] My interactions with both Indonesian government officials and foreign missionaries led me to understand that even long-converted Central Sulawesi highlanders such as the Tobaku are not credible to them as either proper Indonesian citizens or full-fledged Christians. Only the Tobaku seem to consider themselves steadfast Christians and compliant citizens, avid in their devotion to Salvation Army Protestantism and generally compliant with government demands.

The churches of most Tobaku villages are full every Sunday, and there is an infinite array of services led by local Salvation Army officers in the homes and farm shelters of congregation members—averaging more than one Protestant service per hamlet on every day of the year. Christian practice flourishes among the youth as well as the adults in highland Central Sulawesi even as many poorly attended churches have ceased to prosper in Europe. These circumstances suggest that although Western missionaries have had great influence on the cosmologies of colonized peoples in past centuries, these same marginal people in turn are affecting the overall global construction of Christian churches and practices, even if few are praising or publicizing it.

Although there are factions and leaders of both Catholic and Protestant churches who insist upon the absolutely incontrovertible nature of Christian doctrines and practices, this is a perspective that largely denies the evidence of nearly two thousand years of litigious church history. Missionization is not a one-way causal process any more than was the European project of colonialism and modernization of which it was an integral part (Stoler 1985; Sahlins 1994; van der Veer 1996). Both colonial and contemporary missionaries have had to grapple with their own canons of faith to suit their expatriate circumstances. Protestant missionaries in Central Sulawesi have been compelled to reinterpret their own deities, such as Satan, in order to incorporate and explain locals' images of malevolent ancestor and nature spirits. Some missionaries, then, may be pressed to define Central Sulawesi practices in a negative light to preserve a hold on their own orthodoxy, as they struggle far from home to define and communicate it.

Western Protestant missionaries working in Indonesia do not hold uniform views on either Christian orthodoxy or Central Sulawesi highlanders' degree of deviation from those diverse standards (Aragon 1992, 19–25). Rather, their individual views of Central Sulawesi Christianity often reflect personal concerns with immorality in the world and aspects of cultural dissonance or expatriate "culture shock" that are not easily resolved. Although I found myself sympathetic to many views on Tobaku Christianity expressed to me by both

Indonesians and Western missionaries, ultimately, I support Asian theologians like Chung Hyun Kyung when she argues that Western theologians do not retain a copyright on Christianity. Asians, she writes, are destined to ask themselves and their churches some tough questions, such as:

> Who *owns* Christianity? Is Christianity unchangeable? What makes Christianity Christian? How far can we make ourselves vulnerable in order to be both truly Asian and truly Christian? (Chung 1990, 113)[3]

Christian Tobaku, most of whom seldom read, write, or speak Indonesian (much less English) in their daily lives, do not pose these particular theological questions. Yet their Christianity, which builds upon centuries of veneration for ancestral and local nature spirits, is not just a Christian-coated style of animism, a *parvenu Protestantism*, as many missionaries have suggested. Rather, it is an indigenized Christianity built upon almost a century of conversation with national and international representatives of foreign religious orthodoxies. Central Sulawesi Protestantism rests upon a differing set of ecological and historical conditions that are interpreted through an oral society's firm faith in a unified cosmos. Their views, while generally not antithetical to Christian gospel, remain distinct from prominent Western translations and interpretations of that gospel. Contemporary cognitive science argues that Westerners' seemingly most abstract moral values also are inevitably enmeshed in cultural particulars and local events (Johnson 1993). Within any particular local orthodoxy, individuals' exact understandings and new applications of concepts may vary widely even when texts or precedents are fixed and referenced.

Some writers focusing on Christianization in colonized areas have suggested that the central anthropological issue is how an "orthodoxy interacts with, and is changed by, local religious belief and action" (Schneider and Lindenbaum 1987, 2). This statement suggests a perhaps overly monolithic view of orthodoxy, but it usefully shifts the study of religious conversion away from the earlier vision of outside foreign influences being followed by internal reactions of only local relevance. This perspective highlights local agency and the ability of converts to change imported orthodoxies, which is indeed what has happened to Christianity and all world religions throughout history.

That a cultural anthropologist in the 1990s should be troubled by the idea of ethnic minorities being referred to by missionaries or government officials as "without religion" or "primitive" is not surprising. My intent here, however, is not simply to inveigh against these categorizations, but also to examine the criteria and meanings of "Christianity," "orthodox," and "modern" as they have been claimed by, applied to, or withheld from peripheral Indonesian groups such as those in Central Sulawesi. To focus on what social and religious labels the highlanders have received from outside or claimed for themselves is to explore questions about the formulation of group allegiances and religious or ethnic affiliations. Such social, religious, and ethnic boundaries are changing rapidly among Indonesia's hundreds of ethnic minority groups (Kipp 1993). Moreover, in both the Dutch colonial and post-independence Indonesian states, these issues have been a critical matter of practical political concern, not merely questions of customary worship or personal identity.

Visions of the Modern

One of my [Dutch] teachers had said: Just a little while longer, just a little while, and people will no longer have to force their bones and squeeze out their sweat for so little result. Machines will replace all and every kind of work. People will have nothing to do except enjoy themselves. You are fortunate, indeed, my students, he said, to be able to witness the beginning of the modern era here in the Indies.

Modern! How quickly that word had surged forward and multiplied itself like bacteria throughout the world. . . . So allow me also to use this word, though I still don't fully understand its meaning.

Pramoedya Ananta Toer, This Earth of Mankind

Modernity is a subjective experience of achievement and a valorization of the new as much as it is a set of objective social and economic changes related to industrialization, capitalism, and bureaucracies (Brenner 1998; Osborne 1995; Turner 1990). Discussions among Central Sulawesi highlanders illustrate that their ideas about "modernity" often are associated with Christianity, which in turn is associated with foreigners. Highlanders assume that all Westerners are like the Protestant missionaries they know, a reasonable deduction given that missionaries represent virtually all the Westerners most highlanders ever encounter. Thus Westerners, who epitomize modernity, are envisioned as wealthy in material possessions and also as devout and proselytizing Protestants. These two images, wealth and fervent Christianity, have become closely associated in highlanders' minds, creating models for aspiration and emulation.

Few Central Sulawesi people ever have the opportunity to travel overseas, but I met an Indonesian Salvation Army officer who had been privileged to join a religious tour to visit the Salvation Army headquarters in London. Major Lou divulged that he had been shocked by what he saw in England. Before leaving Indonesia, he said, he assumed that all Westerners already were modern and hence Christian. During his travels, however, Major Lou saw that in the West, as in Central Sulawesi, there are many people "who do not yet have a religion" (*yang belum beragama*, Ind.). I marveled how the "do not" or "not anymore" of European agnostics and atheists had become the "not yet" (*belum*) of Indonesians who both anticipate developmental perfection and define modernity as requiring it. As political scientists have noted, Indonesia's process of nationalism has been characterized by its linkage with the concepts of modernity and economic development rather than citizens' common ethnicity or history (Cribb 1998).

This man's unsettling discovery was based on an innocence about worldwide religious devotion that has been cultivated by missionaries and the Indonesian government with a barrier of restricted information sources. What had been destroyed in this man's mind was not just his view of Westerners' uniformly devout Christianity but the entire connection, widely held by Sulawesi highlanders, that Christianity and modernity are inseparably linked. If some modern Westerners were not Christian, what did this say about highlanders and their path toward progress? If Christianity, or "world religion" in the government's broader view, was not a necessary ingredient to define modernity and national development, what was?

Influenced by Max Weber's writings (e.g., Weber 1930; Gerth and Mills 1958; Andreski 1983), Western social theorists of modernization often presume that this process entails increasing rationalization, secularization, and disenchantment with spiritual concerns. Just as Christian mysticism declined in the West subsequent to the successes of post-Enlightenment science, so modernization theorists have assumed that religion, especially its conservative spiritual and mystical aspects, would decline in other developing states. Recent rises in both fundamentalist and new sects in the West as well as in other world regions, however, have called such assumptions into question (Marty and Appleby 1991; Eickelman 1992.)

As Lawrence (1989, 2) argues well, fundamentalism in Christianity, as in any monotheistic religion, requires the material conditions of modernity to make its rejection an ideological possibility. Moreover, the stance of Indonesians who associate the very idea of modernity with world religions such as Islam and Christianity argues that broadly conceived Western concepts concerning the relationship of Christianity and "modernity" are overdue for revision. Once the subjective aspects of the concept of modernity are recognized, then it is easier to understand the alternate paths that different societies have taken in their approach to "new" models for contemporary life (Brenner 1998, 9–14; Comaroff 1994).

Weber's intellectual descendants, including Bellah (1964, 1965) and Geertz (1963), have distinguished world religions from traditional or community religions on the grounds of the former's greater doctrinal rationalization or "disenchantment," Weber's term that Gauchet (1997, 3) characterizes neatly as "the impoverishment of the reign of the invisible." Anthropological studies recently have challenged this division as prejudicial artifice (Comaroff 1994; Hefner 1993a, 14–18). World religions such as Christianity may be more accurately classified by their formalized written doctrines, organized clergy, definitions of membership, compartmentalization of worship contexts, and institutions of reproduction. The extent of any religion's "rationalization," "disenchantment," or interaction with the global "macrocosm" are empirical questions that do not necessarily exclude those faiths commonly defined as "traditional" or community-based religions. The ancestral religion of Japan, Shinto, has endured famously throughout Japan's twentieth-century industrialization process and integration with the global economy.

The study of Christian conversion and its ties to views of modernity also includes issues of state politics as they have unfolded in both the missionaries' home countries and their host domains (Kipp 1990; van der Veer 1996, 5–10). In many cases, Weberian ideas about rationality and personhood have been used by European missionaries and postcolonial administrations as tools to legitimate policies regarding religious and social transformations that were primarily of economic or administrative utility (Wiener 1995). Western discourses about superstition or barbaric practices justify social interventions. And conversion facilitates nationalistic schooling and economic retraining. The very recency of Protestant missions locates them and their progressivist efforts to tamper with the "private" domain of spiritual belief firmly within the modern sphere of European ideology (van Roorden 1996, 66).

When Sulawesi highlanders said I was from a modern world whereas they themselves were "backward" or "not yet modern" (*belum moderen*, Ind.), they generally referred to my possession of foreign-made goods, an unquestioned Christian heritage, and a presumed extensive knowledge of science and technology—possessions not characteristic of all members of our imagined modern Western world. The highlanders melded diverse images associated with Western capitalism and did not consider the importance of their own colonial past to the attainment of that mercantile venture (Sahlins 1994, 412–416).

Just as modernity has been conflated in Indonesia with possessions and Christianity, primitivism has been conflated in the West
with the absence of possessions and the existence of "paganism."
Tsing has written eloquently about how media attention to "primitive
people" is considered warranted only in cases of isolated "Stone Age"
throwbacks or hunter-gatherers who are characterized as our "contemporary ancestors" (Tsing 1993, ix–xi). By parallel logic, missionized ethnic groups such as the Tobaku, who are thereby "tampered
with," were generally of little interest to previous generations of
anthropologists or other scholars drawn to study the exotic. Such
Christian groups were considered too Westernized to be "authentic"
enough for interesting cultural study yet too un-Westernized to be
considered relevant to "modern" social issues, such as the rise of fundamentalist or evangelical religious practices in "developed" areas of
the world such as the United States. Their particular combination of
economic and religious development placed them betwixt and
between primitivism and modernity.

Yet Central Sulawesi highlanders are not only firmly linked to the
global economy—the coffee you drank this morning might well have
been grown in their gardens—they also practice a form of Christianity
that is no less "modern" than that of my rural North Carolina neighbors. Like these Southern Baptists, Central Sulawesi highlanders have
taken a set of originally Middle Eastern and European religious ideas
and practices and adjusted them to suit a contemporary pattern of life
that includes increasing bureaucratization, technological changes, and
the global exchange of material goods. Even certain philosophical
assumptions, such as the idea that all events are controlled by God's
hand, are held identically by both populations (cf. Ammerman 1987,
1990, 1991). Thus the lack of modernity that Central Sulawesi highlanders attribute to themselves and that others attribute to them is
grounded in invidious comparisons of wealth and social evolutionary
teachings that exist apart from any systematic analyses of their local
religious doctrines or integration with the global economy.

World Religions on the Periphery

Until recent years, anthropologists' research favored the examination of "indigenous religious rituals," or what Redfield (1956) called the "little traditions" of religion. Such studies artificially stratified the global, urban, and literate from the local, rural, and illiterate, and thus they skirted postcolonial manifestations of world religions such as Christianity or Islam. This contrasts with comparative religion scholarship that painstakingly considered the doctrines and practices of world religions in the "great traditions" while giving short shrift to the localized reformulations developing in peripheral geographic areas. Following these predilections, both groups of scholars largely ignored the recent realizations of world religions that are absorbing millions of adherents in the present day.

By the mid-1980s, this scholarly lacuna was addressed by scholars of Southeast Asian Islam who were considering the negotiation of Middle Eastern and Asian doctrines (Bowen 1993; Hefner 1987a; Peacock 1978; Rodgers Siregar 1981; Roff 1985, 1987; M. Woodward 1989). A few years later, localized forms of Christianity in Southeast Asia also became discussed more vigorously (Aragon 1991/1992; Kammerer 1990; Keyes 1991, 1993, 1996; Kipp 1990; Hefner 1993a; Russell 1989).

Academic anthropology has undergone well-publicized philosophical transformations (e.g., Appadurai 1990; Clifford and Marcus 1986; Dirks, Eley, and Ortner 1994; Ortner 1984; Said 1978) during the past decades as it abandoned claims to objective scientific documentation of homogenous cultural entities. In its place there has come new attention to the inequities of political economy, transnationalism, multiple layers of social allegiance, and local contestations of race, gender, and class. This anthropological interest in the dynamics of European colonialism missions has generated several excellent studies of Christian missions based on archival histories (Barker 1979, 1990b; Beidelman 1982; Boutilier, Hughes, and Tiffany 1978; Clifford 1982;

Comaroff 1985; Comaroff and Comaroff 1986, 1991; Kipp 1990; Rafael 1993).

My research project, by contrast, extends into the realm of contemporary personages and practices. Because western Central Sulawesi was still an active mission field during the 1980s, I was able to evaluate localized Protestant practices with respect to the often diverse teachings of contemporary missionaries, as well as according to archival reports about past missionaries.

Barker (1990a, 2) notes that Pacific Christianity "possesses both a local and a global face." Yet such dichotomous imagery can mislead because many descriptions of "local" African religions were based on colonial misunderstandings (Ranger 1993), and the transnational factors are not well explored (Beidelman 1974, 1994). Moreover, the tensions between "headquarters" and provincial forces never really cease in the religions of either the colonized or the colonizers. Protestant conversion in Indonesia has never been "a blinding flash of light on the road to Damascus" (Kipp 1991b, 3–4, 1995) nor a simple matter of political expediency under the Dutch colonial or New Order regimes, but rather a set of negotiations that both unite and mutually transform those so-called "great" or "global" and "little" or "local" traditions. In this respect, the Comaroffs' work on South Africa has been seminal in their attention to the shifting European as well as African sociology of the missionization process (Comaroff and Comaroff 1991).

Elsewhere I have used the term "conversion" to refer to a self-reported affiliation with an adopted religious sect (Aragon 1991/1992). I argued that the isomorphism, or lack thereof, between the ideas and practices of missionaries and converts should be considered as a separate issue. I have found "conversion" to be a troublesome term because it suggests a rapid and incontrovertible transformation between distinctive ideologies, when what is denoted by the word often is a lengthy process of renegotiating religious ideas and behavior. (Ranger 1987, 183) identified the problem precisely when he wrote, "[O]ne either has to say that the fact that conversion was incomplete is the truism in which every study of the interactions of mission and society begins, or that the notion of 'conversion' is in itself inadequate to conceptualize the dialectical process." My previous effort to confront the term's inadequacies was to restrict its meaning to matters of self-ascribed changes of affiliation.

More recent writings focusing on Christian "conversion," however, have spoken to these concerns and used the term both to denote and problematize the long-term, interlocal processes of changing religious affiliations (Hefner 1993b; Kipp 1995; van der Veer 1996). These studies include social factors leading to changes of religious affiliation as well as discussions of indigenized Christian ideology and practices. They also consider how Christianity, as an interlocal institution, ultimately draws missionized people beyond their villages into super-regional symbolic and political networks. Bowen is right to argue that the correct method for approaching globalized world religion is to neglect neither regional culture nor the "external, normative reference point" for such localized religion (Bowen 1993, 7). Yet this study will emphasize that such reference points are not necessarily so fixed. Rather, missionary transmissions can shift the "religious reference points" from the written texts such as the Bible or church doctrines institutionalized in Europe to broader cultural prescriptions such as changes in agriculture, households, family names, or personal attire.

Syncretism and the Politics of Religious Synthesis

> . . . if these people regard themselves for all practical purposes as Muslims, it is difficult to maintain that scientific research has come to the conclusion that they are not. . . . [O]ne is inclined to feel that if an Indonesian says he is a Muslim, it is better to take his word for it.
>
> C. A. O. van Nieuwenhuijze, Aspects of Islam in Post-Colonial Indonesia

Echoing Nieuwenhuijze, Roff argues that one problem in the academic literature on religious change is Western scholars' Orientalist habit of suggesting that people are not "really" Muslim — or

Christian—when in fact the key issue is the inevitable tension "between the demands of the ideal and the demands of social reality" (Roff 1985, 8). In both established and missionary congregational contexts, among both Christian and Muslim populations, religious leaders often work to induce the members of their communities to be more attentive to a prescribed faith and set of ritual practices. Moreover, the proliferating denominationalism of both these religions belies any scholarly attempt to establish a simple, culture-free standard by which to judge the behavior of all communities.

Aside from criticisms of people's laxness in following known religious principles, a community may be criticized for not being pristinely Muslim or Christian. This is often the case when longtime members of a world religion evaluate new converts who supplement little-known or vaguely specified doctrines of their new faith with familiar tenets of their old one. Such situations have fostered another problematic concept used in writings on religious change, that is, "syncretism."

In much anthropological, sociological, historical, or comparative religion scholarship, the word "syncretism" is applied loosely to describe any incorporation of extraneous elements into a preexisting religious tradition (e.g., Peel 1968, 29). That definition, however, is so broad as to allow most known religions as practiced in all known places to qualify as syncretic. Because religions do not exist in isolation, the critical issue is not whether foreign elements are introduced into cultural or religious systems, but how they are interpreted (M. Woodward 1989, 17).[4]

"Syncretism" is an Ancient Greek-derived term referring to religious borrowing. The term has a long and checkered history of usage associated with European political strife, strategic Christian missionary allegiances, and fundamentalist backlashes (Shaw and Stewart 1994, 3–6). Thus the concept has been avoided by many recent scholars in favor of discussions of religious reinterpretation, bricolage, creolization, or hybridization (e.g., Aragon 1996d; Bhabha 1985, 173; Comaroff 1985; Hannerz 1987). Shaw, Stewart, and their colleagues, however, have endeavored to revitalize the term by recasting "syncretism" not only as a process of religious borrowing and recombination, but as the complex array of political processes and competing discourses involved in religious synthesis. "Anti-syncretism" is then defined as "the antagonism to religious synthesis shown by agents concerned with the defense of religious boundaries" (Shaw and Stewart 1994, 7).

Within such a revised framework, this study of Central Sulawesi Christianity undeniably concerns the politics of religious synthesis, or "syncretism." Yet I still eschew the term because of its disparaging connotations and its essentialistic ideas of "pure" religions from which syncretic ones could be created (cf. Sears 1993, 9). Sulawesi Protestantism, like all other forms of Christianity, is indeed a synthesis, but to label it so as distinguished from the religion of the Europeans who introduced their version of Christianity to Central Sulawesi is seemingly to accept European premises of authenticity or purity (which of course Shaw and Stewart do not). Therefore, although I support the reconsideration of syncretism as a political as well as intentionally "acculturating" process, one of my aims in this book is to examine contemporary Central Sulawesi Protestantism as an independent theological entity, to reveal a trajectory for Indonesian Christianity that is other than a mere refraction of a presumed singular European orthodoxy.

Highland Places and Peoples

Dutch colonial administrators began their work in Central Sulawesi by formally identifying what they considered distinct languages and ethnic groups. The Tobaku and their eastern neighbors speak a language that linguists categorized as "Uma," after the local word for "no." Like all Central Sulawesi highlanders, the Tobaku also were placed into the generic ethnic category of "Toraja." The panoply of highlanders' ethnolinguistic labels and divergent "autonyms" indicates their ambiguous political status, their long-term evasion of state supervision, and the imperfect population group classifications that all state and mission administrations require.

To call the Tobaku "Uma people" borrows an eccentric colonial linguistic category that classified all groups in Sulawesi after their word for "no." To call them "Toraja" borrows a vastly overgeneralizing colonial category for little-known interior peoples. To call them "Pipikoro" borrows a synecdoche of recent missionary linguists. To call them "Kulawi" reifies a feature of the colonial and postcolonial bureaucratic hierarchy. To call them "Tobaku," as I do, acknowledges these peoples' own name for themselves, although it reveals fewer of their ties to neighboring groups.

Central Sulawesi highlanders name themselves after their dwelling places, usually in reference to rivers, mountains, or trees. Tobaku elders say their autonym, "people of Tobaku" (*to Tobaku*), refers to the waters of a small Lariang tributary near Siwongi, one of the earliest heartland villages. The Lariang River, which runs broad and muddy in the western lowlands, spouts from myriad sparkling sources in the upland domains of the Tobaku and other Uma-speaking peoples. The Uma word for the Lariang, *koro*, also means "river," it being the only waterway in their homeland. A name used by some for the Uma homelands is *pipikoro*, "the banks of the river," and eastern Uma-speaking people simply call themselves *to Pipikoro*, "people of the river banks." Summer Institute of Linguistics (SIL) linguists who worked in the eastern area near Kantewu use the term "Pipikoro" to designate all Uma speakers and their language (Barr, Barr, and Salombe 1979). Tobaku people in the western areas, however, use the term only to define the eastern populations near Kantewu and Peana villages.

Like many peoples of the Indonesian archipelago, including state-level polities such as the Balinese (Lansing 1991, 56), Uma peoples consider the higher waters and mountains—where they happen to live—purer and more sacred than the lower waters and lands below. Indeed, community wastes do float downstream, and everyone knows that the cleanest drinking water is collected upstream from the village. The consort to Tobaku people's experiential involvement with the river is the mountains, which range from 1,000 to over 2,000 meters in their homeland. "It is this way with us mountain people" is a phrase that Tobaku people often use to explain a custom or excuse their modest material circumstances. Their dual identity as both "mountain people" (*to bulu'*, Uma; *orang gunung*, Ind.) and "owners of the area" (*pue' ngata*, Uma) or "original people" (*orang asli*, Ind.) is a verbal means by which the Tobaku and other highlanders distinguish themselves geographically and ethnically from their two kinds of lowland Muslim neighbors, Kaili and South Sulawesi immigrants.

Dutch and Indonesian governments seeking control throughout the twentieth century have pressured highlanders to reside permanently at lower elevations along the major footpaths. Nevertheless, many communities continue to move up and down through the forests along the Lariang tributaries in search of game, forest products, and the swidden garden lands upon which their subsistence depends. This type of local or "internal travel" in which the whole community participates can be differentiated from the "external travel" to regional centers such as Kulawi and Palu, which is conducted mainly by male traders, community leaders, and the occasional visiting outsider. As Tsing (1993) has noted, the ability to travel widely or control settlement mobility can differentiate men from women, leaders from followers, and government officials from rural citizens. The context for these politically contingent conditions of mobility is created or at least exacerbated by the geographical extremes found on the island of Sulawesi.

Environmental niches in Central Sulawesi vary greatly between the coastal shelves and the interior mountain ranges. The narrow strips of coastline are generally flat, hot (frequently reaching 35°C), and extremely dry. The Palu Valley in particular is the driest region in all of Indonesia, with only 40–80 centimeters (15–30 inches) of rainfall each year. The desert-like provincial capital of Palu, with a population over one hundred thousand, is only two degrees south of the equator. Despite its inhospitable milieu, Palu has become the largest city in the Donggala Regency (*kabupaten*). Created in the early 1960s as the provincial capital, Palu now overshadows the nearby port of Donggala, which had been the entry point of South Sulawesi traders for centuries prior to Indonesian independence at the end of World War II.

The hot and dry conditions of the coasts contrast sharply with those of the interior mountains, which are subject to chilly nights, distinct wet and dry seasons, periodic flooding, and disastrous landslides. Although construction on the ambitiously named "Trans-Sulawesi Highway" has improved transportation through portions of the interior, passage in many areas depends on seasonal flooding. The preferred means of transportation around much of the province is by boat to avoid problematic terrestrial conditions altogether. The populations on the coasts depend largely on marine resources, sea trade, goats, chickens, and, in irrigable areas, wet-rice agriculture. By contrast, interior populations depend on shifting farming of rice, maize, cassava, and sago, pigs, chickens, riverine fishing, hunting, and trapping.

Central Sulawesi (*Sulawesi Tengah*, or SULTENG, Ind.) is the largest of Sulawesi's four provinces, with an area of 68,033 square kilometers (26,270 square miles). The province's population was estimated in 1990 at only twenty-two persons per square kilometer, with almost 90 percent dwelling along the coasts, leaving the interior even more sparsely populated. As of 1990, approximately 64 percent of the land was still forested, and over 95 percent of the province's income was said to derive from the export of timber, principally ebony (Acciaioli 1990, 155). Until recently, Kulawi District highlanders have had little direct involvement with tourism or timber industries because of the absence of roads into the interior, but they have contributed to the nation's burgeoning export businesses indirectly through their production and sale of cash crops such as coffee (Aragon 1997).

The mountain villages and satellite hamlets of the Tobaku people rest in the southwest of the Kulawi District, whose administrative center, also named Kulawi, is located approximately eighty kilometers south of Palu. Aside from government offices, schools, and a Salvation Army branch hospital, the village of Kulawi features several general stores, owned and operated mostly by ethnic Chinese or South Sulawesi traders. These unobtrusive establishments, invariably imbued with the aroma of dried fish, are the collection points for highlanders' cash-producing items, including coffee, cloves, cacao, and vanilla beans.

Tobaku people claim they were a politically unified regional group of Uma speakers prior to the arrival of Dutch observers in the early twentieth century. Tobaku populations constitute slightly less than half of all Uma speakers. The Uma total was estimated in the 1980s by SIL missionaries at fifteen thousand people in about thirty villages (M. P. Martens 1988ms). I first visited the Kulawi District in 1984 when I was a graduate student seeking a field project on Central Sulawesi Christianity and cultural change. I returned and visited all Tobaku and most Tole'e and Pipikoro hamlets between April 1986 and March 1989.

As it would have been inappropriate for a woman alone to have her own house, I resided with others—first in the nurses' dormitory, then in both clergy and lay people's village and garden homes primarily around Towulu', the largest village (*desa*, Ind.) of the region. I tried to compensate my hosts fairly in local terms with gifts of supplies that their families ordinarily purchased, such as dry foods, soap, and cloth.

Towulu' is a double-hamlet village (Lida' and Bola' Hae) of over one thousand residents, perched on both sides of the Towulu' River at an altitude of about 700 meters. Towulu' administers the separate hamlets (*dusun*, Ind.) of Wuruwi, Doda, and, during the 1980s, Wana'. I also resided briefly in Winatu, Siwongi (which includes Biro), Rantewulu' (which includes Momi), Banggaiba (which includes Mpehewe and Lompo), and Lawe', a border village between Tobaku and Pipikoro regions. In 1993, I resided in the new village of Noke' (near what was Wana') as well as in Towulu' and Winatu. My movements were aimed to give comparative breadth to my research, to prevent myself from becoming allied too exclusively with any one family or social stratum, and to spread both the burden and benefits of hosting a foreign student guest. I also visited the homes of over twenty missionaries working in the province.

Rugged Ethnic Terrain

> The way people play rummy in a particular fishing village need not have anything to do with their self-identity or with the way others identify them. Yet it is precisely the conflation of these two practices of identity that provides the basis for the equivalence of culture, ethnicity and race.
>
> Jonathan Friedman, "On Perilous Ideas"

Despite Boas' (1911) early analytic separation of people's race, culture, and language, his efforts often have been forgotten when observers confuse observed commonalities of behavior with either outsiders' ethnic identities or insiders' ethnic identities. The literature on Central Sulawesi ethnicity illustrates a confusion derived from the practical efforts of colonial observers to create manageable ethnic categories for administering the colonized. Analyses of Central Sulawesi ethnic groups also tend to overlook the fluid and concentric layering of self-identities well described by Southeast Asian ethnologists (Leach 1954; Moerman 1965; Lehman 1979). As Moerman notes for smaller Thailand groups, individuals within their homeland ascribe to themselves a narrower ethnic identity than when they travel outside their homeland or describe themselves to outsiders as part of larger regional groupings. The small-scale migratory ethnic groups of both mainland and insular Southeast Asia likely never had "any permanent and immutable ethnographic status" (Kirsch 1973, 35; Leach 1954). Such groups indeed may have formed, as James Scott, among others, suggests, as fugitives from state control and related practices such as slave raiding.

In Dutch colonial literature, most museum collections, and even in recent secondary sources (e.g., Lebar 1972; Holmgren and Spertus 1989), the highlanders of Central Sulawesi are referred to as "Toradja" or "Toraja." Along with Indonesian scholars such as Pakan (1977), Masyhuda (1977), and Mattulada (1991), I argue against this usage because Central Sulwesi highlanders use other terminology and reject the label "Toraja." Additionally, Central Sulawesi highlanders are culturally and linguistically distinct from the South Sulawesi peoples who have adopted the term "Toraja" for themselves since the 1930s (Bigalke 1981).

"Toraja," like the labels "Batak" and "Dayak," was an epithet invented by coastal people to categorize the peoples of the interior. The origin of "Toraja" has been traced to the Luwu Buginese phrase "*to ri aja*," meaning "people in the uplands" (Nooy-Palm 1975, 54). The missionary A. C. Kruyt was instrumental in elevating the term to general use among colonial personnel. After a trip to Palopo in 1897, Kruyt decided that the Luwu term "Toraja" was more dignified than "Alfur," which had been used by European explorers to label all the non-Islamic, non-Hindu peoples living on the eastern islands (Pakan 1977, 22). The term "Alfur" derived from the Ternate word "*halefuru*," meaning "wilderness, forest" (Encyclopedië 1917–1939, 1:30).

By applying the term "Toraja" indiscriminately to all highland Sulawesi groups, Kruyt left himself and future scholars with the problem of distinguishing one from another. Not coincidentally, he referentially united all the interior groups he considered available for Protestant conversion. Kaudern criticized Kruyt's widespread application of the label Toraja, especially on linguistic grounds, but felt that the practice was too ensconced in the literature to warrant its removal (Kaudern 1925, 2:1–3). Kaudern only further divided Kruyt's three Toraja categories (South, East, and West) into four categories. He retained the Poso (East) and Sa'dan (South) divisions and then divided the Kaili (West) Toraja into the Palu and Koro categories.

After concerns about nationalism and regional ethnic identity developed locally in the 1930s, the large and relatively united South, or Sa'dan Valley, Toraja group in fact came to identify themselves as Toraja, emphasizing the morpheme "raja," which means "king" or "ruler" in the Malay or Indonesian language (Nooy-Palm 1975, 54; Bigalke 1981, 13–16). By contrast, the more fragmented interior groups to the north and east eschewed the Toraja label.

During the New Order regime, foreign missionaries again turned to linguistics to define ethnic boundaries. The languages of Central Sulawesi were studied intensively in the 1970s and 1980s by SIL/Wycliffe Bible Translators teams. SIL was founded in 1936 by an American missionary named William Cameron Townsend (Moore 1984, 12). Townsend left college in 1917 to sell Spanish Bible translations in Guatemala, only to find that the Native Americans could not read them. He began translating the Bible into local languages and eventually taught other missionaries to do the same. In 1942, Townsend opened a legally separate organization called Wycliffe Bible Translators. Although the same people are members of both SIL and Wycliffe Bible Translators, the former can approach foreign hosts as a scientific and educational organization while the latter can collect donations and support at home for Bible translation and missionary work. Although they receive formal linguistic training, SIL and

Wycliffe personnel are said to "expect their efforts to result in conversion of indigenes to Christianity" (Taylor 1985, 93).

In 1971, SIL signed a contract with the government of Indonesia permitting their members access to Indonesian areas with less well known languages (Moore 1984). On the basis of one hundred-word Swadesh surveys, four hundred-word lists, and considerable fieldwork in particular language areas (Kaili, Uma, and Balantak), SIL linguist-missionaries determined that the largest group of languages in Central Sulawesi belongs to a subgroup that they name Kaili-Pamona (Barr, Barr, and Salombe 1979). Steedly (1996, 459) and Harries (1988, 26) have critiqued the tendency of missionaries to create a validating history, territory, and "ur-identity" for groups sharing a language defined by the missionaries themselves. Yet no outsiders know Central Sulawesi languages better than the senior SIL missionaries who retained permits in the region for decades. Therefore, in lieu of other data or claims for alternate ethnic categorizations, their linguistic groupings have been used by all recent administrations.

On the basis of the SIL linguistic data and his own personal knowledge, a Kaili-Bugis scholar named Masyhuda (1977, vol.1; 1988/1989) proposed to divide all Kaili-Pamona speakers into four main ethnic groups: Kaili, Kulawi (including both Moma and Uma speakers), Lore (including Napu, Bada', and Besoa), and Pamona (formerly called Poso or Bare'e Toraja by Kruyt). Although such ethnic partitions devised by government and mission officials invariably simplify and overextend to create crisp, governable domains, Masyhuda's proposal constructs middle-range groupings that do have historical kinship and political ties as well as common learned routines (Brumann 1999).

Uma speakers will, when visiting Palu, for example, refer to themselves as Kulawi peoples, simply to distinguish themselves from Kaili, Bugis, Poso, or other more different groups for listeners who have no idea about the geography of the highlands. Undoubtedly it is politically expedient for individuals hailing from beyond the end of the roads to present themselves to lowlanders as part of the larger Kulawi group. Moreover, Uma-speaking peoples were placed under the juris-

diction of Kulawi leaders during the Dutch colonial era, so they anticipate this classification of "hierarchic inclusion" (Kuipers 1998). The
shifting nature of their ethnic labels also helps protect them from careful outside scrutiny and interference.

Tobaku and other Kulawi District highlanders thus claim different ethnic allegiances depending upon their listener, using localized
place names for familiars and broader administrative identifications for
strangers. Based on behavioral commonalities, the peoples living in the
Kulawi and neighboring districts may be seen as "chains" of related
cultural groups just as their languages may be mapped as chain
dialects.[1] This shifting ethnic and linguistic mosaic may be understood
as the consequence of swiddening subsistence strategies and fluctuating political leadership framed within a colonial imperative to govern
and identify potential Christian converts.

Land That Moves, and That Which Moves through Land

In many western Meratus areas, rice farming is described as sending the rice
seed on a long journey to find companions and return home with them as the
harvest. Movement is understood as opposing stagnation, not security; it represents the possibility of increase.

Anna Lowenhaupt Tsing, In the Realm of the Diamond Queen

Paralleling Meratus ideas, concepts of stasis and inertness are
antithetical to Tobaku thoughts about land. By contrast, colonial and
postcolonial states thrive on the sedentarization of their citizens and
dislike unauthorized movement (Scott 1998). Tobaku people measure
the larger units of time that we define as solar years according to the
movement of their gardens through the forest landscape. When
Tobaku women are asked their children's age by outsiders, they generally recall the place of their primary rice field when the child was born
and then "count" through the names of subsequent rice gardens
farmed until the present. Thus time is measured by places, and movement through places is what creates life.

Land can change its nature over time just like any other living creature, so Tobaku individuals approach land with care and caution. All places are inhabited by invisible beings. Mus (1975 [1933], 11) notes with regard to Southeast Asian indigenous religions, or "spirit cults," that the earliest deities recorded are "defined above all by localization." Place, and human movement through places, is at the basis of Tobaku spirituality. European missionaries, by contrast, sought to instill metered stability and stasis, in both highlanders' settlements and their concepts of deity. Natural environments and human ecologies thus inevitably affect religious perspective and proposed spiritual solutions to the mysteries of life.

Virtually all Tobaku people work the land, and human fates in this endeavor are regulated by ancestral rules imbued with religious sentiments. While government officials and missionaries talk of industrious farming, fencing fields from damaging livestock, and the regional marketing of produce, Tobaku people talk of ancestral priorities, community transgressions, and land that is "too hot" to use. Outsiders view land in the Tobaku highlands as "jungles" beyond civilization, places of fear. Outsiders also assume that these forested mountains are under the permanent jurisdiction of governments or living individuals.

Tobaku people, by contrast, type their land variously according to its past use, ancestral authority, and most recent spiritual manifestations. Land that has never been cultivated is still owned by deities. Land that has been previously cultivated is under the continued jurisdiction of families of the founders who first cleared that earth of trees, whether these individuals are living or dead. Hence Tobaku families maintain pragmatic yet spiritual ties to what are characterized in the Southeast Asian anthropological literature as founders' cults.

The strength of Tobaku people's religious ideas concerning land and its use has made farming a target of intensive Protestant ritual activity. At the same time, farming is a cosmological niche over which the church and government lack certain controls, given their inability to undermine Tobaku subsistence strategies without starving their citizenry. The highlanders' scattered settlement patterns and the potential of Kulawi District land for future developments in forestry or mining, however, has made the Indonesian government increasingly interested in either tying highlanders to defined and accessible village centers or removing them to sites of lowland transmigration programs that are based in permanent wet-rice agriculture subsistence (Aragon 1997).

State governments discourage uncontrolled mobility among their citizenry for reasons of security and tax collection. Churches also find it difficult to shepherd wandering flocks, and seldom have been loath to tamper with the domestic arrangements of missionized peoples in the name of Christian propriety. Thus colonial Dutch, Indonesian, and mission authorities have applied almost a century of pressure to restrain and alter Tobaku settlements. These communities formerly were not village-based in the contemporary sense, but were a set of fluctuating household clusters reorganized each year in preparation for new rice field centers.

Most Tobaku people now keep an official residence in a government-authorized village, although they spend much of the year in field houses built annually in their shifting dry-rice gardens. Archival documents and oral histories indicate that prior to colonial intervention, the locations that are now official villages were primarily ceremonial sites. Tobaku people only descended from their rice gardens when notified of upcoming feasts or warfare councils. The precolonial "ceremonial village" thus consisted of a large temple (*lobo*, Uma), a small temple (*sou eo*), which doubled as an inn, and a few other multihearth dwellings that would each periodically shelter several families who shared a common horticultural settlement for that year.

The Dutch and Indonesian governments have put pressure on all highlanders to maintain a single, nuclear family-centered residence in officially designated villages. A few families still keep permanent "wild houses" (*hou polompua*, Uma) outside the village near their perennial vegetable gardens, but prolonged residence in these domiciles as well as in the rice garden houses, generally located at higher elevations, is discouraged by officials who find them difficult to monitor, tax, and control.

One of the last remaining pre-Christian temples (*lobo*, Uma) in the Kulawi District, restored at Peana.

In 1911, a Dutch army captain, R. Boonstra van Heerdt, conducted a tour through western Central Sulawesi to survey the extant villages. He then ordered smaller populations in more remote areas to move their settlements and consolidate them with the largest nearby villages along the major footpaths. The settlers of Mangkau, for example, were ordered down from the mountains where they farmed and lived. These Tobaku people then constructed the hamlet of Wuruwi, about five kilometers west of Towulu'. Mangkau continues to this day as a favored rice garden settlement area for Wuruwi, which is now officially a hamlet of Towulu'.

Kaudern's figures indicate that even after the consolidation imposed by Boonstra van Heerdt, the largest Tobaku villages only compared with the average village size in Kulawi, approximately twenty households. This was about half the size of the major Pipikoro village of Peana, estimated at forty households in 1918 (Kaudern 1925, 1:38).

These houses, however, undoubtedly were extended family households that probably contained more than ten individuals on the average—as they often still do today. Besides changes in settlement patterns, new regulations introduced by the Dutch government and missionaries included the prohibition of headhunting, human sacrifices,
burials under houses, and tooth-pulling or tooth-filing ceremonies for
women's puberty rites. After the decrees, many precontact rituals still
were conducted, sometimes with animals or banana tree trunks dressed
as humans substituting for the original sacrifices (cf. George 1996).
The stipulated changes to Tobaku rituals, however, began to alter the
uses of village structures as well as their occupation and constellations.

Present-day Tobaku villages or hamlets (*bola'*, Uma) are much
larger than in precolonial times, ranging from about twenty to over one
hundred houses each. Settlement populations have increased corre-
spondingly from about two hundred to over one thousand individuals.
Following an early Dutch command, village houses now are set in rows
facing the main path running through the village, although the exact
arrangement is somewhat dependent upon the prevailing topography
and local concepts of auspicious home sites. Although the Dutch tampered differently with the villages of Sumba, Kuipers (1998) similarly
describes how formerly autonomous villages were subsumed into a
colonial map that placed them on the periphery of a Dutch-run political hierarchy.

Tobaku people cultivate rice, maize, tubers, and other vegetables
on steep mountain spurs. These staple foods are supplemented by forest game and river fish, plus occasional imported supplies bought with
income from introduced cash crops such as coffee, or more recently,
cacao. The primary crop of any Tobaku swidden plot is rice (*pae*,
Uma), which, being considered symbolically female, is always interplanted with maize (*dagoa*), considered to be male. Maize was introduced from the New World only in the colonial period, so the sym-
bolism of a foreign male fertilizing a local female is suggestive,
although not part of local discourse. Glutinous, or sticky, rice (*pae*

pulu') is planted in a strip along the lower border of the plot and may account for up to one-quarter of the rice crop. Formerly, types of millet (*dale'* and *wilo'*), Job's Tears (*rope*), and black sesame (*sinangi'*) also were planted more extensively. Now these early grains are planted only in small amounts.

Crookneck winter squash, cucumber, cherry tomatoes, papaya, mustard greens, capsicum peppers, Chinese eggplant, and pole beans are planted at the edge of the grain fields. These cultigens, plus wild plants such as ferns, add seasonal variety to the otherwise unchanging bowls of rice or surrogate starches. Patches of chewing tobacco also may be planted. Tobaku people know how to farm with wet-rice agriculture technology, but the steep terrain and waterway patterns allow for only a small portion of their land to be planted with this higher-yielding permanent technique.

Tobaku people describe two types of primary forest that they say has never been cut by humans: *wana'* and *ponulu*. *Wana'* is far from any settlement, used only for foraging, and under the corporate jurisdiction of the village whose ancestors exploited it in the past. *Ponulu* is located nearer to cultivated areas and may be considered suitable for new swidden fields (*role*). In principle, *ponulu* is available to any village family needing new rice fields who can assemble sufficient labor to clear it. In practice, ancestral rules (*ada' to owi*) still warrant that village elders grant permission. Moreover, large animals such as pigs, cows, or buffalo must be sacrificed—formerly for the "owner(s) of the land" (*pue' tana'*) now for the Christian God—and the meat served to all persons, sometimes forty individuals, helping to clear the forest.

As far as I could observe, only one or two areas of primary land are cleared per village in any given year. To open primary land, a family needs to "borrow hands" (*mpoala' pale*) and be prepared later to "give back hands" (*mpohile pale*). More crucially, they must own sufficient livestock to meet not only their other life-cycle feast obligations, but also to feed additional workers on the land at feasts throughout the planting and harvest season. Consequently, headmen and other government officials are most likely to venture opening primary forests today, just as the hereditary leaders (*maradika*) were the ones pioneering new lands in precolonial times.

Once any primary forestland is opened, all future use rights to that named area go to the head of the family who sponsored the initial clearing, and afterward to closest heirs. People often recall which illustrious ancestor first cleared which primary field area. Since the nature of Tobaku swidden farming is labor intensive and kin-based, collateral relatives such as cousins may request and be awarded farming plots on the same mountainside as the individuals with primary control over the land. First cousins are not expected to give any compensation for borrowed land use, but more distant cousins are expected to make a "rental" payment (*sima'*), usually about one-tenth of their total harvest from the land.[2]

Usufruct land rights vary somewhat from village to village. In the Towulu' area, the mountain face farmed by each cluster of households that comprise the work groups (*hantuda*) is officially "owned" (*rapue'*) by one elder, usually a woman, who lends all the roughly one and a half hectare plots (*limo'*) she is not using to close relatives. For example, Tina Tompongi "owned" a farming area because her deceased father and mother had founded a now abandoned hamlet by that mountain. She chose a preferred spot for her household to farm and then offered the next rights of refusal to her closest eldest female relatives, and so on down the line.

After one agricultural year (*hampae*), rights to borrowed land revert to the senior heir of the ancestor who first cleared the land. Swidden land rights thus are owned corporately, and they cannot be sold or otherwise alienated from the descendants of the person first clearing the forest. Obligations also pertain at the village level. Each year the village of Towulu' corporately pays a small percentage of its total crop as rent to the leaders of Siwongi because Towulu' was once just a hunting territory of the older village of Siwongi.

After forestland has been first cleared, it is called *oma*, or "secondary forest." *Oma tua* is secondary forest with sufficient growth that it is considered ready for reuse. Tobaku people report that their swidden cycle runs from about six years for the most fertile, newly opened, land, to about ten years for the more exhausted land near older villages. When I checked individuals' recollections about where they actually farmed for the previous dozen years, however, I discovered a different pattern of usage. Many sites were not reused at all during a ten-year period, while others were used two or even three times. This difference was explained by owners' reports of how good their harvests were at different years at the various sites. If a location produced a bumper crop of rice one year, it would be favored for reuse within five years. A site with a poor harvest, however, was considered inauspicious and so was dropped out of the rotation for a longer period of time.

To'olo', literally "that which is in between," is land that is not considered cultivable either due to infertility, inaccessibility, or a state of "hotness" (*morani'*) signifying its inhabitation by harmful spirits (*seta*). In the last case, anyone attempting to clear the forest is expected to die because of the anger of the "owner(s) of the land." Therefore, before primary forest is ever cleared, the individual planning the deed will consult with village elders to ascertain if the area is considered to be "in between." If a tragic death or accident occurs in a cleared area, those fields also will be abandoned and labeled "in between" for up to ten years, at which time the owning family may try their luck again. Such land is untouchable because it rests in the dangerous zone "in between" the worlds of the living and the unseen spirits.

Besides the primary rice plot (*bonea* or *bonea mpu'u*, "true swidden field"), families try to avoid complete harvest failures by making a second, smaller swidden plot of one hectare or less, which is called a *lora'* and is tilled a month or two prior to the main field. They also tend a perennial vegetable and fruit garden called a *pampa*. *Pampa* gardens are inherited along with the swidden field rights and usually are shared among sisters or matrilateral female cousins. *Pampa* gardens primarily contain cassava and yams of various color (white, yellow, and purple-red), but also cultigens such as papaya, sugarcane, peanuts, pole beans, ginger, shallots, and capsicum peppers. The leaves of tuber plants are used routinely for green vegetable side dishes, and the roots supplement or substitute for rice when necessary. These vegetable gardens are closer to the village than the primary rice fields and are maintained by women for decades, even generations, in the same place.

Primary forest is available to any villager wishing to plant coffee or other cash crops. Once large trees are felled and coffee trees are established, the land is considered under ownership of the cultivator. Cacao was of minimal importance as a cash crop until the early 1990s, when cacao profits began to rival coffee profits. Dutch traders introduced coffee beans that were harvested first by the 1940s or 1950s in old villages such as Siwongi. Yet coffee's use, specifically, its palatability when mixed with sugar, was still unknown even during the 1950s in villages such as Towulu'. Before the local importation of granulated, white sugar, Tobaku people wondered how foreigners could have any desire for that bitter bean brew.

The rules applying to cash crop land rights follow precolonial rules pertaining to valuable trees such as areca, sago, and sugar palms. Areca palms provide the main ingredient for betelnut quids, still chewed by older women and men, especially at ceremonial events such as weddings. Sago, like maize and cassava, is a starchy rice substitute that becomes important during the so-called "famine" season of January, February, and March, when rice supplies from the previous year's fields are depleted. Flour from the pith of either a sago or sugar palm tree can be extracted and processed in a few days. The proceeds are split among the workers and the tree owner, who may or may not participate in the extraction work. Formerly, families also cultivated and tapped sugar palms for sap, which was fermented into palm wine or boiled down into red sugar. Sugar palms now are less cultivated because the Salvation Army discourages the drinking of palm wine (baru). Coffee or boiled water is substituted at Protestant rituals in most villages.

Two young Tobaku men travel the forest paths prepared to hunt and collect sugar-palm sap, 1988.

Economic development enters the Tobaku region informally through consumer purchases of store-bought items that replace locally produced items. Woven cloth, for example, has always been of interest to a people formerly dependent upon barkcloth. The majority of Tobaku villagers wear casual Western (now national Indonesian) clothes with the addition of Javanese or South Sulawesi-style sarong cloths that are loosely wrapped around the waist at formal ceremonial occasions. Within the home, aluminum pots have replaced local clay vessels, and enamel or plastic plates mostly have replaced coconut shells and glossy leaves. Water and palm sap now usually are fetched in plastic jerricans, replacing the two-meter-long bamboo tubes still used in a few areas to carry liquids.

Vendors running tiny shops (*kios*, Ind.) in many highland villages sell kerosene, coconut oil, soap, toothpaste, cigarettes, rolling tobacco, candy, granulated sugar, instant noodle soup packs, monosodium glutamate powder, salt, dried fish, canned fish, canned milk, powdered milk, and camphor ointment to those who can afford to buy. Many people still live without these products or purchase them only in bulk during occasional trips to Kulawi when they sell their coffee beans or conduct other business.

Corrugated iron roofs have become increasingly popular in Tobaku villages. Noisier, hotter, more expensive, but more maintenance-free and fireproof than roofs thatched with sugar palm fibers, iron roofs have become a sign of prosperity and social status. Such roofs, which require many difficult journeys back and forth to Kulawi to fetch the coiled sheets two at a time, were introduced by the Salvation Army for their church buildings and later were sought by locals for their own dwellings. In addition to iron roofs, cement floors and walls, which again model the Salvation Army churches and require additional cash and labor, are considered prestigious and modern.

The absence of vehicle roads in the Tobaku heartlands helps preserve the populace's subsistence-farming strategies. Church officials and government leaders, however, say that Tobaku crop surpluses are "wasted" by being given away to relatives or neighbors because they are too difficult to transport to lowland markets. Regional officials and outside developers also envision roads into the mountains as a means of access to untapped hardwood timber supplies and potential mining resources. For these reasons, supporters of "development" see the precolonial extended kinship exchange and shifting land use patterns as an impediment to initiatives to promote the Indonesian nuclear family as an independent economic unit responsive to marketplace demands. Outsiders' plans to regulate land ownership, intensify agriculture, and modernize transportation, however, overlook the degree to which the distance and movements of highland farmers are tied not only to the economy, but also to religious ideology, domestic arrangements, and leadership hierarchies.

Family Values: Kinship, Marriage, and Naming Practices

Although Western missionaries often laud Central Sulawesi highlanders' devotion to children and elders, they also have found much that is reprehensible, even "unchristian," in the "family values" or kinship practices of the region's ethnic groups. Protestant officials and governments thus have intervened in highlanders' domestic lives, especially with regard to polygyny, marriage to cousins, bridewealth, marriage ages, husbands' obligations to in-laws, wedding rituals, divorce, and naming practices.

One of the common Uma phrases used to explain and prescribe actual or expected kinship behavior is *"ompi' ompi' omea,"* meaning literally, "siblings, siblings, all." Knowledge of local kinship terminology and endogamous marriage practices ushers the saying's meaning into the realm of the literal as well as the figurative. Cousins, like siblings, are termed *ompi'*, and Tobaku prefer to marry cousins. Thus almost everyone in a Tobaku village is either an *ompi'* relative who is too close to marry, or a more distant *ompi'* relative who might be suitable for marriage.

Tobaku people reckon their genealogies bilaterally, counting the relations on their mother's side identically to those on their father's side. To determine their relationship, two people will consider their closest common elder relative or ancestor and then trace down the generational links from that starting point. In this way one person may find him or herself the classificatory grandparent or grandchild of someone of the same age. Two persons may keep in mind more than one route by which they are related, for example via both the mother's and father's sides, but usually the closest tie prevails in any formal evaluation. Most Tobaku adults keep track of the specifics of their own lineal genealogy only up to three or at most four ancestral generations because that is all they need to know to establish the hierarchical links between themselves and any other person. As with most Indonesian societies, chronological age is a key correlate of social status, but Uma genealogical reckoning based on generational layers sometimes may allow a physically younger person to be socially "elder" in their kin relationship.

None of Murdock's classic kinship terminology models precisely fits the Uma language data, although this system may be considered a variant on the Hawaiian typology (Murdock 1949, 228–230). Tobaku kinship terminology distinguishes mothers and fathers from uncles and aunts, but often nieces and nephews of varying degrees (*pinoana'*) are simply described as children (*ana'*). At the zero and other more remote generations, however, Tobaku terminology resembles the "Hawaiian" type insofar as cousins are most often equated with siblings, great uncles and aunts are equated with grandparents, and great-nephews and great-nieces are equated with grandchildren.[3]

Most frequently, newly married couples will live in the same house as the bride's parents, perhaps building a separate but nearby house after several children are born. Sometimes even when village sleeping quarters are separated, kitchens or rice-garden houses still may be shared with parents. While the other children eventually move out, the youngest daughter and her husband usually remain in the parents' house, tending to them in their old age. For this service, the youngest daughter inherits the house and a larger share of the parents' movable goods.

Given the uxorilocal residence practices, sisters and matrilateral female cousins tend to be close and cooperative companions. By contrast, males as they grow older and marry tend to form strong alliances with their wife's brothers (*era*) and their wife's sisters' husbands (*lago*), with whom they may live and work in close proximity. This matrilineal kinship orientation has not always been understood or accepted by the more patriarchal states and churches that have entered the area.

The groom's family pays bridewealth, usually only a down payment at the time of marriage, to the bride's family. The amount paid for any girl should in principle equal the bridewealth paid for her mother by her father's family. The assessed value of a woman's bridewealth may not be reduced without risking a dread disease (*wunto*) incurred by all heinous acts of disrespect to one's elders, ancestors, and social superiors.

Ideally, bridewealth consists of a number of ritual items: buffalo (*bengka*), antique cloth (*mesa'*), and antique brass trays (*dula*), but now these are replaced by smaller animals, commercial substitutes, and token

Most highland households center around related adult women and their children, Winatu, 1986.

cash payments. Tobaku families say that their villages are now poor in terms of bridewealth valuables, and they are willing to accept lower bridewealth in order to see their daughters obtain desirable marriages.

Although first-cousin marriages officially are not allowed by elders, there are always cases to be pointed out in any Tobaku village. The uncorrected violation of such marriage rules is said to cause natural disasters such as earthquakes, fires, floods, and landslides. Drought, flooding, or pests such as insects, mice, and monkeys also are associated with sexual misconduct. These misfortunes are said to be "a beating from the owner(s) or God" (*peweba' pue'*), and villagers begin to wonder who is committing premarital sex, incest, or adultery. Usually someone is discovered and the Christianized ceremony once called "to bleed the sun" (*moraa' eo*) takes place to wash the earth of sin.

At a *moraa' eo* expiation ceremony, the intestines and blood of a sacrificed animal are set in the river to float downstream out of the village, thereby carrying the sin and its evil consequences away with it. As described by George (1989) for the Pitu Ulunna Salu people of South Sulawesi, rivers play a symbolic role as conduits for gaining spiritually fortifying elements and shedding polluting ones. The meat of the animal is divided and distributed to the elders of all the families in the village. No one of childbearing age is allowed to consume the meat, or else the tendency for such sin might continue in the families.

In most cases of discovered premarital sex, whether or not pregnancy occurs, a quick marriage with no engagement is arranged following a cleansing ceremony, rather than a splitting of the headstrong couple. Salvation Army officers now oversee all household ceremonies including expiations, and they withhold the privilege of church weddings from couples with forced marriages. Therefore, the church attaches a permanent stigma to marriages that in former times would have been deemed fully legitimate once expiation rituals were implemented. This exemplifies how missionaries often have introduced a divergent moral meaning to the identical social event, such as a required wedding.

Prior to missionization, Tobaku men could marry more than one wife if they could afford the costs involved. They needed to pay off the bridewealth of senior wives, whether or not these women had produced children, and give them an antique cloth or a buffalo "to oil the goodness of heart" (*molana kalompe' nono*). This was in addition to paying the bridewealth down payments of new wives and housing for them all. Commonly, a wife's younger sister might become a second wife if a sacrificial ceremony to "make them twins" (*moropa'*) was performed. If there was harmony among the wives, they could live in one household with separate sleeping areas. If there were quarrels, then separate households were built. By contrast, women could marry a new husband only if freed from the previous one by death or divorce.

Divorce, or "release" (*hibahaka*), and remarriage are prohibited by the Salvation Army Church, but they still are arranged when necessary by villagers. Relatives of a dissatisfied husband or wife first complain directly to the spouse's parents. The wife's parents often demand further bridewealth payments to assuage any wrong to their daughter. If peace cannot be arranged by less drastic means, a divorce will be adjudicated by the village elders apart from church legitimization.

Kuipers (1998) argues that the shift from traditional namesake patterns and prestige names to Christian and family names on Sumba is a key linguistic element of Weyewa people's social marginalization under the colonial Dutch. Names that once had a social and achieved-status meaning became convenient "modern" indicators for government records. Although Central Sulawesi naming has a greater focus on teknonymy (names based on kin relationships) and much less on prestige names related to possessions, missionaries and colonial officials similarly worked to standardize naming according to European administrative models. They have been daunted, however, by Central Sulawesi highlanders' continuous assumption of new names plus most highlanders' continued reluctance to utter the childhood personal names of elders and ancestors.

Tobaku people utilize five Uma kinship terms of address, one of which can be applied to any individual except one's own parents, who are addressed exclusively as "mother" (*ina'*) and "father" (*mama*, or now, to avoid confusion with European forms, *papa*). All elderly men and women are addressed as "grandparent" (*ntu'a*), older men as "uncle" (*uma'*), older women as "aunt" (*ino'*), younger males as "boy or son" (*uto'*), and younger females as "girl or daughter" (*dei'*).

After being initially called just "son" or "daughter," precolonial children were named with whatever words came to their parents' minds at the time of their birth. Therefore, babies might be called "ant," "green bean," "rat trap," or "ugly." Unattractive names would deter malevolent spirits tempted to steal the child's life (A. C. Kruyt 1906, 71). To this day, if a child is persistently unhealthy, his or her name may be changed to fool malicious spirits and alter the fortune of the child. With the advent of missionization, Tobaku people were urged to take biblical names for their children and bestow them permanently within a month after birth. Since these names tend to be long and adopted from a foreign phonology, a usually unrecognizable one- or two-syllable abbreviation is formulated for daily use.

Despite missionary hopes, this childhood name remains with a person only until marriage, at which time a wife will thenceforth be called "woman/wife of (husband's child name)" (Tobine X) and a husband will be called "man/husband of (wife's child name)" (Tobangke Y). As soon as the first child is born to the couple, hopefully within a year, their names will shift again, to "mother/father of (child's name)" (Tina/Tama Z). This name will be kept, with some exceptions, until the birth of their first grandchild, at which time they will be called "grandparent of (grandchild's name)" (Ntu'a Q).

Only such teknonyms and teknonym-style nicknames are spoken freely because childhood names become increasingly subject to taboos during a person's lifetime. Names of parents-in-law or dead ancestors are not readily uttered for fear of the dread disease of disrespect (*wunto*). Even elderly persons often are spoken about by reference to some physical feature (the gray-haired one), their relation to a younger relative (the parent-in-law of X), or to a physical place where they live (the old one living near the lime tree).

Dutch colonial administrators seeking greater ease of personal identification and nuclear family accountability introduced the novel concept of family names (*nama fam*, Ind.) to be inherited through fathers. The childhood names of men who were living at the time the first missionaries entered Tobaku were selected to become the first local patronyms. These family names, especially those belonging to the prior founders, are considered highly taboo and generally are never employed. The names cause great gasps when demanded from brides and grooms during Salvation Army wedding services. As the daughter of Tama Ena, a former headman of Towulu', married and was made to pronounce her father's childhood name (her official last name) in church, the congregation became extremely agitated. When Tobaku people occasionally emigrate and enter the mainstream Indonesian or Salvation Army work forces, they either change their registered family name to some less dangerous nickname or must disavow the ancestral taboo.

Government officials and foreign missionaries have not altered highlanders' method of genealogical reckoning, but they have pressed for the aforementioned changes in domestic constellations, marriage rules, and naming practices. Although Tobaku people maintain extended family and uxorilocal practices in inheritance rights, both Protestant missions and state governments have encouraged nuclear family and patrilineal practices during the past decades. Polygyny is now very rare, and European-style permanent first names and patrilineal family names have been widely introduced, if not always utilized. Indonesian government and Salvation Army officials insist that marriage licenses and Christian church weddings are the legal and true marriage events, thereby hoping to push ancestral engagement and marriage-related rituals into the background. They also discourage divorce and what they consider excessive animal sacrifices for marital alliance rituals.

Hierarchy, Gender, and Legal Codes

The Dutch colonial government, Protestant missions, and post-independence Indonesian governments worked to dismantle the pre-colonial hierarchies of authority in Central Sulawesi. Although these outsiders often proclaimed more egalitarian ideologies, they also sought to introduce hierarchies more amenable to their administrative aims. Most precolonial highlanders maintained social ranks, but their shifting settlement patterns and the relatively Spartan nature of their material culture resulted in few property or consumption differences among persons of different ranks. Only with the colonial era and increases in imported goods did this situation begin to shift toward the current modest escalation in economic difference between the poorest and most wealthy villagers.

Most Tobaku villagers are still subsistence farmers with few possessions that they do not create by their own hands. Yet a minority of families are distinguished either by the addition of civil servants', teachers', and ministers' salaries or by trading concerns. Each village now includes a few horse-owning merchants who collect and trade cash crops such as coffee or cacao beans, which sell for considerable profit in the lowlands. These nouveau riche trading families give evidence of their distinction through finer clothing, more "modern" houses of cement with corrugated iron roofs, imported foods, larger village rituals, and the ability to send their children to the lowlands for middle or high school educations.

When early Dutch observers such as Adriani and Kruyt arrived in Central Sulawesi, most of the highland groups that they categorized as Toraja evidenced inherited ranks. They included a small upper stratum of what Europeans called "aristocrats," perhaps better described as community founders and their descendants. There were also a large group of free commoners and a small group of slaves. Slaves usually were obtained as war prisoners.

In the Kulawi District, precolonial founders, or "aristocrats," were called *maradika*, or some cognate thereof. Village policy decisions were made by an informal council of male elders led by such a community founder, who would choose his successor before his dotage or death. Kruyt (1938, 1:500) states that the term *"maradika"* is derived through the Bugis language from the Sanskrit term *"maharddhika,"* referring to persons exempted from certain social debts and burdens. Dutch colonial writings also speak of East Indies' nobles from many islands as *mardijker*, linking the term to *merdeka*, the Malay word for "freedom." Indeed, Kulawi District leaders were freed from the tedium of normal agricultural and household chores. As with their Bugis neighbors to the south, the leaders' blood was said to be white, and they often were cast as descendants of gods, birds, or white bamboo. Reportedly, the feet of high-ranking Tobaku women never touched the ground outside their houses.

In some Tobaku villages, commoners were called "the many" (*todea*), while the most respected individuals were and are called "the old of the region" (*totu'a ngata*), indicating their role as founders, or descendants of founders, of the community. Slaves, first taken as war captives (*tawani*), were called *batua*. In contrast to these descriptions, Kruyt (1938, 1:chap. 3) hypothesized that the aristocrats were newcomers, a group of conquering outsiders who introduced buffalo and wet-rice agriculture to the indigenous mountain people of Central Sulawesi. Kruyt's rather weak evidence for this is that some more isolated swiddening groups had no slaves and no aristocrats at the time of his research (A. C. Kruyt 1938, 1:501). He noted that communities without their own aristocracy felt themselves subservient to the leaders of other larger villages on their periphery.

There apparently was a range of social stratification among precolonial highland groups, the specter of which lingers to the present. Those with greater population concentration and more connections to lowland kingdoms evidenced greater internal stratification. This situation likely was caused by factors other than those Kruyt describes, including leadership gained through contact with outsiders rather than any decided conquest by foreigners. The range of stratification and its ritual formation in Central Sulawesi appears similar, although in most cases less grand, to that reported in descriptions of the Sa'dan Toraja people of South Sulawesi (Nooy-Palm 1979; Waterson 1981; Volkman 1980, 1985) and highland groups on the Southeast Asian mainland (Leach 1954; Lehman 1963; Kirsch 1973).

High-ranking individuals were surrounded by taboos of respect, the violation of which was said to result in disease (*wunto*). Commoners were not to touch their superiors' personal effects, disobey their instructions, pronounce their personal names, own certain heirlooms, and so forth. The settlement leader, usually a man, acted as a horticultural advisor to the community, and in exchange he and his family rarely had to work their own fields. His major responsibilities were to conduct farming rituals, give astute guidance, and sacrifice his own livestock for feasts to feed workers on his family's land. Within the village, high-ranking leaders, also called "the ones who sit, preside, lead" (*topohura*), acted as senior judges for legal cases, and they collected a percentage of the fines they imposed. The life-cycle rituals for these individuals were invariably more extravagant than the corresponding ceremonies for commoners.

Other than these general ranks, there were few special offices among the highland groups. The most important were the shamans (*tobalia*; see chapter 7) and the war leaders (*tadulako*). War leaders are said to have been unusually brave commoners who succeeded in designing battle campaigns (A. C. Kruyt 1938, 2:55–223). Although some highlanders proudly claim war leader ancestry, their oracular and military practices have fallen into disuse under Christianity and peaceful conditions.

Two other hereditary ritual offices existed: drumming specialists, who played the *lobo* temple drums (*karatu*) that called the spirits to join the rituals of the living, and persons who handled the heads of human sacrifices and presented them to the community leader. These individuals controlled potentially dangerous aspects of spiritual forces. Some

Tobaku people can still identify the descendants of these ritual specialists, but the pedigree has little significance in the Christian present.

Only one type of pre-Christian ritual specialist still performs regularly: "the one who speaks" (*topolibu'*), also referred to as "the one
who presents the betelnut" (*topotonu pinongo*). Every Tobaku village
has these respected orators, who are invited to make formal requests on
behalf of wedding candidates and other legal petitioners. As one of
their titles implies, they are the ones who deliver the betelnut prepara-
tions, which begin all formal social occasions other than church services. The position of village orator is gained on the basis of rhetorical
skill, although one ritual speaker mentioned the significance of his
high-status background and village of origin, Banasu, which is
renowned for its genteel and calm speech.

Certain aspects of the precontact social hierarchy have been
upheld even within contemporary Salvation Army services. The ranks
of officership are available to those descended from all social strata—a
few officers even pride themselves on being the descendants of Seko
war captives—yet some officers of noble rank still insist on precolonial
rules of deference, such as the escorted procession. One former officer
of *maradika* birth, Brigadier Bohe, insisted on being picked up at his
home and escorted to all church services by other village leaders, or
else he would not show up to preach. In this way elements of the precolonial hierarchy are preserved tacitly in the etiquette of many church
processions.

In Towulu', people say that there are no longer any descendants
of slaves living in the village, that they were all killed as sacrifices or
died with no offspring to succeed them. In some other Tobaku,
Pipikoro, and Kulawi villages, however, there are known descendants
of Seko and Rampi slave captives. Tama Abi', a schoolteacher from
Siwongi, said that when he was a child a certain family in the village
of Momi always inexplicably sacrificed a chicken to feed him when he
visited their house. Only when he was older was he told that these people were the descendants of his family's former slaves, and so they con-

tinued to enact their familial obligations toward him. Individuals descended from some slaves captured in Seko have become officers of the Salvation Army Church, which they see as having championed their ancestors' freedom.

Neither highborn nor slave ancestry is readily discussed by Tobaku residents, but most demonstrate awareness of such ancestral reputations. I once bemoaned that some of my questions about ances-tral practices were shunted from one adult to the next until finally I reached an elder too old, frail, or toothless to talk intelligibly. I then was reminded that those who would speak of ancestral traditions with-out both the age and inherited rights to do so would risk misfortune. Like Volkman (1985, 19), whose Toraja slave acquaintance responded with the words, "Why are you questioning me? You're questioning a cat!" I found that certain types of questions about ritual practices were not welcomed by lower-ranking individuals, who risked cosmological and local community repercussions if they spoke of matters not in their rights to discuss.

Elders are seen as authorities and guides until they are no longer active in farming and political activities. Men are officially in charge of village politics, especially in the form of councils of village elders (*totu'a ngata*). The council convenes formally to discuss pressing vil-lage-wide legal issues, and informally at weddings and other rituals where they are guests of honor. By contrast, women are in charge of the land plots farmed, and most of their politics is conducted infor-mally while working in the fields, rivers, or kitchens. Wives of male leaders, whose birth rank is usually equal to or higher than their spouse's (as judged according to their mother's bridewealth), are expected to have a corresponding influence among their female peers in the village.

Gender ideology in the Kulawi highlands, as in much of Southeast Asia, revolves around assumptions of complementarity in conjunction with some public areas of male privilege (Atkinson and Errington 1990; Van Esterik 1982). As is noted by several Indonesianist

At a "traditional" (*adat*, Ind.) wedding, Towulu' men discuss politics while the bride and groom sit in embarrassed silence, 1986.

scholars (Atkinson 1990; Keeler 1990; Kuipers 1990b; Tsing 1990, 1993), men tend to dominate in the arenas of public political speech and regional trade, while women leverage their interests more from the background. Although female rulers and shamans were rare in the Uma regions, women do perform major roles in farming and life-cycle rituals. All planting and harvesting ceremonies revolve around women. Only women may enter the rice storage bin, so they control this most precious source of life. Ritual chanting over corpses also is the domain of women in Uma-speaking areas, much as it is in West Sumba (Hoskins 1987b) and the Bosavi highlands of New Guinea (Feld 1990).

Tobaku women are responsible for most farm labor, gathering forest foods, pounding and winnowing rice, cooking, washing clothes and dishes, most child care, river fishing, chicken and pig husbandry, plus handicrafts such as basketry and plaiting sleeping mats. Formerly, they also manufactured barkcloth for clothes and blankets, or in some areas such as Winatu produced clay cooking pots with a stone and paddle technique.

Men, by contrast, are responsible for hunting and trapping game, collecting firewood, building and repairing houses, gathering certain palm roots and rattan, caring for cows, buffalo, and horses, slaughtering and cooking animals for feasts, and, where practiced, tapping sugar palms for palm wine. They also perform farm-related tasks such as felling large trees, burning cleared fields, fencing, and planning. Formerly, men were involved in internecine warfare and distant trading expeditions to obtain bridewealth valuables. Now men go primarily to Kulawi to trade cash crops for their routine or ritual needs.

In principle, property can be owned by either men or women although dry-rice fields and houses are considered the domain of women, while large livestock and wet-rice fields are considered the domain of men. According to ancestral practice, only the senior woman of the household may enter the rice storage bin, and she should not speak or otherwise disturb the rice when she makes withdrawals for family meals. Despite, or perhaps because of, their heavier workload, Tobaku women's self-esteem regarding their importance to economic and family life is high. Women pride themselves on being farming and household experts, just as men pride themselves on being good hunters or house builders. Both men and women commonly measure their success in life according to the number of children and grandchildren they have produced. Women and men asserted to me that their rank was equal, although in contexts of particular family disputes some people maintained that a woman should be under the control of her husband. Whether this is a precolonial caveat or not, I do not know, although during the past century it has been advanced by Western missionaries, colonial Dutch, and Indonesian government officials.

In comparison to the Victorian Europeans who missionized

Tina Nase plants maize (field corn) with a ritually carved dibble stick. Towulu' vicinity, 1987.

them, western Central Sulawesi highlanders practicing uxorilocal residence maintained a female-focused household. With matrilineally
inherited swidden land rights and female-dominated farming, they
practiced a more female-centered economy. Thus they had a more
female-focused cosmology, with a female rice goddess, many deities of

unspecified gender, and no high male gods. European missionaries worked to disrupt this relative prominence of women on domestic, economic, and spiritual fronts, although they simultaneously provided women with new career opportunities in nursing, teaching, and the ministry (Aragon 1999a; see chapter 8).

Tobaku parents say they have no preference for male or female children, but rather hope to have boys and girls in roughly equal numbers. Girls, they say, are more helpful and easier to raise, but every family needs sons for heavy tasks. Some people mentioned the expense of financing bridewealth for sons' weddings, but an unusual family with twelve daughters and no sons described the burden of arranging twelve weddings.

I perceived Tobaku women's disadvantaged position relative to men with respect to heavier workloads, certain behavioral restrictions, and their public rights to food. The most highly prized foods, such as meat, were put on females' plates last. This discrimination was particularly disconcerting because, as a foreign guest, I was given what were considered the choicest foods despite my gender. Women and girls are trained from childhood to be "embarrassed" (*me'ea*, Uma) to take or accept the favored, protein-filled morsels of food in public. Just as the best is deserved by elders over their juniors (except for the very elderly, who take and receive less and less as they approach death), so do the finest victuals, particularly meat and fish (*bau'*), go to men over women unless some other element of status, such as age or kinship position, overrides their gender disadvantage. Women, however, oversee food storage and preparation, so they may have some private opportunities to assuage their nutritional needs and desires.

The aging process confers increasing status and independence upon Tobaku women. Most women clearly express that the finest aspect of marriage is the experience of raising children and then grandchildren. When I asked some middle-aged widows and divorcées if they would like to marry again, they scoffed in disbelief, often pointing to their healthy, teenage, or adult offspring. "With these fine children to help me in my old age, why would I want to remarry?" Tina Lidona' asked rhetorically. "If I had another husband," she said, "I would have to prepare his rice every day." As in other regions of Asia, the Tobaku marriage bond is viewed primarily as one of potential parenthood, domestic economic cooperation, kinship alliance, and sexual companionship. Other than teenagers recently influenced by syrupy pop-music cassettes from Palu, individuals evidence few idealistic notions of romance.

Precolonial law, like social hierarchy, was intertwined with religious concepts. Families and community members were expected to redress the errors of their kin and fellow villagers before the ancestor spirits or deities inflicted more serious punishment on the community. Fines (*giwu'* or *waea'*) of material goods and animal sacrifices, regulated through precedents known by oral tradition, were the major form of expiation. Corporal punishment or enslavement was invoked for particularly heinous crimes, such as adultery. Often, however, these sentences could be commuted or replaced by heavy fines.

A basic principle of Tobaku law was and is for each dispute to be solved at the next highest level of social jurisdiction. If a personal dispute cannot be resolved within the family by the elders, one or both sides will take their grievances to a community leader, formerly the *maradika*, today the village headman or the Salvation Army officers. If community leaders cannot bring the matter to satisfaction, the affair will be turned over to the judgment of regional leaders, formerly the leader of Siwongi or Peana and today the district head (*camat*) of Kulawi. The colonial Dutch simply added new hierarchic layers of administration, which they dominated. Now Europeans are replaced by Indonesian government officials from other regions.

Fines, payable to the offended and the dispute mediator, once governed an infinite variety of daily and ritual behaviors, everything from playing a bamboo harvest instrument (*kakula*) out of season to making a speech error at an engagement ceremony. The Salvation Army similarly couches regulations for its students and staff in terms of fines. Although some types of fines, like ordeals, have been dropped, many precolonial fines are still invoked, sometimes on the unsuspecting.

In the late 1980s, when the Javanese chauffeur of a missionary rode his motorcycle in Kulawi following the death of a high-ranking leader, the outraged community demanded a fine of one buffalo. Precolonial mourning taboos at the death of *maradika* forbade activities such as riding horses. By logical extrapolation, locals today argue that motor vehicles should not be driven. As an innocent outsider, the chauffeur refused to pay. The community then reduced the fine to Rp20,000.[4] Ultimately, a nominal payment of Rp1,000 was donated to the grieving family in acknowledgment of the customary taboos governing the driver's accidental slight to the deceased. Public opinion, gossip, and the threat of ostracism still rally a measure of even church cooperation with such ancestral norms.

In recent decades, much of the governing authority formerly held by precolonial community leaders or their descendants has passed to Indonesian government and Salvation Army representatives who have established themselves as ritual and moral leaders. Ethnic identities, land use, kinship and gender relations, naming practices, social rankings, and legal procedures have adjusted to numerous Salvation Army and government constraints. Yet none of these arenas of social life has become detached from its inherent interconnection to local relationships, cosmological well-being, and consequent earthly prosperity. Survival in the Central Sulawesi highlands continues to be based on land, animal, and human fertility. The will of deities, ancestral or Protestant, always is manifested in localized natural outcomes. Community prescriptions and prayers thus are enjoined to alleviate any signs of cosmological imbalance. Given the radically different ecological and social world in which the Tobaku people live, their Christianity was destined to depart from customary European expectations of religious reality.

꩜ 3 ꩜

Precolonial Polities, Exchange, and Early Colonial Contact

> Making history is really a single process with two strands: the practice of fash-
> ioning a future social order entails a constant revaluation of the past.
> Consequently the historical—supposedly factual accounts of what has hap-
> pened—can never be entirely separated from the mythical-persuasive elabora-
> tions of what exists eternally and what might be.
>
> *John D. Y. Peel,* "Making History: The Past in the Ijesha Present"

By 1929, the pioneering Dutch missionary A. C. Kruyt claimed that indigenous Central Sulawesi cultures were disrupted irrevocably through contact with Europeans (A. C. Kruyt 1929). Kruyt saw his mission activities as providing a spiritual and social lifeline for emotionally desperate natives unmoored from their prior cultural stasis and isolation. His view slighted the ecological specializations and precolonial interethnic relations in which Central Sulawesi highlanders had engaged for centuries. By all accounts, including their own, Tobaku always were montagnards, peripheral to larger population centers. Yet their late precolonial political formations, economy, and religion depended upon periodic migrations and regional, often interethnic, exchanges. As the Dutch missionary writings themselves make clear, the ancestors of contemporary Tobaku communities moved fluidly throughout western Central Sulawesi seeking forest produce, potential farm land, and game. They also conducted raids, exchanged goods, and sought mates in their paths to and from the coasts. The current separation between coastal Muslims and Christian highlanders did not yet exist.

This chapter concerns highlanders' precolonial polities, including their spiritual facets, and examines their earliest documented con-

84

tacts with "foreigners." Founders' cults were, and still are, a regional political and religious institution that melds local cosmology with ecologically necessary settlement movements and leadership formation. Highland populations such as the Tobaku had a long history of movement and trade encounters with lowland groups. These regional alliances were poorly understood and quickly dismantled and subsumed by early Dutch administrators.

Central Sulawesi highlanders did not anticipate how Europeans would use material goods and services to unhinge local exchange systems and prevailing patterns of social ranks. In turn, Europeans did not comprehend the significance of shifting settlements and the ritualized orchestration of local political leadership. These precolonial circumstances and contact-era misunderstandings are a little noticed aspect of Christian conversion and Dutch colonial administration in Central Sulawesi. By 1900, Kruyt had forged both a symbiotic and antagonistic relationship with the Dutch colonial government as they constructed policies related to their sometimes common, sometimes divergent, religious and political aims.

Shifting Populations and Founders' Cults

Archaeological materials from highland Central Sulawesi that relate to proto-Austronesian religious life include pottery burial jars with associated bones and grave goods, stone barkcloth beaters, and megaliths. In eastern Central Sulawesi, extensive carved stone remains exist in the form of lidded vats and anthropomorphic statues that are up to several meters in height or diameter (A. C. Kruyt 1938, vol.1; Kaudern 1938, vol.5; Perwakilan Departemen Pendidikan dan Kebudayaan 1973; Masyhuda 1980/1981). Although the megaliths have not been dated with precision, they are estimated to be as much as three thousand years old (Bellwood 1997). Between these spotty archaeological records and early twentieth century mission reports, there exists little specific information on highland groups. Dutch colonial records focus mainly on coastal events, and government reports lump interior "Toradja" groups together in a frustratingly vague manner. In turn, Tobaku oral histories, unconcerned with linear chronologies, do not document specific events much prior to the colonial era.

Tobaku people say they had an established confederation of villages with its original center near Siwongi when the Dutch arrived in the early 1900s. Reportedly, in the late 1880s, about one hundred families from the eastern area near Lonebasa were driven from their home during a battle with Kulawi. About sixty of those families fled west along the Lariang River toward the coast, while forty stopped and settled under the leader of Hungku, a former settlement near Siwongi. They arrived by raft at the Tobaku River and, finding it a good area for hunting, settled in the region permanently.

According to a popular Tobaku narrative, hunters from Hungku then chased an *anoa* (*Bubalus quarlesi*, a wild cow unique to Sulawesi) to the present site of Siwongi, where the animal turned to stone (Tarro 1982). At that spot there grew a *jiwongi*, a fragrant tree with only two leaves. When the hunters cut the tree down, it launched itself into the river and floated to a spot, where it then stood up to become the center post for the first Tobaku temple (*lobo*). This event represents the official beginning of Tobaku history. Once the temple was built, the tale goes, no enemies entered Siwongi successfully, and residents always won their battles. Later, a man from Tompi in the east married a woman from Siwongi in the west. Their daughter married a man from Winatu in the north, and one of their children became the great-grandfather of Tutu', the leader who represented Tobaku under the initial Dutch colonial regime. Towulu' oral histories also reiterate Kruyt's report that several hundred people from Rampi, driven northwest by drought, entered the Tobaku area during the late precolonial period and intermarried with Tobaku residents already settled there. Winatu elders, by contrast, claim that at least part of their ancestral population migrated west from a non-Uma-speaking area, Besoa in the Lore Valley. These oral histories suggest a complicated regional migration history where shifting horticulturists and hunters moved regularly along the Lariang River and its tributaries for a variety of reasons, including war, drought, epidemics, and the search for fruitful land and spouses. The unilateral south-to-north migration theory of Kaudern (1925, 2:68) undoubtedly oversimplifies Kulawi region settlement patterns.[1]

The movement or creation of settlements in highland Central Sulawesi was, and is, a religious matter. Community elders made verbal pacts with the spirit owners of the forested land that was cleared for farming settlements. The pacts promised food offerings to the spirits in exchange for ample harvests. Successful elders were recalled after their deaths to become mediators again between the spirits of the land (see chapter 5) and the deceased elders' descendants. These ritual bonds between community elders, or "founders," and land areas integrated the precolonial religion with political leadership formation. Founders' cults also set the groundwork for intergroup relations and ongoing group segmentation or realignments.

The primary literature describing founders' cults in Southeast Asia concerns mainland societies (Mus 1975 [1933]; Lehman 2001), but similar phenomena have been described for Indonesian societies in both European colonial (e.g., A. C. Kruyt 1906; Meijer 1932) and more recent ethnographic literature (Geertz 1960, 23–28; Jay 1969, 326; Koentjaraningrat 1989, 341; Wessing 1999). Founders' cults concern two different, but often conflated, types of spirits. The first are the unseen guardian deities, often referred to as "owners" or "lords," of a land area (*pue'*, Uma). These spirits permit the land's initial clearing and its transfer from the "wild" to the human domain. The second type are ancestral spirits of those individuals who made successful agreements with the guardian deities.

The conflation of these spirit types occurs both among the followers of founders' cults and foreign observers (Geertz 1960). In areas such as Central Sulawesi, the spirits of founders become so closely associated with the land guardian deities that their discrimination often serves no symbolic or practical value. The agency of these two types of spiritual beings simply is merged. The metaphoric collapsing of land guardians and founding ancestors holds symbolic and practical value by allowing descendants of founders to claim descent from the guardian spirits and deified ancestors as well as mere mortals.

Veneration of guardian and ancestor spirits has been entwined with the construction of community hierarchies in western Central Sulawesi. Those individuals with the spiritual prowess to procure favors from guardian spirits and obtain prosperity from formerly wild lands gained status as settlement founders. Their descendants continued to assume leadership over descendants of junior followers, who in turn ranked above recent arrivals to the community. Such a portrayal of founders' cults inclines us to view the hierarchical political outcomes as ramifications of religious ideology, or alternatively as sheltered by such ideology, and it is worthwhile to examine briefly these well-trodden theoretical paths.

Consonant with Weber's earlier analysis of Hinduism (1958, 29), Dumont's treatise on social hierarchy in India (1980) explained the political vehicle of caste in terms of Hindu religious principles of purity and pollution. Said (1978) and others such as Dirks (1987) attacked Dumont's view. They saw his perspective as emanating from a colonialist agenda that benefited from, and sought to create, a brittle indigenous polity resting on "hollow" religious misapprehensions. One of the more interesting arguments that Dirks makes, applicable here, is that the Hindu caste system could be manipulated by British rulers precisely because it "continued to be permeable to political influence" (Dirks 1987, 8). Similarly, I suggest that Southeast Asian founders' cults are neither the prime movers of small-scale political formations nor merely justifying epiphenomena of them. Rather, they are flexible religious institutions whose rituals perform and display the ongoing construction of regional political formations.

The general description of founders' cults provided above meshes with outsiders' observations and likely would be acceptable to Tobaku elders. Nevertheless, this model omits important facets concerning the parties and territories involved in the founders' cult pacts among various humans and spiritual forces. Rituals, held at the level of the household, swidden farming settlement, and region, often serve as the proving ground for leadership formation and for planning swidden migrations (cf. Kirsch 1973). When the Tobaku hamlet of Wana' was created in the 1960s, for example, its genesis was accompanied by ritual pacts and feasts sponsored through a former Towulu' headman and a splintering leader among his constituency.

Dutch colonial rule, Protestant missionization, and recent development-related migration have introduced extraordinary new conditions to such founders' cult bargains that once mainly implicated kindreds, local leaders, and regional spirits. Although highland settlements and their ties to other similar or larger polities seem never to have been stable in Central Sulawesi, the transformation of founders' cults under missionization and the area's integration into the Dutch colonial and postwar Indonesian states require a reassessment of leaders' pacts and their supposed relationship to local constituencies and physical locations.

Christian conversion has permitted Protestant ministers to infiltrate the bargains made between deities and communities in order to claim a share in founders' authority over highland territories. More recently in the New Order Indonesian state, occasional migration to the lowlands has forced highland leaders to establish novel pacts acknowledging spiritual claims by other ethnic groups over occupied lands (Aragon 2001). Highlanders' revised appraisals of the covenants that formulate community hierarchies and spiritual aspects of land use have altered local perceptions of physical territories or "senses of place" (Feld and Basso 1996). They also are affecting the dynamics of interethnic relations in peripheral zones such as Central Sulawesi, which are being drawn into national development projects—contemporary topics to which I will return in chapter 8.

Highland and Lowland Polities

Precolonial founders' cults in western Central Sulawesi are developed within highland and lowland diplomacy. Tobaku leaders drew on their personal relationships with lowland leaders to impress their own constituencies, and parallels throughout the archipelago suggest this is a widespread pattern (e.g., Atkinson 1989; Tsing 1993). According to both early colonial reports and present oral histories, the Tobaku and other highlanders maintained trade, tribute, and occasional military alliances with lowland Kaili kingdoms (A. C. Kruyt 1938, 1:182–185). Moreover, the elevated exchange value of objects produced or made in each others' regions promoted the status of both highland and lowland leaders who could organize interethnic gift exchanges (Aragon 1996a, 47–49).

At the time of Dutch contact, the interior groups of western Central Sulawesi were involved in trade and tribute relationships with the kingdom of Sigi, a Kaili polity that was vassal to the Bugis kingdom of Bone in South Sulawesi. According to the Makasar scholar Mattulada (personal communication), the Bugis folk hero Sawerigading established relations with the Palu Valley Kaili people in the ninth or tenth century a.d. This claim dates the relations between South and Central Sulawesi coastal peoples to many centuries before the rulers of South Sulawesi kingdoms converted to Islam in the early 1600s (Pelras 1985).

Adriani and Kruyt (1968 [1950], 2:chap. 12) state that the coastal Kaili living around Palu Valley and Tomini Bay became officially Muslim by the late 1800s, but most were dilatory in their Muslim practices. Reportedly, the Arab and Bugis traders of that time found the practice of Islam in Central Sulawesi so wanting that they termed it "shrimp Islam" (*Isilamu mpolamale*). By this they meant that local Muslims, like shrimp—which have filth on their heads while their hind parts are clean—are completely different from what they should be (Adriani and Kruyt 1968 [1950], 2:343). Adriani and Kruyt maintain that besides not carrying out the five pillars of Islam diligently, Muslim converts continued practices such as headhunting uninterrupted until the Dutch colonial government finally interfered (Adriani and Kruyt 1968 [1950], 2:381–382). This reported shallowness of Central Sulawesi Islam was used as a justification by the Dutch government for introducing Protestantism to the region. Paradoxically, the reported superficiality of early Christianity in Central Sulawesi also was used as a justification for increasing funding for the missionization process.

Tobaku oral histories recount that precolonial trade involved carrying forest products such as rattan to traders in Mora, South Sulawesi, who would provide ceremonial items such as round copper alloy trays (*dula'*) or woven cloth in return. Salt also was an item sought by the highlanders, usually via Kaili people in the Palu Valley. Within the Tobaku area, the southwestern villages traded barkcloth produced by women for clay pots manufactured by women in Winatu. Barkcloth from the highlands also was traded to Kaili kingdoms such as Sigi for use as ritual apparel and funeral shrouds (Aragon 1990).

Sigi developed as a kingdom in relationship to traders from South Sulawesi, just as the Bugis, Mandar, and Makasar of South Sulawesi were influenced through trade with foreign court societies such as those in Java. The commoners of Luwu, the oldest Bugis polity in South Sulawesi, speak Tae, the same language as the highland Toraja (Errington 1989, 18). Similarly, the Sigi people speak Ija, a dialect of Kaili, the same language used by Palu Valley highlanders. The founders of the earliest highland settlements thus continued political and marital alliances with the larger lowland polities of Sigi, Banawa, and Dolo, which often made claims to superordinate rank through displays of wealth and access to overseas trade. The interior groups thus became junior partners, described locally as "younger siblings," in a network of regional exchange relations framed in cosmological and kinship terms.

Members of the Lamakarate family, descendants of the colonial-era ruling family of Sigi, describe how a precolonial "raja" of Sigi

Bapak Lamakarate, son of the last colonial ruler of the Sigi kingdom, stands dressed in a golden silk sarong with his nephew, 1993.

formed a sacred pact with the raja of Bone in South Sulawesi. The rulers each performed a human sacrifice and carved ceremonial sword handles from the victims' leg bones. The ruler of Bone sacrificed a woman, and so sent the "female" sword to Sigi. The ruler of Sigi sacrificed a man, and so sent the "male" sword to Bone. In that way their relationship was established, and the largest kingdom in Central Sulawesi, Sigi, became a symbolic marriage partner to the illustrious kingdom of Bone in South Sulawesi.

The royal Lamakarate family of Sigi still claims an elder brother status to the highland groups of the Kulawi District and, like the Dutch and other Indonesians who succeeded them politically, identify all interior groups of the district generically as Kulawi people. Even in recent decades the family has brought Tobaku children from Winatu to work in its household in exchange for educational assistance. Tobaku elders also stress their group's importance to the Sigi kingdom as devoted "younger siblings" who sent their war leaders to pilot some of Sigi's important campaigns into the east and south. The highland and lowland precolonial relationship, therefore, did not entail the religious and social rift that the Dutch colonial government began to create.

Tobaku elders often recall their people's status as feared warriors in the precolonial era, when they sought heads for ritual purposes and raided as far south and east as the Seko and Lore Valley regions for slaves, buffalo, and prestige goods such as woven resist-dyed cloth (*ikat*). Raids also were made on Kulawi Valley villages. Tobaku responsibility for the famous village fire at Bolapapu (literally, Burnt Village) in Kulawi is claimed by both Tobaku elders and Kruyt (1938, 1:185–186).[2] Kulawi warriors in turn are said to have penetrated far into the Tobaku region in search of gold dust, which is panned near the mouth of the Lariang River.

According to Tobaku oral historians, internecine warfare was responsible for many population movements. One section of Kantewu Village, called Lida', is said to be populated with the descendants of inmarrying Tobaku warriors. Descendants of slaves captured in war

A Tobaku hamlet leader, Tama Laura, demonstrates a precolonial war dance, 1993.

with Bada' are still living in the Tobaku village of Rantewulu', although most slaves captured in Tobaku wars are said to have been taken from Seko and Rampi. Tobaku elders say that their forefathers raided as far southwest as Mamuju in South Sulawesi, but then a Mamuju leader gave them a ceremonial spear as an oath of permanent peace. As with all endeavors of Central Sulawesi highlanders, success in war was the sign of its moral righteousness and favor of the deities (see chapter 5).

Like today, Tobaku's closest allies at the turn of the twentieth century were their fellow Uma speakers to the east and north. Their precolonial standing with respect to Moma-speaking Kulawi is somewhat difficult to determine because of Dutch colonial interference. According to Kruyt (1938, 1:147–148), the Dutch saved costs and eased administration in the western Central Sulawesi region by "discharging" (*ontslag*, Dutch) all the "small chiefs," such as those in Tobaku, and subsuming their territories under the leader (*maradika*) of Kulawi, who then was given the title of *magau*, a Kaili term for "ruler" used by lowland polities such as Sigi.

The Pipikoro, Tole'e, and other southeastern Uma-speaking groups reportedly agreed to accept the new circumstances because they were accustomed to being beneath Sigi and perceived Kulawi as their "elder brother" (A. C. Kruyt 1938, 1:148). Tobaku, however, had rather strained relations with Kulawi at the time and initially refused to submit to the hierarchy decreed by the Dutch. The Tobaku instead preserved their own rulers, first Tama Sesa, also known as Makole, then Tama Kalagi (probably a Dutch transcription of Kalaki, a founding family still prominent today). Preferring to unite with the Kaili center of Dolo, rather than Kulawi and the Kaili center of Sigi, Tobaku people reportedly hacked a path in the forest from Tobaku to Bangga to avoid passing through Kulawi on the way to the coast. Although Kruyt does not specify what Dutch government measures were taken against the Tobaku, he says that they finally were forced to accept their incorporation under Kulawi. Tobaku elders report that the first Tobaku *maradika* to serve under the Dutch was named Tutu' (Mountain Peak), sometimes called Lanti' (Appointed [king]).

Uma speakers were united officially by the Dutch under the "top leader" (*maradika malolo*) in Peana while all Moma speakers were united under an "elder leader" (*maradika matu'a*) in Kulawi. Both chiefs were to channel their relations with the Dutch government through the Dutch-appointed *magau* ruler in Kulawi. The first *magau* of Kulawi was Tama Rengke, signatory to the Dutch government treaty of November 30, 1908 (Kaudern 1941). He retired in 1910 and was replaced by Tama Mampe, a Muslim who Kaudern says was not well liked by the Kulawi people but who was efficient in collecting taxes for the Dutch Controleur (controller) in Palu. Tama Mampe was among the four hundred out of two thousand people in Kulawi who died during the Spanish influenza epidemic introduced by Europeans in late 1918.

Such heavy-handed attempts to bureaucratize western Central Sulawesi politics clearly altered Tobaku relations with lowland Kaili kingdoms as well as other groups in the mountains. What had been bilateral relationships steeped in the rhetoric of brotherhood, ritual events, and occasional raids became rigidified by the Dutch into a fixed unilateral hierarchy. Tribute to, and gifts returned from, the lowland rulers were forbidden (Adriani and Kruyt 1968 [1950]), and lowland Kaili groups rapidly increased their conversion to Islam in opposition to Dutch interference. In the next section, I look more specifically at the issue of regional exchanges, placing them within the realm of cosmological constraints and the precolonial ideology of highland and lowland symbiosis.

Precolonial Religious and Political Gifts

Before Salvation Army missionaries arrived from Europe, highlanders in western Central Sulawesi routinely presented offerings or gifts to localized deities, highland leaders, and lowland kingdom rulers (A. C. Kruyt 1938, 1:182–185; Aragon 1992, 126–130, 251–266). These gifts included food, livestock, slaves, barkcloth, or forest products such as rattan, beeswax, and resins. Such gifts were integral to early highland-lowland polity relations and precolonial wealth in Southeast Asia. Archival data and current narratives indicate that highlanders such as the Tobaku exercised autonomy in their lowland exchanges and perceived themselves as benefiting from the interactions.

Mauss (1967, 14) noted on the basis of Kruyt's data that precolonial Central Sulawesi religious gifts were inevitably made to initiate or maintain a bargain with deities, lowland rulers, or ancestors. In Central Sulawesi, good rice harvests, strong houses, war victories, easily caught game, or healthy relatives were requested (or as Mauss put it, "purchased") with offerings. Without promises to the gods, no returns could be expected. Without proper supplication and retribution, the gods would no longer give their favor, but rather would seek revenge. Offerings or gifts maintained relationships that served all parties.

The same ideals of hierarchical reciprocity applied to exchanges between highland commoners and leaders, and also between highlanders in general and their lowland "elders." Linguistic evidence neatly ties the worship of indigenous deities to the homage paid to regional rulers. A term found in many Central Sulawesi languages meaning both "to worship" and "to give tribute" is "*mepue'*." "*Me-*" is an intransitive verb prefix, and "*pue'*" literally means "owner" and connotes indigenous deities who were titled as *pue'*, followed by the name of their domain of jurisdiction, such as land, water, rice, or gold. The taking of a person or a spirit as an "owner" was realized by the act of giving them an offering for which one hoped to receive a beneficial return.

Gifts by highlanders to their own community leaders were a religious as well as political matter because spiritual blessings flowed from harmonious hierarchical relations. Commoners maintained good relations with members of high-ranking families by regularly bringing them small gifts of food, betelnut, firewood, and so forth (A. C. Kruyt 1938, 1:509). Fostering felicitous relations through small gifts thereby

allowed weaker commoner households to call upon the more powerful families in times of need, for example, when they required a buffalo or pig for a ceremonial sacrifice. Requests for such favors perpetuat-
ed for generations reciprocal debt and obligation relationships between
families of leaders and commoners.

Regional concepts of religious propitiation and lowland kingdom
power were so entrenched in Central Sulawesi at the time of the
Dutch conquest in 1905 that some highland groups continued to send
yearly gifts to the lowlands even after the Dutch government prohibited these relations. New Dutch regulations forbidding highland-to-low-
land tribute gifts aimed to replace the authority of the lowland Muslim
kingdoms with their own (Adriani and Kruyt 1968 [1950], 1:191).
Tobaku highlanders treasure the few lowland heirlooms they still own,
and in the absence of that continued ownership, village leaders tell
tales of the objects they once owned as "proof" of their individual and
regional importance in lowland-highland relationships. Such ritualized gift exchanges may have been less significant from the vantage
point of interethnic relations than for establishing leadership ranks
within the individual ethnic groups themselves. This predisposition of
local leaders to invoke foreign connections through imported goods
also benefited colonial Europeans.

Like deities, Tobaku community founders and lowland royal families were expected to attract prosperity for their communities and to
show signs of this ability through their material wealth and generosity.
The notion that the rulers of lowland polities may have blithely
received valuable material resources without having to give anything
substantial in exchange—or only spiritual blessings—runs counter to
the well-documented Southeast Asian regional pattern that necessi-
tates "the distribution of material largesse by a chief to sustain his spiritual aura" (Kathirithamby-Wells 1990, 3; Wolters 1970; Wheatley
1983; Milner 1982). Central Sulawesi, like Java, Thailand, Burma, and
many other precolonial systems, fits into what Adas (1992, 90) calls the
"contest state," where rulers' claims to power and control, over gifts as

well as other matters, are in effect limited by factors such as poor communications, weak administration, a dearth of labor, the mobility of peasant populations, and rivalry among leaders.

In precolonial Southeast Asian communities, an initial gift, even by a social inferior, generally obliged the recipient to accept the offering and thereby become indebted to the giver. Therefore, highlanders were not only giving gifts of subordination and worship to lowland rulers, but also staking economic, political, and spiritual claims. What was exchanged between highlanders and lowlanders may not necessarily have been material gifts of equal value when measured in terms of either internal or external markets. There was, however, a pattern of hierarchical reciprocity with a potential for indebtedness on either side—although local assessments of the debt balance may well have varied between the two groups.

In Central Sulawesi, marriage gifts to a bride's family perpetuate a woman's and her offspring's social rank and simultaneously place the woman's family in a ritually superior status to her husband. When a member of the lowland Sigi royal family married a high-ranking Kulawi woman in the early twentieth century, it was a political and spiritual coup not only for the Sigi kingdom, which obtained tribute promises and increased control at the periphery of its domain, but also for the Kulawi community, which gained not just bridewealth gifts, but a spiritual and kinship claim upon the Sigi court. This is a case of complementary yet divergent perceptions of the significance of a single set of exchanged items.

In sum, the gift-giving relations between highland and lowland kingdoms in Central Sulawesi were a source of economic benefit and prestige to leaders on both sides. As with the highlanders' offerings to their local deities, gifts to lowland rulers sealed bargains to ensure a predictable return and general prosperity. Unlike the exchange relationship later forged by European missionaries, the precolonial protocols for gift giving and the goods that could be proffered and expected by the other were familiar and flattering to both groups.

The "Ethical Policy" and Kruyt's Mission in Central Sulawesi

Recent anthropological research on Sumatra has emphasized that the various European interest groups involved in colonial forays — including government bureaucrats, businessmen, and missionaries — were not necessarily united toward common goals (Stoler 1985, 1989a, 1989b, 1992; Kipp 1990). In Central Sulawesi there was a gradual transition from a symbiotic relationship between the Netherlands Indies government and Kruyt's first Protestant mission toward an increasing dissatisfaction by both parties with the actions of the other. This section looks first at the Dutch government's policy shift from the Cultivation System (*Cultuurstelsel*, Dutch) to the Ethical Policy (*Ethische Politiek*) and then turns to Kruyt's role in implementing and formulating Ethical Policy practices for missions in Sulawesi.

The distinct shift in Dutch colonial policy toward Indonesia that began during the last decade of the nineteenth century resulted in part from Dutch middle-class displeasure with what was perceived in Europe as a lack of moral and economic commitment to the betterment of the colonies. An increasingly engaged colonialist policy in the early 1900s aimed to annex the colony more completely to Holland through the establishment of tighter political, religious, and economic connections (see Schrauwers 1998, 208–213). Paradoxically, the humanitarian concerns of Dutch leaders were realized with military force in order to establish conditions favorable for the desired Indies administration and economic development.

Central Sulawesi inhabitants first experienced military interference from the Dutch in 1905. Troops were sent to "pacify" the region and obtain "short contracts" (*korte verklaring*, Dutch) signed by local leaders who would hand over political authority to the Netherlands. Dutch soldiers entered the interior at the behest of Assistant Resident A. J. N. Engelenberg, supposedly to extinguish intertribal fighting between the Napu and Poso peoples. Engelenberg then instructed the troops to inform all interior chiefs that the ruler of the Luwu kingdom had submitted to the queen of the Netherlands, who would be their new sovereign as well. Resistant communities were subjugated with European guns, and the Dutch demanded corvée labor (*herendiensten*, Dutch) through the now-compliant chiefs (Adriani and Kruyt 1968 [1950], 1:231–237). These demands compelled local men to begin harvesting and trading forest resources such as dammar or rattan for Dutch colonial currency.

According to prevailing social theories of the Netherlands, education was the best medicine to cure the indolence and immorality of natives in the colonies, just as among the working class in Holland (Habbema 1904, 997). Through the introduction of a colonial Christian education system, both the Dutch government and mission initially were united in their desire to invest native societies with three European values: rationality, individuality, and acquisitiveness (Coté 1979, xi). Taxation, school fees, and new agricultural techniques were introduced to dissolve communal interdependence and promote individualistic financial responsibility. The Dutch government intended to civilize and uplift the natives economically while garnering greater tax revenue through closer control of native affairs.

Albertus Christiaan Kruyt, the pioneering missionary-ethnographer of Central Sulawesi, represented the Netherlands Missionary Society (Nederlands Zendelinggenootschap), associated with the Dutch Reformed Church (Nederlands Hervormde Kerk). He was born in 1871, the son of Johannes Kruyt, a missionary stationed in East Java. Albertus Kruyt was raised and educated in the Netherlands to follow in his father's footsteps. His studies, however, were broad enough to bring him into contact with diverse theological perspectives, including Christian socialism and the theories of cultural evolution prevalent in European social sciences at the time (K. J. Brouwer 1951, 26–27).

In 1891, at the age of twenty, Kruyt was formally installed at his Poso Lake missionary field position by the future Resident of Manado, E. J. Jellesma, who informed the gathered locals that helping Kruyt would be tantamount to helping him (J. Kruyt 1970, 68). The

Christian mission was perceived as a piece with the colonial administration, and for all intents and purposes it was in the initial decades of active colonial involvement in the region.

In 1895, the Netherlands Bible Society sent a linguist, Nicolaus Adriani, to join Kruyt and help translate the Bible into the Bare'e (now called Poso or Pamona) language of the Lake Poso inhabitants. Erroneous government estimates numbered the Poso people at approximately 100,000 souls. The first census of 1907 indicated a much more modest population of only 22,977 people within the district of Poso. Nevertheless, the original plans to missionize and actively administer this animist region were pushed forward with vigor. A third Dutch missionary, H. C. Hofman, arrived in 1903 (Adriani and Kruyt 1968 [1950], 1:229).

Adriani and Kruyt thought that knowledge of the local language was essential not only to communicate the gospel, but also to comprehend the indigenous cosmology that they were aiming to supplant. The missionaries' ability to master elements of the regional languages impressed local inhabitants tremendously, sometimes adding to false impressions of missionaries' divinity or common ancestry. The studies begun by Kruyt and Adriani on the Poso population were the first extensive reports of Central Sulawesi conditions available for Europeans, even though, as Downs notes, their monographs are disorganized and full of inconsistencies (Downs 1956, preface). In Kruyt's volume on the "West Toradjas" (A. C. Kruyt 1938), these problems are exacerbated by the author's tendency to conflate information about the numerous ethnic groups he discusses on the basis of brief observations and comments by his Indonesian staff.

Yet Kruyt began his mission field with Pamona speakers almost twenty years before the Salvation Army established their highland posts in western Central Sulawesi. Thus he significantly shaped Dutch colonial policy and local responses during the initial contact period. Moreover, Kruyt's and Adriani's ethnographic scholarship, even on Uma speakers, far excels in both quantity and quality the relatively few writings produced by Salvation Army missionaries concerning Central Sulawesi events and practices. Finally, Kruyt's and Adriani's commentary and letters regarding their efforts, coupled with the subsequent writings of Kruyt's son, Jan Kruyt, and biographer K. J. Brouwer, give the most extensive picture available of a missionization process that appears to have been rather uniform throughout Central Sulawesi.

During the first decade of his mission, Kruyt worked closely with Dutch government officials to advance their common goals of checking the influence of Muslim kingdoms such as Sigi and Luwu, and introducing educational programs aimed to achieve a more cooperative and economically productive interior population. Financial limitations constrained both Kruyt's mission and the regional government such that they were forced to depend on each other's respective strengths. Kruyt's extensive on-the-ground experience and entrenched position within local politics allowed him to have considerable influence over regional government policy into the early 1900s. Moreover, he continued to maintain virtually absolute control over the local school system that was subsidized for many years by the Dutch government.

Kruyt wanted locals to accept Christianity and schooling voluntarily rather than compulsorily, yet he felt pressed to meet all government requests for mission schools in order to forestall the creation of a government school system that would rival his church-based institutions. Ultimately, a solution to the mission's and regional government's financial problems was sought in Kruyt's introduction of new cash crops such as coffee and copra (dried coconut to be pressed for oil), the profits from which were returned to the local church, school, and regional administrators in the form of taxes and fees (Coté 1979, 267–273).

Kruyt argued that the government could only spread its development programs effectively with the aid of value changes introduced by the missionaries, and the missionaries could only put forward their educational and social programs with government decrees, resources, and law enforcement (A. C. Kruyt 1907).[3] Kruyt and his colleague Adriani, however, found that gaining the trust of his mission community, much less converting them, was a difficult task:

> Upon his arrival in the country the missionary was received with great suspicion, because the people could not understand why a Hollander, who in so many respects was so much better off than the Toradja, came to live among them without looking out for his self-interest in one way or another. That another God was proclaimed to them in order that this one be served instead of their own gods was an absurdity to them. They served their ancestors; the Hollanders did this for theirs. The ancestors-gods did not interfere with each other and entertained not the least interest in each other's descendants. Therefore they did not take the preaching of the gospel to heart. (Adriani and Kruyt 1968 [1950], 1:229)

Kruyt progressed slowly in the first dozen years, only gaining his first Poso converts in 1909. According to his own reports, he followed a policy where he commenced with personal contacts, especially visits to chiefs. He made generous gifts and contributions to local agricultural and life-cycle rituals. Eventually, Kruyt began to request return favors, initiate schools, and utter simple sermons (K. J. Brouwer 1951, 79). Only in the final stage did he preach seriously, suggesting to the Poso people that they shared common ancestors with the Dutch and so should worship the same God, who would give their personal souls salvation through faith in Jesus Christ (Coté 1979, 67).

Not only did Kruyt's mission and the Dutch government see their aims as closely allied, but the Pamona highlanders also identified them as one and the same institution. Kruyt was once told, "When we are subject to the Netherlands Indies Government, you [the missionaries] will be our chiefs because you are the first Dutch people who came to us" (Adriani and Kruyt 1968 [1950], 1:136). Such a statement, in retrospect, shows that locals were astute in assessing the power of the missionaries. The statement also illustrates how early missionaries became elevated as spiritual founders, who eventually gained religious authority similar to indigenous founders of land settlements and regional spirit cults.

Kruyt often was frustrated in his efforts to establish schools in the highland Pamona regions. Hamlets were small, usually no more than ten households, and widely dispersed. Swidden farming practices resulted in additional, even smaller, scattered settlements seasonally drawing the population away from the main centers. In 1894, a new, larger "model" village was established when Kruyt convinced Papa i Wunte, the chief of Wayo Makuni Hamlet, and others to consolidate several hilltop settlements into one fifty-household village in the valley (K. J. Brouwer 1951, 60). This Dutch strategy of uniting scattered and difficult-to-control highland settlements into larger, lower-elevation villages is apparent within the administrative boundaries followed by the Indonesian government today, and the strategy continues under current "local transmigration" programs.

With "gentle compulsion" (*zachte dwang*, Dutch), Kruyt tried to use prestige gained from years of financial and medical contributions to persuade village leaders to send their children to school with teachers hired from the Minahasa region of North Sulawesi (Coté 1979, 76–83). The greatest problem Kruyt encountered was local resistance to the idea that the children would be given special foreign knowledge, making them potentially superior to or different from their parents, elders, and ancestors (A. C. Kruyt 1900, 348; Adriani 1919). Adriani inferred that the formal instruction of schools was equated with local notions of private apprenticeships in magic or sorcery. For these varied reasons, Kruyt's efforts to expand schooling in the interior were largely thwarted until military establishment of the colonial administration compelled Poso people to approach school education as a means to cope with the unprecedented political changes being forced upon them by the Dutch government.

To maintain a mission monopoly on schooling, Kruyt even opened schools in Muslim coastal centers such as Mapane and Tojo. He did this not so much to proselytize Muslim peoples, but to maintain a presence in the mercantile centers where the Pamona peoples traded, and also as a kind of damage control measure against Muslim anti-mission propaganda. He began separate schools for Muslims in some religiously mixed areas because he feared Muslim contact might have an adverse effect on the highlanders' fragile Christian values (A. C. Kruyt 1898a, 179).

North Sulawesi teachers who had received four years of instruction at a teachers' training institute were provided with up to six months of further training in the local language before their carefully supervised placement in a village chosen by Kruyt for a school program (Coté 1979, 93–99). Often the veranda of the teacher's house initially served as both the schoolroom and site for Sunday church services. Adriani's linguistic work permitted the early use of Bare'e school books: first a volume of transcribed local stories in 1894, and then Bible stories in 1903. Reading, writing, Malay, arithmetic, geography, church music, and crafts were taught. While the appropriate education for "natives" was actively debated in Holland, Kruyt's vision—emphasizing practical calculations, useful crafts, abstract thought, and religious contemplation—was ultimately the only one to be implemented in Central Sulawesi.

The missionization efforts of Kruyt, in conjunction with the forced government regulations and the rash of smallpox and other epidemics beginning in 1884, resulted in a series of millenarian movements locally called *meyapi*, meaning "to hide" (Adriani and Kruyt 1968 [1950], 1:93–94; van der Kroef 1970). These social movements, which erupted in various eastern Central Sulawesi settlements between 1903 and 1908, were characterized by charismatic leaders who prophesied an escape from bad times and Dutch oppression through dedication to the ancestral religion. The leaders usually gathered their followers at a particular mountain site, waiting in vain for rescue by ancestral spirits. In 1907, some Pamona groups aided the Mori in an overt attack on Dutch soldiers, but their severe defeat signaled once and for all the futility of resistance against the better-armed Dutch forces (Adriani and Kruyt 1968 [1950], 1:94).

The cozy relationship between Kruyt's mission and the regional government began to deteriorate in late 1912 (Coté 1979, 283). The institutional honeymoon was over. Newly stationed government officials, shocked by the almost sovereign power wielded by Kruyt, increasingly tried to assert control over school curriculum, school financing, and mission administration. Government officials began to question the benefit of the schools' curriculum beyond its apparent successes in Christian indoctrination, and to ask why Kruyt's mission provided so little in the way of medical and social services.

Questions about the motives of Kruyt's mission intensified after epidemics of smallpox, cholera, and influenza ravaged the region's newly contacted population periodically between 1884 and 1912. Despite ensuing conflicts regarding schools, hospitals, and economic ventures, however, the central Dutch government's perpetual fear of Muslim encroachment ultimately permitted Kruyt and, after 1921, his missionary son, Jan, to maintain a relatively firm grasp on eastern Central Sulawesi schools and communities until the Japanese occupation in the early 1940s.

Kruyt claimed that by introducing the Christian message, he hoped to achieve just the minimal social alterations necessary for conversion and not to disturb the overall social framework of local communities, a claim still made by New Tribes Mission personnel working in the late 1980s. Kruyt stated that he did not propose a radical alteration of Central Sulawesi society because he saw highlanders as partly conforming to Christian socialist ideals that opposed capitalism and oppressive force. He proposed only sufficient changes to allow for the acceptance of the finer Christian and European ethics (A. C. Kruyt 1929). Missionaries from Kruyt's time to the present have clung to the idea that they could micromanage behavioral changes: altering what they identified as religious practices without changing what they identified as secular customs or economic processes.

It is clear from Kruyt's writings that, unlike many Dutch Reformed missionaries, he had little interest in medical or economic development projects outside the context of evangelization and mission maintenance. Kruyt also never admitted that the facets of Pamona culture he did appreciate might be linked to those he aimed to destroy, with the aid of government force if necessary. Rather than conceding some responsibility for the untoward disruption of local customs, he accused later government officials of meddling insensitively in regional affairs and doing psychological damage that he was at pains to alleviate with his Christian message (A. C. Kruyt 1929). Kruyt maintained throughout that only missionaries understood the Indies people sufficiently to recommend and introduce social changes suited to their needs and character. Both government and mission maintained that they had the Central Sulawesi people's best interests at heart, and they began to accuse each other of exploiting the resources, labor, and schools of the Poso region for selfish aims.

Kruyt's interest in studying indigenous Central Sulawesi religion "was similar to Snouck Hurgronje's interest in Islam: the aim of both was to find the basis for a program of 'spiritual annexation,'" and to prove that the pre-Christian belief was superficial and feeble (Coté 1979, 46). Kruyt disparaged the indigenous religion, arguing that the people had only a vague understanding of their ancestral gods and performed their extensive rituals mainly out of fear (Adriani and Kruyt 1912). Kruyt supported all Dutch government regulations that might unsettle ancestral rituals related to agriculture, the construction of houses, marriage, puberty ceremonies, funerals, and the treatment of illness. Kruyt considered the heathenism of the Poso people to be inextricably linked to their system of rice cultivation (A. C. Kruyt 1898b), so he encouraged new farming methods such as wet-rice agriculture (A. C. Kruyt 1924).

If Kruyt's interest in the culture of the Poso people was motivated by the agenda of conversion, so it seems the interest of Pamona leaders in Kruyt was largely based on hopes that he might provide them with military protection against local enemies, plus assure other economic and political favors from the Dutch government. Although there was resistance to new taxes and corvée labor to build roads and model villages, Dutch troops were easily able to quell dissenters through military operations. By 1907, all of Sulawesi was, for the first time, considered to be under Dutch control. By 1909, baptisms of local Pamona chiefs were followed by conversions of most major household heads in villages where Kruyt proselytized extensively.

The Dutch administration levied a 5-percent income tax on every head of household. This act puzzled highlanders whose precolonial "ownership" was more broadly corporate, spiritually based, and generally included usufruct rights only. The Dutch administration forcibly reduced the number of permissible days for celebrating major feasts, re-ranked local leaders, and compelled the unification and movement of villages to more accessible locations (Adriani 1932). Young men became increasingly absent from the villages as they turned to collecting and selling dammar resin, rattan, and ebony wood for sufficient cash to pay their nuclear family's taxes (Adriani and Kruyt 1968 [1950], 1:239).

The government encouraged nuclear family dwellings, which it thought would simplify taxation procedures, encourage concepts of private ownership, and be more sanitary (A. C. Kruyt 1924). Secondary burial, practiced in the Poso region, also was prohibited for hygienic reasons. In some "model" villages, missionaries even required that crooked houses, or those facing away from the planned road, be torn down and rebuilt according to Dutch aesthetics and specifications (Hofman 1908). The Pamona people's already high infant mortality rate was aggravated by these regulatory measures imposed by Dutch authorities, as Kruyt himself eventually admitted (A. C. Kruyt 1929).

Precolonial dry-rice farming rituals had no equivalent in the Protestant religion, and wet-rice cultivation required high-density settlements rather than the small, shifting populations fostered by dry-rice cultivation. Kruyt considered wet-rice agriculture to do for Poso adults what his schools did for the children: make them rational, practical, cooperative, and freed from the trappings of animist ritual. Despite considerable resistance to the newly introduced agricultural system, the results of which in some areas threatened starvation, the government forcibly required the planting of wet-rice fields. Christian thanks-giving services were introduced after wet-rice harvests to replace the indigenous rituals formerly associated with dry-rice cultivation (Coté 1979, 275–277).

Kruyt's theories on indigenous Indonesian religion were developed in his first major book, *Het Animisme in den Indischen Archipel* (Animism in the Indies archipelago). This volume was written after about fourteen years of fieldwork in the Poso region. It followed a 1905 journey through the Indonesian archipelago financed by the Netherlands government (A. C. Kruyt 1906, vii). Kruyt's second major book, the three volumes written with Adriani on eastern Central Sulawesi (Adriani and Kruyt 1912), has a narrower geographic focus than the book on animism, but a wider range of topics is discussed. Although it largely follows the style of European ethnographic monographs of its day, the book's impressive range of detail and periodic efforts at theorization reveal a scholarly interest seemingly beyond Kruyt's stated goal of pure evangelization.

While Kruyt may have aimed to comprehend the Pamona primarily to convert them, he and Adriani nevertheless expended great energy collecting obscure information on subjects such as kinship and craftsmanship that bear little direct relation to the purposes of his mission or the Netherlands Indies' government. It is certain that such scholarly efforts to define and document diverse traditions and laws throughout the archipelago were designed in part to counter Muslim claims for a unified Islamic state of culturally similar peoples (Lev 1985, 66; Schrauwers 1998, 210–211). Such political purposes were served along with investigations useful to the conversion process. Yet no one can read the corpus of Adriani and Kruyt's writings and view them as less than serious scholars.

Adriani's health deteriorated while in Europe during World War I, and he died in Poso in 1926, a considerable loss to Kruyt's cooperative scholastic efforts (Adriani and Kruyt 1968 [1950], i–iv). A revised version of the 1912 edition of *Bare'e Sprekende Toradja's* (Adriani and

The village of Towulu' as it looked in the 1920s. Photograph by W. Kaudern (A. C. Kruyt 1938, plate 53).

Kruyt 1950) was already underway, however, with more recent field data collected by Kruyt, Adriani, native pupils, Jan Kruyt, and another missionary named J. Ritsema.

Kruyt's subsequent four volumes on the "West Toradjas," which includes information on Kulawi District peoples, was based upon three months of fieldwork per year from 1924 to 1927, aided by local graduates of his mission school (A. C. Kruyt 1938, 1:2–4). Having already written a similar work on the "East Toradjas" of Poso, he knew how to make comparative inquiries. Indeed, his chapters follow the earlier book closely in terms of topics. Some of Kruyt's descriptions are secondhand, but he did travel to Tobaku briefly in 1926. He describes Towulu' as "a slovenly built village" (*een slordig aangelegd dorp*, Dutch), but adds that the site on which it lies is "very inviting" (*zeer uitlokkend*).

By the time Kruyt wrote *De West Toradja's*, naturalists such as the

Sarasin brothers (Sarasin and Sarasin 1905), the German explorer Albert Grubauer (1913), government officials such as R. Boonstra van Heerdt (1914), and the geographer E. C. Abendanon (1917/1918) had completed surveys of Central Sulawesi and reported their findings. So had Walter Kaudern, the Swedish naturalist and ethnologist who wrote five illustrated volumes devoted to Central Sulawesi material culture, which he collected for the Göteborg Museum in Sweden (Kaudern 1925–1944).

Academically, Kaudern and Kruyt became rivals, although Kaudern often depended upon information from Kruyt and Adriani, as well as from Salvation Army missionaries such as Hendrik Loois, Leonard Woodward, and Edvard Rosenlund, who were stationed in western Central Sulawesi beginning in 1913. Although the European missionaries of the Salvation Army provided far less documentation than Kruyt and his colleagues on indigenous practices, they did leave behind noteworthy records of their approach to the Kulawi District highlanders, materials I explore in the following chapter.

4

Onward Christian Soldiers:
The Salvation Army in Sulawesi

> There is hardly a country in the world where the [Salvation] Army has, from its earliest days, enjoyed so much goodwill as in Indonesia.
>
> *Melattie Brouwer*, "Tanah Toradja: Goodwill and Co-operation"

D utch efforts to "pacify" western Central Sulawesi began in 1905, but Kulawi highlanders, who were renowned and feared as headhunters, eluded colonial rule for a few more years. In 1908, a lowland inhabitant led Dutch troops up a little-known mountain pass. The startled highlanders were armed mainly with bamboo blowpipes and spears. After the Dutch conquest, missionaries were invited by the Netherlands Indies government to open new mission fields. Western Central Sulawesi was awarded to the Salvation Army because missions from the more favored Dutch Reformed churches (Nederlandse Hervormde Kerk and Nederlandse Gereformeerde Kerk) were preoccupied with the Lake Poso region to the east and the Sa'dan Toraja region to the south.

In 1909, Assistant Resident H. De Vogel requested that A. C. Kruyt begin work in the Kulawi District of the Palu Regency (Alfdeeling) in order to prevent the creeping encroachment of Islam (De Vogel ms). Although the coastal Kaili populations had long been under South Sulawesi influence, Kruyt reports that active adoption of Islam in Central Sulawesi only became widespread following the Dutch "pacification" (A. C. Kruyt 1938, 3:3). Bugis or Makasar merchants and farmers were given positions of authority by the Dutch colonial government. While they served as middlemen in developing the region economically they began to dominate the indigenous Kaili people religiously and politically as well. Kruyt scarcely had the staff and financial resources to complete his goals in the eastern Central Sulawesi regions around Lake Poso, much less take on responsibility for a different language area many days' march away. Therefore, about 200 square kilometers of western Central Sulawesi, including what is now the Kulawi District, were turned over by Governor-General A. W. F. Idenburg to the Salvation Army, which had been permitted to work in Java since 1894.

This chapter outlines how the first Salvation Army missionaries from Europe approached and were received by their potential flock. Missionaries aimed to separate "bad superstition" from "good culture" in order to retain local behaviors they favored while eliminating those ideas and behaviors they defined as "unchristian." European gifts and services were essential to a conversion process that began by unhinging local patterns of economic reciprocity, especially between highlanders and lowlanders. While Central Sulawesi highlanders generally desired European goods, missionaries varied greatly in terms of their interest in local material culture. Kruyt and other Dutch Reformed missionaries working in the eastern Central Sulawesi highlands actively collected indigenous material culture, both to remove "idols" and for the "scientific" benefit of Dutch museums. By contrast, most Salvation Army missionaries working in western Central Sulawesi had much less interest in local artifacts. Similarly, the writings that Salvation Army officers produced are presented less as scholarly descriptions than as inspiring tales of missionary pioneers who confronted savages and tropical perils with God's help.

The general dissimilarity in approach both to collecting and writing by members of these two missionary orders can be correlated with differences in their national policies, class backgrounds, education, religious training, and preparation for fieldwork overseas. The Dutch Reformed missionaries, more directly linked to the ruling colonial government, were selected and trained to produce information that was in scholarly form but also useful for regional political administration.

Salvation Army missionaries, by contrast, were a more distant arm of the Dutch Empire's political and educational system. Their writings are oriented appropriately to home churches and mission fund-raising.

Salvation Army officers' initial written impressions of Central Sulawesi people and their spiritual beliefs bare the philosophical and psychological complexities of their cross-cultural encounter. Early missionary reports range from joyous claims of instantaneous conversion to confessions of miserable living conditions among uncomprehending native bystanders. Their statements disclose misunderstandings of indigenous theology and a distinctly European view of the boundaries between the religion they wished to abolish and the cultural features they wished to leave undisturbed. For the early missionaries, the premises and practices of Christianity and European civilization were impermeable entities that could be inserted bit by bit into the less developed, more porous cultures of Central Sulawesi.

As with Kruyt's mission in Poso, gifts, medical service, and education were key strategies for gaining converts in western Central Sulawesi. Yet Salvation Army leaders held good works as a major goal, not simply a felicitous by-product of the salvation of souls. The relatively brief (less than twenty-five years) colonial mission effort in the Uma-speaking areas was eclipsed by the strange events of World War II and its aftermath. Oral histories, military documents, and colonial reports suggest that the intrusions of the Japanese occupation and postwar rebellions catapulted many highland populations from being reticent colonized converts to becoming enthusiastic followers of a more indigenized Protestant church.

The following brief history of Salvation Army missionization in western Central Sulawesi documents the contradictions of conversion outlined in chapter 1. The foreign religion that Europeans brought neither readily suited the local ecological and social conditions, nor could it be translated quickly and understandably within them. Missionaries were left with unanticipated dilemmas in selecting local behaviors to extirpate or conserve. Moreover, as the missionaries sought to make the highlanders more like them in terms of spiritual ideas, moral values, and social habits, they coincidentally forged the conditions for the converts' economic and political marginality both within the Dutch colonial empire and in the future Muslim-majority nation of Indonesia.

The Salvation Army's Origins and Establishment in Sulawesi

The Salvation Army began as the East London Christian Revival Society in 1865, when a Wesleyan Methodist preacher named William Booth took his message to the street people of East London. Booth quickly discovered that these lower-class individuals, often alcoholics or scofflaws, were unwelcome in established English churches. When their roving street evangelism was discouraged by Methodist Church institutions, Booth and his wife, Catherine, founded their own sect (Carpenter 1957). They recognized that their prospective audience was not attracted to the staid atmosphere of conventional churches and organ music, so they created a circus-like environment of tents thrown up in public squares with vivacious music played on guitars, banjos, trumpets, and bass drums (Neal 1961, 6–7). In this context, Booth and his wife preached eternal salvation through Christian faith and discipline to individuals who were considered the most sinful members of British society.

Booth remained doctrinally faithful to Wesleyan principles: faith in both Old and New Testament scriptures, the Trinity, original sin, and the atonement of Jesus Christ. Booth emphasized the possibility of salvation through belief in and obedience to Jesus Christ, as well as belief in a final judgment where the righteous will receive eternal happiness and the wicked eternal punishment (Salvation Army 1976b, 240). It was less a matter of doctrine than Booth's constituency and approach to them that made the Salvation Army a distinctive sect apart from Methodism.

Because many of his original followers were alcoholics, Booth eliminated the sacraments, which he saw as tempting his followers with sips of wine. Salvation Army members are forbidden alcohol and tobacco in order to purify their physical and spiritual selves from sinful habits. Booth also encouraged, yet disciplined, the charismatic expression of penitence among his followers by restricting their confessions of faith to moments in the service when all were called upon to volunteer their "witness" to the greatness of the Lord (Carpenter 1957, 47). Upon the preacher's request, congregation members stand up and relate the magnificence of God's role in their daily lives.

The East London Christian Revival Society changed its name to the Christian Mission and then, in 1878, to the Salvation Army. Booth found military references in the Bible evocative of the kind of energetic and disciplined movement that he envisioned (Sandall 1948, 17). Hence the organization's chosen processional hymn became "Onward, Christian Soldiers!" Once the Salvation Army name was chosen, the way to structure and clothe the organization's members became clear to "General" Booth, who began to assign military ranks and adopt used British Army garments that later were altered to create a distinctive Salvation Army uniform.

By the late 1880s, Salvation Army congregations, or "corps," were opened in other parts of the British empire and European continent. Given the organization's early statement that "[t]he Salvation Army makes religion where there was no religion before" (Salvation Army 1976a, 35), missionization in Europe's overseas colonies was a natural next step for the Salvation Army's expansion. Methodists already disavowed the high Calvinist view of strict predestination, which made missionary work more purposive, merely another extension of the desired *corpus Christianum* (van den Berg 1956, 84–86).

In 1909, A. W. F. Idenburg, the newly stationed governor-general of the Dutch East Indies, contacted Gerrit Govaars, the first Dutch Salvation Army officer ever commissioned and the newly assigned Indonesian territorial "commander." Govaars was assigned to travel from an established Salvation Army headquarters in Semarang, Java, to assess the possibility of opening missions among the "pagan Toradjas" of Central Sulawesi. A 1970s interview with Govaars indicates that once he arrived in the Palu Valley, he met a German named Zuppinger.[1] Zuppinger, who was married to a "native" woman and could speak some local language, accompanied Govaars on a journey to Kulawi's pagan temple, where Govaars became "the first Christian to preach the gospel in Kulawi" (M. Brouwer 1973a, 4). Of his travels into the interior farther south, Govaars said:

> From place to place we hired carriers, and so traversed the country. We spoke to the heads of the tribes. One of them listened interestedly to what I told him about Christ, serving the Lord and not doing bad things. Then he asked: "Are we allowed to eat pig's meat?"
>
> Upon my affirmative he said: "Oh well, that is all right. Wild pigs eat our harvest, so we ought to be allowed to eat pigs." (M. Brouwer 1973a, 4)

These comments, familiar ones to all missionaries in Indonesia, encapsulate one of the primary objections that highlanders have to Islam. By initial comparison, the Christian religion seems less of a dietary hardship. Unlike the coastal Kaili, most of whom gradually gave up eating pork to forge alliances with Muslim merchants from South Sulawesi, highland Kulawi people never found a sufficiently good reason to renounce their major feast food in favor of a foreign religion.

On September 15, 1913, Salvation Army activities formally began in Sulawesi when two missionary couples were sent to Central Sulawesi stations via Palu Bay. The Jensens were assigned to work with Kaili people in the Palu Valley, while the Hendrik Loois family was assigned to work with Moma-speaking people in Kulawi. A letter written by Captain Charles Jensen a few months after his arrival suggests that acquiring formal conversions in western Central Sulawesi went more easily than it had for Kruyt in eastern Central Sulawesi:

> Under these circumstances we feared the people would not come to the meeting, but at the signal they gathered around us. They were a little shy at first because some Mohammedans had told them that the "Captains of Jesus" had come to put pig's meat in their mouths and to tease them and punish them in all kinds of ways.

> While speaking I tried to make them understand different things and at
> the end of the meeting I asked whose followers they wanted to be: Jesus,
> Mohammed or heathenism? Deep silence. I asked those who wanted to
> follow Mohammed to rise to their feet. Nobody moved. The question was
> asked again, with the same result.
>
> When the question was asked: "Who will become a follower of Jesus?" I
> saw something I will never forget. They jumped up, men and women,
> young and old, more than 500 in number.
>
> "I will follow Jesus; I will be a Christian," they called out. With folded
> hands stretched out towards the clear blue sky, full of stars, we closed this
> memorable meeting, singing "Glory to His name." All night the people
> kept singing, but we were tired enough to sleep all the same. (M.
> Brouwer 1973b, 4; also Salvation Army 1915)

Why did initial conversions proceed so much faster in western
Central Sulawesi than in the eastern areas? Being the first highlanders
proselytized, the Pamona were the least prepared for either the white
man's gospel or his military reprisals. They did not anticipate the forces
that would be brought to bear against them if they did not submit, at
least nominally, to the new ideology. The western groups, by contrast,
had roughly twenty years to hear of events transpiring in the Poso
region. Undoubtedly they knew about the fantastic material wealth of
the Europeans and about their persuasive guns.

The first large mission center developed by the Salvation Army in
Central Sulawesi was at Kalawara, a village of one thousand penurious
Javanese who were relocated midway between Palu and Kulawi by the
Dutch colonial government in 1906 (M. Brouwer 1973c, 4). In 1915,
Ensign Gerrit Jan Veerenhuis and his wife were stationed at Kalawara
to run this self-supporting agricultural colony of Javanese indigents and
juvenile delinquents. That same year, Assistant Resident H. J. Grijzen
established regulations concerning the combined mission-government
financing of schools. The regulations called for community plantations
to be farmed by villagers in the Palu Valley. The plantations were
designed to finance schools operated by the Salvation Army at the invitation of the colonial government (Coté 1979, 313). In subsequent years
the Kalawara settlement prospered commercially. The colony sold

Tama Gempo (*left*) with two other highland "chiefs" and Salvation Army Commissioner Palstra in the 1920s. VIDOC (*Visuele Documentatie*), Koninklijk Instituut voor de Tropen, Amsterdam.

copra, kapok (a plant fiber used for bedding), maize, eggs, and meat to markets in Palu. Some Javanese graduates of the school also were trained to missionize indigenous people deeper in the island's interior.

According to Salvation Army documents, the first direct contact that Uma-speaking people had with missionaries was between 1913 and 1917, when Kantewu men were required to perform four days per month of government-mandated road labor in Kulawi (M. Brouwer 1974c, 4). During those work assignments, they heard from Kulawi Valley people about the Christian meetings and attended some of them out of curiosity:

> Much impressed, these sons of the fierce warring clans of the head-
> hunters listened eagerly. Although the language differed somewhat from
> theirs, they got the message all right and forthwith invited "Tua i Heni"—
> Ensign Loois—to come and preach the "word of life" in Kantewu. They
> promised him safe entry to their village. (M. Brouwer 1974c, 4)

Pursuant to this reported local demand for more Salvation Army officers, a British officer named Leonard Woodward was sent in 1917 to open a mission in the Uma-speaking village of Kantewu, a relatively large population center in the Pipikoro region three days' walk south of Kulawi center (Salvation Army 1924a, 1925b; Kenyon 1952). Loois accompanied Woodward on the journey to Kantewu. Upon their arrival through the single fortified entrance to the village, startled local people fled into their homes (Kenyon 1952, 34). Shortly thereafter, the headman, Tama Gempo, appeared and led them to rest in the indigenous temple, which also was used as a travelers' hostel.

Woodward reports that they were brought presents of food: bananas, rice, coconuts, eggs, and a chicken (Salvation Army 1919, 67). Using the Moma language from Kulawi, Loois requested a formal audience with the headman and village elders. Most Uma speakers also know some Moma language; thus the Salvation Army officers and their Kulawi assistants conveyed to a gathering of fifty or sixty elders that Woodward wished for land sufficient to build a school, a meeting hall, and a personal residence (Kenyon 1952; M. Brouwer 1974c, 4). The officers promised that the mission's arrival would bring many special advantages to the village.

Kenyon writes that Tama Gempo, the skeptical chief and senior warrior of Kantewu, agreed because he feared that the white men might be associated with powerful spirits. Another Salvation Army report suggests instead that the Kantewu leaders saw Woodward and Loois as Dutch government officials whom they needed to treat with caution or risk military retaliation (Salvation Army 1924b, 5). In either case, before they returned to Kulawi, the two European ministers treated sick villagers, adding to local people's impression of their extraordinary abilities. The beard—a great rarity among Sulawesi people—that Woodward had grown on the trip was looked upon as a sign of special wisdom. He was given the local name Tua Jangku', meaning "Grandfather Beard" or "Sir Beard" (Kenyon 1952, 38–39). Woodward

Majors Leonard and Maggie Woodward, the first officers to the Pipikoro and Tobaku regions. The Salvation Army Heritage Centre.

rapidly gained the cooperation of Kantewu people such that every able-bodied male performed eight days' work in felling and moving timber for Woodward's buildings (Salvation Army 1924b, 5). During the next two decades, Woodward, his wife, Maggie, and their Menadonese teacher, Philippus Nelwan, worked tirelessly to convert the Kantewu area population into Salvation Army "soldiers."

After Woodward's first two years in Kantewu, the Loois family in Kulawi was replaced by a Finnish officer, Edvard Rosenlund. Rosenlund accompanied Woodward into the neighboring Tobaku region in 1919 to contact the villages of Biro and Towulu' for the first time (Caddy 1982, 13–14). During that visit, according to Salvation Army records, fifteen inhabitants of Biro and forty-three in Towulu' agreed to become Christians. In cooperation with the headman of Towulu', Woodward planned the first school for the Tobaku area.

Majors Leonard and Maggie Woodward dressed in highland ritual attire. The
Salvation Army Heritage Centre.

Missionary Positions: Salvation Army Writings Back Home

The writers and editors of missionary publications are motivated to tell stories that elicit financial and labor support from their home congregations. Salvation Army writers such as Raymond Caddy often make the early conversions in Sulawesi sound both instantaneous and miraculous, proof of the potency contained in the gospel and European civilization:

> At last, covered in mud, they [the party of Rosenlund] arrived at Kolomanta [Kalamanta]. After a river-bath and a meal they gathered the people to hear the gospel. Most of the local inhabitants had never heard the story of Jesus before. Edward's sciopticon pictures were a novelty too. The robustness of his machine on such a trek must be another marvel!
>
> Delighted with the story of Jesus' love, begging Edward to tell them more, the villagers stayed long after the meeting singing and rejoicing over the good news until dawn. (Caddy 1982, 16)
>
> Three further days of forest trekking brought them to Rampi. The people of this area had been notorious headhunters not many years previously, and the explorers were to see skulls and scalps hanging in the old lobo (temple) where they held their meeting and told the story of Jesus and His love. The villagers had lost nearly three-quarters of their number during the world-wide influenza epidemic which had penetrated even this isolated corner. Quite demoralized, they were clearly ready for someone to lead them into a new and better life. (Caddy 1982, 17)

In conjunction with Kruyt's reports from the Lake Poso region, this last quote, describing a nearly decimated and "demoralized" indigenous population, further suggests why less resistance to missionization was met in western than in eastern Central Sulawesi. Salvation Army missionaries encountered populations already disrupted by new settlement regulations, corvée labor requirements, and inexplicable plagues such as the Spanish flu epidemic of 1918. Western highlanders thus were more open to the anticipated appearance of missionaries promising a finer future. The foreigners displayed awesome wealth, offered useful gifts, controlled unknown medicines, and arranged novel entertainments in the form of music Victrolas and moving-picture displays.

By 1919, after only two years' work, Woodward reported that 126 adherents were enrolled in the Pipikoro region, including the primary ritual leader (*mardika malolo*, Uma) from Peana, and all the village headmen (Salvation Army 1919, 68). Among the first converts was one of Tama Gempo's schooled sons, Buli, whose Christian fellowship with members of the Seko group reportedly convinced his father to end his headhunting and slave raiding in that region (Kenyon 1952, 57–59). Tina Idjo, one of Tama Gempo's daughters, whom I met in the 1980s, said that Woodward entered Kantewu about ten years before some Bugis arrived and asked her father to convert to Islam. Therefore, she said, Christianity is known by Kantewu people as the prior, or "elder," religion.

Some of the more difficult and unpalatable aspects of the missionization endeavor are described in writings by Captain William Harris, an officer who left Kulawi prematurely due to health problems. Harris candidly describes his troubles with the "impenetrable jungle," the locals' "personal habits [that] leave much to be desired," the "indescribable filth" of native homes, and tropical diseases that "often present a very nauseating spectacle" (Harris 1925). He also admits to a lack of interest and understanding on the part of many congregations, saying, "[O]ne felt that even after some years of effort only a curious interest in the white Officers had been aroused, while the people's understanding of things eternal remained dormant" (Harris 1925, 117). This frank admission of obstacles is rare in the missionary writings for this region, yet it is a significant counterpoint to the tales of unbridled success that continue to the present. Harris is also one of the few Salvation Army missionaries to admit publicly that the Protestant message might not be comprehended in its intended form.

Some officers' stated goals with regard to the Sulawesi population sound much like Kruyt's idealized plan not to create "pseudo-Europeans" (Caddy 1982, 19) or damage local culture:

> Many officers seem to consider that the age-long customs of primitive peoples—so-called heathen customs—are all of the Evil One, and must therefore be rooted up. To my mind this is a great mistake. In the ancient customs of the Torajas in the interior of central Celebes, for instance, I

have found much that is good, and, if properly adapted, they will provide a structure into which one can fit all the new practices belonging to the Christian life—after the Spirit of God has changed the people's hearts, of course. (Rosenlund 1933, 302)

The message from Kruyt, the early Salvation Army officers, and the other evangelical Protestants working recently is basically the same: everything that the missionaries like need not change. Everything that the missionaries do not like needs alteration "after the Spirit of God has changed the people's hearts." These premises left individual missionaries throughout the twentieth century with the dilemma of deciding which ideas and practices need extirpation and which need preservation in the face of government plans for development. Missionaries' solutions to this quandary reveal their vision of the supposed boundary between religion and culture and the separation of both of these domains from economic and political concerns.

Like Kruyt, early Salvation Army officers saw native Central Sulawesi religion as a superficial and trivial faith:

> Time is no object, for they have no special goal in life, while they vaguely suppose eternity to be spent in some sort of spiritworld where happiness is largely dependent upon friendly relations with Satan. They worship the devil, generally at feast times, and some of their children, specifically chosen, are set aside to become priests and priestesses in the evil one's service.
>
> The Kailies [sic] have no strong religious instinct, so that even their devil and spiritworship is not well sustained, except in times of trouble. On the track to the entrance of most villages a bamboo altar will be noticed, on which offerings to the devil can be placed, but as a rule there is such a scarcity of offering on that altar that I think the devil must be disappointed. When they become converted, however, they make sterling Salvationists. (M. Brouwer 1973/1974, 5, 4; also Harris 1923, 86)

European notions of Satan are far distant from indigenous Central Sulawesi concepts of the nature spirits they termed *seta*, as will be explored in the next chapter. These local spirits were not inherently evil, but rather powerful protectors of ancestral laws. Moreover, the criticism that locals made only minimal offerings to their roadside spirits misapprehends the conditions under which large and small offerings were warranted. Such comments reveal the extent to which some Europeans were deeply ignorant of the indigenous cosmology they thought could be replaced with voluntary conversion.

Salvation Army writings often emphasize the brutal aspects of indigenous worship, particularly headhunting:

> Prior to the coming in of the white people among them, they were head hunters, savage and cruel. Such worship as they practised was a sort of spiritism, similar to that practised by the Red Indians. Their temples were adorned with the heads of slain enemies. (Unsworth 1922, 10)

> Practically all the people in our district in Mid-Celebes totally lack any religious background. The terrible practice of headhunting, for which the island has been notorious, arises out of the belief that evil spirits in the ground have to be appeased so that they do not interfere with the growth of crops. Human heads or scalps are therefore buried under the temple—generally by the *tobalia*, or "witch doctor," who represents what little "religion" the people know of. But, especially in the interior, strict moral standards, or *tabus*, are maintained, putting to shame the conduct of many so-called Christians in Western lands. Moreover, the people of Celebes are intelligent, and when they understand the better way, many are prepared to follow. (Woodward 1933, 14)

Woodward's "evil spirits in the ground" is his gloss for the spirit "owner(s) of the land" (*pue' tana'*). The heads of captured enemies were consecrated at the temples, particularly to end mourning for leaders or to curtail crop misfortunes, but contrary to Woodward's impression, these practices were only an occasional element of warfare tied into a much broader local cosmology (see chapter 5). Woodward's comments define indigenous Central Sulawesi religion as virtually no religion at all in European eyes.

Another premise upon which both Kruyt and the Salvation Army officers agreed was that Central Sulawesi religion was founded on tremendous fears, from which the Christian message would free them:

> Toradjas, who are animists, believe in evil spirits and therefore they live in constant fear. These evil spirits are all around them, in their house, too, in spite of the many charms or talismans they keep, and of the exorcists who take advantage of the people who think that all disease and disaster is caused by the evil eye of the spirits. In all sorts of ways they try to cheat the spirits. For instance, when they go to the fields to harvest the

paddy, they hang little straw dolls in the trees, hoping that Satan will think they are people and enter into them. Animals are given other names. A horse they will call a dog, a buffalo, a sheep. Women are not allowed to speak [during the rice harvest] outside their house. An expectant mother may not be seen, for fear Satan takes revenge on the unborn child. The people are in constant fear of death, fear for the women and children. They are never free.

It is only when the gospel becomes clear to them, that they feel free and happy. (M. Brouwer 1974b, 4)

European missionaries saw fear of indigenous spirits as more heinous than the fear of God and hell they proposed in its stead. They did not discern that highlanders were well versed in the ancestral rituals required to palliate cosmological disruptions. From a local standpoint, Central Sulawesi people already understood how to cope with their deities and ancestors. Coping with the Protestant God, by contrast, initially was puzzling, if not more onerous. Only in the context of increasing government and mission demands, unfamiliar epidemics, and rapidly changing material circumstances did the highlanders show a gradual willingness to accept new Protestant methods for contending with the spiritual hazards of their environment.

The Salvation Army encouraged patience toward new converts and an optimistic, teleological vision of their spiritual development. This approach, although patronizing, contributed to the dialogue that helped highlanders negotiate their own visions of Protestant faith:

There is an obvious difference between the converted man and the sanctified man, but it should be only the difference between the child and the man, the blossom and the fruit; the one should be a natural development of the other.

As God in nature frequently works in stages, it is not surprising that a similar development is seen in spiritual life. In nature, the blossom naturally, yet quite distinctly, precedes the fruit, the caterpillar is a complete form of life, but only the forerunner of the lovelier butterfly. In each case there is a distinct change yet a continuing life.

Thus it is in the spiritual realm. The converted man, realising that forgiveness of sins is only the beginning and that perfection lies before, should move normally and naturally into the experience termed holiness. (Blackwell 1949, 15)

European Salvation Army officers working in Central Sulawesi from the 1920s to the Japanese occupation in the 1940s took their converts wherever and whenever they could get them, confident that someday the blossoms would turn into fruit and the caterpillars into butterflies. In this pragmatic, long-term approach the Salvation Army leadership moved prudently and predicted trends rather accurately. The vast majority of Kulawi District highlanders became Christians. They abandoned many features of their precolonial life that were objectionable to Europeans, and they accepted the foreigners' definitions of a valid religion. It was only, to push the poetic analogy further, that the local varieties of mature fruit and butterflies could never become the same as European ones.

Gifts as a Strategy for Conversion

The writings of pioneering Salvation Army officers include specific remarks about their use of gifts to attract attention and motivate Christian conversion. Woodward writes:

> At Kantewoe [Kantewu], as in most places in our district, where we have first to learn the people's language, we began by making friends with the children. This is generally achieved by distributing beads among them. (The ladies' support is won by the gift of a large-eyed needle; they otherwise sew with the hollow bone of the wing of a bat, which, however, has to be threaded after every stitch!) Another much coveted gift is salt, which is very scarce in the mountain districts; the children are as fond of eating salt as white children are of sweets. (Woodward 1933, 13–14)

Salvation Army missionaries distributed previously unknown goods such as European clothing, white sugar, beads, candy, soap, matches, and medicines supplied by the Dutch government. They established an elementary school system in which the Malay (now Indonesian) language was taught, and they introduced biblical illustrations as teaching and preaching devices. To this day, the Uma-language term for attending a church service is "*mogampara*," literally, "to use pictures." This term is derived from the Malay word "*gambar*," meaning "picture," although pictures now are rarely used in adult services.

The variability of indigenous peoples' fascination with European goods reveals that Western commodities are not always deemed superior to local goods and that imported objects are not invariably an irresistible force in the colonial encounter. Yet the ability to provide a high-ranking valuable, such as a gun, to those who have no other access to such an object does create a basis for social inequality (N. Thomas 1991, 101–104).

This latter example represents the type of situation in which western Central Sulawesi highlanders found themselves. Woven cloth, metal objects, salt, and glass beads, which were scarce and highly valued in precolonial times, were suddenly available in abundance from the missionaries. Matches could create a fire much more quickly than indigenous friction techniques. Dutch medicines, even simple antiseptic formulas and aspirins, could achieve impressive results. Sugar and candy held great allure, especially for highland children, who normally scoured the mountain forests for every available morsel of wild fruit. In sum, European goods were very appealing to highlanders who were accustomed to receiving useful exotic goods from exchanges with lowlanders.

Protestant missionaries were interested in teaching the value of money to highlanders, so Dutch coins were given to children to reward their errands and attendance at school. The same coins later were solicited as church donations (Salvation Army 1925b, 177). Tama Gempo's daughter said that Woodward introduced Dutch money to Kantewu in exchange for the local eggs, rice, and chickens he needed to feed his family and staff. Then the Dutch colonial government requested Tama Gempo to collect the money back in the form of taxes. Eventually, Woodward introduced a rice-threshing mill and mechanical sewing machine that he rented to Kantewu people, providing yet another incentive for them to pursue cash through Dutch-oriented services and products.

Kulawi and Tobaku elders recall how Woodward, guarded by military escorts, used to throw Dutch coins of low denominations into the rivers to entice children to bathe and congregate for religious instruction. Woodward brought bags of granulated sugar to the Tobaku region and showed the children how to dip their fingers into the bag and then lick the sugar off. Initially, the children were so frightened that they held hands in a line and only the most courageous youths would reach out for the sugar, trusting their comrades to pull them back from the foreigner's clutches if necessary. Gradually, the children found Woodward harmless and approached him easily to receive presents and be entertained by pictures and Bible stories.

The Salvation Army's policy of freely dispensing medicines and other items generated great excitement among the Central Sulawesi populace. Major Arigje Both, a divisional secretary during the 1920s, gives this description of her trip to the Pipikoro area:

> A crowd of people came up from the surrounding kampongs [settlements] that night. We heard them talk and felt them gazing at us. We knew ourselves in the hand of God, but it is understandable that we did not get much sleep. At daybreak I found out what was on.
>
> The divisional commanders had a habit of taking lots of medicines and all sorts of trinkets with them, like little mirrors, safety pins and needles. He had given me, too, a plentiful supply. There was a lot of malaria, goitre and ulcer of the legs, so we had bandages, quinine, eucalyptus oil, aspirins, tincture of iodine, and other items—not to forget laxatives. And that was what the people were after.
>
> All sorts of dirty tins and jars appeared, which had first to be cleansed, and then each got what he or she needed. Goitres were painted with tincture of iodine, an excellent remedy which brought much relief.
>
> After all the people were helped and we had something to eat, we got on to our ponies and were off to Kantewu, where after a three hours ride we were given a hearty welcome. The whole day we were surrounded by children and adults from local and higher up kampongs, so that we had a terrific crowd for the open-air meeting. It was held on a high plateau. I saw several women who were wearing the safety pins in their ears! (M. Brouwer 1974b, 4)

The goods provided by the missionaries were not always put to the purposes the Europeans intended. Nevertheless, their exotic paraphernalia, everything from safety pins and bottles to European-style clothes, took on a prestige value comparable to the bronze boxes, bronze trays, and woven sarongs formerly introduced by the lowlanders of the Sigi kingdom. Similarly, close relationships with the mission household resulted in the acquisition of more status goods and indicated local ties to greater foreign powers. Gradually, the power and wealth of Western churches became the external axis point to which Tobaku political leaders would draw connections, just as they had formerly invoked ties to the lowland Kaili kingdoms. Western goods were showered on the populace to draw crowds and give the impression of "free" gifts before the inevitable material and spiritual returns were defined. By opening the exchange relationship with valuable and exotic gifts and services—and insisting that there were no exchange obligations involved—the Europeans were later in a favorable position to specify the material or behavioral returns necessary to ensure the continued flow of imported valuables.

The Europeans' ability to give desirable gifts was perhaps at least as important to their long-term colonial strategies as their ability to back up their requests for cooperation with military force. Gifts were cheaper and easier to justify in the homeland reports than battles. Gift-giving strategies by the Netherlands Indies government and early missionaries exemplify the use of gifts not to create a particular exchange interaction requiring the return of gifts in kind, but rather to forge an unequal relationship whereby precolonial strategies of religious and political gift giving were gradually rearranged to suit the designs of the foreign gift givers.

Contemporary Tobaku individuals are not ignorant of the role that gifts initially played in the mission's abilities to attract their attention and elicit their compliance with church directives. When I once asked Mrs. Major Isa' if her people converted because they were forced to do so during the colonial period, she answered:

> No, they were just pulled in. With money, beads, sugar. That was the way of Colonel Woodward back then. When many people gathered to see what he was doing or giving out, then he began a Christian service. In that way, religion (*agama*, Ind.) entered our lives.

Tobaku people, who are now 99 percent Protestant, generally support the programs of their local Salvation Army churches and clinics, as long as too many demands are not made upon their already fragile subsistence base. Nevertheless, Tobaku individuals clearly understand that the Salvation Army no longer provides free gifts. They describe clinic medicines as expensive, and every ritual blessing by a church official has its known costs in rice, meat, coffee, or cash.

Even the rubric of gift exchange largely has been eliminated from church transactions. Once given freely, Indonesian-language Bibles and hymnbooks must be bought by those highlanders who can afford them as symbols of prosperity, spiritual power, and ties to the church. Few Tobaku have the Indonesian reading skills or leisure to read the Bible outside of church (see chapter 7). Yet as Thomas (1991, 4) observes, "[O]bjects are not what they were made to be but what they have become." Similarly, the missionaries' proclaimed greatest gifts, the Bible and Christianity, are best examined not for what they were made to be, but for what they have become in the western highlands.

As in other mission territories, such as India (see Tolen 1991, 118), the Salvation Army leadership in Central Sulawesi decided that goods made available only through purchase are more highly regarded than those received for free. Even medicines donated to the Salvation Army through foreign aid now are sold at some minimal cost to highland villagers to ensure that they are "properly valued." Thus Protestant mission economics has followed the procedures of Western merchandizing in general, whereby initial "free" samples are used to create a perceived need that leads to a more profitable pattern of compensated exchange.

Western goods continue to be associated with Christianity, and more recently, under the initiative of government development programs, they have become associated with modernity as well. Many elements of Tobaku material culture have been eliminated from production due to their association with "paganism," while many imported goods have been accepted not necessarily for their pragmatic virtues, but rather for symbolic reasons associated with Protestant conversion. Dress shoes are a good example of an imported product heavily associated with Christianity. Although expensive, unnecessary for the tough-footed Tobaku, and impractical on the wet and rocky trails of Central Sulawesi, they have become widely desired for their association with Christian propriety and correct church attendance practices as taught by Europeans.

Salvation Army ministers now say they do not give anything away to congregation members because only God gives freely. Ministers do, however, request villagers to make food and cash offerings to God, which are used to maintain the ministers' own worldly households as well as God's church. Tobaku people show that they are aware of this verbal subterfuge at times when they resent the rapaciousness of a particular minister. Nevertheless, they normally contribute the weekly collection money and yearly post-harvest crop tithes requested by the Salvation Army Church.

Just as the Tobaku no longer receive free gifts from the church, they do not give them as unobligated religious offerings. Careful written tabulations are kept by Salvation Army officers detailing the expected versus actual harvest contributions made to the church by each Tobaku household. These church "donations" are viewed less as gifts than as payments required of all community members. Those who work directly for the church as ministers, teachers, or nurses are the only Tobaku individuals, outside of a few civil servant teachers, who earn their living from a wage, locally connoting servitude, rather than subsistence farming and family exchanges. Thus wages and formal payments have replaced the services and products that were presented as precolonial religious offerings. Salvation Army officers still speak in their sermons of the countless blessings of the Lord, yet Tobaku individuals are aware that the pattern of their precolonial regional exchanges as well as the early Christian promises of free gifts have been altered by their colonial history and affiliation with Protestantism. Most now accept these changes as a price of modernity and world religion.

The Central Sulawesi data contest the often unquestioned notion that gift givers become the superior participants in an exchange hierarchy. In the precolonial Central Sulawesi situation, giving and receiving were perceived to elevate the status of both lowlanders and highlanders. In the colonial situation, the seeming inability of highlanders to counter European gifts compromised their position as participants in an exchange relationship. The Central Sulawesi evidence moves the concept of "alternating disequilibrium" (Strathern 1971, 222) in political exchanges from narrow regional contexts into a cross-cultural one and shows how the presentation of supposedly free gifts constructed a new and lopsided form of colonial disequilibrium (Aragon 1996a). It also substantiates how the subversion of local reciprocity became an integral facet of Christian conversion.

The Salvation Army's Early Medical and Educational Work

The Salvation Army in western Central Sulawesi and Kruyt's mission in eastern central Sulawesi viewed their obligations to provide social services very differently. Kruyt saw medical, economic, and higher educational services as ancillary, sometimes even disruptive, to his primary task of evangelization. By contrast, the Salvation Army views such activities as within the New Testament's call for good works as well as faith, citing James 2:14–16 (M. Brouwer 1974b, 4). The Salvation Army was eager to accept the Dutch government's offer of free medical supplies in order to attach dispensaries to each of their mission centers.

Woodward reports that he dispensed government medicines every day from 6:00 to 8:00 a.m. (Salvation Army 1919, 65), and according to a 1924 report, Woodward's clinic treated an average of 1,250 patients per month (Salvation Army 1924b, 5). As the Kantewu environs hosted only about 1,000 people at that time, the clinic's reputation apparently drew clientele from other Uma-speaking villages, some of which were located several days' walk away (Salvation Army 1924a, 56). In this fashion, missions based in primary population centers could attract and forge contacts with those who lived outside the range of their daily sermons.

While medical treatment attracted adults, mission schools aimed to influence the young apart from parental supervision. As in Poso, the first Salvation Army schools in western Central Sulawesi employed teachers from Minahasa, at the north of the island, the first Sulawesi area missionized and "civilized" by Europeans (Henley 1996). These teachers introduced a Manado-influenced Malay dialect and other Minahasan features into Central Sulawesi. The indigenous end-blown, four-holed bamboo flute largely was replaced with a side-blown, six-hole Manadonese flute producing European pitch scales suitable to play Protestant hymns. With government financial support and North Sulawesi teachers, a large network of Salvation Army primary schools was opened prior to World War II (M. Brouwer 1974a, 4).

The most quickly converted individuals in Kantewu were the students, who were provided with religious teaching prior to each day's school lessons (Salvation Army 1925a, 42). Promising primary school graduates were trained as teachers to open schools in adjacent Uma-speaking regions such as Tobaku. Schoolchildren, called "Junior Soldiers," were given new Christian names because Europeans considered local names to have either a negative or ridiculous meaning. One cadet "was formerly named 'Burned Rice,' now he is Elisha" (van de Werken 1924, 4). Not realizing the venerable tradition of name switching that already existed in Central Sulawesi societies, the missionaries were pleased with how readily the locals accepted their new Christian names—and often distraught at how easily they changed them again.

The Salvation Army stressed Malay, rather than local languages, for schooling and religious instruction. While Kruyt saw local language as the key to the Central Sulawesi native's consciousness, the Salvation Army early envisioned a widespread missionizing effort that would allow easy movement of personnel throughout the archipelago and prepare isolated highlanders for their inevitable integration into the national mainstream. While Kruyt emphasized the changes in comprehension and consciousness necessary for separate tribal groups, the Salvation Army emphasized the potential for a united, Indonesian-speaking Christian population. The Salvation Army vision was to prove more consonant with the independent Indonesian nation, whereas Kruyt's vision better supported the Dutch colonial divide-and-rule politics of his day.

Despite the Salvation Army's policy of preaching and teaching in Malay and the early officers' lack of linguistic training, some Central Sulawesi officers did make efforts to prepare gospel texts and hymns in local vernaculars. Rosenlund translated over one hundred Bible stories into the Ija dialect of Kaili. Observing Woodward's heavy reliance on printed illustrations to accompany Bible stories read in poorly understood Malay, a Finnish captain, Heikki Juutilainen, translated Luke and portions of Acts and Genesis into the Moma language of Kulawi (M. Brouwer 1974a, 4). For advice and translation assistance, these Salvation Army officers repeatedly contacted Kruyt, Adriani, and the Dutch linguist S. J. Esser, who conducted a study on Kulawi grammar (Adriani and Esser 1939).

Esser arrived in the 1930s to study lesser-known Central Sulawesi languages such as Uma. He resided periodically with Salvation Army officers stationed in Kulawi and assisted them with their own language studies (M. Brouwer 1974e, 4). After four years in Kantewu, Woodward managed to translate the Lord's Prayer and the Ten Commandments into Uma. He also had a small songbook of ten hymns translated into Uma by Esser to use in his services (Salvation Army 1924b, 5).

The early gospel translators ran into the types of cross-cultural semantic difficulties that the SIL Bible translators still encounter today. Captain Harris reports problems in translating European Christian concepts such as "salvation" and "confession" into local terms (Harris 1922, 10). It took Woodward four years to deliver his first Bible address in Uma and to gain his first oath-taking convert, or "soldier" (Salvation

Army 1949, 98). After eight years, however, hundreds of villagers raised their hands when asked if they would follow Jesus. "Many, however, continued some of their heathen practices" (Salvation Army 1925a, 42).

Other missionaries, no doubt including Kruyt, questioned Woodward about the depth of these early mass conversions, but Woodward replied smartly that some of his first Kantewu converts became faithful officers for the next thirty years (Salvation Army 1949, 98). In all likelihood, the early Salvation Army officers did require less stringent criteria for "conversion" than Kruyt, who waited eighteen years for his first official convert. In 1932, Woodward described the Kantewu conversion process this way:

> Naturally, considerable patience is required in teaching these lovable people the plan of salvation. It has been our practice after some time to invite those who are deeply interested in our message to become Army adherents. We then devote special attention to them and expect them to attend our meetings regularly. Generally we do not invite folk to seek salvation until we believe that they really understand what is meant; their very awe of the white man might easily lead them to come forward wholesale.
>
> At Kantewu my wife and I had been at work for four years before we rejoiced over our first two converts, both of whom were older schoolboys. One of them is an officer. We have now in Celebes several thousand adherents, also about 600 fine Salvationists and 16 Celebes-born officers. (Woodward, quoted in M. Brouwer 1974c, 4)

By 1931, after only eighteen years of work in Central Sulawesi, the Salvation Army had fifty officers, both European and locally trained. Church meetings were held at seventy-one locations. Eighteen schools taught some thirteen hundred pupils (Hatcher 1932, 24). In 1923, Woodward organized the first formal training session for indigenous Central Sulawesi teachers and officers. During the initial six months, Woodward trained cadets for Salvation Army field officership. During the next six months, he prepared them to pass tests for government teaching diplomas in reading, writing, geography, and Malay language (Salvation Army 1925b, 176). During the first two years, only male cadets were taken. Then, women were added so that there would be trained wives for the men officers. The Dutch government was prepared to pay the salary for any teacher with a diploma who was installed by Woodward. Fifty years later, in 1973, Brigadier Philipus Laua, one of the first two Kantewu-area boys to convert under Woodward's tutelage, described his training process as follows:

> On October 17, 1917, the school at Kantewu was opened, the first in the Pipi Koro area. I was among the first scholars. I was about 19, and went to school for three years. On May 21, I became an adherent, and went to live with the officers. While at school, I often accompanied the officer to far-away and nearby kampongs [hamlets], carrying mattresses and food. At every kampong, even when only passing through, a meeting had to be held. I served as translator. Often, too, I had to speak from the Bible. Probably this made the officer think I might work in the Lord's vineyard.
>
> In 1921 and 1922 I was a voluntary teacher at the school. On March 1, 1921, I was converted and on April 3 I was sworn-in. One day in 1922 the officer asked me: "Is Philipus Laua willing to become an officer?" I could not answer that question. At first in my heart I said, can anyone like me work for the Lord? I become an officer, just like Tau [sic] Djanggu [Leonard Woodward]? Impossible!
>
> In the beginning of 1923 six of us young fellows were sent to fetch materials from the jungle to build a house for the teacher, and for an officers' training school. In October the training session began. I certainly did not think at that time I would remain an officer until now. On September 15, 1924, we were commissioned and two days after I went to open the corps at Banasu. (M. Brouwer 1974d)

In addition to giving Christians Western-style names and a career alternative to rice farming, Woodward involved himself in marriage negotiations for his graduates. Young teachers asked Woodward's advice on a marriage partner, sometimes to the dissatisfaction of their parents who had another candidate in mind. Woodward insisted that no "heathen" ceremonies should be conducted in association with an officer's wedding. He thus denied officer couples' parents the anticipated buffalo sacrifices, postmarriage uxorilocal residence, and bride service (Woodward 1933, 15–16). In such fashion, serious converts continued to be distanced from the influence of their families.

According to J. Ph. Tarro, a 1980s Tobaku government official in Palu, the first Towulu' school opened in 1925 and was run by a Kulawi-born teacher named Demas Tandaju. He was nicknamed "Crying

Teacher" (*Guru Geo*, Uma) because the torturous mountain path from Kulawi to Towulu' brought him to tears. Then, as now, the remote Uma-speaking areas were considered hardship posts for indigenous Central Sulawesi people as well as outsiders. Another early teacher in Tobaku was Bapak Salla from Sangir, North Sulawesi, who married a high-ranking woman from Towulu'. Their son, Hendrik Salla, became village headman (*kepala kampung*, Ind.) from 1975 to 1990, when he was replaced by Tama Alce, a son of Tama Ena, the previous headman (*kepala tua*), whose daughters work in Salvation Army hospitals. The history of Salvation Army education and medical training is thus entrenched in the pedigrees of village leadership.

The officer-training program begun by Woodward in Kantewu in 1923 was soon superseded by a national training program in Java. In 1930, an officers' training college for all "natives" was built in Bandung, and four men from Central Sulawesi were initiated. From 1930 until the political disruptions of World War II in 1942, promising Central Sulawesi candidates were sent annually to Java for training, coincidentally exposing them to early facets of Indonesian nationalism. More germane to Salvation Army interests, these initiates were removed from the constraints of their home villages for European-style religious training.

Prior to World War II, the Salvation Army was the only Christian organization with Dutch government permission to operate missions, schools, and medical clinics in western Central Sulawesi (M. Brouwer 1974d, 4). With this monopoly on Christian missionization guaranteed, their only possible rivals in religious proselytizing were Muslims, who had increased trade in the interior once the Dutch government established better roads and more peaceful traveling conditions. Kruyt felt that commerce was not appropriate to evangelization and eventually forbade his staff to run stores. Many Salvation Army officers, however, found trade activities useful in eliminating their rivals' proselytizing opportunities. When Muslim traders were perceived as covert missionaries for Islam, one officer simply acquired and began to sell identical goods, thereby encouraging the Muslim traders' departure from his Christian territory (Unsworth 1922, 10).

Muslim merchants still find Tobaku villages difficult places in which to flourish. Muslim traders can get no aid on Sundays or other Christian holidays, and there is no sympathy for their dietary restriction on pork, the key component of most highland ritual meals. Mercantile ventures such as clothing sales and food auctions are actively pursued by contemporary officers to increase their income beyond ordinary church revenues. The professed aim of avoiding the imposition of "nonreligious" aspects of Western culture notwithstanding, missionaries always enjoin highlanders to participate in the region's expanding formal capitalist economy because higher local incomes result in increased church revenues.

In general, Uma-speaking people present favorable recollections of the Dutch era as a time when regional warfare ended, new goods arrived in abundance, and "religion" entered their lives. Their positive attitude to Dutch sovereignty is no doubt colored in part by the fact that their remote location, pacifist compliance, and meager natural resources left them relatively undisturbed by the harsher aspects of Dutch colonialism. Kruyt notes that although the government ordered Uma speakers to move to more centralized village locations, most evaded the regulations by residing almost continuously in their swidden farming settlements (A. C. Kruyt 1938, 1:155). At the very least, Tobaku individuals make a relatively favorable assessment of the peaceful and orderly "Dutch era" in comparison with the tumultuous "Japanese era" and the "era of gangs" (gerambolan, Ind.) that ensued as the shadow of World War II darkened their homeland.

The Japanese Occupation during World War II

During the Japanese occupation, highlanders had their first startling view of airplanes overhead, although some had heard from traders about the existence of "flying ships" (kapal terbang, Ind.). Uniformly, however, Tobaku elders recall the occupation not with mere astonishment, but with abhorrence. Towulu' people describe over two years of virtual slavery to Japanese soldiers who administered a mica mine outside their village. The "Japanese time" now is recalled as a puzzling historical nightmare with little but an abandoned mica mine to corroborate elders' war stories.

When I began fieldwork in the 1980s, Tobaku people said they still did not have the slightest idea why the Japanese had wanted their mica, a resource they had used previously for decorative sequins on barkcloth clothing. Only subsequent research of U.S. government documents and geology texts revealed that wartime Japan, with its limited mineral resources, was desperate for new mica sources needed for electronics and related military equipment (Aragon 1996b).

Elders in Towulu' describe over two years of forced labor in the mica mines. Japanese soldiers centralized residents of the scattered highland villages to excavate, process ore, and carry cleaned mica to the nearest road in Kulawi. People were relocated to work the Towulu' mines from as far north as Kulawi, as far west as Banggaiba, and as far east as the Pipikoro region, distances of about fifty kilometers in every direction. Every month, about one hundred men and women, reportedly ten from each population center, were compelled to move to Towulu' and work nine hours a day in the mica mines.

The local and relocated populations were divided by the Japanese soldiers into men's and women's teams. Males worked outside the village digging, blasting, and hoisting rocks from the mines while females worked inside the village to trim, select, and pack the mica blocks in wooden boxes for transport. Small weekly payments were made to mine workers and porters for their services, but all able-bodied villagers were forced to perform mine work when requested or risk beatings by Japanese soldiers. The boxes containing mica were carried through the mountains to Kulawi in caravans of twenty to forty persons. From Kulawi the mica was trucked via Palu to the shipping port of Poso, then on to Japan.

Towulu' villagers describe canings they received from occupation soldiers either for innocent mistakes in their work activities or for infractions of unfamiliar Japanese rules. Soldiers demanded that highlanders demonstrate absolute subservience by bowing before any Japanese present and also to the Japanese flag. Highlanders recounted that they were compelled to entertain their captors by staging dances and jumping competitions. Towulu' men were struck with rattan whips to force them to jump higher and higher as Japanese soldiers laughed at their humiliating predicament.

During the two-and-a-half-year occupation several villagers reportedly were slain by soldiers. More died in the mines, killed by falling rocks blasted with Japanese dynamite. Rumors spread among the highlanders that there was a Japanese plan, to be implemented once the mines were exhausted, to murder all local inhabitants over eight years of age so that news of the mining atrocities would not leak beyond local borders.

Besides the terror and physical stress of mining work, the Japanese soldiers interfered in Central Sulawesi farming practices. Labor was diverted from farm fields to the mines, and the soldiers demanded that highlanders modify their planting habits. While the highlanders interplant rice and maize seeds in their swidden gardens, the Japanese insisted that they plant the two crops separately. According to villagers, rice planted under this Japanese restriction could not thrive because maize is the "male" plant that fertilizes the "female" rice plant. Although maize was introduced to western Central Sulawesi only during the colonial era, highlanders consider the combined planting of rice and maize to be a basic tenet of ancestral law. In their view, violating that prescription doomed their crops to failure. The neglect of farming duties occasioned by the shift of labor resources to the mines likely also contributed to the poor harvests that reportedly occurred during the occupation.

In the vicinity of Kulawi Village, the Japanese forbade the planting of dry rice altogether. They insisted that all hills be planted with cotton, most of which was requisitioned by the Japanese for their own clothing needs. This interference in subsistence practices coupled with wartime trade embargoes made food and clothing increasingly scarce commodities as the occupation progressed. Local rice supplies were appropriated and then rationed for each household at rates far below usual consumption levels. Only some village leaders and personal assistants to the Japanese received access to woven textiles.

Most families were compelled to resume their formerly dwindling efforts to manufacture barkcloth. Processed by women with wood and grooved stone mallets from the inner bark of a variety of trees, barkcloth was the main source of highlanders' clothing until the Dutch colonial administration. Barkcloth also held precolonial significance when it was painted and used for ritual offerings, ceremonial flags, and feast apparel (Aragon 1990; Kotilainen 1992, 220–227). Under Dutch rule, machine-woven cotton cloth became widely available in the highlands for the first time as indigenous regional warfare was curtailed and coastal-to-highland trade activities increased. Barkcloth and imported *ikat* cloths then became reserved for certain ceremonial occasions while imported loomed cloth became the everyday fabric of choice. With the Japanese occupation, access to this beloved commodity and element of bridewealth exchanges suddenly was impeded.

Many poignant stories about the humiliation of occupation conditions revolve around this desperation for proper attire. A Tobaku man, Tama Bugu', described how he finally was reduced to just one ragged woven sarong that he wore proudly around his shoulders over his barkcloth loincloth. One day, as he was walking through the mountain paths, he encountered someone dressed in barkcloth leading a large cow. As the stranger spotted the sarong Tama Bugu' was wearing, he offered to trade the cow outright for the piece of woven cloth. Tama Bugu' steadfastly refused. As Tama Bugu' related this story some forty years later, he laughed because now a cow is many times more valuable than a threadbare cloth. During the occupation, however, that woven textile represented the fragile sheath of his personal dignity.

After hearing such stories about the misery inflicted by occupa-tion soldiers, it was startling to learn what a small number held the entire southern Kulawi District hostage. Different individuals reported that three to eight Japanese men were resident in Towulu' along with their Kaili servants and Javanese wives or concubines. Tina Sori recit-ed the names of six Japanese men she remembered personally. Apparently the soldiers' guns and their willingness to shoot trouble-makers on sight, perhaps coupled with the highlanders' prior acquies-cence to the Dutch colonial administration, made the thousands of highlanders in the Kulawi District an easy target for wartime slavery.

Almost all the economic changes of Japanese rule were reversed as soon as the occupation was ended by Allied forces. The mica mine was abandoned, rice and maize plants were interplanted once again, production of barkcloth again declined in favor of imported textiles, and cotton was no longer farmed in the Kulawi area. Indonesia, which was not a significant region for mica exploitation prior to World War II, turned its efforts to develop other, more lucrative, natural resources.

Yet the Japanese occupation left other types of scars and influ-enced postwar social patterns in unexpected ways. Changes to local ethnic and religious identities occurred that were more durable than the changes in subsistence patterns described above. Kulawi high-landers began to view themselves with humiliation as a continuously subjugated people. They also started to compare their various foreign oppressors. Ultimately, their negative impressions of Japanese culture, coupled with the forced wartime indigenization of Salvation Army leadership, drew highlanders closer to the Protestant religion they had assumed with some vacillation during the Dutch administration.

The narratives I recorded indicate that the Japanese occupation dramatically transfigured highlanders' ideas about foreigners, religion, and their own ethnic identity. With the arrival of Japanese soldiers, Central Sulawesi highlanders began to look back on the Dutch admin-istration as relatively benevolent. The Dutch, they say, interfered to some degree with their political administration and settlement patterns, but at least they brought order—secure trade routes and regional peace. The Japanese, they say, just brought chaos—fear of corporal punishment, forced labor, hunger, and clothing shortages. This invidious comparison of the two foreign overlords matches highlanders' subsequent evaluation of the foreigners' religions.

After the occupation, highlanders no longer compared their precolonial religious practices only to European missionary teachings, but also to what they perceived to be Japanese belief and practice. Echoing European disparagement of their own indigenous faith, many Tobaku stated that the Japanese had no real religion, but only worshipped their national flag. They spoke mockingly of the Japanese "flag religion" (*agama bandera*, Ind.). The Japanese stipulation that Sulawesi villagers bow in the presence of a Japanese flag was cited as evidence that it was the Japanese people's god. Although Towulu' villagers and Japanese soldiers reportedly cooperated to conduct spirit offerings to improve their fortunes in the mica mines, by the war's end Central Sulawesi highlanders concluded that the Japanese were without true religion and that they themselves were not. They identified their own morality and spiritual authority with the European ministers expelled by the Japanese.

Many residents of large highland villages such as Towulu' and Kantewu were officially Christians prior to the arrival of the Japanese, yet the two indigenous temple buildings (*lobo* and *sou eo*, Uma) still were used for rituals, and the Salvation Army primary school was used for Sunday services. Once the Japanese soldiers seized control, villagers were expected to work the mines on Sundays the same as other days. Given that European missionaries had modeled their interdiction against Sunday work on local calendrical taboos entailing cosmological sanctions, Kulawi highlanders inferred that Sunday labor and the termination of Protestant services also might have unfortunate consequences.

Mining accidents and intermittent difficulties in locating adequate veins of mica led locals, and reportedly the Japanese soldiers as well, to conclude that their mining activities were causing offense to indigenous spirits. Some suspected that the spiritual power(s) ruling the mountains wanted revenge for the plundering of mica resources without proper ritual compensation. The headman of Towulu' was convinced to sacrifice one of his own buffaloes at the mining site. Either the ancestors, the indigenous spirits, the Christian God, or some combination of deities was displeased with the highlanders and their captors.

The Japanese soldiers seem to have interfered with ancestral rites in such a way as to prompt local reevaluation. To communicate with local deities, highlanders performed circle dances and accompanying songs (*raego'*) at all major precolonial religious rituals (Aragon 1996c). The Japanese soldiers found these coed dances seductively entertaining and commanded what were formerly ritual performances for their personal amusement. The forced enactment of ritual sacrifices and dances at the behest of their Japanese captors seemingly alienated highlanders further from their ancestral ritual practices and inclined them toward Protestant devotions.

Just prior to World War II, the Salvation Army was running 140 corps and outposts, 19 schools, and 5 clinics in Central Sulawesi.[2] These mission bases were supervised by sixty-six Salvation Army officers under the direction of Leonard and Maggie Woodward, who resided in Kantewu (Kenyon 1952, 77). During the Japanese occupation, most European Salvation Army officers—except for a few German and Scandinavian personnel—were removed from their posts and interned in prison camps. From 1942 until the war's end, the Woodwards were sent to separate men's and women's camps in Malino, South Sulawesi, near Ujung Pandang.

In the Europeans' absence, de facto responsibility for all the Salvation Army divisions in western Central Sulawesi fell to an Ambonese officer, Adjutant Eliza Sahetappy, who kept the mission organization running despite difficult financial conditions and occasional Japanese threats (M. Brouwer 1974f, 4). Without Salvation Army subsidies, most indigenous officers simply left their assigned posts and returned to their home villages, where they tried to continue Protestant meetings. Reportedly, Mrs. Sahetappy was commanded to provide village girls to "serve" and "entertain" Japanese soldiers, but she refused even in the face of threats to her life (M. Brouwer 1996, 144).

Some highlanders inferred that the tragedy of war and the oppression of the Japanese were brought on by the neglect of ancestral customs in the wake of Christian conversion (Kenyon 1952, 77). Indigenous Salvation Army leaders endeavored to dispel these notions and make Christianity a rallying point of opposition to the Japanese invaders. Although Tobaku people now speak of their dislike for the occupation soldiers and their programs, highlanders in fact did emulate the Japanese proposal of "Asia for Asians" by beginning a more thorough indigenization of the church, at first under duress but subsequently by design.

In early August 1945, the Indonesian replacement officers were called to Palu and informed that the war had ended. The Woodwards had survived in their South Sulawesi prison camps but were released in a weak condition. Within the next year, the European officers, in good health, returned to their Central Sulawesi divisions, often following furloughs to their homelands. Fifteen out of about 150 foreign officers in Indonesia had died during the occupation period. The Woodwards traveled first to Australia for recuperation and then made a return tour of welcome to Central Sulawesi. They then retired to England in 1949 following the formal opening of the Salvation Army hospital in Kulawi (Kenyon 1952, 92–101; M. Brouwer 1996, 169). Leonard Woodward died, or as Salvationists prefer to say, "was promoted to glory," in 1950, within a year of his return from Sulawesi. One of Woodward's assistants, Officer Laua, took over leadership in Kantewu and achieved impressive results in school attendance. Prior to the war there were 120 children attending three primary school grades. By 1949, there were 250 children attending six grades (Salvation Army 1949).

If Dutch colonial administrators had nudged and pressured Kulawi District highlanders into half-hearted acceptance of Europeans and their demands, the Japanese occupation startled highlanders into realizing the potential tyranny that an outside force could wreak upon their livelihood. Soon after World War II, the highlanders became unsuspecting victims of the *Permesta* and Kahar Muzakar rebellions, which infiltrated their regions from North and South Sulawesi, respectively, in the years between 1950 and 1965. Again the highlanders were subjugated by foreigners whose guns easily overwhelmed their locally manufactured weapons. This time they pointed to their Protestantism to convince the invaders that they were neither savages nor infidels. The ancestors and deities who had protected them since time immemorial then appeared feeble compared to the ancestors and deities of the foreigners who conquered them so easily.

The Postwar Regional Rebellions

Was everything going smoothly and according to plan in this wonderful land, you would ask? Of course not. It never does in this world. There must needs be temptations, testings and trials. These were multiple in Sulteng [Central Sulawesi].

Wrong influences had their effects during the occupation, and after. On the whole strong drink, mercifully, was practically unknown in these parts, though there is a palmtree whose intoxicating juice is drunk. Smoking was only indulged in by those who had mixed with Europeans in Java. Other Protestant churches now free to enter did not take these matters so seriously, and their example brought quizzings and temptations. . . .

Our own people had undergone a change of mentality, which the Japanese had fostered: Asia for the Asians. Some were no longer submissive, but reckoned they had a right to everything belonging to the Army.

Melattie Brouwer, "Tanah Toradja: A New Start—Then Civil War"

After the Japanese were expelled in 1945, conditions initially were more settled in Central Sulawesi than in war-torn Java. There, foreign Salvation Army officers were required by the revolutionary Republic battling the Dutch for independence to confine their work to

four coastal cities (M. Brouwer 1974g). Therefore, the first postwar officers' training courses for the Indonesian mission field were held in
Kalawara, south of Palu. This arrangement continued until 1948,
when regional rebellions began disrupting Sulawesi as well.

Groups of demobilized soldiers in both Christian North Sulawesi
and Muslim South Sulawesi felt disenfranchised by the new, largely
Javanese, government of the Indonesian Republic. Both groups
rebelled against the national Republic's armies between 1948 and
1965, even joining forces briefly before being suppressed. The name
"*Permesta*" (an Indonesian acronym for *Perjuangan Semesta Alam*,
meaning Inclusive or Universal Struggle) was derived from a 1957
charter issued in South Sulawesi that demanded provincial autonomy.
The name later was adopted by rebellious groups in North Sulawesi
(Harvey 1974, 1977).

The picture that western Central Sulawesi people present of the
postwar era is one of continued chaos and confusion. Certain villages
were heavily plundered or burned by Muslim rebels who supported a
South Sulawesi man named Kahar Muzakar in his revolt against the
new Indonesian Republic. Some highlanders supported the Christian
Permesta rebels from North Sulawesi, believing that these Christians
had come to protect them from the Muslim attackers entering from
South Sulawesi. Other highlanders, including Salvation Army officers,
were drafted and sent around with the Republic's army during operations aimed at quelling the Christian rebels. Most highlanders, however, merely did their best to hide or flee from all three kinds of soldiers,
in a desperate effort to keep their families, crops, and homes intact.

During the Kahar Muzakar rebellion, Muslim guerrillas entered
Central Sulawesi from the west via the Lariang River and from the
south via the Seko Valley corridor. Muslim rebels passed through
Banasu, where they reportedly sliced peoples' arms and applied salt
while commanding them to pray to Allah. The western periphery of
the Tobaku region suffered most when Muslim guerrillas from South
Sulawesi entered the Lariang River from the coast by boat in 1958.

Tobaku people who were settled near the mouth of the river fled upstream, poling their small water crafts in caravans. Many traveled north all the way to the Palolo Valley, where they stayed until the 1970s before returning home.

The same South Sulawesi rebels plundered their way to the interior as far as Momi, which they burned to the ground. The inhabitants of Momi, after trying unsuccessfully to defend their village with blowpipes, fled east to Ntipe (near Rantewulu') and Towulu', taking refuge with their relatives. The Tobaku settlements at Banggaiba, which previously had converted to Christianity, were converted anew to Islam, and one remains Muslim today. The Muslim invaders forced conversions to Islam in villages as far east as Ntipe, but both Rantewulu' and Momi later reverted to Christianity. Siwongi inhabitants, some of whose houses were burned to the ground, fled to Towulu' for safety and thereby avoided the forced conversion to Islam.

Tobaku people farther inland heard news of the guerrillas ahead of time from refugees running from the west, and they fled to higher elevations, hiding in their rice gardens. Seven Muslim guerrillas with guns terrorized Towulu' and threatened the village headman for several days before finally moving on. Two Christian Manadonese *Permesta* rebels with guns later came through and gained assistance from local leaders who had been terrified by the Muslim rebels. The men from Manado led a local war party to free Momi from the Muslim guerrillas. Employing guns, swords, blowpipes, and spears, the Tobaku and Manado men killed two of the Muslims. The remainder of the Muslim rebels fled, and Momi was liberated. A few Towulu' leaders later were jailed for three months in Palu by the Indonesian government during the 1970s for aiding the two *Permesta* rebels from North Sulawesi. Their sentences were light, however, in recognition of the confusing difficulties of the highland situation. These men in fact returned to positions of village leadership after their prison time was served.[3]

The two rebellions ended in the Tobaku area in the mid-1960s, when about one hundred soldiers in Company B of the Republican

Army entered the region to restore order and supervise the first election of the New Order government's GOLKAR (Golongan Karya, or Government Workers Party). Repercussions in the Tobaku region from the Indonesian government coup of 1965 that ended President Sukarno's regime appear mainly related to this election, where government troops were strongly interested in the success of the GOLKAR party. Pockets of support for the rival Indonesian Christian Party, PARKINDO (Partai Kristen Indonesia), led to scattered outbreaks of fighting, even among close family members. Unhappy recollections of that period of community disharmony were used sometimes to explain and justify strong GOLKAR party support in the highlands through the end of President Suharto's regime in 1998.

Christian Consolidation in the Postwar Period

Once the Indonesian Republic seized independence from the Netherlands, a new set of competing political forces came to bear upon Central Sulawesi Christianity. In 1945, President Sukarno's "five principles," or *Pancasila*, national philosophy, which prescribed monotheism, further encouraged any remaining "pagans" to convert to a world religion. On the other hand, the suspension of colonial policies favoring the established missions allowed other churches to enter the western Central Sulawesi playing field. In that changing political arena, which dramatically highlighted all non-Muslim areas of the archipelago, foreign churches began to compete for souls, as well as for government favors based on economic assistance packages.

When the New Order government gained control in 1965, the national administration was firmly grounded in west Java, the provincial administration was centered at the coast in Palu, and any hope Kulawi highlanders had of regaining full-fledged political autonomy dissolved. Their fate, rather, was to join the nation's hundreds of small, peripheral, and relatively weak ethnic minorities. The highlanders' new overlords were mostly Muslim Indonesian government functionaries invariably originating from larger ethnic groups. Yet although highland communities now admitted to political frailty and relative poverty within the nation, they also claimed new spiritual and ethnic strength through their ties to international Protestantism.

Initial postwar efforts by the Salvation Army in Indonesia concentrated on reparation of war-damaged materials, consolidation of church territories, and furtherance of local devotion to Western Christian ideals. New translations and school texts had to be developed because all standardized study materials had been burned in the Javanese headquarters at Bandung during the war (M. Brouwer 1974d, 3). By 1950, a new officers' training institute (*Pusat Latihan Bala Keselamatan*) was opened in Jakarta, and the training center building in Bandung was converted into a hospital and national administrative headquarters, as it is today. The Salvation Army also upgraded its Central Sulawesi school system. The area's first junior high school was opened in Kalawara during the 1960s, and the first high school and a teachers' college were opened in Kulawi in 1971 (M. Brouwer 1974a, 4).

Some more remote areas, for example, the Tole'e village of Onu, which had not been actively missionized prior to the war, received new attention in the 1960s. Elder shamans in the highlands still occasionally came forward to convert to Christianity, although most new Salvation Army members by that time were children (M. Brouwer 1974h). Because of its late conversion during the postwar period, when the Salvation Army no longer maintained an exclusive mission field in the district, Onu is the only Tobaku village to harbor three different Protestant sects: the Salvation Army, the Donggala Protestant Gospel Church (Gereja Protestan Injil Donggala, or GPID, the localized Dutch Reformed Church), and the Pentecostal Church (Gereja Pantekosta).

Like Kruyt, Salvation Army missionaries considered non-Christian contacts, such as those instigated by the Japanese occupation, postwar rebellions, and the New Order regime, to be detrimental to the moral fiber of the Central Sulawesi people under their stewardship. Nevertheless, they also recognized that these events challenged the capabilities of local Salvation Army officers and soldiers and served as a growth experience. For this reason, as well as the relentless demand for self-administration unleashed through Indonesian independence, the Salvation Army mission acceded to indigenization from that time forward. By 1973, only 4 of the 76 Salvation Army officers and 265 teachers in Sulawesi were foreigners (M. Brouwer 1974I, 4). As the New Order period progressed, more Western officers returned home without replacements, until the last one departed in 1994.

Critical reformation phases occurred under indigenous officers during the 1950s and 1960s. In Siwongi, for example, regular church services were held only beginning in 1952, and these were held in the indigenous temple for want of a church building. According to reports in Towulu', female puberty rituals and the associated teeth filing ended only after World War II, probably in the 1950s. The last pre-Christian ritual feasts (*motaro*, Uma) with *raego'* dancing took place at about the same time. In 1959, only two years after the last public curing ceremony with trances was held, the Salvation Army school in Siwongi was converted to a church.

Key figures in the extermination of ancestral rites and their substitution with Salvation Army rituals in Tobaku were Brigadier and Mrs. T. Tantu, who later retired to Palolo. In 1954, the Winatu-born officer and his wife took charge in Towulu', determined to uproot all the old heathen practices. When they arrived, there was still no church building, only the indigenous temple and a Salvation Army school building that was used for Christian services. Ancestral feasts with spirit possessions aimed at curing the sick were still being held under the leadership of the officially Christian village headman and the leading shaman.

For about three years, Brigadier Tantu said, he got little result from his efforts to end heathen practices. Then, in about 1957, the headman opened a mountain for farming and, as usual, made a pact with the "owner(s) of the land" to sacrifice a buffalo if the fields were successful. The crops did not grow well, so the headman opened another field and asked Officer Tantu to make a Christian blessing ceremony. Others opening fields near the headman's watched and wanted to follow their leader's example. The headman suggested that the other villagers wait to see how his crops turned out first. The harvest proved abundant, and after that, Brigadier Tantu claimed, all the villagers were eager to try the Protestant methods.

According to Mrs. Tantu, the villagers initially were so afraid of revenge from the owner(s) of the land that they spoke of the Christian-blessed fields as "the fields owned by Mrs. Tantu." In this way, they thought that if the owner(s) became angry, any revenge would fall upon her, the minister's wife. Later, when the fields continued to prosper, fears diminished and villagers abandoned the taboo name.

Brigadier Tantu pinpointed his greatest moment of success in Towulu' to a massive ritual transition he created. With the consent of both headman and shaman, Officer Tantu staged an ancestral-style ritual to end all non-Christian rituals. Each household in the village was called upon to sacrifice either a pig or a cow, and everyone was told to eat foods that violated their personal pre-Christian food taboos. Contrary to the rules of certain pre-Christian feasts, youths and children were invited to attend and eat the meat provided. Verses from the Bible were read throughout an entire night of feasting in the temple to end the bonds between villagers and their old faith.[4]

Brigadier Tantu said he convinced not only the general populace, but also the community shaman, Tama Mulu', to give up his personal food taboos and refrain from passing on his shamanic knowledge before his death. After the Christian ceremonies, Brigadier Tantu said, the harvests became better and better, and some elders who had never converted relented and signed up as Salvation Army soldiers. The planting of mission-supported cash crops such as coffee also intensified in the 1960s once peace was established and more trade opportunities were provided by the world market.

Salvation Army Protestantism in western Central Sulawesi thus evolved in three initial stages. During the colonial period prior to 1940, Dutch government disruptions and new diseases were introduced and then ameliorated by the teachings and technology of European missionaries. This is the period when the first behavioral and cognitive negotiations between Europeans and Uma speakers were made. During the intermediary period of political chaos between World War II and 1965, European ministers were removed temporarily and locals had to reanalyze their nascent Protestant faith under threats from Japanese occupation forces and Kahar Muzakar rebels. Finally, in the post-independence period, indigenized Christianity became an official goal, foreign missionaries gradually were sent home, and ritual acts were reformatted with Protestant substitutions. In the next three chapters I more closely examine the logic and practice of European negotiations with precolonial ideas and rituals before returning, in chapter 8, to the role of the New Order government in "developing" world religion and the moral behaviors of a "modern" citizenry.

5

Precolonial Cosmology and Christian Consequences

The precolonial religion of the Central Sulawesi highlands not only drew the approbation of Europeans, but puzzled them as well. Local ideas related to spiritual facets of people, animals, places, and things contested European Christian certainties about the divine, personal, and exclusively human soul, as well as commonsense assumptions about property ownership. Europeans even had trouble defining highlanders' pre-Christian deities in order to place them within or outside the Protestant Trinity. Their makeshift solutions to these classificatory dilemmas often served as justifications for European claims that Central Sulawesi people had no true religion of their own, just misguided superstitions about vaguely known demons from which they should be saved. To ease practical administration and allay concerns about increasing Muslim strength, Dutch colonial officials sought and created for Indies people official boundaries between "religious belief" and "secular" cultural habits.

The European comprehension and public manipulation of Central Sulawesi cosmology was a philosophical Procrustean bed with distinctive consequences for contemporary local Christianity. Early missionaries' skewed representations of local religion swayed Central Sulawesi spiritual ideas and practices as they increasingly were drawn into the Christian armature. Yet from persistent ideas about unseen and often nonpersonified forces of the universe to unflagging concepts of divine justice,

Tobaku narratives illustrate local contributions to an indigenized and, for Europeans, somewhat unmanageable Christian theology.

This chapter explores a local cosmology, one that becomes refracted through colonial European lenses. Whereas world religions of the past millennia, including Protestantism, elaborately portray the personalities and words of their gods, precolonial Sulawesi cosmology is rather silent on such matters. Thus missionaries pursued a difficult search for analogues to God, even analogues for what they could accept as religion. My aim here is to break apart the cosmological aspects of conversion by delineating the Europeans' reclassification of Central Sulawesi spiritual ideas, and locals' appropriation or sometimes refusal of these newly categorized concepts.

Adat "Traditions": Once Unified, Now Fragmented

Before the European category of "religion" entered the Indonesian archipelago during the colonial era, it was preceded by another borrowed concept that encompassed precolonial cosmological frameworks and related canons of appropriate behavior: *adat*, or one of its cognates. The term derives from the Arabic *'ada*, meaning "habit, wont, custom, usage, practice" (Wehr 1976). The word likely entered the Indonesian archipelago when frequent trade with the Middle East commenced between the seventh and thirteenth centuries A.D. The nearly universal adoption of the term throughout the archipelago and the infrequency of indigenous synonyms suggest that centuries of extensive Middle Eastern and Malay trade encounters required a means by which a variety of island peoples could represent and justify their heretofore locally known philosophies and practices to outsiders familiar with the Arabic term. The Tobaku and other Uma speakers of Central Sulawesi use the cognate term *"ada'*," which they, like many Indonesians, now distinguish from "religion" (*agama*, Ind.), with its "world religion" connotations.

Early European accounts, developed with a pragmatic eye toward colonial administration, cast *adat* as either custom (*adat kebiasaan*, Ind.) or traditional law (*hukum adat*). Although the more holistic nature of *adat* as both cosmology and regional practice was comprehended by both late colonial scholars and Christian missionaries (e.g., Cooley 1962; Schärer 1963), the efforts of administrators to codify traditional law (*hukum adat*, a gloss of the Dutch *adatrecht*) and the efforts of Christians to define pre-Christian religion (*agama adat*) resulted in a new fragmentation of the *adat* concept not only among foreign scholars, but among local people as well (Whittier 1977, 1978). Through the imposition of colonial regulations, local communities were obliged to accept the segmentation and reification of their formerly more expansive and not necessarily internally consistent category of *adat*.

Scholarship and bureaucratic documentation in President Suharto's New Order government only increased this fragmenting tendency because regional offices of the Department of Education and Culture (Departemen Pendidikan dan Kebudayaan, or DEPDIK-BUD) were charged with issuing documents describing the *adat*, or "traditional culture," of various Indonesian ethnic groups. These ubiquitous booklets, usually based on descriptions drawn from Dutch colonial texts or from interviews with a few local elders, inevitably codify uncontroversial portions of region-specific *adat* codes and present them in a laundry-list fashion, as if they represent an entire cultural matrix or definition.

In fact, pre-colonial *adat* systems were open to reinterpretation under changing conditions in a way that is concordant with subsequent scholarship on the continuing invention of what social science scholars once unthinkingly designated as "tradition" (Hobsbawm and Ranger 1983; Borofsky 1987). As Steedly notes when discussing the Karo of Sumatra, "[T]he rhetorical *reproduction* of Karo adat as a transhistorical social object should not be mistaken for its *continuation* as a timeless structure of human social relations independent of actual human agency" (Steedly 1993, 50; emphasis in original).

Local Indonesian depictions of *adat* as timeless rules of authority undoubtedly masked its constant readjustment to social circumstances. Colonial Dutch officials grasped the static rhetoric while overlooking or suppressing the pragmatic aspects of *adat* flexibility. Dutch fears of the potentially unifying force of Islam also promoted a divide-and-rule strategy of elaborating innumerable "micro-adats" of regional law that were presented to show how culturally fragmented the archipelago would be apart from Dutch rule (Lev 1985, 66; Schrauwers 1998, 208–213).

European philosophical systems such as Christianity and the externally imposed bureaucratic administration overstretched the inherent flexibility of earlier *adat* frameworks and required a cognitive segmentation of *adat* by the indigenous people themselves. The colonial bureaucratization of *adat* law in Indonesia ruptured the former holistic and comprehensive moral quality of *adat*. Fines and other compensatory measures became legal measures to punish the guilty instead of efforts to repair a violated cosmological harmony.

Christian conversion thus had a splintering effect upon some populations such as the Kenyah Dayak of Borneo (Whittier 1977, 1978). Christian converts divided their *adat* into two segments: religious *adat* (*agama adat*) and traditional customs (*adat kebiasaan*). They maintained their ethnic identity and local habits through their ties to the latter while retaining their right to take exception to the former. Christians no longer saw their personal moral behavior as capable of disturbing the cosmological balance such that, for example, Christian commoners might wear tiger teeth ornaments formerly sanctioned only for aristocrats without fear of personal misfortune. Meanwhile, dedicated followers of the pre-Christian religion feared cosmological disturbances were being created by the Christians' aberrant behavior. Thus segmentation and migrations of Kenyah populations occurred on religious grounds (Whittier 1977, 8; 1978, 108–109).

Steedly reports that *adat* rituals declined dramatically even among non-Christian Karo in Sumatra after some of their relatives

A renowned highland elder, Tama Roti, poses with Salvation Army Sergeant Subagio beside a miniature ancestral temple (*lobo*) in 1986. Tama Roti built the temple not to challenge Christian religion (*agama*, Ind.), but to demonstrate historical tradition (*adat*).

converted. After these conversions, specific categories of kin who were needed to perform particular ritual roles would no longer participate. This prevented the achievement of an entire set of ritual exchanges (Steedly 1993, 60). The continuity of Karo *adat* was left by Christians to the "traditionalists," who increasingly found themselves unable to mount complete rituals without their Christian relatives.

The physical segmentation of communities described by Whittier for the Kenyah and Steedly for the Karo did not occur in western Central Sulawesi because community decisions to convert were more or less unanimous, not individually based. Community leaders or elder councils passed resolutions to convert, and their constituencies loyally followed, at least in principle. One by one, communities agreed to Christianity until even the smallest ones deferred to the wisdom of their relatives in larger population centers hosting more missionary attentions.

Both colonial pressures and postcolonial government policies or opportunities have forced decisions about which ideas and practices are to be included within various categories of *adat*. Tobaku people now regularly distinguish between *adat*, meaning age-old customs or traditional rules and *agama*, meaning legitimate world religion. They now understand that the state philosophy of *Pancasila* (see chapter 8) is supposed to take precedence over Christian religion, which in turn is supposed to take precedence over the local "customs" they call *ada'*. Yet they also understand that they can claim certain ritual performances or behaviors as legitimate—and in principle not in competition with religion—by insisting that these practices belong to the domain of historical or secular custom and not world religion.

The contemporary category of *adat* gives Central Sulawesi highlanders a recognized philosophical and behavioral domain in which to store important elements of pre-Christian cosmology that are not readily assimilated into Protestant doctrine and practice. For example, most Tobaku accept the missionary assertion that the essential marriage event is the Christian church wedding, yet families also mount a series of preliminary and subsequent "traditional" events that allow them to negotiate the necessary economic, social, and cosmological aspects of household alliances and fertility.

If, then, *adat* in western Central Sulawesi was something more than what it has become to both outsiders and locals, what did it originally encompass? Below I approach this question of cosmology through European apprehensions, local responses, and postcolonial transmutations.

Soul Concepts of Breath, Shadows, and Efficacious Forces

Austronesian conceptions of souls or invisible realizations of visible entities are diffuse, complex, and alien to current Western thought. The conceptual divide is manifested in the confusing nature of outsiders' reports about Southeast Asian or Pacific concepts of spirits and souls. After evaluating and comparing some of these analyses with Sulawesi concepts, I conclude that Tobaku names for "soul elements" often represent various aspects or manifestations of spiritual forces rather than individuated types of spirits. The differences between Central Sulawesi and European Protestant notions about souls demonstrate one area of misapprehension between missionaries and converts.

Kruyt (1906) writes that "tribal" Indonesian people have two soul concepts. The first one is a life force that dwells within living humans, animals, and even inanimate objects such as rocks. The second one Kruyt describes as a less-developed concept of a personal immortal soul that comes into being only at a person's death. Kruyt called the first concept, often labeled with a word meaning "shadow" in Indonesian languages, "soulstuff" (*zielestof*, Dutch) and the second concept, often labeled with a word meaning "breath" in Indonesian languages, just "soul" (*ziel*). Kruyt considered the Indonesian idea of two entirely separate kinds of souls, the former accompanying life and the latter beginning around the time of death, as a vague and primitive understanding of the true unified human—that is, Protestant—soul.

Kruyt devotes most of his book on animism in the Indonesian archipelago (1906) and sections of his books on the "East" and "West Toradjas" (Adriani and Kruyt 1912; A. C. Kruyt 1938) to detailed discussions about local concepts of soulstuff contained in human secretions, possessions, plants, animals, and minerals. To develop his theories about Indonesian animism, Kruyt relied on his personal knowledge about Central Sulawesi populations, which was gleaned from his efforts to convert them. Insofar as Kruyt uncritically lumped all concepts about nonimmortal souls or animating forces into one Dutch category (*zielestof*), we need to reassess his conclusions, not only about the role of soulstuff in motivating headhunting, but also about his merger of diverse local ideas to create a dualistic soul model.[1]

Roseman posits a Malaysian view of the permeable person, conceived as a number of "potentially detachable selves" (1990, 227). Although Roseman's analysis concerns the Austro-Asiatic Temiar, a rain forest-dwelling population of interior Malaysia whose soul concepts differ somewhat from those of Sulawesi populations, her approach is germane to Austronesian cosmologies. Using Scheper-Hughes and Lock's (1987) concept of an interactive or "sociocentric self" that does not end at the boundaries of the individual, Roseman's view of souls accounts for their presence in both human and nonhuman forms. She thereby better explains the data concerning Southeast Asian souls—including those presented by Kruyt—than Kruyt's dualistic model. As Bird-David (1999) suggests, even anthropological theorists often do a poor job of assessing "animism" when they cling to modernist views of personhood and the separation of spiritual life from the natural environment.

Kruyt (1906, 1938; Adriani and Kruyt 1912) recognized the feature of multiple souls, or soul elements, and documented their association with inanimate objects or human secretions. Nevertheless, he was constrained by cognitive blinders to lump everything unfamiliar into one "soulstuff" category placed in opposition to the personal soul known to European Protestantism. Kruyt also failed to see that the multiple aspects of souls that he termed "soulstuff" are characterized by a linkage to individuals or objects in their everyday or resting state, but become detached and mobile in specific contexts such as illness, dreams, ritual, and physical or emotional disturbance (cf. Roseman 1990, 231).

From his standpoint as a social evolutionist and Protestant missionary, Kruyt claims that world religions such as Christianity and Islam diminish the "superstitious" concept of soulstuff among Indonesians and develop the higher concept of a single, immortal human soul (A. C. Kruyt 1906, 5). The first missionaries among the Uma speakers tried to provoke this transformation by labeling an immortal human soul with the local term for the personal "breath" soul (*inoha'*, Uma). Then the Holy Spirit was called *Inoha' Tomoroli'*, literally, "Breath/Spirit that is Clean/Smooth." As MacGregor (1987, 455) notes, some original Judeo-Christian concepts of the human soul referred to breath (e.g., *spiritus*, Latin), as do Indic concepts (*brana*, Sanskrit) and those of East African groups such as the Dinka (Lienhardt 1982).

By contrast, the "shadow" aspect, or soul element (*kao'*, Uma), which was recaptured by pre-Christian shamans curing the afflicted, is little mentioned by missionaries in connection with the establishment of Protestant doctrines. The concept is, however, still widely invoked by Tobaku people, especially when they perceive these "shadow" souls wandering their villages. Peoples' experience is that the corpse or ghost (*kiu*, Uma) can return to the village after death. They are told in Christian sermons, however, that the corpse (*mayat*, Ind.) stays always in the cemetery ground while the soul (*roh*, Ind.) departs the village at death. Thus villagers often described to me a dissonance between the church's claims about transformations at death and their own empirical observations of wandering souls.

A third aspect or soul element described by both colonial and postcolonial scholars of Malay and Indonesian societies is called *semangat*, or a cognate term (*semanga'*, Uma). Endicott, whose analy-

sis of Malay religious concepts remains more useful than many
(including Skeat 1901; Winstedt 1982 [1951]; Cuisinier 1951),
describes *semangat* as similar to the Polynesian notion of *mana*, a pervasive force that can inhabit inanimate as well as living beings
(Endicott 1970, 2–32).[2] Endicott (1970, 47) concludes that contradictions in previous writers' discussions of *semangat* derive from their confusion of three Malay aspects of soul: *semangat*, *nyawa* (breath), and
roh (shadow). Only humans have *roh*, and only living, breathing animals have *nyawa*, while even inanimate minerals may possess *semangat* (Endicott 1970, 47–80; Laderman 1991, 41–44).

Errington describes the Bugis concept of *sumange'* as a cosmic
force concentrated at the human navel and secreted in human waste
products. Although all people have and shed some *sumange'*, high-
ranking individuals produce more and must guard it more carefully to
retain their exalted position. It can be gathered through rituals, protected by talismans, and stored in personal effects such as clothes or
regalia (Errington 1989, 51–63; Acciaioli 1989; Adams 1993). Such
Austronesian terms, in contrast to Indo-European notions of "soul,"
present themselves as relational categories that are employed to comment upon the unseen aspects of natural things. These invisible
aspects of the natural universe, often categorized as "souls" by
Westerners, are manipulated by Austronesian ritual specialists often
without regard to specific understandings about their composition,
their gender, or their relationships among each other.

Several other important differences between Sulawesi and
Western concepts of souls can be noted. Coville (1988, 163) and
Adams (1993) describe how Toraja ideas of the "breath" soul (*penaa*)
involve the connection between individuals and their community,
whereas the Western concept of soul has a purely individual focus.
Sulawesi ideas of soul are based in assumptions about the continuity of
relations between the living and the dead, and assumptions about hierarchy, which destine the souls of important individuals to become
higher spirits. Toraja sense that their pre-Christian spirits have been
banished by Christianity to some other geographic region and that

their land of the dead is merely becoming underoccupied as Christian converts send their dead relatives to heaven instead (Adams 1993). Such ideas often seem more accurate in terms of real-life experiences than the foreign ideas about souls and afterlife taught by missionaries.

Kruyt classifies Indonesian concepts of *semangat*, along with "shadow" souls, under the rubric of "personal soulstuff" (*persoonlijke zielestof*, A. C. Kruyt 1906, 1–2, 66–68). Thus Kruyt created "soulstuff" as a catchall category in which to place diverse types of unfamiliar Indonesian soul elements that did not match his Christian view of the human soul. "Shadow" souls that escaped to cause illness or avenge the newly deceased, mysterious efficacious forces in everything from saliva to kings, even the power of headhunting trophies, all became "soulstuff," a superstitious concept to be subdued by godly religion. Contemporary narratives, however, reveal that Kruyt's classificatory gambit failed to give a good account of the unseen entities routinely perceived by Central Sulawesi highlanders. Missionaries were faced with similar cognitive hurdles when they tried to master Central Sulawesi concepts of "owner" deities, ancestors, and other tutelary spirits.

"Owner" Deities, Ancestors, and Dangerous Spirits

The crux of conversion in colonies is the translation of ideas and desires under the pressures of conquest (Rafael 1993, xvii–xx). Greater than any other conceptual problem for the European missionaries in Central Sulawesi was the translation of the entities that they would replace with the Protestant notions of God, Jesus, and the Holy Spirit. Conversely, they were forced to delimit their application of the concept of Satan so that it did not include absolutely every being that Central Sulawesi people revered. The missionaries' inability to locate a hierarchically privileged, creator god in Central Sulawesi left them troubled by the relative importance of what appeared to them to be an inchoate and physically mobile mass of dangerous minor spirits and lingering ghosts.

In this section I seek to find comprehensibility in what the early missionaries found so perplexing. I also identify where the missionaries' impetus to find an indigenous Christian order violated ethnographic realities. I argue that the Europeans' hierarchical and personal images of their own God(s) and Satan confounded their impressions of local deities. In addition, their private-property notion of "ownership" interfered with their comprehension of "owner" spirits, the most significant deities that Europeans could draw on for their proposed translation of local ideas about "God."

Kruyt (1938, 2:422–494) explains western Central Sulawesi gods and spirits in a discussion that begins with sky gods and creators and moves downward to the nastiest demons. His implied comparisons with the heavenly High God of Protestantism and the lower sources of satanic evil are never far below the surface. Kruyt presents his findings in a list, noting that some spirits are tied to the earth, water, or skies, and some are more important than others for certain ethnic groups. Although Kruyt never fathoms any relationship of one set of spirits to another, Uma categories for pre-Christian deities and spirits can be sorted into three types of beings that vary according to their domains of control. Rather than forcing a comparison of local spiritual forces to Christian ones, I suggest that Tobaku concepts show their own internally coherent order as long as Sulawesi concepts of ownership and concentric hierarchies are given priority over European concerns with a linear hierarchy, private-property ownership, and Good versus Evil.

According to Tobaku people, the pre-Christian world was inhabited by localized "owner" spirits called *pue'* (or the synonym *tumpu*), deified ancestor spirits called *anitu*, and a group of wandering fearsome beings now identified as *seta*. This last group of apparitions includes trickster spirits of the forest (*tau lero*), angry souls of women who die in childbirth (*pontiana'*), demons sent by sorcerers (*tope'ule'*), nocturnal flying creatures that eat human livers (*popo'*), and invisible forest monsters (*tope'tilinga*).[3]

Pue' are the spirits with the largest spheres of authority. The term literally means "owner(s)," but like the Indonesian word "*tuan*" or the

Burmese word "*nat*," it also connotes "master(s)" or "lord(s)." Central Sulawesi languages do not use specific pluralizers. Thus *pue'* can refer diffusely to one or many beings who oversee or "own" a particular domain such as a mountain, a waterway, or a stand of trees. Kruyt, however, was led by European linguistic conventions to envision each *pue'* as an individual god or demon. Missionaries also favored the European political connotation of divine "masters" or "lords" over the less-understood indigenous custodial concept of "owners."

In Uma, these localized tutelary spirits are titled only according to their domain, such as "owner(s) of the trees" (*pue' kasu*). The use of personal names for high-status individuals is considered impertinent and dangerous in Central Sulawesi. Positional titles are the safer and more respectful means to address or refer to powerful individuals such as parents-in-law, elders, or ancestors.

In the Da'a Kaili language, *pue'* is not only a spirit title, but also the kinship term for grandparents (Barr 1988). The same is true in the Winatu dialect of Uma, reflecting a regional view that one's grandparents are the true owners or guardians of the world passed on to the present generation. The use of *pue'* as a kinship term suggests that *pue'* spirits, like the deified ancestor spirits (*anitu*), are the focus of the founders' cults discussed in chapter 3. *Pue'* represent the guardian land spirits with whom the founding ancestors made their pacts to clear the land.

Apart from Christian teaching, Central Sulawesi people generally do not personalize the unseen forces that affect their local universe. Unlike the Judeo-Christian God and son Jesus, whose characteristic behaviors are known from the Bible and whose humanized images are thoroughly conveyed through Western portraiture, Central Sulawesi deities are known primarily through the behavioral codes they expect from humans, not through literary or visual representations of themselves. The personal characters of the myriad unseen forces that organized the Central Sulawesi universe were essentially irrelevant. Only their domains of authority and requirements for human behavior were requisite knowledge. Thus it was a challenge for missionaries to unify and personalize deity concepts, as well as to capture highlanders' interest in the biographical details of European deity representations.

A final issue related to missionary misunderstandings of the *pue'* spirits revolves around discrepancies between European and Central Sulawesi concepts of ownership. Europeans envisioned deity "owners" of places or resources to be like European human owners: that is, individual beings who held private and comprehensive authority. For Central Sulawesi groups, however, ownership is corporate and constrained by overlapping usufruct rights and orders of precedence. The spirit "owners" they knew were temporary occupants of a place, or guardians representing those entities whose usage was prior to the present one. Local representations of spirit ownership were not modeled on patrilineal feudal lords or biblical-era slave owners, but rather on shifting cognatic groups of horticulturists whose movements through time established their authority in any particular region. These spirit owners, like Central Sulawesi people themselves, expected their rights over a resource to be acknowledged with supplicatory words and food offerings when the resource was sought. They did not expect continual obeisance outside an immediate dominion or season. These limitations on the owner deities' authority made Central Sulawesi cosmology both bewildering and meager in the eyes of Europeans.

Kruyt writes that in contrast to the rather occasional interaction sought by highlanders with their "higher" land- or sky-owning deities, the ones who seemed more akin to the Christian God, spirits of ancestors are perceived and consulted on a daily basis. He also notes the sharp difference in attitudes toward the spirits of the recently deceased and the spirits of individuals who have been venerated with a complete set of death feasts (Adriani and Kruyt 1968 [1950], 2:102). He observes correctly that while the former generally are avoided as well as feared, the latter are honored as deities and sought out with offerings for more routine contacts.

What Adriani and Kruyt did not comprehend is that the spirits of deified ancestors hold claims over people of particular kindred groups rather than physical domains or resources. The *anitu* are a difficult class of spirits to investigate because there is now variation among descriptions of them given by various Tobaku people. Some confirm that they are ancestor spirits, while others deny that idea. Some assign them to the "evil spirit" category of *seta*, while others say they are good because they can help in times of family illness.

My conclusion that *anitu* are deified ancestor spirits of powerful people is based partly on field narratives and partly on the pervasiveness of the term's cognates in other Austronesian-speaking regions (e.g., Molnar 1990). For example, the term *"anitu"* is used in the Philippine Cebuano Visayan language for beneficial spirits (Wolff 1972, 47). The term *"antu"* among Borneo Maloh people and the term *"nitu"* among Timor Atoni and Moluccan Tanimbar people also refer to ancestor spirits, or sometimes literally to corpses (Bernstein 1997, 54–57; Schulte Nordholt 1971, 503; McKinnon 1989, 39). The Malay or Indonesian term *"hantu,"* usually translated into English as "ghost," shares this common history of meaning. For Uma-speaking groups, *anitu* were, and for many still are, a category of elevated ancestors with moral authority over particular bilateral kindreds, or hamlet communities.

Some Tobaku people deny that *anitu* are "ancestor spirits" (*arwah orang tua dulu*, Ind.), possibly because *anitu* is not a term that applies to everyone's deceased relatives. Rather, *anitu* are a special type of ancestor spirit, the deified kind. There is no single Uma language term for "ancestor spirit" that includes all possible manifestations of human essence following death. Spirits of ancestors include *kao'*, a newly dead person's "shadow" spirit, *kiu* or *rate*, corpses or spirits of people whose mortuary rites are incomplete. Most ancestors (*to owi*, "those long ago") never become *anitu*, but simply go to the afterworld (*sirowi*), which, unlike the Christian heaven, closely resembles a village of the living. Early missionaries had difficulty convincing Sulawesi natives to strive for the salvation of God's heaven when they already knew where they were destined to go (the earth-like villages of *sirowi*) and anticipated being reunited there with their deceased relatives.

Anitu, in contrast to those more ordinary spirits of the dead who farm rice in the afterworld, are described as deified spirits of very "powerful people" (*to baraka*) who are extensively honored by their living relatives in mortuary feasts. The Central Sulawesi term "*to baraka*" comes from "*to*," referring to a person, and "*baraka*," from Arabic, meaning "divine blessing" or "supernatural power" (Geertz 1968, 44–45). As spirits of powerful people who held sway over large groups of their relatives, *anitu* become deified guardian spirits of bilateral kindreds, able to intervene positively or negatively in community affairs when living individuals uphold or violate ancestral moral codes.

The third pre-Christian category of spirits, the ones with no legitimate physical or human domain, are now called *seta*, a name with clear implications for Christian observers who identified them with Satan. The Central Sulawesi term, however, most likely derives from the Arabic word "*shaitan*," adopted early into the Malay language. Uma speakers also use a cognate (*ji'i*) of the Arabic word "*jinn*" to refer to particular harmful spirits or *seta*. Although the majority of Central Sulawesi highlanders may have had little direct contact with Islam until the early twentieth century, they traded with lowland kingdoms such as Dolo and Sigi, which became Muslim centuries earlier through their relations with the Luwu kingdom of South Sulawesi (Adriani and Kruyt 1950, vol. 1; A. C. Kruyt 1938, vol. 1; Andaya 1981).

Kruyt (1938, 2:269, 274) describes *seta* as harmful "lower nature-ghosts" (*lagere natuurgeest*, Dutch) as if they were just a more trivial version of the "owner" spirits. There is no way to know how specific the terms "*seta*" and "*ji'i*" were before Christian missionaries entered the region. We may even question whether the spirits now called *seta* were identified collectively before contact with Muslims. Recent narratives portray some of the harmful spirits called *seta* as vassals of more powerful spirits such as *pue'* and *anitu*. Others wander unattached as forest demons or vengeful souls. Ultimately, this congeries of dangerous, unseen entities was to become lumped, personified, and elevated by missionaries into a Christian vision of Lucifer.

To summarize, the guardian deities called *pue'* oversee specific natural resources such as land, rivers, gold, or rice, which they allow humans who petition them respectfully to use. The deified spirits of important ancestors called *anitu* may be considered the owners, or tutelary spirits, of the family kindreds. Like *pue'*, they help or harm on the basis of their approval of human actions relating to ancestral rules. The various harmful spirits called *seta* own nothing themselves, and hence desire to take from, or punish, the living. These three classes of pre-Christian spiritual entities can be viewed on a continuum in terms of their domains of authority. Only a few are specifically conceived as male or female, or as appearing to humans in a particular physical form. The Owner of Rice, *Pue' Niu*, is considered female like the grain itself. The "owner" of waterways, *pue' ue'*, is sometimes described as appearing in crocodile form, a feared creature thought to punish ill-behaved humans.

Most owner spirits, however, are not defined according to number and gender. Nor are they visualized in any specific form. Without fully understanding the spirit beings' essential characteristics or local concepts of property ownership, Protestant missionaries concluded that these seemingly ignoble and imprecise ideas comprised something less than the gods of a true religion. They thus aimed their efforts toward dismantling what they considered erroneous and primitive concepts while translating as many potent unseen beings as they could into the Protestant categories of God, Jesus, Satan, and the Holy Spirit.

Constructing the Trinity

European missionaries faced the daunting linguistic challenges confronting Christian missionaries everywhere: How was the great and good Protestant God to be called in a language containing words only for lesser malicious spirits? By default the term *"pue'"* (owner, or lord) was chosen by the first European missionaries to speak in Uma about the Christian God as lord of the universe. Jesus also became referred to as *Pue' Yesus*, "Lord Jesus" or "Owner Jesus." The Uma word for "breath" or "life force" (*inoha'*) was selected to discuss the Christian concept of an immortal human soul with a personal relationship to God.[4] The Holy Spirit was called "Breath/Spirit that is Clean/Smooth" (*Inoha' Tomoroli'*). Likewise, the Holy Bible was translated literally as the "Book that is Clean" (*Buku Tomoroli'*).

By contrast, European missionaries lumped the regional guardian deities (*pue'*) and venerated ancestors (*anitu*) into the base category including nasty forest spirits and vengeful souls of the unhappy dead (*seta*; cf. Hoskins 1987a, 157). Only one terminological exception was made: the name of the pre-Christian "owner(s) of the skies" (*pue' langi'*) was accepted as an Uma synonym for the Christian God. There likely was local resistance to putting all indigenous owners into a repugnant category, and the sky lord was accorded exceptional treatment because the biblical God too is termed Lord of the Heavens.

The Arabic-derived term "*Alatala*" also became used as an Uma gloss of the Indonesian word for the Christian God (*Tuhan*, Ind.). *Alatala* comes from the Arabic *Allah Ta'ala*, meaning "God the Great One" (Adriani and Kruyt 1950, 2:chap.12; Weinstock 1987, 78). The use of this term, which even prior to Christian missionization referred to a distant creator god, again indicates the presence of some Muslim influence in the highlands before the arrival of the Christian missionaries. The fact that Christian missionaries did not eliminate the term suggests that they may have accepted its value in conveying the concept of a supreme high god despite its prior association with Islam. The Indonesian cognate borrowed from Arabic, *Allah*, also is used daily in the conglomerate phrase that begins all Protestant prayers in the region: "*Allah, Bapak kami, Tuhan yang Maha Esa*," or "God, our Father, God the Great One."

The reformulation of deity categories in the Kulawi highlands is less a change in deities' and ancestors' expected behavior than in their titles and individuality. The Tobaku, like many Indonesian peoples, often employ evasive titles and taboo words, especially when addressing or referring to powerful or endangered entities. Central Sulawesi peoples readily substituted Christian for pre-Christian deity terminology through an ongoing sociolinguistic process not readily appreciated by the European missionaries who promoted it.

Precolonial Central Sulawesi groups regularly changed the uttered names of deities, ancestors, aged elders (who have almost attained the status of ancestors), newborn babies (who are vulnerable to attacks by spirits), important animals, and plants to avoid giving offense or tempting an eavesdropping spirit to harm the person or valuable named. A rather extensive Uma replacement vocabulary was used each harvest season in order to protect the rice crop. Even in the 1980s, the residents of one highland Kaili region never uttered the word for coffee because their village headman had a similar personal name, which should never be spoken out of respect and fear of cosmological retribution.

The management of names is one of the symbolic struggles that often takes place between more and less powerful segments of a society (Bourdieu 1985, 731–735; Kuipers 1998). At the same time, local terms and missionary meanings are mutually defining, and it may require many generations of consistent external pressure before ambiguities in the newly introduced concepts are resolved, only possibly in favor of foreign interpretations (Lienhardt 1982, 90–94). The potential for feedback of local deity conceptions into earlier Christian categories is generally overlooked in missionization studies.

Europeans' efforts to dump all ancestor and nature spirits into the negative category of Satan required Westerners to begin thinking about the Christian devil as a multiform entity including "ghosts" of the dead, fantastic monsters, and evil spirits lurking in the tropical forests. Even Protestant missionaries working recently in Central Sulawesi have constructed views of Satan that are realized in terms of spirit categories learned from the highlanders. An American missionary in Central Sulawesi once said to me candidly, "It is much easier to believe in ghosts here than it was back in Leavenworth, Kansas."

Interpreting the Bible

> The man who doesn't read good books has no advantage over the man who
> can't read them.
> *Mark Twain*

Policies of religious conversion through local vernacular or national languages are studied political decisions on the part of missionary organizations (Rafael 1993; Steedly 1996). Although early Dutch Reformed missionaries such as Adriani and Kruyt were committed to working through local languages, the Salvation Army moved in a different direction to foster uniform church activities. The Salvation Army decided early on that church and home services throughout the archipelago should be conducted in the regional lingua franca of Malay, now Indonesian, to promote a unified Christian community rather than a linguistically fragmented one.

The Salvation Army's policy carries with it the practical advantage that officers assigned to Indonesia are never required to learn more than one foreign language. Thus both Western and Indonesian officers can be moved readily from one post to another without great linguistic retooling. Another advantage for the Salvation Army is that, at least in public church forums, local congregations tend to be pushed away from their regional concepts toward nationally established terms of religious dialogue. The disadvantages from a mission viewpoint are that in many regions locals have never understood even the basic content of services. They then easily carry on their own potentially subversive religious conversations (cf. Rafael 1993, 1–22).

In the Tobaku region, officers usually preach in Indonesian, even when the majority of listeners, especially older women, have a weak grasp of the language. In an effort to extend comprehension of Protestant doctrines, the Salvation Army allows the inclusion of some prayers and biblical exegesis in local Central Sulawesi languages such as Uma. The effective realization of this permission, however, depends upon the assignment of an Uma-speaking officer to each congregation, something that is usually but not always the case.

A family of SIL missionaries based in the village of Kantewu began working in the 1970s to translate the New Testament into the Pipikoro dialect of Uma. A translation of the gospel of Luke and Acts was issued in 1987 (Wycliffe Bible Translators 1987), and a complete Bible was published in 1996 (Wycliffe Bible Translators 1996). Although a few Tobaku villagers I encountered in the late 1980s and early 1990s owned the Pipikoro translation of Luke and Acts and were proud of its existence, I never saw them use the book. This in part reflects the lack of leisure time that Tobaku villagers have to devote to reading. Perhaps also the volumes sat neglected because they necessarily elevated the dialect of one non-Tobaku region to become the biblical form of the Uma language. Choices of particular dialects for gospel translations invariably have unexpected political as well as semiotic implications.

SIL missionaries are granted Indonesian visas to work on the "educational" endeavor of translating the Bible. Their parent organization gives them some freedom about which Bible books to translate, and in which order. The SIL translators begin by finding a native speaker who can complete a preliminary translation of the selected Bible book from Indonesian to the local language. Then they check the translation with the native speaker and, if possible, also directly with a Greek version. In English, they work with the *Living Bible*.

Once an initial Bible book translation is prepared by the regionally assigned translation team, an independent SIL specialist comes to check it with native speakers not directly involved with the first translation. Sometimes the Bible specialist will legislate on matters of acceptable translation. For example, with the story in Luke (8:43) where a woman has been bleeding for twelve years, a SIL linguist had trouble locating Kaili words that would allow for the possibility that a woman who was bleeding for so long could still be living. Finally, an indigenous assistant suggested the word for "menstrual bleeding." The SIL Bible translator initially adopted the usage, but then the independent specialist objected, saying that there was no precedent for such an interpretation in the biblical commentaries. In this way, native interpretations are edited to match prior European ones.

As far as possible, SIL translators seek to find the closest local terms for Christian concepts and then draw out the Christian contextual meanings to refocus the local language terms, thus enlarging or coopting their semantic references. For example, a Pipikoro story about the ancestral punishment for adulterers led a SIL Bible translator to a term he decided was suitable to convey the Protestant concept of "redemption" through Jesus Christ. In the precolonial era, both adulterers were to be killed unless their "bodies were replaced" (*tolo' woto*, Uma) by the sacrifice of a white buffalo in a ceremony arranged by relatives. The adulterous man then would have to crawl beneath the buffalo's legs as it was slaughtered in his place. Now the preachers of Christian liturgy try to stress the Western Protestant concept of "redemption" from sin in place of that derived from the "bodily substitution" ritual for adulterers, which is no longer practiced.

Indonesian translations of the Bible are available through the Salvation Army, but they too are difficult reading for most unschooled villagers. Although highlanders know biblical stories from a variety of sources, including Sunday school meetings for children, the Bible as a book—in either Pipikoro or Indonesian versions—is rarely a directly consulted source. Few Tobaku people have the leisure time to read or the inclination to do so. Reading silently, outside of a group context such as a church service or a schoolroom, is considered a peculiar or antisocial act only practiced by the odd visiting ethnographer. Most Tobaku individuals sit and rest only when ill or eating, or after the sun sets. Few find the use of kerosene lamps or reading glasses affordable. I never encountered a Salvation Army Bible reading and discussion group like Morris (1996) describes for Central Java, although such groups exist in urban center like Palu, where migrants are not so busy farming, hauling drinking water, fetching firewood, making tools, or washing clothes in rivers.

As Morris (1996) describes, even when Westerners and Indonesians read the same Bible passages together, they often retain rather different ideas about how God has instructed them to act. A good example of fertile ground for divergent interpretation is to be found in Matthew 21:28–31, where two brothers are asked by their father to work in his vineyard. The first brother tells his father he will not go, but later changes his mind and does the work that his father requests. The second brother promises politely that he will complete the task but then does not. Westerners invariably conclude that the first brother is the better son. Indonesians such as the Tobaku, valuing harmony and deference to an elder far more than work achievement, invariably view the second brother as the better son.

Kruyt and Adriani published many Central Sulawesi stories and cosmological myths, a few of which continue to bear on Protestant interpretations of biblical doctrine (Adriani and Kruyt 1968 [1950], 2:chap. 9; Adriani 1933). Adriani and Kruyt describe how Pamona creation stories often involve an original human couple whose children populate the world by committing incest. This angers the deities, but the couple is forgiven when they float an animal sacrifice down the river to purify the community (Adriani and Kruyt 1968 [1950], 2:15). Some Pamona stories, like the Bible, present humanity as originally living in a paradise where food grows without toil until the idyll is spoiled either by human misstep or the action of an evil spirit (Adriani and Kruyt 1968 [1950], 2:22–24). There is also a pre-Christian flood story that Adriani and Kruyt say locals support by pointing to the fossilized sea shells found up to 600 meters high in the mountains.

Adriani and Kruyt see these and other parallels between "indigenous" myths and Christian ones as divinely inspired. Another more earthly explanation is that some biblical stories were introduced prior to missionization through contacts with Muslim traders. This proposal seems especially likely given the number of stories about Mohammed (some telling how Mohammed and *Alatala* argued over this or that policy regarding humanity) that have been adopted and transformed by people living near the coasts of the Tomini Bay (Adriani and Kruyt 1968 [1950], 2:319–321).

Although most Tobaku individuals do not own Bibles, they do

work through ministers to find verses supporting their views on disput-
ed behaviors because the sanctity of the biblical word is never questioned. For their daily sermons indigenous Salvation Army officers
choose passages recommended by Salvation Army monthly guide-
books published in Indonesian, as well as other locally favored passages
that help to cast Central Sulawesi moral problems in Christian terms.

Biblical stories elevating the meek and the poor find support in
Uma people's own philosophy that ill-gotten or quickly acquired rich-
es lead to misfortune. "Don't wish to become rich," they say, "or you
won't live a long life." Highlanders also favor an interpretation of the
Adam and Eve story that they associate with their mortuary feast schedule. Like a few of my Protestant college students in North Carolina,
some suppose that men have fewer ribs than women do because one
passage of Genesis (2:21–23) says that a rib from Adam was taken to
make Eve. Highlanders note that even before their people became
acquainted with the Bible, they made the major mortuary feast one day
later for women than for men because of woman's extra rib.

The Old Testament offers support for many Central Sulawesi
ideas that are discouraged by missionaries. The existence of sacred
trees, marked as places for communal gathering and ritual reverence,
are mentioned several times in the Bible (for example, Genesis 12:6–7;
13:18; 18:1). More important, the idea that a select group of ancestors
can have a special place beside God as his council is described in
Psalms 89:5, 7; Psalms 82; Deuteronomy 33:2–5; and Zechariah 14:5.
These ancestors are described as "the assembly of holy ones," and they
represent forefathers of the Israelites, who are called "the right hand of
God" (cf. Hutchinson 1977, 4). The second book of Samuel 21:9 discusses a case of seven human sacrifices that serve as blood revenge for
the Gibeonites wronged by Saul. These human sacrifices become the
means to end a three-year famine of punishment and are performed at
the start of the barley harvest. As such Old Testament texts describe
scenes that closely resemble precolonial Central Sulawesi practices of
revenge warfare, headhunting, ancestor worship, and human sacrifices

to promote crop fertility, they are bypassed by missionaries who prefer New Testament passages that reinforce contemporary Western Christian ideals.

An individual's direct contact with God and unmediated access to gospels are considered distinguishing features of Protestantism. Yet missionary filters and the difficulties of upland farming strive against such meditation and scholarship. Therefore, Tobaku people's reverence for the Bible has not resulted in its extensive personal use as a written document. More often, I saw it tucked away among a household's valuable heirlooms or placed inside a rice storage bin as a protective talisman. Bibles are physical valuables akin to other types of heirlooms. This sets Bibles *as books* in a different category of being than the spoken "holy" or "smooth" words that are contained inside. As will be discussed in chapter 7, only when uttered aloud do the gospel verses and other Christian texts achieve their potential as powerful words that bring the worlds of the living and the unseen spirits into balance.

Metaphysical Misunderstandings and Doctrinal Conflicts

The conceptual distinctions between European and precolonial Central Sulawesi cosmologies often rest undisturbed within contemporary Christian ritual practice. Yet these politically unified perspectives sometimes diverge unexpectedly when Tobaku are faced with metaphysical questions not recognized by missionaries. One example is when "shadow" spirits of the newly dead upset family members of the recently deceased. According to pre-Christian views, a newly dead person's shadow spirit remains in the village for several days before traveling to the afterworld following mourning rituals. In Uma-speaking areas, the major rites usually are held at nine days after death for a man and at ten days for a woman. Under Muslim or Christian influence, an additional mortuary ritual may be held for prominent persons at the fortieth day after death. In such cases, Tobaku individuals complain of being bothered by *kao'* spirits for up to forty days.

Western missionaries consider the spirits or sorcerers that high-landers complain of as fallacies of the pagan imagination; or worse, as devil worship. Yet the Western concept of the devil is one topic about which missionaries disagree among themselves. There has been a resurgence of belief in the personification of evil among North American evangelicals during this century (Zehner 1996), and these ideas often resonate with Central Sulawesi notions of evil spirits. English publications translated into Indonesian and circulated by the Salvation Army explore the issue of the devil's role in daily life (e.g., Orr 1977). By contrast, many Dutch Reformed Protestant missionaries working in Central Sulawesi try to minimize talk about the devil incarnate, aiming instead to place responsibility for good and evil within the human individual. In either case, Sulawesi narratives about the acts of witchcraft or malicious spirits that make them ill or ruin their crops meet with disbelief or disapproval from missionaries of every persuasion.

One source of these conflicts is that most missionaries do not recognize the limitations of biblical Christianity in addressing and resolving local metaphysical questions concerning evil and suffering. Rather than considering Tobaku ideas and practices in terms of biblical doctrine per se, they tend to criticize Tobaku interpretations on the grounds of their divergence from current Western concepts. A rebellious Tobaku teenager named Isak who sickened and died during travel to the mouth of the Lariang River was said by neighbors to have violated an ancestral taboo against baking prawns in that region. Missionaries considered this an "unchristian" interpretation of events because baking instead of boiling prawns cannot cause death. Although they judged this Tobaku "superstition" according to criteria based on prevailing Western science, the missionaries suggested they applied a Christian litmus test.

To give another example, the Bible makes no mention of whether mixing swidden-grown rice and wet-field rice in storage bins will produce sickness, but Tobaku folk knowledge traces a certain illness precisely to violation of that ancestral taboo. Although it is familiarity with Western scientific principles that convinces missionaries that mixing two varieties of rice or their associated tools cannot cause illness, they identify Tobaku concepts as poor Christianity rather than as poor science. On questions where the canons of science cannot be invoked, such as the difference between Tobaku ideas of traveling to the afterlife and Western concepts of passage to heaven and hell—neither of which can be deemed particularly scientific—Tobaku ideas also are judged by missionaries as deficient Christianity rather than as deficient in Western cultural ideas. In such ways, the boundaries between what is religious doctrine and what is not are drawn to suit Western cultural presuppositions that are neither biblically based nor etiologically Christian.

While locals and missionaries do not always agree about the cause of an illness, they may reach concordance regarding a Christian cure. Interpretive unification, or at least parallelism, is achieved when both parties agree that Christian prayer or ritual will rectify an illness or misfortune, no matter what its source. One elderly woman, convinced that her illness was caused by the sorcery of a jealous person, said she was cured only when her family played cassettes of Christian pop songs around the clock at her hospital bedside. These Christian pop songs are recorded in Manado, North Sulawesi, the homeland of many Christian teachers sent to Central Sulawesi. Although Western missionaries such as Major Carron do not themselves invoke sorcery as a cause of illness, they look favorably upon the use of Christian music and prayer in the face of any adversity. They, too, endorse spiritual healing when they warn patients at the Salvation Army clinic that biomedicines alone will not cure in the absence of faith and prayer to God.

Some Tobaku people claim that punishments for moral violations such as stealing family heirlooms still are carried out by angry local spirits. The *seta* spirits involved, however, now are construed as vassals of the Christian God rather than of pre-Christian deities. Tina

Abi' argued that Salvation Army officers are mistaken when they disparage ancestral techniques of eradicating demons or spirits. She said this was not a case of taking false gods above the Lord, but rather a matter of recognizing that the Lord makes the demons (*seta*) who torture humans, and that the ancestors who lived long ago, heathen though they were, developed some effective methods for repelling these demons. In such instances, Tobaku people defend pre-Christian empirical solutions to cosmological problems, and their ritual practices may differ, privately at least, from those that the missionaries prescribe.

Missionaries complain that highlanders do not confront the contradictions between Protestant concepts and ancestral concepts. The SIL missionary Robert Carter argued that highlanders conflate the "tradition" versus "religion" (*adat* versus *agama*) distinction by overlapping diverse practices to cover all possible truths, thereby evidencing their true lack of Christian understanding. He does not recognize the artificially imposed distinction between "tradition" and "religion" upon which the colonial missionization process was based.

A Dutch Reformed missionary named Henrik Rinkes summed up his problem for me when he reported how one of his congregation members complained that after giving generous donations to the church for three years, his crops were still poor, so what was the point? Central Sulawesi people expect positive results from their religious practices and will escalate ritual activities until results are achieved. Western missionaries find these expectations signs of sinful pagan bargains rather than pragmatic actions reminiscent of sixteenth- and seventeenth-century European Christianity (Thomas 1971). A Manadonese minister was known to answer the question of why Westerners are so much richer than Sulawesi people by saying it is because Westerners pray to the Christian God before planting so they always receive bountiful harvests. Missionaries who criticize such aspects of local Christianity acknowledge neither the scriptural basis for motivated offerings nor the extensive European history of such practices. More important, they do not recognize the crucial historical and cognitive shift from earlier religions' perception of success as a sign of cosmological balance or grace to a more recent European view of an omniscient but inscrutable God whose actions are discontinuous with the ritual actions of humans and disengaged from the remainder of the natural world.

Today's evangelical missionaries often make philosophical statements about their mission's aims and methods that closely resemble those of early missionaries such as Kruyt and Woodward. A New Tribes missionary named David Southard, working with a recently converted Lauje group, said, "The community accepted Christianity very readily. We don't touch their culture, except in the areas of Satan and sin. Aside from that they can marry the way they want and all that kind of thing." Robert Carter made a similar kind of statement, saying that he finds it acceptable for locals to maintain their ancestral dibble-stick planting rituals and chicken dinners as long as Christian prayers are added and stressed. Unlike his peers, Carter compared these Central Sulawesi syncretic practices to the use of Christmas trees by Europeans, thereby acknowledging a longer and more historically nuanced view of Christian history.

Despite the elimination of many precolonial concepts and practices at the missionaries' urging, there continues to be both public and tacit negotiations over acceptable ideology when indigenous ontology chafes against European preconceptions of appropriately modern Christian practice. The pluralistic streams of practice, and the churches' vacillation over whether to overlook and incorporate or actively purge heresies, mirror records of early Christianity in Europe (Chadwick 1967; McNeill 1933). As Asad (1983, 244) notes, the medieval Catholic Church was more concerned with placing all practices under a unified authority than it was in making those practices uniform. Similarly, Central Sulawesi Protestantism holds currents that diverge somewhat in practice while acquiescing to the unified authorities of the churches and the Indonesian government.

Divine Justice or Right Makes Might

It is perfectly clear that behind all the forms of curses and war-cries, there looms up an efficacious and vivid belief in transcendental justice, and the tendency to help its manifestation by means of weapons in cases where this manifestation of transcendental justice lingers in revealing itself.

Pieter Middelkoop, Curse-Retribution-Enmity as Data in Natural Religion

A pervasive certainty in divine justice flourished in precolonial Central Sulawesi ontology, just as it did in the precolonial Timor described by Middelkoop. The righteousness of the unseen forces revealed itself routinely in natural and social outcomes. If necessary, it also could be called into play by highlanders who sensed the need for it. Divine justice explained otherwise puzzling cases of exceptional good fortune (*rasi'*, Uma), such as abundant harvests, healthy offspring, or financial prosperity, as well as bad fortune (*hala'*), such as illness, calamity, warfare, or harvest failures.

The principles of Central Sulawesi theodicy were in large part familiar to European missionaries, who carried their own ideas of God's righteousness and punishments. Where the European and local views required alignment was in regard to exactly which behaviors warranted rewards or negative sanctions. The wrongful nature of some behaviors, such as adultery, could be readily agreed upon. Other issues could not be so easily resolved. Central Sulawesi transgressions such as parent-in-law avoidance and food taboo violations, or European transgressions such as polygyny and working on Sundays were not meaningful across the cultural borders.

Uma speakers say that victims of cosmological retribution have been "hit by the owners(s)" (*peweba' ba pue'*). Punishments are said to occur when transgressions (*sala'*) go unpunished by human communities. The term "*sala'*" is cognate with the Malay or Indonesian *salah*, meaning "fault, mistake, wrong." The Central Sulawesi term more often carries the connotation of social error or ritual misstep rather than the European idea of personal moral guilt. Another Uma term referring to transgressions is *"jeko'*," which under missionization has been translated more specifically as a moral "sin" (*dosa*, Ind.).

Tobaku individuals evaluate violations according to a scale of individual, family, or community involvement and responsibility. Divine punishments are meted out accordingly. Certain crimes committed by an individual will result in the individual's downfall. For example, a man's poor health may be traced to years of incestuous adultery or the use of sorcery against his fellows. Other transgressions, however, are said to result in illnesses or misfortunes that befall members of the family or community of the guilty one(s). As Kuipers notes for the Weyewa of Sumba, the search for understanding is less a matter of "finding a single agent who *caused* the calamity than in exploring the ruptured relationships among specific actors" (Kuipers 1990a, 42; emphasis in original). Similarly, Tobaku theodicy seeks to repair a fractured social order.

Villagers often grope for the source of their own misfortunes. After Tina Abi' described several recent deaths in both her husband's and her own extended families, she commented that they were beginning to wonder what sin they had committed to receive such misfortune. When individuals cannot trace any wrongs to themselves, they consider their immediate family members, then their extended family members, and finally their larger community or representative leaders. The rules for assigning cosmological fault clearly are flexible enough to allow families to trace their problems to various sources.

Community-wide cosmological curses such as flooding, landslides, earthquakes, epidemics, or pestilence are termed *"silaka."* In the extreme case, untoward actions by one important individual are said to result in the downfall of an entire village. A now abandoned western Tobaku village was ruined by monkey raids, landslides, and earthquakes. These calamities reportedly were caused by father-daughter incest followed by the long-term adultery of a leader. Tobaku individuals say that neither sexual crime was punished by the families or community, so the deities wreaked destruction upon the entire village.

The tale of a former Pipikoro village named Kaliua, purportedly destroyed for its inhabitants' moral crimes, is described by Kruyt (1938, 1:162–163) and is still told in Uma-speaking areas. Tama Ena noted that *kaliua* means "overlooked," signifying that the people of Kaliua had overlooked their community members' transgressions, but the deities ultimately did not. Reportedly, the village sunk into the ground while the surviving population moved to live in the present village of Lempe Lero. Often stories about the destruction of villages include violations of "natural laws," such as the bathing of cats. Such unnatural acts are said to bring down the anger of the owner deities, inciting them to decimate whole settlements. Stylized plots involving animals hint at other types of "unnatural" moral transgressions that have taken place in the ruined villages.

Schärer recognized early that *adat* law in Borneo was more concerned with averting cosmological repercussions to the community, such as reduced crop fertility, than with punishing guilty parties (Schärer 1938, 563, as cited in Middelkoop 1960, 66). Tina Abi' explains that the village council of elders must quickly mediate in all land and family disputes for the safety of all: "It is taboo to violate land boundaries because calamity will arrive" (*Palia mosoro pobika', mporatapi silaka*, Uma). Similarly, I was told of a case of first cousins, raised in the same household, who engaged in sex and were then married without the proper expiation rituals. When the young wife soon died, people agreed that there had been divine retribution in the form of the *silaka* curse on an unpunished transgression.

Some types of divine punishments result from violations of respect or hospitality rules (*solora'*, Uma). A young relative of Tina Abi' was gored by a wild boar reportedly because he boasted at the start of the hunt that he would catch game. Then, to make matters worse, he cursed the owner(s) of the land when he returned empty-handed. The wild boar that attacked him was "possessed by the spirit owner(s) of the land" (*kahawea seta tumpu tana'*). The young man's braggart behavior resulted in his being "eaten by the curse of disrespect" (*nakoni solora'*). The curse of disrespect also includes infringements of what might seem to us to be minor rules of hospitality. If an accident befalls an individual who has just declined a neighbor's friendly invitation to sit and drink coffee, the misfortune is viewed as a cosmological retribution.

The outcome of precolonial warfare in Central Sulawesi, including headhunting raids, likewise was conceived as the arbitration of transcendental justice, a kind of ordeal (Downs 1977 [1955], 118). Schärer early hypothesized the historical and psychological unity of headhunting and human sacrifice among the Ngaju Dayak of Borneo. Unlike Kruyt, Schärer understood that

> head-hunting in Borneo originally was never practised by parties concerned to acquire or to strengthen their own life powers or magical energies; that is not why they went out head-hunting, but they wanted human skulls for personal or collective offering for a purge from disaster and restoration of the disturbed cosmical balance. (Schärer 1940, 6, as translated by Middelkoop 1960, 70)

The volume edited by Hoskins on Southeast Asian headhunting (1996) and related writings (Hoskins 1987c, 1989; George 1991, 1996) cogently argue for attention to the wide variety of indigenous rationales and circumstances that contextualize the seemingly unitary phenomenon of headhunting. But still, it is exactly the ritual attention associated with what otherwise might be common murder or internecine slaughter that marks the headhunting act or its intermittent postcolonial echoes as a peculiarly Southeast Asian solution to widespread cultural problems of cosmological balance and justice.

Most Tobaku assume that the Christian God punishes and rewards humans for the same reasons the indigenous deities did. Such reinterpretations are possible because the Christian doctrines presented by missionaries have not addressed and answered all the issues regarding correct behavior and suffering that concern highlanders. Like the Azande described by Evans-Pritchard (1937) and the Sumba people described by Kuipers (1990a, 42), Tobaku say there are not only physical reasons that an old granary building might collapse, but also cosmological reasons that a certain person happened to sit below it and be killed when it fell.

Some Pamona told Kruyt that every child chooses his or her own death while still in the mother's womb. Tsing (1993, 291–294) records similar ideas from the Meratus of Kalimantan. Other Pamona told Kruyt that the gods decide the fate of every human being, also just before the infant's birth. Kruyt considered it a paradox in the indigenous cosmology that everyone espoused this predestination of fate, while also holding the conviction that misfortune and death are punishments for sins or ritual errors (Adriani and Kruyt 1968 [1950], 2:21). He did not consider the possibility that the initially planned fate, the default-value death if you will, is merely overridden in some cases by later actions. I was told by Tobaku that the time of everyone's death is decided by God. Thus, they say, medicine from the Salvation Army clinic will avert an impending death only if God Himself wills it, thereby changing the course of events.

Like many of their American counterparts, more enthusiastic Tobaku congregation members often say, "God arranges everything" (*Tuhan mengatur semua*, Ind.), or "It is humans who plan but only God who determines" (*Manusia yang berencana tetapi hanya Tuhan yang menentukan*). Unusually good events as well as misfortunes are considered for their cosmological causes. Moreover, the necessary and sufficient causes to which any disasters are traced are expanded to include contemporary Christian violations such as shirking church on Sundays or the perceived misuse of birth control pills.

European missionaries working in Indonesia long have struggled with the issue of divine justice. Middelkoop writes that, as a missionary, he found it best to avoid teaching the Old Testament because it too easily supports the pagan "curse-beliefs" intrinsic to "Timorese natural religion" (Middelkoop 1960, 9). Middelkoop is himself troubled by God's vengeful actions in the Old Testament:

> The conception of the divine law in the O.T. [Old Testament] is linked up with the threat of a destructive curse in case of transgression which

aroused the belief of enmity on God's part against the sinner who must be condemned to suffer death. This enmity is also directed against the peoples who refuse to subdue themselves to the divine law of the God of Israel. (Middelkoop 1960, 11–12)

Middelkoop saw disturbing parallels to biblical concepts of divine vengeance not only in indigenous Indonesian philosophy and practice, but also in sermons of the 1940s delivered in more conservative Protestant churches in the Netherlands. He found such harsh philosophy to be antithetical to God's forgiving love as revealed in the New Testament by Jesus Christ and his crucifixion. For this reason he recommended against emphasis on the Old Testament or divine retribution in Indonesian missionization, a view and practice that I saw followed by Dutch Reformed missionaries working during the 1980s. Other missionaries and many indigenous ministers, however, do interpret events of good and bad fortune as signs of God's pleasure or displeasure with congregation members. Sometimes they use this ideology as a weapon to demand unquestioning compliance to the directives of church leaders.

After a calamity or unusual windfall, Tobaku assessments of God's judgments are made strategically, often with indigenous Salvation Army officer cooperation. In 1986, when the yearly rainy season resulted in excessive flooding in the Winatu area, many locals attributed this to sinful behavior (*mosala'*, Uma; *berdosa*, Ind.). Salvation Army Captain Silase gladly cooperated by increasing ritual attention to expiate the supposed sins. Conversely, when a Towulu' man successfully panned for gold and bought a horse with his profits, Salvation Army officers presided over the "thanks to God" service (*pengucapan syukur Tuhan*, Ind.) and praised the man for having been so worthy of God's favor as to become rich enough to purchase a horse.

When one village obtained a poorer harvest in 1986 than they had in 1985, Major Isa' told them during the "thanksgiving" church service that they were being "fined by God" (*didenda oleh Tuhan*). Not only did Major Isa' imply that the villagers were being punished for moral crimes with a bad harvest, he and his wife also argued that the villagers were being punished by the Christian God because they had planted months later than tradition or *adat* specified. Hence God now punishes for violations of ancestral law as well as missionary rules.

Tobaku villagers tell stories about how individuals striving for ill-gotten gain are foiled by God's intervention. Tina Abi' said that there are now so few buffalo and other large livestock left in her home area because of the moral turpitude of the village leaders: "Their hearts are not straight [upright, just]" (*Uma monoa' nonona*, Uma). She described how the five buffalo once owned by the senior elder all drowned in a flood because of his dishonesty. Another village head-man, Tama Sori, watched his horse fall in a ravine, and the cow he obtained in an unfair deal died almost as soon as it was in his hands. It was "struck by God because his heart was crooked," Tina Abi' claimed.

Church and government leaders often self-servingly trace the misfortunes of villagers to the victims' lack of participation in church-prescribed ritual. In 1987, a flood killed twenty-one residents of a Bada' village who were camping by the river in which they were panning for gold. A government official explained that the people from that village never went to church on Sunday. Moreover, they had conducted a pagan ceremony for luck before beginning their gold-searching expedition. Similarly, a Tobaku teacher's wife, Tina Kola', suggested that her neighbor's rice fields had turned red with disease because the neighbor had not sponsored a second round of Salvation Army—led blessing ceremonies after planting. She pointed out that someone in a neighboring hamlet also had refused to contribute and had likewise been cursed with diseased rice plants.

Such post facto evaluations of divine justice can be highly self-righteous and somewhat merciless. A Christian living in the Banggaiba area had a good harvest while his Muslim neighbors culled poorer harvests despite planting more seed. The Christian man concluded that the Muslims' harvests were worse because "they do not truly know God" (*mereka tidak tahu Tuhan secara betul*, Ind.). When a pregnant girl miscarried as she was bearing a heavy load of coffee to sell for cash to buy her marriage license, Major and Mrs. Isa' claimed that the girl had received divine punishment for engaging in premarital sex. Salvation Army officers and other Tobaku people often comment on cases of personal misfortune by saying that "God has a plan other than those of humans" (*Tuhan punya rencana lain daripada manusia punya*). These notions of transcendental justice also served Europeans' interest in naturalizing the power of their colonial rule.

Interpreting Acts of God

Concern with transcendental justice is as characteristic of Tobaku church leaders as it is of lay people with the most fragile grasp of church doctrines. Salvation Army officers quickly travel to make graveyard improvements for their deceased relatives when personal misfortunes appear to signal a higher authority's anger over a neglected ancestral cemetery. Similarly, Mrs. Major Isa' often wondered aloud what terrible wrongs she had committed to have deserved her bizarre fate of motherhood. First, she had never been able to bear any children of her own. Then, when she adopted a baby son, he grew up to be the most troublesome and irresponsible of teens. As Mrs. Major Isa' was unable to see any transgressions committed by herself or her husband, she concluded that her adopted son became a beast because he had been nursed with the breast milk of a beast: a cow rather than a human. When the officer's wife adopted the orphaned baby, she received powdered infant formula and powdered cow's milk from the mission canteen and so did not enlist a local wet nurse. Later, she decided that her teenage son's currish behavior must be derived from his body's having received its earliest sustenance from a nonhuman animal.

I once was invited to a household "thanks to God" ceremony in Kulawi sponsored by a school administrator, Guru Daud, who had just received a promotion. After the local Salvation Army officer finished some standard prayers and hymns, Guru Daud stood up and explained the nature of his blessing, how God had rewarded him for doing the right thing. His job had been troublesome, and all had not been well with his school's administration. When his regional supervisors inquired, however, he did not tell them the unpleasant truth, but feigned that everything was running perfectly. In the end he received a promotion and an increase in salary, all for telling what we might call a lie. In his eyes, he had behaved absolutely correctly, as the reward from God proved.

In this case the irony of the divine justice interpretation presented will be more apparent to a Westerner—raised to believe that deceptions aimed toward personal benefit are wrong—than to an Indonesian who is raised to believe that deferentially maintaining harmony by telling one's superior what he wants to hear is more noble than creating disharmony through the reporting of any literal truth. The other guests present at the ceremony evidenced none of the uneasiness I experienced at this man's admission. They, too, thought it reasonable that God would reward the schoolmaster for such optimistic and faithful behavior.

The principle of theodicy is one by which Western as well as indigenous church leaders often measure their own behavior. Major Carron, a registered nurse and missionary, suggested that her continued health and vigor despite years of exposure to the foulest of disease conditions must be due to God's special protection over her good works. Although the logical connection is rarely made overt by religious leaders, this hypothesis can imply the converse: that the seriously ill have sinned or have no grace from God. This reasoning matches that of locals who often blame victims or their families in cases of severe illness. To mollify these harsh assessments, missionaries strive to reduce the stigma of repugnant illnesses such as leprosy by invoking notions of Christian charity and salvation. In these arenas, Protestant missionaries, like locals, do not recognize the logical conflicts in the diverse religious premises and conclusions that they apply to interpret events separated in time and space.

European church leaders seek to take the sting out of suffering by appealing to God's greater wisdom. When an Indonesian staff member of a Dutch Reformed church was badly injured in a motorcycle accident, Reverend Hans van der Kers took pains to convince his congregation that although God had not caused the man's accident, "none of us ever leave the hands of God" (*kita tidak pernah keluar tangan Tuhan*, Ind.). Similarly, when Major Carron was distraught over a family struck by a series of calamitous physical accidents, she concluded that only God could know why such terrible circumstances befell these individuals. The rest of us must simply trust in His omniscience. This determination not to cast a moral judgment regarding misfortune is rare among highlanders. Most do not ever envision God's or gods' will as serendipitous or incomprehensible.

Upon occasion Tobaku people invoke divine justice as a means to extricate themselves from uninvited debts. When I spontaneously helped people without means or gave them small gifts, they sometimes would simultaneously bless me and release themselves from any future indebtedness by saying, "Not I, but God will repay you later" (*Bukan saya tetapi Tuhan akan balas nanti*). In this way, Christianized notions of divine justice can be used to evade debts not required by ancestral law.

A Tobaku Salvation Army officer stationed near Lindu Lake, Major Sampei, told me that he anticipated a reward from God after he provided hospitality to two Western backpackers who asked directions to a hotel. No guesthouses existed in the area at that time, so the officer brought the Westerners home with him. When the tourists departed, they asked how much they should pay for their night's lodging. Major Sampei told them, "There is no need to pay me. God already sent angels to our house for one night. Therefore, God will compensate me later" (*Tidak usah. Tuhan sudah kirim malaikat kepada rumah kami untuk satu malam. Jadi Tuhan akan balas saya nanti*). This statement epitomizes the high esteem in which Westerners are held by many Central Sulawesi Christians schooled by missionary teachers. For some, all Westerners who enter their lands are anticipated as angels of the forest. The officer's statement also rationalizes gifts given outside of the obligatory exchange networks through an invocation and expectation of divine justice.

One transformation in the Protestant approach to theodicy is the extent to which Tobaku people now feel confident to interpret the causes of misfortune without the benefit of pre-Christian shamans and possession ceremonies (*mobalia*, Uma). Tina Abi' provided the following examples of how lay people decide ritual actions for themselves:

> If the rice fields look good, the harvest seems plentiful, and then suddenly at the rice storing ceremony (*ngkolompe*', Uma), the storage bin is half empty, everyone knows it is an ancestral curse (*nasesa'*). So we make a Protestant thanks to God ceremony. If a person is frequently ill, feels afraid of the unseen forces (*kingkima*), then makes an entreaty (*pokimaa'*) and is quickly well, we know that we must carry out the necessary deeds: cleaning graves, cutting livestock in honor of deceased relatives, and so forth.

Although this readiness of lay people to interpret the causes of cosmological problems also may have existed in pre-Christian times, reportedly shamans were the final arbiters of such judgments, just as now Salvation Army officers are the experts usually consulted. In some cases, however, villagers do not consult the officers, but merely seek advice from family elders.

Another means by which Central Sulawesi highlanders comprehend and convey information about cosmological retribution is through the retelling of dreams. Dreams often are reported as omens of God's will, and they incorporate pre-Christian symbolic elements, such as a mountain ridge path to the afterworld (*sirowi*, Uma), as well as newer images of biblical characters and electric lights. A dream reported during a church testimonial (*kesaksian*, Ind.) in the 1980s went as follows:

> Tama Leli' told how he became ill after sponsoring a sorcerer's malicious acts against someone else. Tama Leli' then had a dream where first he was taken below his house to be tortured, but then was rescued by the prophet Abraham (*nabi Ibrahim*). Abraham sent him walking along the top of a mountain ridge [to the afterworld] and instructed him not to look back. Finally, Abraham asked him what he saw. He said that he saw a

great light ahead, as if it were a city with electric lamps. The prophet said that, yes, he could go there but it was not his time yet; that first he must return to his home village and mend his ways. Abraham told him that he must not be stingy any longer, and must persuade the sorcerer in the village to use his knowledge only for good, not for Satan to hurt people.

Reportedly, after the recounting of this dream in church, the social behavior of Tama Leli' improved. Even the conduct of the alleged sorcerer improved temporarily, but he later fell back into his reprehensible ways and so died of a terrible illness.

The mingling of indigenous and Christian notions of divine justice results in some conclusions that no holder of either religion prior to their contact would share. One emergent religious concept involves the use of fish poison. In the past, Tobaku people often placed a local root (probably *Derris* species) in the water to stun fish for capture. Some Tobaku say that excessive use of this poison angers the "owner(s) of the water" (*pue' ue*), who will cause blindness in the user. Mrs. Major Isa' once countered this statement, insisting that use of the poison will not anger any deity and cause blindness—unless it is done on Sundays, in which case its use will anger God.

Perhaps the most ironic instance I encountered of competing concepts of divine justice was when Major Carron told of a calamitous flood in Palu that had badly damaged the Salvation Army hospital's physical plant. She told sadly of staff members displaced from their residence halls and of ruined food supplies. When she further expressed anxiety about where she would turn for monetary aid, I asked if the hospital was not insured. Startled, she replied that, yes, it had been fully insured, but that the insurance company refused to pay. "They called it an act of God, and said that the insurance policy does not cover acts of God!" Major Carron uttered these words with chagrin, clearly understanding the statement's local implications regarding God's possible displeasure with her establishment.

Although Tobaku people's discussions of divine justice or acts of God follow recognizable narrative patterns, these patterns are flexible enough to allow for guilt to be assigned variously by individuals with diverse interests and alliances. Moreover, future events allow people opportunities to change their interpretations and assign guilt to new transgressors. This flexibility is demonstrated by narratives concerning the most terrible calamity described for a certain Tobaku village: the great fire of 1973 or 1974. The villagers themselves are not certain about exactly which year the momentous fire occurred, which indicates again that the Tobaku past is remarkable less as a series of chronological markers than as moments of epistemological significance. Natural disasters are read by Tobaku people primarily as barometers of their community's cosmological status at a particular moment, not as a calibration of linear time.

The case of the Tobaku village fire exemplifies the local politics of interpretation devised by villagers to see their community history in terms of divine justice. It also illustrates how villagers readily reinterpret responsibility for past local events in light of present occurrences. In the course of seven years (between 1986 and 1993), the villagers moved from a divisive strategy of mutual blame to a united interpretation focused on a single moral transgressor, Salvation Army Major Wile. In 1993, the offensive behavior of this one protagonist in the original drama led many to enlarge his culpability for the fire.

The devastation of the great fire is attributed to losses of wealth and the physical evidence of villagers' pasts. No one was killed in the blaze because most residents were harvesting rice in distant fields when it occurred. In material terms, however, the conflagration was disastrous. Houses, food supplies, clothes, and virtually all ancestral heirlooms such as woven cloth, jewelry, and bronze ceremonial trays were burned beyond recognition. Most inhabitants lost everything but the clothes on their backs and what few possessions they had stored in their garden settlement houses. Inside the main village, only the two Salvation Army buildings and two houses at the extreme west end of the village were left undamaged by the flames.

Everyone agrees about who set the thatch houses ablaze: a widower who went insane after the death of his wife. But the story never ends there. During my 1986–1989 fieldwork, other stories about the fire emerged involving both ancestral and Christian moral violations that precipitated the fire. A few people implied that the madman's family was cursed because of evil deeds his forefathers had committed during the precolonial era. Others insisted that the fire was caused by misdeeds that occurred in the village during the decades just prior to the misfortune. People had slept with other people's spouses. Incest had been committed. Individuals had even been known to kill one another. Hence, God had punished all the villagers with the devastating fire. Espousing a moral position familiar to Europeans from the Old Testament, residents felt that there was a common responsibility among all the villagers for the individual evil acts committed within their community.

A different interpretation was posed by one of the local Salvation Army officers, Mrs. Major Isa'. She maintained that all the villagers, except her family members, whose houses were untouched by the fire, had been punished by God for failing to cooperate with Major Wile, the minister assigned to the village at the time of the fire. Mrs. Major Isa' related how all the village houses had burned to the ground, except that of her father and her older sister, descendants of a known village founder. She told how her father's domesticated pigeons miraculously rose up and flew around the family property, flapping their wings furiously so as to fan the fire away from their residences. She added that while many other villagers had failed to cooperate with and obey the directives of Major Wile, her father always defended that officer and upheld his causes. She implied that her family, already blessed by their ancestral founders' status, had achieved special favor in the eyes of God, who punished the rest of the disobedient community. Mrs. Major Isa' had her ancestral pedigree, local Christian moral logic, and all material evidence to support her argument. It was undisputed that her family's houses were the only ones spared by the fire.

Shortly before leaving Central Sulawesi in 1989, I heard a

Sunday church sermon in a different Tobaku village that again invoked the memory of the great fire. The presiding Salvation Army minister admonished the local populace not to make difficulties for him, especially not to question how he used the funds just collected at the annual harvest thanksgiving ceremonies. He said that was what the people from the burned village had done, and that their refractory behavior toward Major Wile had angered God to the point of cursing them with the fire.

He recounted how, over a decade earlier, Major Wile had left the fateful village carrying sacks of the newly donated rice to sell in Kulawi. Before the minister traversed half his journey, the cursed village burned to the ground behind him. In this way, many years later, the tale of the fire had been turned into a warning, one might even say a threat, to elicit the cooperation of villagers with their local church leaders. Both indigenous Indonesian and Old Testament concepts of transgression and curse are bound similarly to the idea of disobedience to gods (Middelkoop 1960, 118). Therefore, as the Salvation Army officer was alluding to his own congregation's sins of disobedience, in local terms he simultaneously was cursing them with a potential disaster if they refused to cooperate with him.

When I returned to the Tobaku region in 1993, I found to my surprise that Major Wile had been reassigned to the rebuilt village that he had overseen before the fire. As I listened to local gossip, it was clear that neither the minister's temperament nor his popularity had improved.

My visit coincided with the annual harvest thanksgiving ritual, a lengthy church service followed by the sharing of coffee and cakes, and an auction where donations of produce from the congregation are sold to supplement the ministers' annual salary. To my astonishment, Major Wile publicly cursed members of his congregation who began to depart after the service, but before the refreshments and auction. Only the few individuals who earn a salary, such as Salvation Army teachers or officers, make many bids at church auctions. Therefore, most of the women and those without cash wanted to depart after the service once they had delivered the crops and prepared snacks that each household was required to contribute to the event.

As Major Wile saw some women exiting the back of the church, he shouted out, "Whoever leaves early, your rice fields will not succeed" (*Siapa yang berangkat duluan, padi tidak akan jadi,* Ind.) The minister's disgruntlement was comprehensible in that a successful auction equaled money in his own pocket for the upcoming year. Yet I was not the only one taken aback by this reckless use of church power. Other people commented afterward that such behavior was unacceptable, and some said that type of curse was exactly what led to the fire that had razed the village when he was displeased with them so many years before. The blame for this local tragedy quickly was shifted from the backs of sinful fellow villagers onto that of the greedy minister.

A few weeks later in another village, I encountered Mrs. Major Isa', the officer who earlier had criticized her fellow villagers for disobedience to the church. When she heard the news of Major Wile's curse at the auction, even she was critical of her colleague's tactics. Her argument was not that it is immoral for Christian ministers to curse their congregations, but rather that it is foolishly self-destructive to do so. She said simply, "If they do not eat, we do not eat." Salvation Army ministers do not work their own fields, but depend heavily upon donations of food by congregation members. Therefore, to curse the congregation's harvest is indeed to bite the hand that feeds you.

Local analyses of the Tobaku village fire of 1973 (or 1974) illustrate the ongoing entanglement and reapplication of founders' cult legacies, the political negotiation of highland Christian theology, personal agency, and public consensus. In the next chapter, I shift focus from deities, souls, and the cosmological interpretation of events to the precolonial ritual practices that missionaries reformatted with introduced substitutions.

ᕇ 6 ᕇ

Sacrificial Dialogues and
Christian Ritual Qualifications

In short, the term "sacrifice" designates a complex ritual action, during which an offering made up of animal, vegetable, or artificial components having symbolic values is consecrated to one or several deities, on certain occasions and with certain ends in view. Thus every sacrifice must be described as a function of the following features: (1) its end and the occasion on which it is made; (2) the deity or deities to whom it is addressed; (3) the content of the offering and its symbolic value; (4) the way the offering is treated and apportioned in the rite.

Valerio Valeri, Kingship and Sacrifice

Ritual cycles in the Central Sulawesi highlands enact the relationships of religion, eclipsing abstract cosmologies and the particularities of individual deities, both autochthonous and foreign. Highlanders' spiritual life continues to be steeped in moral assessments and practical strategies. That highlanders turn to rituals for "worldly benefits" (Reader and Tanabe 1998) does not significantly divide their religion from that of the Protestant missionaries. I prayed before meals with American evangelical families who thanked God for blessing them with the imported ingredients to make their pizzas, and for creating a beautiful waterfall *for them* to have beside their mission school. They regularly prayed for God to keep them healthy, deliver their supplies on time, and keep their Cessna plane rides safe.

The assumption that Asians' pragmatic rituals are "magical," and hence less a "religion" than those of doctrinally focused faiths such as Protestantism, is challenged readily by showing missionaries' own pragmatic concerns with religion. Moreover, the salvation of supposedly "world-renouncing" religions such as Christianity and Buddhism has been shown to be merely a spiritual and chronological extension of a good and happy life in this world (Reader and Tanabe 1998). Finally, asking for worldly benefits does not absolve petitioners of a moral code or obligations to deepen their faith. On the contrary, requests for worldly improvements draw followers into ties of debt. And efforts to validate their prayers' results often draw them to rationalize how their petitions were answered, even in the face of events that could be interpreted otherwise.

The Central Sulawesi religious rituals explored in this chapter are public vows or promises (*pohanga'*, Uma) and the animal sacrifices (*tinuwu'*) they entail. The rich anthropological literature on theories of sacrifice extends from W. R. Smith (1889) and Hubert and Mauss (1897/1898), who focus on the human-deity transactions and moral violations, to Leach (1976) and Valeri (1985), who focus on how the entities sacrificed variously symbolize deities, sacrificers, and their hierarchical relationships. Leach and Valeri question why animals are killed and whether the sacrificed symbolically represent the deities or the beneficiaries of the sacrifice.

Keesing reorients Leach's suggestion that the sacrificed animal's life substitutes for the beneficiary by saying that sacrifice is basically a human-deity "dialogue through the doors of death" (Keesing 1982, 141). The point is that offering life to the unseen powers ensures future life for humans. Christianized rituals in Central Sulawesi continue their past dialogues through the channel of sacrificial deaths, but the deities officially addressed are swapped: Protestant for indigenous ones.

There is another, more subtle, point to be made about Central Sulawesi's Christianized rituals. Perspectives concerning how the universal order is harmonized by sacrifices changed radically between early Judaism and later European Christianity as sacrifices shifted from effective acts, such as Abel's, to largely symbolic ones, such as Holy Communion (Herrenschmidt 1982). That shift from effective to symbolic sacrifices is not realized in Sulawesi Christianity, which often leaves a tension between missionary and native interpretations of ritual events. Western missionaries expect ritual meals to be essentially a solemn format for prayer, whereas Tobaku view these meals as necessary vehicles to transmit those prayers and safeguard their potency.

Indigenous sacrifices that fulfilled personal obligations to relatives, living or dead, and achieved practical solutions to worldly problems made their union with Protestant services imperative for early missionaries. Even contemporary missionaries working with fully converted populations recognize the centrality of religion's practical performance in Central Sulawesi. As the SIL missionary Robert Carter said to me, "Crops, sickness, and evil spirits are the most important things to these people. Christianity must deal with these matters to have any meaning here." Despite their loftiest theological ambitions, Protestant missionaries in Central Sulawesi always have had to cope with local concerns and confidence in the pragmatic aspects of ancestral rituals. Defining a major gulf between community and world religions, O'Connor observes that "when one is confronting a failing crop or a sick child, salvation is not yet a need, and still less a solution" (O'Connor 1996, 221).

Whereas Protestantism introduced limited channels to communicate with God, basically prayer and hymns, Central Sulawesi religion bustled with vows, effective ritual offerings, shamanic trances, public curses, and other media that missionaries were at pains to stifle. Yet although much of the diversity, overt bargaining, and bucolic festivity of precolonial rituals was dampened by the formulaic application of Protestant services, few of the key features of their sacrifices, as outlined by Valeri, were altered. They still are needed to make human life prosper.

Below I outline the precolonial ritual calendar to provide an ethnographic context for discussions of Salvation Army rites that sometimes disorient the foreign observer's expectations of Protestant practice. Many indigenous rites have been reinterpreted "offstage" so they still can arrange or fulfill ancestral vows of sacrifice yet publicly be subsumed under standardized Protestant rituals presented as a symbolic thanks to God. Three specific cases of Salvation Army "statement of thanks" (*pengucapan syukur*, Ind.) ceremonies illustrate how ritual efforts to cope with misfortunes such as illness are managed under Christianity. Salvation Army officers now replace precolonial shamans as interpreters of misfortune and managers of ritual sacrifices. I also look at Salvation Army Sunday services, not for their departure from Western models—because there is little—but from their local interpretation as analogous to taboo days on the indigenous ritual calendar.

Calendrical Rituals

Pre-Christian highland rituals are described in the colonial literature primarily by Adriani and Kruyt (1968 [1950]; A. C. Kruyt 1938). More recent Indonesian writings also describe some local ceremonies in the Kulawi District (Soelarto and Albiladiyah n.d.; Masyhuda 1977; Yunus and Mahmud 1986/1987; Garang 1985). Where not otherwise specified, however, the following details about Tobaku rites are drawn from my observations of modified rites performed in the late 1980s and early 1990s, plus additional information from oral histories about the more elaborate shamanic rites of the past. Ritual procedures clearly varied over time and from one Tobaku community to another, but they are described in specific form here to provide a comparative baseline for assessing Protestant rituals in other regions. As I outline the ritual year in writing, I sometimes find it necessary to shift between past and present tenses to convey which aspects of precolonial rituals are abolished and which are still practiced in modified form.

Most calendrical rituals in the highlands have the annual primary rice harvest as their focus. Tobaku harvests are initiated with a ritual called "to work (or descend into) the rice paddy" (*mohompo pae*, Uma). Village shamans, now replaced by Salvation Army officers, accompany the female owner of the plot and her household to where she begins to pick rice in silence. After three days of mute harvesting, the leader is freed from her lonely task and joined garrulously by other women of her garden settlement. Cut rice sheaves are carried in backbaskets to each garden house, where teenagers remove the stems by stomping energetically on the stalks.

The first rice is picked near a woodpile where special plants and the first rice seeds were ritually sewn at the planting ceremony. The initial rice plants harvested are tied in three bundles before being cut with a hand knife. Women store these bundles separately for later blessing rituals. After the rice around the special woodpile is picked, a taboo is lifted and the family is allowed to use this wood for cooking fires.

At a harvest-opening ceremony (*mohompo mepae*) performed in the late 1980s for the Towulu' headman's wife, Mrs. Major Isa' led hymns and read a brief biblical passage. The verses, which concerned reaping the rewards of God's earth, were followed by a short sermon describing how formerly the first corn or rice harvested and cooked was rubbed on peoples' stomachs to prevent them from becoming ill. Mrs. Major Isa' concluded that those who now "have religion" (*punya agama*, Ind.) no longer need to do that because the prayer service to God she was conducting would serve the same purpose. Such efforts still are made to eliminate household customs considered "non-Christian" while assuring families that the dangers of life still are being addressed.

At the precolonial opening rite of harvest, shamans examined the viscera of chickens to predict the success of the forthcoming harvest. The flowers and herbs grown for ritual purposes (*wunga bonea*, Uma) were cut and blessed by the shamans, who inserted them into each family's garden-house roof to protect the rice stored there. Presently, Salvation Army officers hike up the mountains to each harvest site to hold group prayer meetings, which are followed by the slaughter and cooking of chickens by individual households. The inspection of chicken viscera for purposes of divination and the use of sacred plants for protection are discouraged although continued privately in some households.

Roasted chicken thighs and drumsticks that formerly were delivered with rice to the shamans' homes now are delivered to the Salvation Army officers. During the several weeks of harvest, each household of each garden settlement sends one portion of its morning and evening meal to every other household. This custom, called "to offer to each other" (*mositonui*, Uma), is still practiced in some but not all Tobaku areas. While the meals shared on some days may be nothing more than rice and boiled cucumber all around, the practice compels the frenetic harvesters to stop and eat two meals a day. Moreover, if any family catches game in their traps, all will receive at least a taste of meat.

The sharing of meals also ensures that families observe precolonial taboos that prohibit certain vegetables from being consumed during the harvest period. I discovered these food taboos by accident when, hoping to interrupt the seemingly endless repasts of rice and boiled cucumber, I mentioned a ripe winter squash I had spotted in the field. After this and several other hints for modifying our gastronomic monotony were ignored, I learned that the squash and virtually every other available vegetable were taboo for the ancestors during the rice harvest. Those food taboos, as well as now abandoned precolonial linguistic taboos against employing the usual words for desired foods such as rice or deer, mark the special quality of the harvest season when all hopes of prosperity rest on the compliance of humans with the constraints of unseen spirits.

Prior to mission intervention, when all the rice was picked from every related garden settlement, a ritual was performed to secure the safe storage of rice in harvest bins. The storing ceremony, called "making good" (*ngkolompe'*), and a chicken feast (*mosese'dea*) were held where a genre of harvest songs titled "busy people" (*sese'dea*) was sung. The shamans made the rounds of each household and ritually led the pouring of the rice grains from a house platform (*poropo'*) into a cylindrical bin constructed just prior to the ritual. The lead shaman entered the bin to make a blessing and contact spirits who could deliver a good harvest.

Currently, this ritual in modified form is allowed by Salvation Army officers in some Tobaku villages but is abolished in others. Where the *ngkolompe'* ritual is still held, Salvation Army officers sanction and lead the event, seeing it as part and parcel of the annual harvest thanksgiving to God. The officer holds a brief public prayer for God's blessing at each house and then enters the rice storage cylinder where formerly the shaman (*tobalia*) stood. The pre-Christian shaman uttered a prayer to encourage the Owner of the Rice (*Pue' Niu*) to create abundance as the rice grains were dropped from the upstairs storage platform into the cylindrical bamboo storage barrel set up below. The Salvation Army minister similarly offers prayers to God and invokes blessings upon the rice paddy dropped in an identical fashion. A sacrificial meal of rice and chicken or game then is served by each household to ensure a satisfactory harvest.

The four-foot-tall cylindrical rice bins constructed at each garden house vary in width from as little as three feet to as large as nine feet in diameter. The appropriate size of the bin is estimated by the male head of household according to how much seed was planted. No one considers the harvest outcome to be fixed until the moment the rice is poured down a plaited mat chute into the bin. Male relatives standing on the platform push the rice off into the bin and those below stomp wildly on the falling rice as onlookers crowd around and cheer. The event radiates a giddy excitement and chaotic frenzy as people race from house to house through a haze of churning rice dust to see the outcome of each neighbor's harvest. If the bin is filled, the family feels both spiritually and economically satisfied.

If the harvest bin, no matter what its size, is not well filled, people consider it to be the result of tampering by an angry spirit or a sorcerer. No one ever faults the human estimate that determined the size of the bin. Occasionally, a family will be so disappointed with a partly empty bin that they will repeat the ceremony, hauling the tons of grain back up to the platform and pouring it again into the bin. Before doing so prayers are uttered, more chickens are sacrificed, and the chickens' blood is smeared on the bin. These acts are intended to rectify whatever cosmological imbalance caused the interference in the first place. Villagers insisted that a second pouring could result in a fuller bin, although the one such event I observed did not. The ministers presiding traced the repeated poor outcome to the sponsoring family's consistent acts of dishonesty and greed.

After the rice-storing ceremony, people still are not allowed to return to the village because, they say, "the rice stalks are not yet asleep." Formerly, when all the households had stored their grain in bins, lively festivals called "the summit of rice" or "the summit of endeavor" (*katebuaa' pae* or *katebuaa' powia'*) were held in each garden settlement. Afterward, when all the families descended from their scattered gardens, a village-wide feast (*mobalia mowunca*) was performed at the new moon. For three nights prior to the village feast, shamans entered trances to heal the sick, who gave them live chickens in appreciation.

The focus of this now largely abolished harvest festival was a symbolic tree (*wunca*) made from bamboo or palm wood. The tree was decorated with betelnut, barkcloth, antique woven cloth, shields, and packets of sticky rice. Offerings of freshly picked grain, betelnut, and food were placed at the base of the tree. Throughout every night of the three-day feast, people performed songs and circle dances (*raego'*; see chapter 7). At the feast's culmination on the third night, guests from other villages were invited to join the festivities.

Large livestock such as buffalo and pigs promised to the owner(s) of the land when it was cleared were sacrificed. Life-cycle ceremonies such as puberty rites also were conducted. On the morning after the third night, the head of a sacrificed buffalo was mounted on the *wunca* tree, and the *raego'* songs and dances began again in a rite called "to go around" (*melili'*). After these dances, the guests requested and were granted their leave. They then were splashed with water and mud by the hosting villagers "as a sign of respect" when they departed. These messy honors, I can attest, are still practiced. Villagers explain that they so value their visitors' presence that they become unhappy and protest their guests' departure.

In most Tobaku areas, precolonial-style harvest feasts with dances and songs have been eliminated by church regulations. Only a few elderly people remember how to perform *raego'* songs (Aragon 1996c; Smithsonian Folkways Recordings 1999). Occasionally in Towulu', locals declare a *mowunca* ceremony when a village leader sacrifices a buffalo after harvest, but the rite now is performed as a Salvation Army prayer dinner. Before Christian conversion, however, *mobalia mowunca* harvest festivals sometimes were combined with longer propitiation festivals called *motaro*, where more buffalo or even humans were sacrificed to appease the forces that cause misfortune. If there was sickness in a village, the shaman would enter a trance and try to cast out the affliction by drawing it into a figurine (*pinotau*) made of banana trunk.

The irregularly performed *motaro* festival, which could last for eighteen nights, was conducted only when harvests or other community events were not going well. The last shaman-led *motaro* possession ceremony in the region was held in 1957. Betelnut and livestock offerings were presented by the shaman, and ancestral spirits were asked to inhabit his body. In the precolonial era, if a slave was bought or captured for sacrifice, the violent act was performed in a ceremony called "to carry" (*mokoloa*). The Dutch government ordered that banana trunks be substituted for human sacrifices, and this change reportedly took effect in Tobaku prior to World War II. After the war, most harvest ceremonies were phased out and replaced with church-supervised "thanksgiving" events.

The annual church thanksgiving, or literally, "statement of thanks," service (*pengucapan syukur gereja*), requires families to deliver a portion of their harvest as a tithe to the church. Before the service, each family places donations of produce near the altar. These foods are witnessed during the service, and then most are auctioned back to congregation members to supplement the resident officers' annual income. British officers say that Salvation Army harvest ceremonies in Indonesia follow those practiced in rural England, where first fruits of harvest still are brought into the church and blessed by officers. Thus there were preexisting parallels between the European and Central Sulawesi harvest blessing ceremonies.

Rites called "appearance of the earth" (*mobere' tana'*) formerly succeeded the harvest and concerned the choice of land for the following year's rice plots. Male elders tossed their machetes into the soil of a proposed field to examine the color and consistency of the residues that adhered to the blade. Shamans sacrificed chickens and examined their hearts and gall bladders as a another means to assess promising sites (cf. Kuipers 1990a, 100–102).

An essential facet of these abolished land-opening rites was the promise (*hanga'*) of future offerings to the owner(s) of the land. The promises were formalized in the village "sun temple" (*sou eo*). In Pipikoro, the leader's barkcloth banner was borrowed for divination ceremonies of other families, who carried it out to their proposed fields for good fortune (A. C. Kruyt 1938, 4:chap.15). When the land was cleared, pigs were sacrificed to feed the workers and land spirits whose cooperation was sought, with promises of more offerings after the next harvest.

During the dry season, while cut foliage was left to desiccate prior to burning, Tobaku men traveled westward to pan for gold dust. Before departure they would call the owner(s) of the waters and owner(s) of the land to partake of animal sacrifices and hear vows promising more offerings in exchange for their success. Presently, Protestant prayers are spoken for safety and luck, but these prayers include promises to make a ritual of thanks to God if the expedition is auspicious.

Before the cleared and dried fields were burned there was a now eliminated ceremony to inform the owner(s) of the land about the upcoming conflagration. Farmers sacrificed a pig again to bargain for a productive crop. Men burning their family's fields would wear special headdresses with stalks of red cordyline (*Cordyline terminalis*) protruding from the top. As they lit the fire, they called out to it, "You with the royal shirt, triumph and take over. You the brave one, triumph and take over" (*Iko, tomobaju sakala, mengkalela ko. Iko, to barani, mengkalela ko*, Uma). Then they shouted a whoop of happiness (*mongare*). Some men still wear the cordyline headdresses, and all continue their shouts to the fire when the dried brush is ignited.

After the land is burned and cooled, the planting ritual

(*podungkua*) is held in the rice gardens. Shamans formerly held a second ceremony (*mobalia*) in the village to celebrate the bargains with the owner(s) of the land and to cure sick community members. Today, the curing rituals are omitted and ministers officiate at planting ceremonies, in villages where they are allowed. In the wee hours of the morning, ritual plants are unearthed in the house yard or old farm plots for transplanting to the new fields. Each family also carves a ceremonial dibble stick from a certain hardwood tree (*kasu konore*). Then, by the first light of dawn, the entire garden settlement group climbs the mountains to their proposed farm site.

At present, Salvation Army officers deliver blessings and sermons on the mount. Then, following older customs, one woman of the household begins planting rice by poking and tossing seeds into three adjacent holes. These represent the three stars of Orion's Belt. The stars we identify as the constellation Orion are considered part of a larger Chicken (*Manu*) constellation whose appearance is used by many Central Sulawesi highlanders as a sign to plant. After planting these three holes, the woman pokes and plants in a spiral of points as she walks seven times counterclockwise around the pile of wood and ritual plants. After that, seven more holes are made and filled with maize seed, the male companion to the female rice. Then the carved digging stick (*ntujaa' pae*) is "planted" down slope from the open seed holes.

Formerly, a woman was allowed to sow only these first shaman-blessed seeds and plants around the woodpile before stopping for the day to celebrate with her household. She was not permitted to handle firewood or cook, and a white chicken was sacrificed and inspected as an omen of the upcoming harvest. One or more chickens were cut open, depending on how many birds were necessary to discover healthy viscera that would indicate good fortune. At present, women continue planting all day on the first day, although they continue to eat chicken handled and cooked by others for their evening meal. In some Tobaku villages, a man precedes each woman and makes the holes into which the woman tosses the rice seeds. In the western Tobaku area, however, elder women say that they once tried letting men poke the seed holes, but their work was considered insufficiently precise.

During the growing period, smaller phase-marking rites (*mokareke* or *balia dagoa*) were held when the rice and corn began to fruit. Tobaku sacrificed chickens and consumed them with baked sago or sugar-palm flour, drinking palm wine. Portions were set out in the fields for the owner spirits. Another feast (*mowerai'*) was held when the rice grains began to yellow. A paper mulberry barkcloth flag, dyed yellow with turmeric, was flown in the fields, and men wore matching yellow barkcloth headscarves (*siga*). These smaller rites are now absent, absorbed by Protestant statement of thanks services held in the garden settlements to mark the growth process.

Even the earliest European missionaries understood that a Protestantism that had nothing to offer in the way of farming rituals could have little appeal in Central Sulawesi. Therefore, they coopted the major horticultural rites into their statement of thanks services while forbidding the more objectionable rites and ignoring sacrificial promises and many smaller ritual activities. In this way, Protestant farming rituals came to look European while interpretive differences concerning the effective or symbolic nature of sacrifices generally were overlooked. A similar approach was taken to life-cycle rituals.

Life-Cycle Rituals

Most circumcisions, engagements, marriages, house raisings, and other rites of passage that permit flexible timing occur in a festive month that follows the primary harvest. These life-cycle rites also have received Protestant pressures. For example, the rites that formerly marked phases of pregnancy (Soelarto and Albiladiyah n.d.) now are absent. Certain precolonial birth and postpartum rites have been retained, however, and most Tobaku women, fearing unwanted episiotomies, refuse to accept help from clinic "sisters" until after their babies are born. Only following delivery are nearby Salvation Army nurses invited to examine the baby, deliver an injection of vitamins to the mother, and pray over a small shared repast.

Tobaku women are attended by elder female relatives or an informal community midwife. This person "who has handled blood" is compensated with a live chicken or a bolt of cloth and receives a seat of honor at postpartum ceremonies.[1] Women deliver their babies in tube-shaped sarong cloths, which formerly had to be of red or black bark-cloth. The midwife sits on the floor behind the mother-to-be, holds her around the ribs to support her back and head, and then presses on the top of her belly, if necessary. Laboring women also walk around and sometimes squat, while suspending themselves slightly from a rope tied to a roof beam. Relatives, even children, freely wander in and out during labor. The husband's duty is to carry away soiled cloths and wash them in the river. If labor was difficult in pre-Christian times, a shaman would be summoned to "blow" (*motuwui'*) on the woman and recite spells (*mogane'*). This man, however, was not permitted to view her genital area and was expected to leave before the birth. Emerging babies are splashed with water and fluid is sucked from their noses. Midwives sever the umbilical cord (*pohore ana'*) with a sliver of bamboo cut from the roof of the mother's kitchen, a practice opposed by Salvation Army medical personnel, who consider it unsanitary. No medicine is applied to the navel area. The baby is just cleaned and wrapped in cloth. When the umbilical cord stump falls off about a week later, the mother saves it. If the child later suffers from upset stomachs, the stump is boiled and the broth used as a curative bath.

The remains of the placenta (*daa'*), also called the "elder sibling" (*tuaka*), are considered dangerous both to the mother, who may die if it doesn't come out properly, and to the community, which may be bothered by blood-eating spirits if it is not disposed of properly. It is the father's task to pick up the placenta with bamboo tongs, cover it with fireplace ashes to eliminate odor, and insert it into a package of areca-nut bark. Before the next sunrise, the father carries the package out of the village and hangs it in a fruit tree. Villagers say these packages disappear within a few months, although no living human or animal ever takes them. Rather, the placenta packages satisfy the bloodthirsty appetites of unseen spirits.

There are no food taboos for pregnant women, but new mothers enter a three-day period of rest and restrictions, eating only plain rice porridge. They sit beside a fire and are not allowed to bathe or have physical contact with their husbands. The colostrum, or first yellowish breast milk, formerly was considered "dirty" (*babo'*), so newborns often were wet-nursed for three days by a sister, cousin, or neighbor. Salvation Army medical staff discourage this waste of nutritious colostrum, although most Tobaku women still do not like to use it.

Formerly, a set of tools was placed outside on the ground in front of the newborn's house to indicate the infant's sex. Farming implements and barkcloth beaters were displayed for a girl, and weapons and shaman's bells were presented for a boy. After three days, a shaman would bless the new mother and baby by "blowing" on them and reciting words of protection. A first birth obligated the groom's family to pay an installment of the bridewealth, called *peroro*, no longer paid today.

After three nights, a now abandoned ceremony called "to bring down the child" (*mopehompo ana'*) was performed. The child was stood on a flat river stone placed outside the house, touching the earth for the first time while an elder blessed (*mogane'*) the child and requested that he or she bring good fortune. The baby then was placed inside on a barkcloth sling hung from the roof. This rite, called "to be slung" (*rabintiu'*), symbolized the mother's freedom to return to her normal tasks.

These precolonial postpartum rituals have been eclipsed by a single Protestant household service. After a "three-day" (*tolu eo*) postpartum statement of thanks to God ceremony, the mother and child enter a one-month period of lighter restrictions. The baby is then allowed out of the house, although the mother still carries special leaves such as those called "sleep soundly" (*tutu leta'*) to protect the infant from disturbance by spirits. An infant's hair and fingernails are not cut during the first month for fear of weakening the child. Until the Salvation Army ceremony of baptism, the child is called just "girl" (*dei'*) or "boy" (*uto'*). These impersonal gender labels were used until another child was born before Christian missionaries emphasized the importance of permanent personal names to identify the individual soul.

Formerly, a baby was bathed outside the home only after four or five months, depending on the size of the child and the omens of the indigenous lunar calendar. The first ritual bath (*moniu tawuna*) was held at the new moon and usually performed by the mother's father or uncle. An herbal bath was concocted and the elder recited a blessing to bring good fortune to the child. After one year, a first haircut (*pokoku bulu woo'*) was given by the mother at the new moon. Many Tobaku families still informally continue these small rites of passage for their babies as part of their "secular" customs (*adat biasa*, Ind.).

Precolonial puberty rites (*mpowati'*, Uma) entailed tooth filing (*mpokeso*) for girls and circumcision (*potini'*) for boys. Girls and boys undergoing ceremonies at the same time were ritually bathed at separate locations in the river. Afterward, they exchanged old, ragged clothes for new, painted barkcloth attire. They returned to the village and entered the large temple (*lobo*), where the girls' front teeth were cut with a machete and filed with a stone to make them more even. Boys were circumcised with a small subincision to their foreskin. They recovered together on separate sides of the temple for three days and nights.

While the children were confined to heal and fed only rice porridge, adults celebrated just outside the temple, singing and dancing (*moraego'*) every night. One animal was sacrificed for every girl and every three to five boys. Whether the animal was a buffalo, cow, or pig depended on the child's social rank. The parents of girls who contributed animals expected to receive an equivalent animal from the groom's family when the girl's bridewealth was paid. In Kulawi, girls' front teeth were knocked out completely during the rituals. The Dutch government forbade these female puberty rituals and punished offend-

(*left*) Sister Elsi, a Salvation Army nurse and daughter of a former Tobaku headman, dressed for her traditional (*adat*) wedding ceremony, 1987. (*right*) Sister Elsi dressed for her "white dress" (*baju putih*, Ind.) church wedding.

ers with heavy fines, although minor female puberty rituals without dental mutilation continued in the Tobaku region through World War II. Presently, only male puberty rites occur. Boys of about eight years are circumcised by a male elder in conjunction with Protestant rituals of thanks at which small pigs are sacrificed.

In the present context of increasing migration from the Sulawesi highlands, pre-Christian religious practices are suffering further attrition because ancestral ceremonies are not readily portable (Volkman 1980, 1985). Tama Abi', a Tobaku teacher living in Palu, had his preadolescent son circumcised at the Salvation Army hospital at approximately the same age as he would have undergone a communal circumcision ritual in their home village. Although the family bought a pig and attempted to create a small circumcision feast in their urban home, other ancestral requirements had to be dropped. The ceremony was scheduled for the boy's school vacation rather than at the new moon, and postcircumcision food taboos could not be followed because the boy was fed in the hospital according to standard patient menus. Moreover, the placement of circumcised boys in a temple group or by a household hearth to "dry" their wounds could not be undertaken. There were no open fires in the hospital nor comrades to share the boy's ritual experience. What was once a community ritual of special intensity among youthful peers had become a medical procedure and an isolated family dinner.

Precolonial engagement and wedding rituals are more elaborate and intact than almost any other type of life-cycle ritual (Aragon 1992, 85–102, 261–265). Engagement ceremonies with ritual speakers are conducted at the homes of both bride and groom, negotiations over bridewealth are held, a large feast is mounted, a separate public ceremony to give advice to the newlyweds is staged, and two more ceremonies held at the house of each of the parents-in-law are performed prior to the birth of the first child. Now an Indonesian translation of the standard Salvation Army wedding service is inserted between the precolonial wedding feast and the ceremonial giving of advice to the newlyweds.

The Indonesian government requires that a marriage license be purchased at the district office. In turn, Salvation Army officers insist that only the Christian "white dress" (*baju putih*, Ind.) wedding performed in church legitimizes a marriage. Yet highlanders expend considerable time and resources to complete a larger array of indigenous marital rites. The explanation for this resides in the complex economics of bridewealth and family alliances, matters not to be shunted aside in the name of Christian conversion. The government's demands for revenue and population surveillance through marital documents, as well as the church's demands for authority over sexual unions, simply have led to the addition of government and church events within the prior sequence of marital milestones.

Family disputes that once required a pre-Christian peace-making ceremony (*modame*, Uma) are now mediated by Salvation Army statement of thanks ceremonies. If, for example, a father utters an oath

Women wail and keen as family members grieve over Tama Tobe's corpse at home before burial, Towulu', 1987.

against his son and orders him not to call him "father" any longer, no further contact or ceremonies can take place between them until the peace-making ritual is performed. Ministers perform a Christian version of the reconciliation ceremony where a pig is sacrificed, hymns are sung, and prayers are offered. Afterward, the curse is considered dissipated, and any life-cycle rituals that should have been conducted among disputants may proceed or may be deemed unnecessary.

Death rites have been altered and minimized under Protestant influence. A wide variety of primary and secondary mortuary practices are known from Sulawesi, although Kulawi District highlanders claim always to have buried their dead permanently after death. Corpses of important individuals were kept wrapped in their homes until relatives could arrive from far distances. For hygienic reasons, the Dutch government insisted that burials be carried out within one day of death. Graves formerly were dug under the elevated family house or beside it, shaded by the roof, but the Dutch also objected to that. Colonial regulations required the creation of cemeteries outside village limits.

Nevertheless, until recently Tobaku families quietly buried stillborn babies or deceased infants beneath their parents' houses to keep them nearby and avoid funeral expenses.

Before an ailing person's death it is taboo for kin to cry, but as soon as the breath is gone, women begin keening. Formerly, deaths also were announced by striking a particular rhythm on a wooden rice mortar. Now, where available, the church bell is rung to broadcast the news, and the same named rhythm, "the drum of lowering" (*tinti' pohu*), is played. Male relatives construct a wooden coffin beside the house of the deceased and collect contributions (about Rp 1,000 in the late 1980s and about Rp 5,000 in the early 1990s) from each household that comes to pay its respects. Usually, men socialize outside the house where the corpse lies, while women enter and wail as they first sit beside the corpse. Funeral keening is performed by women only and has formulaic auditory and lyrical patterns. The performer invokes the role that the deceased has played in her life, asking such rhetorical questions as, "Who will make sure that I have a crumb to eat, now that my grandmother is gone?" or "Who will prevent my brother from beating me now that you are no longer here to prevent it? I cooked your food and now no one will be left to defend me" (cf. Feld 1990; Hoskins 1987b).

Corpses are washed and dressed in finery by close relatives. Formerly, the face of the deceased was decorated with spots or stripes of a black pigment called *nompi*, or, in the case of high-born individuals, gold dust. At every meal until burial, relatives placed a portion of food beside the corpse. Outside the house *raego'* songs and dances were performed. Missionaries discouraged these practices, but the corpse still is guarded until interment by wakeful relatives who play games and tell riddles to cheer the crowd throughout the night. It is taboo for anyone guarding the corpse to fall asleep. Charcoal is rubbed on the faces of any individuals who doze off during the night watch. According to Kruyt (1938, 3:chap. 14), this is to keep the spirit of the dead from seeing them and being able to harm them in the vulnerable condition of slumber.

The shaman's role at mortuary rites is taken over by Salvation Army officers, who lead prayers and funeral services at the home and the grave. After a procession to the cemetery, the coffin is placed above a grave pit, suspended on bamboo poles. The ministers read biblical verses about death and eternal life, mentioning little about the deceased individual.

On the third day after death, a ritual feast is held, now preceded by a Protestant service in the deceased's home. Another service and feast are held on the eighth, ninth, or tenth day, depending on the region and sex of the deceased. For some important individuals, a forty-day ceremony is added. Major Isa' said that this ceremony is not ancient, but rather was introduced by a Menadonese minister. He contended that the forty-day ritual was inspired by Jesus' resurrection after forty days. The fact that forty-day mortuary rites occur in many Muslim regions of Indonesia, however, suggests that this ceremony may have an earlier Mediterranean heritage. A one hundred-day ceremony now is added in some areas for wealthy individuals.

One mortuary ceremony revised under Protestantism is called "assisting at the graveyard" (ngawa'hi dayo). Formerly, when rats attacked the crops or someone became ill and ancestral anger was taken to be the cause, graves of relatives were refurbished. Now, Protestant thanks to God ceremonies are performed in conjunction with grave repairs. Often these repairs are scheduled communally between Christmas and New Year's Day, associating the birth of Jesus and the new year with attention to the dead. Ancestors formerly were considered largely responsible for the blessings of each harvest year, and Jesus is viewed by many as caring for the prosperity of the living in the same immediate sense.

In the precolonial era, the deaths of leaders (maradika) were followed by extensive mourning taboos (mo'omo). All work stopped and behaviors such as climbing trees, carrying firewood on the shoulder, wearing hats, and riding horses were forbidden. These proscriptions still are followed, as are some stringent eating and seclusion taboos incumbent upon widows and widowers (M. A. Martens 1993). Precolonial mourning for leaders was lengthy unless ended by the ritual capture of a human head. Tobaku say that if an enemy head was planted on a leader's grave, the deceased would be satisfied, and other mortuary taboos and rites could be curtailed. High-ranking individuals were buried dressed in sartorial splendor, and their passing was marked by the slaughter of numerous pigs, cows, or buffaloes.

At present, just one or two animals are killed to feed kin who donate money and rice toward death expenses. Usually it is the grown children who sponsor mortuary feasts and contribute the animals to be sacrificed, although sometimes parents arrange beforehand to give additional inheritance to particular children in exchange for this service. All the life-cycle rituals, except possibly marriage, have been curtailed under Protestantism, yet the motivation for efficacious animal sacrifices has never been deterred by Salvation Army services. On the contrary, ministers have had to assure congregations that their services, too, would bring blessings or relief from misfortune.

Three Cases of Sacrificial Rituals Giving Thanks to God

The Bible is a text with marvelous potential for multiple interpretations on an infinite variety of behavioral issues. The following three cases illustrate how Protestant rituals featuring locally interpreted biblical doctrines are employed with animal sacrifices to expiate ancestral transgressions. These examples indicate that indigenous cosmological causes for misfortunes readily can be perceived and accepted by all parties involved, including the Salvation Army ministers. Additionally, they show the potential for ancestral moral crimes to be reinterpreted as Christian sins that can be expiated by ancestral-style atonements and oblations made in the name of the Christian God. Major violations of behavior that were thought punished by the owner gods or deified ancestor spirits now are said to be punished by the Christian God. These crimes include land border violations, inadequate mortuary ritual contributions, heirloom thefts, acts of sorcery, the breaking of oaths, and adultery. Christians atone for these sins through Salvation Army statement of thanks rituals accompanied by animal sacrifices.

In the first case, a Tobaku infant was afflicted with severe pneumonia-like symptoms and the parents organized a Salvation Army statement of thanks household service, including the sacrifice of a pig for the ritual meal. The biblical passage read by Major Isa' referred to God's anger against those who steal and lie to their neighbors (Ephesians 4:25–28). After the ceremony, villagers mentioned that the parents of the ill child recently had moved logs marking their swidden borders, thereby effectively stealing land from the wife's siblings who worked the adjacent plot. They noted that this mother had lost a previous child and reasoned that the woman's land violations had not been discovered in time to save her first baby. Another woman who "pushed" (*mosoro*) her land borders over into her first cousin's fields recently had died along with her husband, so this mother was considered fortunate, especially when her child recovered following the Christian ceremony and clinic treatment.

In Tobaku ancestral law the surreptitious alteration of hereditary land borders is among the most heinous of crimes, one said to lead to a curse (*silaka*) such as an unexpected family death within a year. Border crimes are said to be punished by the owner(s) of the land. Since the Christian God now is viewed as the owner of the universe, Tobaku people expect God to punish land-rights violators similarly. Mrs. Major Isa' said that the mother of the sick child confessed to the land transgression as soon as her second baby became very ill — hence the officer's opportune selection of a biblical passage concerning God's anger about a land theft within a family to illuminate the punishment of an ancestral crime in Christian terms.

On a second occasion, a severely ill teacher, Guru Eli, who had migrated from Tobaku to the Palolo Valley, was carried on a stretcher for three days back to his home village to conduct a statement of thanks ritual. Guru Eli suffered from severe diarrhea, fever, and weakness. The man's nearest kin in his home village helped Guru Eli sponsor the renovation of his parents' graves, the household feast, and a second Protestant service at the cemetery. The elders of his family believed that Guru Eli's illness was caused by his meager participation at his parents' funerals. After the graves were re-cemented and a large pig for the feast was obtained at the teacher's expense, the Salvation Army officer read a Bible passage about the necessity of honoring one's father and mother (Ephesians 6:1–3). The anger of the ancestors over Guru Eli's failure to his parents had been recast as the anger of the Christian God.

At the feast of thanks, God and Guru Eli's deceased relatives were entreated (*rakimaa'*) to take mercy on his condition. The man also was treated with rehydration fluids and an antiflagellate (Flagyl) through the Salvation Army clinic. His subsequent recovery was interpreted primarily as a result of the successful mollification of his ancestors by the grave improvements and pig sacrifices performed with the Christian ceremonies. Villagers also praised the attentions of the visiting doctor who administered the Flagyl, a medicine not normally stocked by the local clinic. The fortuitous medical treatment was considered warranted because of Guru Eli's contrite penance.

Although Salvation Army leaders have convinced highlanders that they must hold a Protestant ceremony in order to consecrate grave constructions and pig sacrifices, the reverse is also true. That is, graves must be renovated and animals sacrificed in order to empower the Christian prayer gatherings aimed to cure the sick. This fact remains tacit because Christian religious leaders wish to emphasize the canonical aspects of village services rather than their fusion with complementary ancestral ritual elements. Western missionaries have seen animal sacrifices in Indonesia as a kind of fetishism, the improper conflation of material and immaterial consequences (Keane 1996; Pietz 1985). This problem of interpretation emanates from their differential views of sacrifices as effective versus symbolic, as well as the exclusive doctrinal focus of European definitions of religion.

In a third case, a Tobaku village headman summoned the local Salvation Army officer, Captain Tance, to hold a Protestant rite of thanks to cure his fever-ridden adult daughter. Beforehand, a sizable pig and a chicken were tied up for display outside the headman's house. This act represented their promise, or consecration, prior to the actual sacrifice. Captain Tance introduced the ritual meal with prayers and a recitation of Matthew 8:14–17, which describes Jesus' healing of the sick and demon possessed. Captain Tance then asked Jesus to descend into the midst of the gathering and heal the ailing woman, just as the indigenous shamans once called upon the senior ancestor spirits. In this case, the pre-Christian curing role of the deified ancestor spirits (*anitu*) was reinterpreted by Captain Tance and his audience as akin to the miracles of Jesus as healer.

The above cases follow a distinct pattern where the wrath of the pre-Christian owner spirits and ancestors concerning indigenous moral violations is reinterpreted as the wrath of the Christian God, and the aid granted by the pre-Christian deities is reinterpreted as the grace of God or Jesus. Sacrificial feasts that were promised formerly to pre-Christian spirits on the grounds of good fortune such as births, financial windfalls, and so forth also are redirected to the Christian God. These contemporary understandings clearly are biblically grounded even if the highlanders' view of the efficacy of sacrificial acts differs from those foreigners who delivered their Bibles.

Christian Services, Holidays, and Indigenous Lunar Taboos

Apart from farming rituals held in the garden settlements and life-cycle rituals held in village households, the primary community ritual is now the Sunday church service (*kebaktian gereja*, Ind.; *mogambara*, Uma), which mirrors the format of British Salvation Army services in most respects. Highlanders' Sunday Sabbath, however, is founded on a proscription, or taboo, against performing normal work as much as on a prescription to worship God. The taboo on routine activities and the positive injunction to worship in church mutually define each other.

Most villagers attend church enthusiastically, although a few absentees make excuses when preoccupied with other activities or fearful of a public shaming. During harvest, weekly church attendance produces hardship because farmers wish to cut rice at its peak ripeness and thus are loath to "commute," often several hours, from their distant gardens. For children, the elderly, or infirm, long trips back to the main villages with churches are physically trying. Moreover, some individuals must remain in the gardens to guard the voracious pigs, chickens, rice plants, and houses. Most people, however, do descend to the village briefly for the church service rather than risk criticism or cosmological sanctions. Many thoroughly enjoy dressing up in their best clothes, socializing, and leaving behind the toils of farming.

The emphasis on constant attendance of church services advocated by evangelical missionaries meshes easily with Central Sulawesi interests in correct ritual practice. Some Dutch Reformed missionaries criticize the evangelicals, saying that their focus on formulaic church rituals reinforces the "ethnic religion" (*agama suku*, Ind.) of the local people rather than turning natives' thoughts toward a true understanding of the Bible and the practice of good works every day of the week. Here there arises another contest to define what is "proper religion," even among the foreign missionaries themselves.

The seven-day week was introduced to Indonesia by the Dutch. Hoskins writes that for the Kodi of Sumba it was "the *ritual temporality* of the first Christians—the way they demarcated sacred time—that set them apart from their fellows" (Hoskins 1993, 276; emphasis in the original). Like the Kodi, Sulawesi highlanders formerly used a lunar calendar that, like the Christian week, designated certain appropriate work and ritual days during each cycle (A. C. Kruyt 1938, vol.4).

The temporal rules for conduct introduced by missionaries gained meaning through association with prescriptions familiar from precolonial time keeping. The indigenous lunar calendar was essentially oracular, indicating favorable times for particular events and warning community members not to marry, hunt, or plant on days when their efforts would be doomed to failure. The missionaries' taboo on working on Sundays parallels the lunar calendar's specification that certain days in the moon phases are unsuitable for particular activities. That the missionaries' definition of work includes all food gathering is irksome for villagers who collect fresh produce daily for their meals. Ministers encourage families to plan ahead, to borrow food if necessary, but some ignore this Christian taboo by wandering the land on Sunday afternoons to collect foodstuffs such as cassava, ferns, and hot peppers for their next meal. They cannot believe that God expects them to go hungry the evening after church.

Prohibited activities carried out on Sundays are considered risky, likely to result in failure at best, or disaster at worst. Mrs. Major Isa' tells scolding stories of women who fish on Sunday instead of attending church. Some, she says, catch nothing. Others are victims of terrible accidents, crushed by falling trees. Mrs. Captain Silase, too, recounts how her husband was punished by God when he traveled for trade early one Sunday, leaving his assistant to deliver the sermon. The captain's packhorse, laden with bags of coffee beans, slipped on rocks in the mountains and tumbled to death just as the ten o'clock church bell rang back in his home village. After that, Captain Silase never went anywhere on Sundays. Instead, he sent hired workers early on Sunday morning to perform his trade business for him. Neither the captain nor his hired hands seemed concerned about the consequences of the workers' evasion of church services, all avoiding guilt by shifting sin to those of less importance. Like those lay people who destroy life so that the Buddhist monks of mainland Southeast Asia receive food while remaining pure in deed, the Sulawesi underlings who sin for their masters receive absolution or even merit for their actions.

Another event demonstrates both the unforgiving nature of the Sunday travel prohibition and its association with indigenous taboos. A Salvation Army clinic nurse received an emergency call early Sunday morning to aid a patient in a distant village. During her journey, the nurse fell from her horse and suffered a concussion. Mrs. Major Isa' insisted that it was the nurse's own fault for leaving unannounced before the church service. The nurse and her assistants left hastily without asking permission of the village officers, who could have prayed for her, thereby ensuring the safety of her journey. The nurse not only transgressed the Christian prohibition against traveling on Sunday, but she also violated the pan-Indonesian prescription to ask permission of one's elders before departures. The nurses' dormitory was adjacent to the officers' house and the officer couple viewed themselves as surrogate parents of the young, unmarried nurses. The officers' interpretation of events portrayed the ax of divine retribution falling doubly hard upon the nurse because of two ritual violations: one of ancestral rules and one imposed by European Christian teachings and rigidly upheld by local interpretations.

Aside from Sunday services, other European Christian holidays such as Christmas, Easter, and a harvest Thanksgiving are highlighted in the Tobaku calendar by distinctive events. In addition to candle-lighting services, Christmas entails a village-wide feast or at least special desserts eaten together in church. Presents are not exchanged. New Year's Eve (December 31) in Central Sulawesi is viewed as a continuation of Christmas services that begin at 4:00 a.m. on Christmas morning and are repeated throughout the day and week. Salvation Army adherents attend church on New Year's Eve from 11:00 p.m. through midnight, at which time, in many churches, a second consecutive church service is begun to celebrate the new year. At the stroke of midnight, all in church pray silently for their relatives, near and far, as instructed by the Salvation Army officers. In the Palu church, there are five officers specially appointed to pray for the five Central Sulawesi regional divisions of the Salvation Army Corps. It is believed that prayers at these marathon holiday services are unusually potent, just as petitions to the pre-Christian deities were most potent when issued communally at precolonial rituals such as the *mobalia* and *motaro*.

Shamans to Officers: Christianizing Sacrifices and Rites

The construction of Christianized rituals in Central Sulawesi required transformations along logical and linguistic pathways, and new clerical institutions. European ministers first focused on eliminating the most unacceptable elements in highlanders' rituals, such as headhunting, human sacrifice, dental mutilation, the overt feeding of spirits, and seemingly promiscuous dancing. While they attacked these events, they worked to insert European forms of Protestant services into the local religious calendar. Ultimately, Tobaku communities and missionaries compromised to create a set of unspecialized ritual gatherings and "thank you" feasts, led by ministers, to which both ancestral and Protestant messages could be attached.

Prior to European contact, Tobaku shamans (*tobalia*) performed rituals (*mobalia*) to end misfortunes such as illness. A similar verb root, *bali'* in Uma, means "to change, to alter," and indeed the shaman's task was to undergo a personal transformation during the ritual so that the situation necessitating the ritual also would be altered.[2] During these rites, shamans asked the *anitu* ancestor spirits to enter their bodies and divulge the causes and cures of the sickness. At present, Christian family members themselves speculate on the cosmological sources of illness and other troubles such as death or crop failure. They then often present their problem to the nearest Salvation Army officer and propose to sponsor a service.

Hoskins (1993, 291) was told that the divination of cosmological problems and solutions among the Kodi of Sumba was more precise in the pre-Christian system, where ancestral priests, through rituals, were able to reveal the anger and desires of spirits in an incontestable fashion. Hoskins compares this with the Christian situation where preachers recognize God's displeasure in the creation of community misfortunes but cannot identify exact causes or paths of reparation for their Christian followers. This differs markedly from the Tobaku case where both local elders and Salvation Army officers seemingly excel at identifying various causes and solutions to misfortunes. If there are diverse interpretations about a particular misfortune, the families involved often combine suggestions regarding animal sacrifices or corrective behavior.

Salvation Army officers even are called *tobalia* in Uma because they lead the agricultural, life-cycle, and curing ceremonies that would have been handled by the pre-Christian shamans. The vernacular Tobaku use of the term *"tobalia"* for officers is not officially sanctioned by the Salvation Army Church, but likely was adopted independently by locals according to their sense of the ritual specialists' functional similarity. In addition, the ranking of Salvation Army officers is viewed by some as parallel to the status of the senior and junior shamans in the pre-Christian situation. A Tobaku elder explained that the "great shaman" (*tobalia peligi bohe*) was equivalent to a Salvation Army major or captain while the "small shaman" (*tobalia kedi*), who set out trays of betelnut and food offerings to the spirits, was an apprentice, like the Salvation Army sergeant.

Salvation Army officers in Central Sulawesi mainly are supported by their local communities. In Towulu' in 1986 the resident officer couple received about Rp 20,000, or US$17.50 per month, from the Palu headquarters to purchase household supplies. As with Indonesian civil servants, officers' salaries are not sufficient to support their families. Much of the officers' support came from a monthly church collection for "officer welfare" (*kesejahteraan opsir*, Ind.), the family's own entrepreneurial enterprises, and food payments for their "house call" services—the innumerable rituals labeled as "giving thanks to God."

Officer families generally do not maintain regular rice fields, but rather depend on the congregation members' support in the form of food. In areas where the officers receive goodwill, villagers will provide and work separate fields for the officers' families. Village women also bring the officers baskets of their first ripe maize, vegetables, and rice, which are blessed by the officers in the hopes that the giver will receive an ample harvest. Contributions of the "first fruits" (*buah pertama*, Ind.) of harvest from every plot are expected by all officers.

Household-sponsored rituals led by Salvation Army officers have prescribed remunerations similar to those paid to the precolonial shaman. Cooked food and a live chicken are given at weddings. Six to eight liters of unhusked rice (one large tin can, or *blek*) and a live chicken are given by each household at the paddy-storing ceremony in the garden settlement. Giving less than the expected compensation may anger the officer, who, like the former shaman, is considered to hold spiritual leverage. Every time an officer ministers at agricultural or life-cycle ceremonies—and there can be several per village per day—he or she is fed, and an additional portion is delivered to his or her home. The same applies for clinic nurses, who are honored guests at ceremonies for patients they have treated.

Special collections for building projects and produce auctions (*lelangan*, Ind.) are held after some Sunday services. Villagers bring produce to the church, and the minister auctions off the donations. Officers are required to file monthly activity and financial reports with their divisional headquarters, which for the Tobaku region is a two-day walk away in Kulawi. The largest annual contribution to officers' incomes occurs at the post-harvest thanksgiving ceremony. In church, every family is expected to make a contribution "to God" in the form of unhusked rice, vegetables, livestock, and coffee beans. Officers sometimes mention that 10 percent of a harvest (the biblical tithe) should be given, but the proceeds are invariably somewhat lower.

In 1985 in Towulu', ninety kilograms of unhusked rice and seventy-three kilograms of dried, unroasted coffee beans were obtained by the officers. They reportedly gave 10 percent to the Palu headquarters, 10 percent to the divisional headquarters in Kulawi, and 10 percent to the sergeants, volunteers who assist in their services. The remaining 70 percent of the donations were the officers' to sell, trade, or consume privately. Separate thanksgiving ceremonies for coffee began in the late 1980s, which provided ministers with a valuable resource that they could transfer directly to cash in Kulawi.

Officer families depend upon their communities not only for generous contributions of food, but also for labor services to build or repair

A man (*center*) draws his machete to sacrifice a pig as the Salvation Army officers (*right*) bless the construction of a new Tobaku Corps church building, 1986.

Salvation Army property, including their own homes. Officer couples are posted in particular villages for about three to five years at a time, a policy that aims to diversify their experiences as well as prevent entrenchment, which can lead to corruption or laziness. These reassignments, however, prevent officers from making long-term investments, such as planting tree crops, in areas where they do not have family members from whom they later can make claims.

Officers sometimes complain that their congregation members do not contribute enough to give them a satisfactory living. This situation can be a sign of genuine village poverty or else resistance on the part of villagers who find the constant requests of officers for donations to be overwhelming. Some officers then resort to trading or cash loan enterprises that net them considerable yearly incomes in addition to church donations.

Peripheral villages that do not yet have their own officers are served periodically by staff from the larger regional villages. To open a new Salvation Army Corps with a full-fledged officer, there must be a sizable settled population with a willingness to build church buildings and provide sufficient donations to support the officer's family. Salvation Army officers carefully review villages' past and potential harvests when considering where new outposts could be opened. There is a constant negotiation between officers trying to make a living and their congregation members, who either reward them abundantly in exchange for their blessing or resist their efforts to draw community resources into the church's coffers or their own pockets. In essence, Salvation Army officers who are appointed through a distant church bureaucracy must become as useful as their indigenous shaman predecessors in order to survive economically.

Like the pre-Christian shamans, Salvation Army officers continue to consecrate words with flesh. Whenever prayers are uttered outside the Sunday service, some food—usually meat and rice—is blessed, or promised to God at a future occasion. The necessity of sacrifices to support officers and the church was confirmed at the consecration of a new church in a growing Tobaku hamlet. Residents formerly had traveled by foot each week to attend Sunday services in a larger neighboring village. Now officers came to the hamlet to inaugurate a new branch church. The cement foundations had been laid, and the wood beams were cut and ready for assembly. Future congregation members gathered at the perimeter of the foundation, seating themselves on beams of timber. The officer couple stood inside the foundation, using a makeshift table to rest their Bibles, hymnals, and collection plate. The only other living being inside the perimeter during the rite was a large black pig, its feet tied to a wooden stake.

In most respects, it was a typical Salvation Army service: hymns were sung, a biblical passage describing the ideal church was read, prayers for the new church's success were spoken. The moment the ministers' final prayers were over, however, several men rushed to the pig's side and stabbed it to death with machetes. The church consecration service ended with the death squeals of the pig, whose blood fed the ground of the new Protestant house of worship. A promise to

God was fulfilled, and a future commitment to God and the officers was made as the pig departed the land of the living.

The notion of sacrifice (*tinuwu'*, Uma; *korban*, Ind.) is invoked routinely by ministers when they urge congregations to be more generous with their donations. At a harvest-time thanksgiving service, one hamlet was scolded for its meager contributions to the church by a schoolteacher named Tama Kola'. He declared that although pagan highlanders made extensive blood sacrifices to achieve farming success, now as Christians they were too stingy to donate a proper share of their rice harvest to the church. He warned them that if they neglected to sacrifice sufficient livestock and part of their poor rice harvest to God now, they should accept their unsatisfactory harvest as a herald of worse things to come. At the same service, Major Isa' read the story of Cain and Abel from Genesis. Afterward, he rhetorically asked the congregation why God rejected Cain's sacrifice but accepted Abel's. He answered that God knew Cain did not have true faith and was not making his sacrifice in earnest. Major Isa' implied that the villagers to whom he was speaking were not making their harvest sacrifices in good faith either. He reminded them that God is the true owner of all fruits of the land, but only requests a tithe of 10 percent. After the service, Major Isa' took out a notebook and recorded all the produce, coffee, and animals delivered to the church by particular givers.

The officers encountered overt resistance from that congregation, whose local sergeant insisted that there were no pigs available to be slaughtered for the church thanksgiving feast, only chickens. The sergeant also claimed that the thirty measuring cans (*blek*) of rice promised beforehand to the officers had been "eaten by mice." Major and Mrs. Isa' were furious, saying this was a gift "without contents." They said that given the villagers' earlier promises, the expected gifts were "already owned by God, not by us anymore, so we are no longer involved." With this pronouncement they suggested an ominous future for the wayward hamlet, which would bear not only their anger, but the wrath of God as well. Sacrifices promised or consecrated in public by Tobaku people no longer remain just symbols from the human realm. They become incontrovertible cogs in the cosmological wheel.

Salvation Army officers, too, feel obliged to carry out their promised animal sacrifices to God. Mrs. Major Isa' declined a request to sell a pig to her older sister, a refusal that ordinarily might be construed as disrespectful to her elder. She explained that this particular pig was already promised to God for a household ceremony as thanks for her husband's recovery from illness, and their recent purchase of a new clove orchard in her husband's home village. Conveniently, perhaps, she was able to refuse a loan through her prior promise to God.

Similarly, Captain Tance was chagrined to discover before Christmas that his only pig was pregnant. He said he had promised it to God for the upcoming feast and now would be forced to kill the fetal pigs along with their mother. When I asked if he couldn't substitute a chicken this once, he said sadly that the promise had already been made and, besides, a chicken just would not do for the Lord's birthday. Promises of animal sacrifices must not be reneged upon or in any way compromised from their original terms. Generally, chickens are dedicated only to smaller agricultural events, while large livestock or wild game is required for major rituals.

During the precolonial period, animals and occasionally humans were sacrificed by repeatedly stabbing the victim with spears or machetes until unconsciousness occurred. At that point, the victim's head was sliced off and presented to the event's sponsor. Salvation Army missionaries report that women would attend with babies, whose hands were placed on the weapons so that they would become brave warriors like their fathers and uncles (Hatcher 1932, 25). The first missionaries insisted that these practices stop, and now animals are slaughtered quickly, although still enthusiastically, by a few direct stabs to the neck or torso.

Among all highlanders, however, livestock are slaughtered only for ritual occasions, never to obtain daily food. The Uma term for sacrifice, *"tinuwu'*," specifically refers to the cutting of animals for ritual feasts, especially when the ceremony is held for a third party's benefit. The only socially sanctioned, nonritual sources of meat are trapping and hunting, although occasionally a ritual reason may be invoked when it is apparent that there is a practical motivation to consume meat, such as when a family member is ill and weak. In Kulawi proper, Salvation Army officers complain about the number of large livestock killed for life-cycle ceremonies. Nevertheless, the missionaries never have managed to stop the association of specially cooked meat and rice feasts with the major agricultural, life-cycle, and curing rituals that are now held under Protestant auspices.

At present, all household or community ceremonies should be carried out, if possible, under the guidance of a Salvation Army officer. This ensures that ritual protocols meet church specifications. For example, the surgery of circumcision is carried out by a village elder, but an officer will read prayers and carefully supervise the elder if there is any chance that "magic" or "invisible power" (*pake'*, Uma) is to be employed.

Protestant missionaries and church leaders have used two methods to enforce ritual changes: demand their elimination or coopt them by providing Christian interpretations and supervising revisions. Some officers still take the initiative to curtail or abolish particular ancestral ceremonies. This is risky, however, because the extent to which locals request officers to participate in events will vary according to their comfort with, and trust of, the officers. If the officers are too harsh in forbidding particular rituals, villagers may perform rites surreptitiously without inviting and paying the officers to lead the ceremonies. Hence, theological and economic negotiation between the Protestant clergy and lay practitioners continues, contributing to varied Protestant practices among different highland villages.

I attended a Christianized planting ceremony in 1988 where a newly assigned Salvation Army officer altered past procedures because he was suspicious that some of the community elders might be using pagan magic or oaths (*pohanga'*) to nature spirits to ensure their crop's

A dawn sermon in the rice gardens where a Salvation Army captain exhorts his congregation to address their planting rituals only to God, 1988.

success. The officers formerly assigned to the community conducted
an annual service to bless the rice seeds and special ornamental and
medicinal plants to be set in each swidden plot. The officers performed
this seed-blessing service in church so that they would not have to travel for many miles to bless over one hundred garden plots.

Although this saved the aging officers the difficulty of individually supervising the planting rites of every household, they encountered
another problem. They became convinced that, after they blessed the
seeds in church, a few of the elders were secretly "blowing" (*motuwui'*)
on the rice seeds, a pre-Christian technique to enhance their potency.
All the officers felt they could do was issue stern admonitions to the
elders and their followers during Sunday church services.

When a new captain replaced the elderly officers, he initially
refused to bless the ornamental and medicinal plants altogether. The
swidden community's council of male elders heard about the captain's
reformist platform. The evening before planting, the senior hamlet
elder, Tama Dona, called a meeting at his house and instructed every-

one not to bring their sacred plants to the Christian blessing ceremony. He joked that the new captain was afraid that they would make magic with the special plants to contact *karampua tampilangi*, one name for the pre-Christian owner(s) of the skies. Early the next morning, however, the captain arrived and informed the group that the service would be held in the fields rather than the church and that the families could bring their special plants along—although he would not give the plants his blessings.

The captain's decision to consecrate the rice seeds in the fields instead of in church allowed him more complete supervision of the villagers' planting procedures. During a prayer service in the mountain fields, he gave a long sermon warning the villagers not to give any more thought to their pre-Christian means of calling the ancestors and deities. In essence, he said, "Don't worship your old gods, worship my God. The ancient procedures and symbols such as the ornamental flowers and woodpiles you may keep as long as you pray first to my God and don't call up your own gods in the pre-Christian way. The ancestors did not know any better, so according to the Bible they will be forgiven. But if you sin with Christian knowledge, God will be angry and take revenge on you."

The captain then pointed to me and my husband as examples of Christians who did not fear evil spirits. To prove his claim, he called attention to the fact that we were the only ones present who traveled through the forest without machetes or other weapons. He claimed (to our surprise) that we carried no knives or weapons because we were more devout in our faith to God. We thought instead that we simply were transient and well-cared-for guests with little need on that day for the standard equipment required to farm and defend oneself in the rainforest.

The next day, when the captain had returned to his main village post, I went to a planting ceremony at another, more isolated mountain site. This event was conducted by Tama Dona, leader of the previous day's planting group. A similar ritual pattern to consecrate the seeds was followed except that the blessing prayer was spoken in Uma to *Pue' Alatala* rather than in Indonesian to *Tuhan*. Also, the special ornamental and medicinal plants were prayed over along with the rice seed. By planting at a distant site, the owners of this field were able to have their land consecrated by a lay elder who, while following general Protestant practice, could pray freely in Uma and speak a blessing more akin to that of the ancestors.

Unlike the previous day, when families showed discomfort at being mistrusted, supervised, and scolded by the Salvation Army officer, those who participated in the second planting ritual maintained that this event represented their true customs, even though their impromptu service followed most of the usual Protestant steps. The use of their own vernacular, its style and tone, plus the leadership of their hamlet elder, a spiritual guide descended from the community founder, provided this group with their tiny pieces of freedom, their Christian "weapons of the weak" (Scott 1985).

Clearly, Protestant rituals in the highlands are still an arena for both public and unspoken negotiations. Although missionaries and Salvation Army officers seek to limit blood sacrifices and turn them into mere symbolic events and commemorative meals, highlanders still view them as effective performative acts. Christianization of highlanders' ritual sacrifices has altered much: the deities invoked, the priests' institutional affiliation, aspects of ritual format, the external doctrines invoked, even the language of invocation. Yet, as this chapter's examples demonstrate, resident ministers' theological and ritual negotiations with congregation members are underlain and constrained by the economics of the ministers' own households. Moreover, the concept that ritual slaughter of precious sacrificial animals is necessary to the effective dialogue with deities through the doors of death has never been shaken. In the next chapter I examine how spoken words leverage the dialogues fulfilled by animal flesh.

ᗖ 7 ᗘ

The Powers of the Word

A Tobaku Salvation Army officer once told me his child heard at school that Islam was superior to Christianity because Muslims hold their services in "God's language" (*bahasa Tuhan*, Ind.) while Christians use only human language (*bahasa manusia*), that is, Indonesian. Captain Silase found it comical that Muslim children thought Arabic was the privileged language of God rather than just a foreign country's language in which an imported religious text was written. The Indonesian schoolchildren's intense concern with the religious efficacy of words, however, was neither foreign nor farcical to the Tobaku religious leader.[1]

The Judeo-Christian-Muslim awe of "the Word" has its parallels in indigenous Central Sulawesi religious practice, although highlanders' momentous words were never written. Like the original words of biblical texts, highlanders' decisive words were spoken—spoken eloquently or spoken imperfectly, spoken in good faith or spoken disingenuously. Any words uttered aloud instantly became contracts with performative repercussions far beyond the control of their human speakers or listeners. These often ritualized verbal genres show what Becker calls "word magic" (Becker 1989, 3), a material efficacy closely associated with ancestral authority. The utterances of this still primarily oral society always are a part of, and speak to, natural forces. Inopportune words may imbalance social and cosmological relationships. Appropriate speech may mend them.

Ritual speech in eastern Indonesia mediates between ancestral order and immediately occurring events. It suggests repetition of the past while constructing present claims for the past and the future (Fox 1974, 1988; Keane 1997a; Kuipers 1990a). The marked formality of ritual speech also "suggests that interaction is often a difficult and agonistic as well as a cooperative and dialogic enterprise" (Keane 1997a, 96). Central Sulawesi oratory does not display the wealth of standardized formulaic couplets that characterizes Lesser Sunda speech. Yet highlanders do appreciate paired lines in certain ritual genres, and they characteristically use one spoken topic—such as clearing new farmland—to refer metaphorically to another—such as seeking a bride. Uma language has a range of terms for "speaking" that focus on different facets of narrators' utterances. Some terms emphasize word content (*mpo'uli'* or *nguli'*), while others emphasize the act of speaking or telling a story (*molibu'* or *mololita*). Differential use of these terms shifts listeners' attention to semantic or performative elements of a speech act.

As mentioned in chapter 2, every community has at least one ritual orator, "the one who speaks" (*topolibu'*), who arrives with betelnut gifts at all formal occasions other than church services. Errors in speech at life-cycle rituals such as weddings were, and still are, decried and even fined. Thus a groom's family invariably hires a speaker to carry their proposals and negotiations to the bride's family. Fluidity of speech, using words that are "smooth" (*roli'*; now also "holy"), is thought to be directly correlated with outcomes. If an orator falters or speaks incorrectly, the desired marriage, harvest, or recovery from illness may not take place. During formal occasions such as weddings, it is considered too risky for the interested parties to speak alone without the mediation of skilled orators.

Public speech and leadership positions have been analyzed in relation to gender roles in "centrist" or cognatic Indonesian societies (Atkinson 1989, 1990; Errington 1990; Keeler 1990; Tsing 1990). A favored theme in Atkinson and Errington's volume is that women who become ritual leaders have not violated the rules, but merely beaten the odds. Women are not socialized to become public leaders and do not have men's vast travel experience, which often serves as the source of males' privileged or sacred knowledge (Errington 1990, 40, 55; Atkinson 1990). This situation also holds in the Tobaku region, where female ritual or political leaders are rare although not unknown.[2]

Aside from the ritual speech of specialists in family alliance negotiations, utterances or song lyrics are presented directly by all highlanders to persuade the unseen powers. These unmediated forms of word use also anticipate an imminent impact upon the cosmos, even in their distinctive Christian form. Tobaku individuals now pray (*berdoa*, Ind.) to God as well as make vows or oaths (*mohanga'*, Uma) to God, just as they formerly made such oaths and bargains with their ancestral deities. They also still utter a variety of curses (*mpototowi, metuna, mehapu, pehoma', metipo', mpotipo'*, Uma) when it is necessary to ask God to pass judgment over a human dispute. Tobaku also voice complaints about other villagers through "testimonials" (*kesaksian*, Ind.) in church as well as gossip or other less spiritual public forums. For religious music, Tobaku mostly sing Indonesian translations of European Protestant hymns instead of the indigenous *raego'* songs largely forbidden by early missionaries. In all these cases, highlanders associate the aesthetics of ritual oratory and song with spiritual efficacy and evidence of divine guidance.

Abram (1996) argues that the contemporary Western dichotomy between humans (including their anthropomorphic gods) and the remainder of the natural world has its roots in the Mediterranean origin and spread of literacy.[3] Abram suggests that human societies moved from "reading" patterns and tracks in the clouds, waters, or earth to creating their own visual signs that early mimicked these natural icons but later departed from them to capture and distance the realm of human words from their nonhuman reflections. Central Sulawesi highlanders are now in that liminal moment where most adults still can "read" the signs of nature—the rats in their fields that signal divine retribution, the mocking laugh of the kingfisher that reveals adultery—yet they also know at least the basics of alphabetic writing and its use in government documents, hymnals, Bibles, and Salvation Army handbooks (e.g., Bala Keselamatan 1981).

Tobaku highlanders have adopted Protestantism wholeheartedly and yet never banished themselves—or, significantly, the Christian God—from the realm of a single interactive cosmos. Although the young learn to read and write Indonesian in school, most speak Uma at home. And Uma is rarely written, despite the best efforts of SIL missionaries over the previous decades. Abram's thesis concerning the effects of literacy on religion implies that missionaries' interest in increasing literacy not only spreads the gospel and economic development, but also creates the necessary cognitive conditions for formerly oral peoples to accept a duality between deities and the remainder of the natural world.

Published materials in Uma are few. Both the Salvation Army and the Indonesian government would prefer that citizens master and use Indonesian, at least for church and government occasions—hence the lack of effort these institutions have made to support literacy in Uma or other Kaili-Pamona languages. The political question becomes whether the Indonesian government and churches will allow smaller ethnic groups to retain their regional languages as primary communicative media, or conversely, whether they will strive to eliminate current preferences for these oral vernaculars. Even if the national government does not intend any Machiavellian language policies, the attrition of local languages continues as an ancillary result of other development programs. Both spontaneous migration and government-promoted transmigration atrophy local languages in favor of Indonesian. Kuipers (1998) describes various other facets of "linguistic marginalization" occurring on the island of Sumba.

This chapter explores how spoken and sung Uma words, which were designed as influential communication with unseen forces, have been reshaped under colonial Christian and recent government policies. Many communications with deities have changed ostensibly from bargains to prayers or thanks, from precolonial ritual speeches to church testimonials, from indigenous ritual songs to Salvation Army hymns and "secular" regional art. Yet in all these cases, the indigenous ontology of words and their presumed spiritual efficacy have been retained despite modifications in their presentation or characterization.

The *raego'* song genre provides a good example of how ritual words used to persuade unseen forces were strongly opposed by the colonial government and early missionaries. These ancestral songs have been replaced not only by Protestant hymns, but also in some villages by revised *raego'* versions proclaimed by the New Order government to be regional art rather than religious worship. The example of *raego'* illuminates how missionaries' suppression of ritual forms was rationalized and executed. It also shows how New Order efforts to elevate nationalism and control ethnic diversity sometimes have been at cross-purposes with church efforts to purge indigenous petitions to ancestral deities. Although the linguistic marginalization by state and church that Kuipers (1998) describes is at work in Central Sulawesi, highlanders are notoriously stubborn in their preference for local vernaculars over Indonesian, for oral over written expression, and for performative word uses that invoke the actions of deity.

Smooth or Holy Words: Promises and Prayers

A pre-Christian Tobaku invocation to the deities that invites comparison to the Christian concept of prayer is *mohanga'*, which means "to vow," and is derived from the root noun *hanga'*, meaning "name." *Mpohanga'* means "to name something [as part of a vow]," "to put under oath," or now, under Christian influence, "to bless." Uma speakers ask unseen spirits or God to help them with a problem such as a sick relative or a poor harvest. An animal sacrifice is carried out immediately as a motivating action, or else a sacrifice is promised for a future time such as the harvest period. The proposed sacrifice must be carried out irrespective of whether the requested outcomes occur, but the person making an oath reminds the deities that the feast will be meager and likely unsatisfying to all if the harvest is insufficient or a household member is too ill to work. These bargains were enunciated within the precolonial genre of *raego'* songs, and I draw on these song texts as the earliest documented examples of bargaining with deities.

Although most Protestant churches now look unfavorably upon words or prayers that overtly try to bargain with God, this is a well-known aspect of historic Christian practice. The Basilica of the Sacred Heart at Montmartre in Paris, for example, was built to fulfill a vow to God made in 1870. At that time, French citizens asked God to deliver France successfully from war with its European neighbors and promised a grand church if they were delivered, which they were. Indeed, the English word "prayer" is derived from the Latin *precarius*, meaning "obtained by begging" and the Latin *precari*, meaning "to entreat." Medieval Catholic and precolonial highlanders' prayers simply and explicitly add a promise of future human actions to their entreaties.

Precolonial highlanders—for example, men preparing to hunt—engaged in other motivating communications with spiritual forces. Some of these messages now are realized as private prayers. In a slumbering household just prior to dawn, I awoke to see Tama Kulu kneeling across the fire pit from my sleeping mat with his hands clasped in Christian prayer position. With no one (except me, unsuspected) awake to listen, he was mumbling an incantation to God, *Pue'*, asking for blessings on his day's plan to hunt and collect wild foods. To my surprise, the prayer ended with the ritualized act of spitting into the hearth, a technique used, among other things, to seal bargains during pre-Christian contacts with deities and ancestors. Because of missionary objections, ritual spitting is now rarely a part of public ritual, but this household event suggested its continued domestic use by some to cap prayers or promises.

Missionaries tried to eliminate ritual spitting for hygienic reasons, and also because, like the verbal formulae of shamans it often accompanied, spitting and blowing during rituals evidenced how highlanders envisioned their own potential to affect unseen forces through inherited techniques of efficacious communication. Dutch missionaries viewed such Indonesian behaviors as a fetishistic misunderstanding of appropriate human communication and agency before the Almighty (Keane 1997b; Pietz 1985).

Most highlanders do not say Christian prayers in a daily routine, but mainly during Protestant services or hazardous times, which evoke the need for additional ritual actions. In 1988, when rains were excessive in the Tobaku highlands, Captain Silase was beseeched to pray publicly so that the storms would cease. Only after he prayed for improved weather during church services for three Sundays in a row did the rains end, but villagers were confident that it was his pronouncement of the "smooth words" in church that finally gained their request.

Highlanders learn a standard set of Salvation Army prayers by heart, usually in Sunday school. These prayers are spoken as rapidly as possible, generally in whispered tones. Those families who do pray before meals ask God's blessing over the food and make requests for help with the day's planned activities. Most often, the father or mother of the family will say the prayer, but sometimes guests, teenagers, or children are assigned the task. I often was at pains to catch words whispered across the table at lightning pace, and I had difficulty praying in such a rapid manner when called upon to do so. I once apologized to a local officer about my unusual verses and relatively slow speed at this task, and he consoled me by saying that Central Sulawesi highlanders enjoy Westerners' style of praying because it is "more deep" (*lebih dalam*, Ind.) than that of Indonesians.

Along this same line of argument, Major Carron complained that she could never teach Central Sulawesi people to improvise their daily prayers in a creative fashion. Rather, she said, they just repeat whatever they have been taught in Sunday school and follow a routine formula for every type of occasion. What Major Carron could not appreciate was the pragmatic nature of eastern Indonesian ritual speech and its idealized identification with ancestral precedents. As with all precolonial arts, ritual speech was aimed toward perfection through the idealized repetition of ancestral models, not individual innovation or originality.

Rapid speed and an unbridled performance are considered indicative of words that emanate from unseen powers, rather than from the less exalted creation of unguided humans. Major Isa' claimed that if his prayers for a sick person emerged fluidly, recovery occurred. If not, the patient likely would die. He said he had seen these results repeated many times throughout his lengthy career as an officer. Major Isa' seemed certain that ancestral evaluations of the efficacy of eloquent verbal performances were equally valid under God.

The importance of ceremonial eloquence is not foreign to European Christian history or to its Jewish and Greek origins. We have only to recall the plight of Roman emperor Claudius, whose unfortunate stutter forced him to begin his incantations over and over until he could complete them in their entirety without imperfection. What is required then for all Salvation Army ministers or elders who wish to make claims of religious authority is the memorization and regurgitation of ritual formulae that then seem to emerge from the mouth naturally, as if directed by unseen forces. The words should appear without any apparent contemplation or personal improvisation; that is, the performance should be "entextualized" (Kuipers 1990a, 7).

The focus on perfect repetition is illustrated also by highlanders' obsession with the hymn "Silent Night" which must be sung repeatedly at every Christmas candle-lighting ceremony. In chapter 1 I emphasized how this Christmas service is a vehicle to highlight contemporary as well as early Christian spiritual and political authority. Here it may be added that it is the memorized words of the hymn, repeated more times than any Western congregation could ever imagine, that lend otherworldly authority, aesthetic perfection, and assumed efficacy to the hierarchy of candle lighters presented to the congregation.

Another distinction between precolonial petitioning practices and those taught in Indonesian by the Protestant churches concerns the custom of saying "please" and "thank you." Congregations now are required and reminded to use words for "please" (*mohon* or *minta*, Ind.) in their prayers and always to say "thank you" (*terima kasih*) to God for their health, crops, meals, and so forth. Yet there are no indigenous words for "please" or "thank you" in Uma or any other Central Sulawesi language. Oaths were uttered directly as requests, and offerings were promised and provided in recompense. Therefore, although the Indonesian words for "please" and "thank you" now are utilized and well understood as verbal ornaments, Tobaku prayers still wrap these recent and inherently empty words around the material solidity of sacrificial offerings to instill efficacy.

Some highlanders suggest that the addition of Salvation Army-style words of prayer will Christianize virtually any pre-Christian endeavor. Tina Abi' says that she knows an ancient ritual to avert the consequences of ancestral anger (*nasesa'*, Uma), but, as a Christian, she always prays to God before reciting the pre-Christian mantra. She notes that the last official shaman of the Tobaku region, Tama Mulu', converted and became an excellent Christian because he, too, always recited a prayer to God before he practiced his ancestral "knowledge" (*pake'*, Uma; *ilmu*, Ind.). This perspective of Tina Abi' evidences not her ignorance of Christian teachings or gospel verses, but rather her confidence in the continued spiritual potency of ancestral, spoken words.

Curses and Other Verbal Invocations of Divine Justice

> Especially, the war-cry but in general other curse-formulas also—born from the emotional sphere—seem to be inspired by the belief that it is possible to switch on the punishing power of a cosmical demand for justice, in which heaven and earth, together with the ancestors as a collectivity, manifest themselves.
>
> Pieter Middelkoop, Curse-Retribution-Enmity as Data in Natural Religion

Several Uma terms designate types of oaths and curses that carry performative weight. Their utterance calls upon deities to enforce ancestral rules of divine justice. The verb *mpototowi* means "to call down a curse on something or someone" (*mengutuk*, Ind.). *Metuna* means "to curse someone with ill fortune by predicting his or her calamitous future." *Mehoma'* is to make an oath or curse in the form of an if-then statement, such as "If my child becomes ill again, your sorcery clearly has done it," or "If that land you farm is really mine, you will die from eating my rice." *Mehapu* is to curse oneself by swearing an oath that says, "May ill fortune befall me if I do not do such and such." *Metipo'* is to invoke ill fortune simply by speaking about it, and *mpotipo'* is to lay a specific curse or hex upon someone else. Missionaries viewed all these attempts to control events through language as subversive of God's unique agency, and they did their best to suppress them. In Central Sulawesi, the Dutch also outlawed the ordeals that formerly were used to test the power of oaths.

Yet despite missionary efforts, Uma curses and oaths still are used by elders who are not able to settle disputes in other ways. Moreover, Tobaku people say that the Christian God defends their ancestral rights to utilize these curses to locate the truth. A village headman named Tama Sori claimed that a beautiful cow possessed by an elderly man really was his. Reportedly, Tama Sori was incorrect in his identification of the cow's ownership. The men argued, and the elderly man finally uttered a curse, saying, "If it is your cow, headman, then it will flourish when you take it. If it is really mine, then it will not live." Tina Abi' said that because the elder's words were heard by God, the cow died quickly once it was in the headman's possession. Then everyone knew who had told the truth.

While righteous outcomes desired by God may be invoked by human utterance, negative outcomes also push suffering individuals to admit publicly their violations of moral laws. For Timor, Middelkoop compares admissions of *adat* transgressions and the Christian concept of confession (Middelkoop 1960, 27). Specifically, Middelkoop describes Timorese confessions of wrongs by women suffering in childbirth, by the severely ill, by men about to engage in hunting or warfare, and by members of a community struck by calamity. In such cases, the Christian notion of verbally confessing sins is equated with the indigenous expectation that transgressions are exposed by divine retribution. Thus admissions of wrongdoing spoken under duress are common in Christian Central Sulawesi.

Tobaku individuals also will protest their innocence in the face of misfortunes to divert the assignment of possible guilt. Captain Silase humorously described local reactions to an unusual and severe hailstorm. When the hail began, villagers ran out of their houses and called loudly up to the sky, "It is not me, Lord, who has committed the sin!" The officer chuckled over his seemingly cowardly congregation, commenting, "Really now, which one of us has not committed a sin?"

Local ministers, too, however, seek to formulate narratives of divine justice that cast themselves in the most favorable light. One time while I was traveling through the mountains with Major Isa' and Bima, his deaf-mute assistant, there was a near disaster as we crossed a hanging bridge. Precolonial bridges over rivers in Central Sulawesi were constructed cleverly from interwoven rattan strands, giving the overall appearance of a spider-web tunnel. The few bridges that remain now are open at the top, and the rattan sometimes is reinforced with metal wires and wooden planks to make them sturdy enough to allow small horses to cross in single file. In principle, residents of the nearest hamlet should take care of bridge maintenance, but repairs often are neglected until accidents occur.

On the occasion in question, the bridge seemed rickety, so the packhorse was relieved of its saddlebags before being led across the bridge. Then Major Isa', Bima, and I carried our baggage across the bridge on foot. When this was done, I waited on the far side as Major Isa' and Bima returned to fetch the horse and lead it over the bridge. About halfway across, one, then two, of the horse's rear legs fell between the bridge's open slats. As the trapped horse began to neigh and struggle in panic, I realized the gravity of the situation. The horse's violent movements could tear the bridge's rattan suspension cables loose, dropping both horse and men onto the boulders protruding from the swiftly flowing river below.

I glanced around for my camera to capture this incredible image, but then chastised myself for the thought, knowing that I might be needed immediately for life-saving assistance. Although it seemed perilous to add my weight to the shaking bridge, I began to walk slowly toward the shouting men and horse swaying wildly at the bridge's center. Suddenly and amazingly, Major Isa' and Bima were able to push the horse's rump up to where the animal could pull its legs back onto the bridge's planks. Once we crossed to the far bank, we proceeded on our journey, extremely thankful for our safety.

The next morning, during Sunday services, Major Isa' retold the tale of our precarious bridge adventure. To my astonishment, I became the heroine of his story. Major Isa' recounted how the prayers that Dei' Ngea' (White or Gleaming Daughter, one of the local names I received) spoke at the side of the bridge had made the rear end of the horse suddenly so light that he and Bima (both slight men even by local standards) could effortlessly lift the flailing beast to safety. The post facto nature of the officer's rationale was not unusual for Central Sulawesi moral assessments, but the invocation of myself as a bearer of some unusual Christian power was disconcerting. My cameo presence at an averted disaster was used to convey an image of God's special blessing on the Salvation Army officer who temporarily hosted me, another Western angel of the forest. Instead of considering what transgression had caused the bridge accident, Major Isa' emphasized good fortune: our escape through Christian salvation. His words resonated with Major Carron's proclamation that "in the Salvation Army we have no problems, only challenges." The tale of Major Isa', in its optimistic and thankful elements, precisely suited the Salvation Army genre of "witnessing," or testimonials.

Church Testimonials, or Witnessing

The Salvation Army church event that demands the most personal participation is the practice of witnessing or testifying (*kesaksian*, Ind.). During every Sunday service, congregation members are called upon to testify to the greatness of the Lord. Given local ideals regarding smooth words in ritual presentations, most people, especially women and youths, say they are too shy or embarrassed to stand up and give such a speech from the pulpit. Church leaders, however, persist in their requests until congregation members "volunteer."

Village leaders associated with the church, government, or schools are most apt to proffer the initial testimonials at any service, providing models for the rest of the congregation. Thus an old association between village leadership and performative oratory, usually by men, is continued within the Salvation Army framework. Usually the presiding minister contacts one or two church or village leaders in advance to solicit and plan their testimonials. If no individuals volunteer to testify, the officers resort to drafting unprepared audience members. Foreign guests or visiting Salvation Army staff can expect to be nominated.

Ministers also select villagers who they believe have cause to open their hearts in front of the congregation. Such uncomfortable pressure to discuss domestic matters publicly leads some villagers to hide at the back of the church, or avoid Sunday services altogether. Tina Pangana uncharacteristically refrained from attending church when she learned that a visiting officer planned to call her to testify about her daughter, who had become pregnant by a coastal Muslim youth. The minister hoped Tina Pangana would discuss the misfortune openly in church and thereby receive pressure to prevent her daughter from marrying the Muslim. Tina Pangana, however, thought that the marriage, although not ideal, should take place to legitimize her daughter's child, and she did not wish to bear additional community opprobrium.

For those who do consent to present testimonials, the narrative formula employed moves predictably. The speaker draws upon events of the recent past and vividly describes a personal experience that incited fear or pain. The speaker then tells how God either brought the experience to a positive outcome or at least strengthened the speaker to endure the inordinate difficulty. The narrative ends with praise for God or Jesus and confirmation of the speaker's wholehearted faith in God. Within the framework of this formula, Tobaku residents still find potential for adopting a political stance, making moral accusations, venting sorrows to gain pity, or enacting some of the ancestral oaths that invoke retribution.

On a Sunday following two funerals, a father whose unmarried daughter died prematurely rose in church to thank all who took time from their harvest work to assist with his daughter's funeral. He told of the pain of his family's loss and thanked God for seeing them through their troubled time. This was an exemplary local testimonial. A Salvation Army sergeant then rose and spoke in a different tone regarding the second recent death, that of an elderly woman of distinguished pedigree. He scolded the congregation for not helping enough at the time of their "grandmother's death." He said that people just sat around and ate the family's food when they should have been helping to carry the coffin and attending the Christian service at the graveyard. He concluded by saying, "It is not the elders who call us to the ceremony of mourning, but rather the dead who call us" (*Bukan orang tua yang panggil kita ke pesta kedukaan, tapi orang mati yang panggil kita*, Ind.). With these words, he voiced a warning and insinuated a curse of ancestral misfortune (*nasesa'*, Uma) from within the speech genre of the Salvation Army testimonial.

At least one of the three to four testimonials presented each week is planned and performed by the ministers or their assistants according to approved Salvation Army Church standards. Ministers' efforts to persuade particular people to volunteer allow the church leaders to emphasize community issues of their own choosing. Spontaneously volunteered testimonials, however, can become unpredictable as villagers occasionally get on soapboxes about issues that the ministers do not think are appropriate. Major and Mrs. Isa' would cringe with discomfort as the somewhat deranged son of a village founder would regularly volunteer to testify, usually about the sins that were leading his father on the path to the Christian hell (*neraka*, Ind.). In point of fact, the son's opinions about his father's activities often coincided with official Salvation Army pronouncements, such as the prohibition against drinking alcohol. Nevertheless, public chiding of fathers by sons is not appreciated by highland villagers or even by the ministers themselves. Despite biblical injunctions to the contrary, Tobaku and other Indonesians are not socialized to criticize their parents, especially in public.

Dissatisfied congregation members also use testimonials to critique village headmen or Salvation Army officers indirectly. The testimonial genre, although designed by Europeans and adapted by local ministers to praise God in the most pat and Panglossian way, sometimes serves as a vehicle to express local discontent. No matter to what end these testimonials are put, however, they are considered — like all ancestral ritual speech — to be cosmologically effective injunctions to call down deserved future blessings or wrath.

Precolonial Raego' Songs and Dances

[T]he *moraego* is begun by the men with verses in which the girls are invited to participate in the round dance. . . . Once the women are inside the circle, then it becomes *raego*, and they sing with the men. One of the men starts a line, and as soon as his comrades have recognized it, they sing along, and now the women also join in and sing together with the men. The song is interrupted repeatedly with loud cries, such as ihihi hihi hi jo hijo-hijo, during which there is stamping on the ground with the right foot, while the elbow of the right arm is thrust forward horizontally, and afterwards the whole arm is stretched out, so that the hand points directly toward the face of the women. Then the line just sung is taken up again, or a new one is begun.

N. *Adriani and A. C. Kruyt,* The East Toradja of Central Celebes

Words presented publicly to the precolonial deities and ancestors were uttered primarily by the community leaders (*maradika*) and shamans (*tobalia*), who were prepared for the risks involved in communicating with unseen forces. Other names for the shaman were "the one who speaks" (*topouli'*), "the one who recites spells" (*topogane'*), and "the one who performs the *raego'*" (*toporaego'*). Matching songs and circle dances generically called *raego'* in the colonial literature were performed at life-cycle and calendrical rituals in many regions of Central Sulawesi. Many of the song lyrics were esoteric, understood mainly by the shamans even during their active performance during the precolonial era (Aragon 1996c). The verses, sung in counterpoint by male and female choruses with respective solo leaders, were contoured to the type of ritual held and the specific occasion at which they were performed. The shamans orchestrated the singing of these texts and introduced event-specific lyrics. Other adults familiar with the genre followed along by imitation.

Although circle dances are widespread in Sulawesi and neighboring islands, the genre called "*raego'*" is known primarily from western Central Sulawesi.[4] In precolonial times, the dances and companion songs were performed throughout the night—often over the course of many nights or even weeks—in association with most agricultural, warfare, curing, and life-cycle rituals that occurred between the dry-rice harvest and the seed planting for the following year. Early Dutch colonial officials and Protestant missionaries found these coed circle dances and songs sufficiently disruptive, licentious, and idolatrous that they sought their suppression and ultimate abolition.

Examination of colonial-era *raego'* texts transcribed in Uma demonstrates that most songs were religious chants that borrowed linguistic terms from different ethnic regions to increase their ritual effectiveness. These songs were suppressed by the Dutch state and missions, but later were resurrected and revised for New Order government and church purposes. In essence, the songs retained their potential spiritual powers while the religious and political institutions around them altered and conspired against one another for control of this potent verbal medium.

European photographs taken in the 1920s and 1930s reveal one of the features of the dance to which Protestant missionaries objected: close physical contact between men and women. Even in the late 1980s, Major Carron spoke about "those dances connected with immorality." Her comments concerned not only the arm-around-shoulder position of adjacent couples, but also the dance's role in pre-colonial men's courtship of first and additional wives. When polygynous marriages occurred, they usually were made with a wife's younger sister or maternal cousin who had shared farmland and houses from birth. Married women did not dance the *raego'*, although they and their young children were audience to these public events. In fact, wives participated in the choice and invitation of their husbands' dance partners. The *raego'* songs and dances were ritual procedures, among other things, to augment the agricultural and human fertility of highland families.

Adriani and Kruyt emphasize the flirtatiousness of the songs, writing that

> The content of the verses sung is in the first place mutual courting, expressions of amorousness, desire, jealousy, admiration, and infatuation. Other lines contain an invitation, still others express joy, some have a mocking character. There are also not a few moraego lines that are part of the occasional poetry. (Adriani and Kruyt 1968 [1950], 3:586; Adriani and Kruyt 1950, 3:396)

Not all *raego'* songs were oriented toward courtship activities. Rather, like other ritual speech forms in eastern Indonesia (Coville 1988; Fox 1988; George 1996; Kuipers 1990a; Traube 1986), the songs served more generally as performative elements of religious rituals, and as hallowed words that had binding effects on human and deity relations. Some types of *raego'*, for example, entailed trance-like chanting aimed to cure the ill. Foreign missionaries, however, focused particularly on what they considered the lascivious and idolatrous aspects of the *raego'* song and dance genre.

Both the Dutch colonial government and Protestant missionaries sought to reduce or eliminate *raego'* performances, although their primary motives for doing so differed. Kaudern reported that when he visited the Kulawi region in 1918, the colonial government "for the benefit of more useful work" had passed an ordinance that *raego'* performances were to be limited to once a week (Kaudern 1929, 383–384). He noted that the highlanders eluded this attempt to increase their agricultural productivity and decrease their leisure-time activities by creating a staggered schedule for the *raego'* rituals. By this ruse, *raego'* was sung and danced in a certain village on one night and then performed again the following night at the nearest neighboring village—and so on throughout the nearby communities until the festivities could cycle back to the first village after the seven-day interval specified by the Dutch decree.

Missionaries agreed with Dutch government officials that the *raego'* dances promoted the sin of idleness. Yet they were more concerned about other moral issues. To prohibit the practice of *raego'* on religious grounds, missionaries needed to justify its wickedness in European Christian terms. They did this first on the basis of their initial physical perceptions, what their eyes told them that the highlanders' bodies were doing during the *raego'* dances—namely, creating the conditions for illicit and immoral sex. Second, Dutch missionaries worked to comprehend the regional languages so they could understand the song texts. Some then saw reasons to forbid *raego'* songs on the basis of their interpretation of the lyrics.

The first European missionaries and scholars working in the highlands debated among themselves whether the *raego'* dances and songs indeed held a religious component or were mere secular entertainment. The missionary-linguist Adriani concluded that *raego'* was principally a playful art or pastime associated with the courtship of youth (Adriani and Kruyt 1912, 3:607; Adriani 1915, 333). Adriani wrote that "nothing of any of the religious significance that the moraego might ever have had is left anymore now, either in the form or the content of what is sung or in the memory of the generations now living" (Adriani and Kruyt 1968 [1950], 3:584; 1950, 3:394–395)

The naturalist Kaudern (1929, 417) and the Dutch Reformed missionary Ten Kate (1915) disagreed with Adriani and suggested a greater religious significance for the songs. Kaudern interpreted the taboos and prescriptions surrounding *raego'* performances as evidence that at least some types of *raego'* were spiritually potent. Kaudern also pointed to Adriani's finding that "there are songs that the natives themselves do not understand and cannot explain" (Kaudern 1929, 417). That this is true today is not surprising because *raego'* songs are no longer widely and regularly performed. Nevertheless, the fact that the meaning of many *raego'* songs was described as opaque at a time when they were sung weekly or even daily (Kaudern 1929, 383–384) suggests another social and religious aspect of the *raego'* texts, namely their inherently esoteric nature.

A 1970s Indonesian publication on the cultural traditions of Kulawi lists fourteen named types of *raego'* songs. These were performed at different kinds of ritual events such as harvest, puberty, engagement, marriage, death, warfare, and the construction of new houses (Soelarto and Albiladiyah, n.d.) Six Uma language texts that the Dutch missionary-linguist Esser collected in the Pipikoro area circa 1940 represent examples of five of these song types. Although Esser was the major linguist of the Uma language at that time and was able to write a grammar of the language and translate many folktales, he never prepared a translation of his own *raego'* song transcriptions because of the difficulty of the "priestly speech" (Noorduyn 1964, ix).[5]

Below are twelve lines that open one Uma harvest song (*raego' wunca*) transcribed from Esser's handwritten manuscript, followed by my free English translation.[6]

1. *Inepa merue ntaliku' muli*
2. *Eimo ngkuparata kalompe' lara*
3. *Pogingkiko tumpu tana' ngkiporaego'*
4. *Tumpu lore ine mempokadua*

5. *To i lore ine mengkatirema*
6. *Kamai mate nteteka oni*
7. *Kuwoiwako santeke lele*
8. *Pangale apa kawe ntonuma*
9. *Lawi' kami mpinolilika bonea*
10. *Kuliuwako oni tonci wori'*
11. *Raliwomoko rampa konia'*
12. *Polele lako mbabotu' oni*

1. Do not request anything more from my offspring;
2. This I say goodheartedly.
3. Step aside, owner(s) of the land, we intend to perform the *raego'*.
4. Lord(s) of the mountains, do not cause us illness;
5. Creature(s) of the mountains, do not eat our crops;
6. Come kill the wicked omens of the cuckoo bird.
7. I bring their foreboding news to your attention.
8. Which virgin forest will beckon us, and when?
9. Now only we humans circle the swidden gardens,
10. And I elude the evil omens of many forest noises.
11. We already plan for you to feast on our food offerings;
12. Spread that good news and block those bad omens.

A translation of these few lines of one harvest song indicates that Kaudern and Ten Kate were correct in positing a spiritual significance to some *raego'* songs. In the text above, the singers inform the spirits of the land that the community has provided them with ample food offerings at this harvest feast. These offerings should satisfy the deities and constrain them from retaliating against either the feast sponsors or their descendants. The singers petition the spirits to rid the area of evil omen birds, which herald poor harvests in the future. The singers then promise more offerings if food resources are ample for the living. Finally, they ask the spirits to circulate this message among themselves and cooperate by curtailing further ominous signs in the forest.

One element not apparent in the English translation of the *raego'* text is the number of non-Uma words, even whole lines, that are incorporated into the verses transcribed by Esser. Many of the words in Esser's transcribed "Uma" song lyrics are drawn from the neighboring Moma, Kaili, or even Bada' languages.[7] As Feld notes, the borrowing of foreign terms in religious speech "serves to force a stratification of interpretive knowledge, since familiarity with the borrowed forms is not the same for all users and listeners" (Feld 1990, 140). Thus the Uma and other regional *raego'* forms provide additional evidence of regional fraternization and its pragmatic association with internal community stratification.

Tambiah characterizes esoteric ritual speech as disjunct from secular speech in that it is "broadcast but not understood" by the general populace (Tambiah 1968, 179). Scholars of Indonesia have noted the importance of Sanskrit and Arabic elements that are incorporated into formal Javanese and Malay, just as Latin was borrowed in European languages for ritual use in the Middle Ages (Geertz 1960; Gonda 1973; P. M. Taylor 1988, 429). Words borrowed from Kaili and other regional languages similarly held a prestige status marking cosmopolitan erudition in certain Uma ritual contexts.

In the case of the Wana people of Central Sulawesi, Atkinson writes that the Islamic words incorporated into shamans' spells are not viewed locally as "cultural borrowings, but as an integral and potent part of Wana magic" (Atkinson 1989, 64). Thus the *raego'* texts' obscurity signified their otherworldliness and potential efficacy. This same process of lexical borrowing, which Fox calls "dialect semantics," is an effective linguistic technique for achieving poetic parallelism through the expansion of synonym forms (Fox 1971; 1974, 80–83).

Foreign words are not the only basis for the opaqueness of the early *raego'* texts. When I discussed the songs transcribed by Esser with Uma adults fluent in the dialects from which some lines are borrowed, they still faltered at the meaning of most Uma lines. Many of the Uma words employed are archaic and obsolete. Moreover, even familiar Uma words are juxtaposed in such a way as to make phrase meanings vague or ambiguous. I was able to pursue possible meanings of the song texts only with the aid of a rapidly disappearing generation of elders who had danced and sung the *raego'* in their youth or were raised by pre-Christian ritual leaders.

Although Dutch missionaries and linguists working in Central Sulawesi never completely understood the *raego'* texts, some could discern references to pre-Christian deities (such as *tumpu tana'*, owner of the land) who they supposed, quite correctly, were being called to the ceremony to receive offerings. More to the point, they knew that the ritual events to which the songs and dances were tied were antithetical to the church services that they hoped to establish in their place. Eventually, European missionaries urged converted communities to eschew *raego'* songs and dances altogether. By the 1970s, all performances of *raego'* songs or dances were forbidden in the Christian villages where I conducted most of my fieldwork, although some versions were performed sporadically in outlying hamlets where the supervision of world religious leaders was less comprehensive.

The obscurity of precolonial *raego'* lyrics and their creation by shamans undoubtedly aided Protestant leaders in fomenting the genre's alteration or demise. As the majority of community members were little involved in constructing, preserving, or leading the performances, only indigenous leaders and shamans needed to be targeted for control in campaigns to eliminate performances and even memories of the genre's earlier details. The opaqueness or ambiguity of *raego'* lyrics to the general public, however, not only aided the genre's suppression by early world religious leaders, but also made it easier to revive the songs and dances in new forms once New Order political and religious leaders found it acceptable or expedient to do so.

Revivals of the Raego' Genre and Other "Regional Arts"

In the decades since Adriani and Kruyt spoke of *raego'* as the "national dance" of Central Sulawesi, this formerly ubiquitous genre has been marginalized much as the *tayuban* has in Java (Adriani and Kruyt 1968 [1950], 3:583; Hefner 1987b; Hughes-Freeland 1990), and for many of the same causes. What were once mainstream performances associated with precolonial religious rites, social hierarchy, and community fertility have become largely taboo for contemporary religious and political reasons. In Central Sulawesi, recent performances of *raego'* have been manipulated by government leaders, churches, and rural communities of several ethnic groups to make varied statements about ancient history, cultural continuity, religious identity, and regional autonomy. This situation is part of the Indonesian state's and religious leaders' efforts to deny the ideological aspects of cultural arts while simultaneously using them for political consolidation (cf. George 1998, 695).

The changing relationship of authority, ritual performance, and religious thinking in Central Sulawesi can be analyzed by comparing data from colonial-era *raego'* song texts and records with recent oral narratives and observations of revised *raego'* performances from both coastal Muslim and highland Christian regions. During the 1980s and 1990s, songs from this genre were altered in radically different directions for performance in various ethnic and religious strongholds of Central Sulawesi. Although twentieth-century religious and political authorities have endeavored with some success to suppress and coopt the *raego'*, their continued occasional performance allows local people to renegotiate their relationship with ancestral cosmological ideas as they struggle to retain control over their indigenous ritual practices, bodily expressions, aesthetic presentations, and prosody.

Musical "revivals" usually are not the resurrection of truly dead customs, nor do the so-called revivals necessarily bear much resemblance to earlier musical forms with which they are historically associated (Slobin 1983, 37). Rather, a group's past presents "a synchronic pool of source material" from which motivated individuals, often outsiders, can adapt genre elements to fit new images of a community's ethnic past and future (Slobin 1983, 40). The reuse of remembered musical and performance elements to create recent forms of Central Sulawesi *raego'* songs and dances exemplifies such an inventive process.

Following Indonesia's independence in 1945, the religious and political contexts for manipulation of *raego'* songs and dances changed markedly. The question was no longer if the genre thwarted Protestantism or Islam because all Central Sulawesi communities had been, or rapidly were being, swept toward conversion to one or the other of these two world religions. The question became one of religious leaders' assessments about the acceptability of *raego'* songs and dances in a coopted form.

The New Order government sought to promulgate national concepts of "art" (*kesenian*, Ind.) and "tradition" (*adat*) that could be divorced from the domain of "world religion" (*agama*). Just as monotheistic religions should reach throughout the archipelago on a national scale, by the 1970s there was government interest in monitoring, and if necessary engendering, regional arts and traditions that innocuously supported the national motto of "Unity in Diversity" (*Bhinneka Tunggal Ika*, Sanskrit).

Beginning with the Republic's first constitutional committees of 1945, Indonesian government documents have vacillated about whether indigenous regional arts and cultures are the foundation and continuing source of Indonesian national culture, or whether national art and culture must be created anew by the government to replace the former heterogeneity found in the archipelago (Yampolsky 1995). The ambivalence, or more accurately the combination, of these policies may be observed in the Central Sulawesi cases where *raego'* performers are enlisted and supported yet retrained to make their songs, costumes, and movements conform to national goals of regional art performances.

As many scholars have noted, the Indonesian promotion of regional arts appears designed to generate "the impression that ethnicity is a relatively simple aesthetic matter of regional and spatial variations rather than a matter of deep emotional or political attachments" (Kuipers 1993, 100). This "politics of culture" is illustrated famously by President and Mrs. Suharto's 1970s construction of the Beautiful Indonesia in Miniature theme park (Taman Mini "Indonesia Indah") in Jakarta. In the theme park's displays, each province and its ethnic groups are represented uniformly and ahistorically by "traditional" costume and house exhibits that seem to define and encapsulate the essence of ethnicity and superficial cultural differences (Kipp 1993, 110–113; Pemberton 1994, 152–161; Siegel 1997, 3–6).

In the shadow of these religious and political changes, Central Sulawesi communities have been involved in local negotiations about how to maintain their individual ethnic and cosmological identities while also becoming part of the national citizenry as "modern" Indonesians affiliated with either the Christian or Muslim faith. Once again, regional arts such as the *raego'* songs and dances have carried symbolic weight in defining local attitudes toward ethnic differences, religious compromises, political autonomy, and participation in national development schemes (Aragon 1994, 73–74).

In the 1980s I observed a variety of *raego'* performances held sporadically in highland Christian and lowland Muslim areas (Aragon 1996c). After almost two years of fieldwork in the Protestant highlands, I first heard a *raego'* song only in 1987. It was a harvest song blaring from a portable audiotape player in a house near where I was residing. I soon found a group of villagers clustered in the dark around one of the few cassette players in the village. Men, women, and children were listening intently to these rarely heard songs. The recording had been made by household members who just had returned from visiting Muslim relatives in a distant Uma-speaking village where a "traditional," or precolonial-style, harvest festival still was celebrated.

My discussion of the taped music with Mrs. Major Isa' led her to arrange a second performance of the same type of *raego'* song for my benefit. She and I already were scheduled to visit another village for a post-harvest thanksgiving ceremony. After the church service, Mrs.

Major Isa' cajoled four men and two women to sing a harvest song for the purpose of recording "ancient history." She instructed the elders to sit in rows on benches, as if the *raego'* dances rather than the songs were the offending aspect to her Protestant sensibilities.

The women involved acted particularly embarrassed. They had not sung *raego'* songs in roughly forty years because women did not perform this genre after marriage. The village spectators, however, showed great excitement over the tentative musical presentation. Even Mrs. Major Isa' said afterward that the performance brought tears to her eyes because it evoked strong memories of her deceased parents and grandparents, who had sung *raego'* when she was a child.

Overhearing the taped harvest song being played privately in a Christian village where it was not allowed and hearing reactions to the song supervised by the Salvation Army officer indicated that *raego'* still was symbolically and emotionally a part of Tobaku verbal practice even if it was not permitted as an acceptable Protestant ritual genre. In the Uma-speaking highlands, these occasional performances—even as "dance-less songs"—trigger aesthetic pleasure, spiritual intrigue, and recollections of ancestral cosmology. They remain as a subaltern pattern of ritual word use that exists in shadowy counterpoint to the routine Protestant hymns and services.

Raego' also has surfaced in larger population centers in the form of elaborate, staged revivals that proclaim local politicians' ancestral glory and the Indonesian government's control of regional arts. When local performance genres are sponsored or regulated by government supervision, the Indonesian administration thereby manipulates public discourse and definition of what qualifies as official "regional art" (*kesenian daerah*, Ind.). The political organization of such performances also makes claims about what is supposedly "authentic" or original (*asli*) custom for each region, just as the exhibits at the Beautiful Indonesia in Miniature theme park do.

The Western creation of "authentic primitive art" or "tribal art" has been the subject of incisive scholarship in recent years (Clifford

1988; Errington 1994; Price 1989). Many of the same arguments about art by appropriation rather than intention can be applied to the New Order Indonesian government's selection and classification of "traditional regional art" (Aragon 1999b). Just as Errington argues that what qualifies in the West as "High Primitive Art" is that which bears the closest resemblance to Western modern art (Errington 1994, 215–220), so I suggest that Java-oriented government officials seek regional performances that most closely match Javanese (or Balinese) forms classified as "High Art," which in turn are evaluated according to their formal parallels with Western performance art genres.

By the early 1980s, each Indonesian province was expected to demonstrate its "authentic" native dances, and given the absence of many other options, *raego'* was selected as a regional representative from Central Sulawesi. A series of contests was held in the province to determine which performances from which villages could be videotaped effectively and compete regionally and then nationally in contests judged in Jakarta.

In 1981, *raego'* was danced and sung at a wedding that was staged in Kulawi for a television program produced by the North Sulawesi television station in Manado (Acciaioli 1985 and personal communication). An elite (*maradika*) wedding, with *raego'* songs and dances oriented in a straight line for the television cameras, was chosen by the provincial Department of Education and Culture to represent the "traditional" arts of Central Sulawesi.

This type of contrived spectacle is what Acciaioli (1985) has called "Culture as Art," the government-manipulated performance of cultural presentation. "Regional diversity is valued, honoured, even apotheosized, but only as long as it remains at the level of display, not belief, performance, not enactment" (Acciaioli 1985, 161). Despite the sense of irony with which anthropologists and perhaps some locals may have viewed this staged presentation of *raego'*, I heard from Protestant missionaries several years later that the event disturbed them. They considered the rituals' Muslim sponsors as hindrances in their efforts

A chaperoned school group in Kulawi singing and dancing a revised form of *raego'* in a straight line, 1993.

to move the locals' Protestant faith toward greater orthodoxy. Although the Kulawi District is largely Protestant, many recent political leaders have been Muslims who became brokers of native "traditions" as they cooperated with provincial and national officials to define and control public images of regional arts and culture (*kebudayaan*, Ind.).

The objections by Protestant ministers notwithstanding, a coed *raego'* song and dance group was established circa 1991 in one of the Kulawi-area junior high schools. Music, lyrics, and performance techniques were taught by a male elder, and the Muslim headman's wife and female relatives became adult chaperons for the teenage group. This was to ensure decorum among the young male and female dancers. The elder women, like the teenage singers and dancers, don neotraditional ceremonial costumes and participate on stage as silent witnesses to the performances' social propriety and intended authenticity. When I observed one of their rehearsals in 1993, I was assured that they were preserving the ancestral form of Moma-language *raego'* songs.

Some concessions were being made, however, in the interest of winning regional performing arts contests. Once again, the Kulawi singers and dancers were instructed to perform *raego'* facing forward in a straight line for the ease of photography and television recording. The youths did not know how to perform *raego'* in rotating concentric circles. The teenagers also were instructed to sing and dance in a measured, disciplined fashion that contrasted with the zesty and exuberant performances by elders I had witnessed in neighboring Kaili regions.

Song lines performed by Uma and Kaili elders are characterized by voices dropping in and out as well as by the frequent use of rubato, deviating from the main tempo. Kaili elders said that when *raego'* songs and dances became out of control, such that girls or members of the nobility were caused to stumble or even be knocked over by the vigor of neighboring performers, that was an auspicious omen for the community's future. No such roguish behavior or ritualized cosmological disorder was permitted in the Kulawi school group's rendition. Those dances were revised to uphold the standards of sobriety and modesty prescribed for all regional arts by contemporary New Order policies (cf. Yampolsky 1995, 711).

Another type of transformed *raego'* song that I observed was performed in 1987 by Protestants in the North Pamona District near Lake Poso. These songs were designed for a fortieth anniversary celebration by the local Dutch Reformed Church. A church elder was teaching revised Protestant *raego'* songs to men and women standing in line, in separate rows, as if they were in the Sunday church chorus. During practices, the elder and a local schoolteacher took turns standing before the group at a blackboard, drilling the pupils with the revised song lyrics and melodies.

The village elder was commissioned to rewrite Pamona-language *raego'* lyrics to praise the Protestant church and local ministers. At the rehearsal I attended, one line was rewritten because the parish minister thought that new verses describing the church as "a ship sailing in the wind" did not present a strong enough image of the church's spiritual direction.

The *raego'* performed in the Pamona District was "Christianized" not only through its revisionist lyrics, but musically as well. It included an instrumental introduction redolent of Manadonese Christian pop music (*kolintang*) and a diatonic style of choral singing that clearly was influenced by church hymn singing. There is always a tension in Central Sulawesi Christian hymn singing between the codes of European song styles, which include diatonic scales and unison choruses, and the patterns of indigenous song styles. The latter are contrapuntal, not diatonic, and choral leaders begin melodic lines as solo voices that are joined by other singers in a staggered fashion. Western visitors or missionaries often comment that Central Sulawesi congregations sing "off key" and begin hesitantly, supposedly displaying their poor sense of pitch and timing. To eliminate these "problems," the Pamona men and women sang the same musical lines in unison, unlike the polyphonic coed performances I heard in other Central Sulawesi regions.

Versions of the post-harvest *raego'* that were closer to precolonial forms in terms of lyrics, music, and ritual context were performed on several occasions about a year later (in 1988) in a Muslim Kaili region. Several villages mounted harvest festivals (*mobalia mowunca*, Uma)*,* and about ten elder men sang at each performance. Young unmarried girls, reportedly their partners' close relatives, danced silently in the female positions.

Supported by regional government officials, one Kaili village even built a new precolonial-style temple (*baruga*, Kaili) and performed a set of ancestral rituals that reportedly had not been carried out for forty years. As stated in the festival's official program, the rituals performed included "The Smearing of Chicken Blood on the Columns of the Temple," "The Feeding of the Ancestors in the Temple," "The Shamans' Dance to Elevate the Nobles," "The Feeding of the Land Spirits," and "The Traditional Harvest Dance," that is, the *raego' wunca*.

Given my experiences in the puritan Protestant highlands, I was amazed that such rites were being permitted by local government and Muslim leaders. I was the only foreign visitor in the audience, so clearly these rituals were not just a show for tourists but were designed to impress a Kaili audience. An official from the Department of Education and Culture explained to me that the community wished to build a full-sized model temple while an elder who knew the architecture was still alive. She added that the purpose of the event was to introduce the traditions of the biggest kingdom in Central Sulawesi, Sigi, to wider public recognition and to provide recreation (*hiburan*, Ind.) for the local residents. She said that Muslim officials in the Department of Religion (Departemen Agama) understood that this was just "ordinary or secular tradition (*adat biasa*) because people do not believe in the old spirits anymore." Her comment made explicit the recent cognitive separation between ideas of world religion and secular performances of customs based upon ancestral rituals. In this way, the Indonesian government was able to rationalize the concomitant promotion of world religion to appease fervent Muslims and foster development festooned with "traditional" arts to manage regional ethnic differences and potential tensions.

The two days of Kaili events showcased speeches by provincial government leaders emphasizing their ancestral ties to the Sigi kingdom. In fact, many of the regional politicians in attendance were related to descendants of the last colonial raja of the Sigi kingdom. Through their speeches, modern politicians drew authority from ancestral founders while the direct descendants of ancestral rulers maintained their continuing sacred relevance to political affairs. This symbiotic relationship between the old and new political powers of western Central Sulawesi parallels on a regional scale the efforts by President and Mrs. Suharto to trace their connections to the Surakarta kingdom of central Java. In both cases, the secular politicians of the present cloak their distant associations to ancestral grandeur in the pomp of "traditional" performances that carry a spiritual weight of authority (Pemberton 1994).

Both evenings of the two-day Kaili festival included danced performances of *raego'*. A transvestite shaman (*bayasa*) entered into a trance, and an official used a portable loudspeaker to explain obscure details of these purportedly ancient traditions to the crowd. This was a government-supervised performance, but it also struck me as the only possible resurrection of pre-Muslim Kaili rituals that usually lie dormant, much as pre-Christian ones do in the highlands. Although suppressed by missionaries, the rituals are kept vital through their connection to an ancestral cosmology informally taught by elders. Revised versions of precolonial rites are mounted whenever there is an opportune occasion, even under contrived circumstances. In essence, the sponsoring institutions come and go, but the sacred words and performance patterns retain vigor for popular use.

Official disclaimers noted that these Kaili rituals were only historical and entertaining performances. Yet a founding village family seized the occasion to stage privately a long-eliminated rite (*nabau*) involving a buffalo sacrifice to bless their household. Moreover, one local government official commented, "For forty years now Palu Valley has been far too dry, and only this year, when many *raego'* dances were performed, was the rainfall sufficient to grow good crops." Another government official mentioned that Kaili people often complained when they saw songs and dances from other regions on television, while they formerly were forbidden by Muslim authorities to perform their own rites. Clearly, *raego'* still retained its performative efficacy and legitimacy in local eyes.

Even revised ritual performances can be risky for a government trying to juggle the establishment of monotheism with the promotion of regional arts. The cooptation of ancestral rituals has the potential to result in the reactivation or uncontrolled reconstitution, rather than the elimination, of the religious concepts with which they were once

A government-sponsored arch decorated with a miniature pre-Christian temple that was erected beside the Salvation Army church in Kulawi, 1988.

associated. As a Dutch missionary remarked, "When the government promotes *adat* rituals, even as a show for the tourists, it makes a lot trouble for us." In her view, *raego'* songs and other demonstrations of precolonial rituals still agitate an underlying "paganism" that threatens the churches' control over their followers.

The missionary complained not only about the *raego'* songs and dances, but also about a set of miniature "traditional houses" (*rumah adat*, Ind.) and temples that were erected on arches over roads near Kulawi in 1987 by the Department of Education and Culture. These displays were designed to promote regional architecture, largely demolished in recent decades, and make an attractive presentation for any future tourists that might someday visit the district. Missionaries claimed that within a week of the arches' construction, Kulawi people were sneaking out and climbing up the monuments at night to leave food offerings for their ancestors.[8] I cannot confirm or deny the allegation, but they indicate the continued lack of trust by many foreign missionaries. Missionaries question both local Christians' compliance with church directives and Indonesians' ability to resolve these religious choices themselves.

The institutions and individuals holding the reins of social authority in Indonesia have great leverage in promoting their view of history by forbidding, permitting, or sponsoring certain types of public performances. The New Order government was particularly concerned that religious interests always served nationalist ones (George 1998, 702). Yet religious and political leaders could not succeed fully in their rivalrous endeavor to manage cultural expression because they could never control all the evidence—that is, the *raego'* performances and texts themselves. *Raego'* songs were created and used by pre-Christian and pre-Muslim social authorities to unify and control religious petitions within a medium of poetry and a veil of obscurity. The Protestant churches suppressed these tools of their religious rivals with considerable success in most missionized villages. In a few Protestant areas, the songs are still performed, but they usually are hidden from the authorities or rewritten to praise the new God rather than the old ones. In a few Muslim areas, the songs are no longer viewed as sinister, but *raego'* rituals are cast only as reenactments of historical customs within the garments of Islam.

The residents of western Central Sulawesi have retained their own interests in reconstructing ancestral words and performances. The capacity of ritual speech and songs to be remembered by revered elders, to bring tears to the most staunch indigenous Protestant minister, and to be recorded and carried from free territory to restricted territory gives *raego'* a potential for continued viability apart from the constraints of regional political and religious regulations. That some Muslim lowlanders suggest that a government-supervised performance of *raego'* can influence the weather and crop harvests, and that Protestant highlanders will hide in their homes to listen to bootleg tapes, represents a popular spiritual counterpoint to the recent use of ancestral words and performances for status claims and national policy implementation by government and world religion leaders.

❧ 8 ❧

Constructing a Godly New Order

The New Order government of President Suharto promoted its human engineering programs through godly means—that is, aided by the institutions of world religion. Christianity, formerly promoted by the Dutch colonial state, became supported by the Indonesian state for many of the same reasons. Christian ethnic minorities have been viewed as population "buffers" between Muslim groups, preventing and justifying restraints on Islamic influence over national policies (Kipp 1993, 213). President Suharto's government also gave regulatory support to Christian churches because they enhanced the state's program of nationalism, which was based in economic development as the most essential "rite of modernization" (Peacock 1968, 6).

Missions have implemented development schemes in concert with the state to extract highlanders from their localizing domestic, ritual, and political practices. Church cooperation has been cautious, however, because the churches pursue regional and transnational aims that are potentially distinct from those of the Indonesian state and the nation's Muslim majority.[1] Thus the seeds of recent Christian-Muslim tensions have been sown by state policies from the beginning of Dutch rule to the present. In the 1970s, after mass conversions to Christianity followed the anti-communist attacks that ensued upon President Sukarno's ouster (H-J Kim 1998; Willis 1977), Muslims increasingly resented proselytizing Christians.

In this chapter, I examine how Central Sulawesi Christian institutions interfaced with the development policies of President Suharto's government. These issues set the highland case within a broader provincial context of Christian denominational competition and national political pressures in favor of world religions and modernity. The Indonesian government and Christian churches have been united by their common interests in monotheism, nuclear family-based economic growth, patriarchal domesticity, biomedicine, and intensive agriculture. These interests have led church and state to denigrate highlanders' knowledge and skills while praising the idealized image of a modern Indonesian citizenry. In Sulawesi as elsewhere in Indonesia (Blackwood 1995; Brenner 1998), women's roles in the family unit have been targeted to transform families into the key constituent elements of the state (Suryakusuma 1996). These human-engineering efforts have utilized a rhetoric emphasizing the internal or spiritual improvement of individuals.

As a complication, the varied Christian sects that proliferated during the past decades now compete among themselves, as well as against Muslim groups, to become the essential handmaidens of economic development. Even in the face of government directives they deplore, the foreign-based missions must defer to the government in exchange for work permits. The churches thus have become entrenched in the worldly development of their congregations as these groups became subject to New Order policies and philosophies.

If "backward" people in marginal places are troublesome for governments who seek control over their citizenry, governments can implement two possible strategies: move modernizing programs into the margins, or move backward people out of the margins to centers where they can be influenced more easily. The Indonesian government has tried both methods simultaneously in Central Sulawesi, with local transmigration programs supplementing village leadership and development initiatives. Christian churches are involved with both strategies for political as well as philosophical reasons. The churches and government continue many cooperative patterns of social engineering established during the late stages of the Dutch colonial regime. These patterns also alienate Christian communities, usually ethnic minorities, from common ground with neighboring Muslim groups.

National development proceeds vigorously, if unevenly, in highland Central Sulawesi. A village headman in Kulawi chose to spend the government's "village help" development funds (*Bantuan Desa*, or *BANDES*) on a solar-powered television set for his own home. Meanwhile, he and his neighbors continued to use an increasingly polluted stream nearby for all washing, drinking, and toilet activities. Foreign missionaries oppose such "lopsided" development initiatives. Yet in these small ways, village headmen exercise choice in their required moves toward the government's vision of a higher national standard of living. In most matters, the national government defines the policies of rural transformation while church leaders act as implementers, and sometimes partial financiers. The agency of local villagers often is confined to such creative acceptance of new options, or to foot-dragging, absenteeism, or other tacit forms of noncompliance (Scott 1985, 1990).

In most cases, however, highlanders complied with development projects as much in the service of the Protestant God as in the service of the state. And when they shied away from the state's emissaries of development, they generally needed to hide from their Protestant ministers as well. Highland churches effectively became proxies for the New Order state, as well as the major educators dispensing national codes for personal, family, and village behaviors.

Developing the Outside and the Inside

President Suharto's New Order government (1965–1998) departed from that of his predecessor, President Sukarno (1945–1965). Suharto's state presided over the eclipse of Sukarno's zealous geopolit-

ical nationalism in favor of an ideology more focused on unprecedented economic development (*pembangunan*). Indonesia's limp
economy and rampant hyperinflation in the early 1960s made the
practices imposed under this policy shift appear both urgent and attractive. The Indonesian term "*pembangunan*" literally means "building
construction," as well as "development" in a more figurative sense.
Foreign observers have been quick to notice the New Order regime's
spending emphasis on massive monuments and showy buildings rather
than on the development projects' ostensible functions (Mulder 1978,
91; Robison 1986; Tsing 1993, 90–91).

This untoward concentration on structures and appearance presented itself dramatically when I visited the first Central Sulawesi public library building erected outside of Palu in the mid-1980s. None of
my local acquaintances had ever been to the library, and I enthusiastically traveled there only to find that the gargantuan building, visible for
miles through the valley, contained no books available for public
perusal. I found a few cards in one catalog drawer, but even these volumes, the apologetic clerk informed me, were not in the library. He
explained that the books they had stocked initially already had been
stolen. This and similar regional tales of project corruption belied the
official rhetoric of successful development and foreshadowed some of
the infrastructure problems precipitating the national financial decline
of 1997.

The library building towered in the Palu Valley desert as a testament to the power of the state: a repository that defined valuable
intellectual activities in the region. An outward physical appearance,
or "skin" (*kulit*, Ind.), which suggested important contents, had been
funded grandly without any concomitant budget for maintenance or
an activity plan to support the building's purported internal function.
As Scott notes, a key characteristic of many failed high modernist
plans for social engineering is the dependence upon a clean, geo-
metric, imposing aesthetic that implies efficiency and scientific
measurement but actually is implemented in the absence of any ver-

ification of locally appropriate functionality (Scott 1998, 133, 224–225).

Although the "insides" or "contents" (*isi*, Ind.) of many government projects have been exposed as wanting, the New Order also formulated policies that explicitly concerned the insides or internal workings of the Indonesian citizenry, which were considered wanting. Indeed, the term for development, "*pembangunan*," connotes the idea of social engineering as well as civil engineering (Robinson 1989, 21). The New Order thus also administered programs of "leadership" or "guidance" (*pembinaan*) to propel "backward" (*terbelakang*) villagers toward attitudes and behaviors that supported the state's "modern" initiatives. The family unit, particularly the woman's role in that unit, has been a major focus of the Indonesian state's regulatory and media interventions (Brenner 1998; Suryakusuma 1996). The family being the "insides" of the nation, the state can only be orderly and modern if its family units are orderly. Such self-assured, unilateral state projects for upgrading citizens' behavior denigrate finely tuned local knowledge while promoting the control of the intervening government (Scott 1998, 305).

Churches are involved intimately with "leadership" initiatives in Central Sulawesi. Government officials recognize that foreign Christian missions are still one of the most promising and cost-effective methods to extract knowledge, cooperation, and products from remote interior areas. Favorable government relations with the missions also often ensure their congregations' unanimous political support in the next elections.

In the mid-1980s, an official from the Department of Religion in Palu publicly praised the New Tribes Mission on the grounds that, in their mission fields, voting was 100 percent in favor of the government political party (GOLKAR).[2] A Dutch Reformed missionary who heard the praise commented that although the New Tribes missionaries are strong on technological developments such as airfields and hydroelectric power, they are politically naive because "they think that only heaven matters." The Dutch Reformed minister implied that the New Tribes missionaries were self-serving in their sycophantic service to the government and naive about the Indonesian state's concerns with religion.

Those missionaries—and they come from several denominations—who seem to preach that "only heaven matters" do not involve themselves directly with any political issues related to their congregations. By default, however, they promote an unquestioning allegiance to national programs planned for their mission fields. Governments focused on economic development ostensibly give priority to science over politics (Scott 1998, 4). In this light we may further understand the government-controlled media's, and many churches' denigration of "politics" (*politik*, Ind.).

Even docile and cooperative missionaries are potential victims of their own successes. Once converts are considered suitable for national integration, as evidenced by permanent villages, intensive agriculture, mission schools, and mission clinics, the missionaries themselves often are requested to return home. By the late 1980s, several American, European, and Australian missionaries who had worked for years in Central Sulawesi were struggling to keep their visa permits in the face of what they considered mounting harassment by Muslim government officials. By 1993, most of the missionaries I had known in the 1980s either had returned home after their visas were not renewed or had moved to neighboring countries. Those who remained were stationed in the areas considered to be most intransigently backward and in need of exceptional strategies.

In sum, while most reports on New Order development programs have focused on the "outside" aspects of economic infrastructure, both the Indonesian government and the missions have been intensely concerned with the "inside," or domestic aspects, of "modern" development. In this arena, recent Christian missions have followed an anti-Muslim, "modernizing" pattern set up in the Dutch colonial regime, yet additional conflicts have arisen among the multiplying Christian sects themselves.

Mission Heterogeneity and Competition

In 1945, President Sukarno established monotheism (*bertuhan,* Ind.) as the first of five principles (*Pancasila*) to guide the newly formed Indonesian nation. The call for monotheism was a compromise solution in the face of Muslim groups advocating an Islamic state and other leaders advocating a secular state, given important populations such as the Hindu Balinese and Chinese Buddhists and Christians. Toward the end of his presidency, Sukarno declared that Islam, Hinduism, Buddhism, Confucianism, Protestantism, and Catholicism were to be the six officially sanctioned religions, or *agama* (Mulder 1978, 6). In the past decades a few ancestral religions, in Kalimantan (Schiller 1997; Weinstock 1981) and in South Sulawesi (Volkman 1987, 166), have been registered within the Hindu category. In most regions, however, Indonesian people are encouraged by government schools and on bureaucratic application forms to reject ancestral attachments and affiliate at least nominally with one of the five world religions (which no longer include Confucianism).

Under the new regulations of the Republic, the Salvation Army lost its Dutch-protected religious monopoly in western Central Sulawesi (M. Brouwer 1974d, 4). The government's declared freedom of religion (among the chosen five) allowed other Protestant sects to open their own churches within the formerly exclusive Dutch Reformed and Salvation Army territories. Many of the new Christian sects were introduced by Indonesian migrants. Already missionized in their homelands, these immigrants opened branches of their own ethnically identifiable churches rather than meld into Salvation Army congregations. Some Western missionaries note correctly, and disapprovingly, that most of the churches in Central Sulawesi are ethnically segregated, parallel to the old "ethnic religions" (*agama suku*). These circumstances allow Christian institutions to preserve local community practices, as well as to instill national or transnational Christian values and practices.

Despite Muslim majorities in the provincial capital of Palu (estimated at over 75 percent) and the nation as a whole (estimated at 87 percent), acceptance of Christian missions in Central Sulawesi continued throughout the New Order. Foreign missionaries entered the country variously under the rubric of economic development, medical, or educational programs. Salvation Army officers distributed birth and marriage certificates for the government and operated schools in most highland regions. Although only a few European Salvation Army officers remained in Indonesia through the 1980s (about seven individuals in medical and administrative positions), dozens of Western families representing SIL, the New Tribes Mission, the Overseas Missionary Fellowship, the Missionary Aviation Fellowship, and other independent churches from the United States, Australia, Canada, and Europe had worked in highland Central Sulawesi during the previous fifteen years.

Western representatives of the newer missions to Central Sulawesi either worked with previously established churches or else founded new ones, such as the Assemblies of God. According to government policy, their visas could be renewed for up to ten years. In some cases in the 1980s, foreign missionaries had managed to remain in the province for almost fifteen years, but a less lenient policy in the early 1990s sent several mission veterans out of the country against their will.

The present array of Christian church sects in Palu is impressive. Palu's Catholic Church mostly serves Chinese and Manadonese who converted under Portuguese influence during the early colonial period. Manadonese also are the most heavily represented ethnic group in the congregations of the Gereja Protestan Injil Donggala (GPID; Donggala Protestant Gospel Church), a sect introduced from the Dutch Reformed churches of North Sulawesi. Pamona and Mori people form the core of the Gereja Kristen Sulawesi Tengah (GKST; Central Sulawesi Christian Church), which originated from Kruyt's mission in Poso. The GKST opened a branch in Palu in the 1960s so that Poso people would no longer have to worship at the GPID church dominated by Manadonese. The Gereja Kristen Indonesia (GKI; Indonesian Christian Church) is a recent Protestant church from South Sulawesi, and its core members are Chinese. The Toraja and the Batak Protestant churches in Palu are clearly identified according to the ethnicity of their members. Other newer churches include the Assemblies of God opened by U.S. citizens, and the Seventh Day Adventists tied to branches in Australia.

Chinese and Javanese immigrants form a majority of the Pentecostals in Palu. Morris (1991) describes the introduction of the Pentecostal Church from Seattle to Java via two Dutch couples funded by the Bethel Temple in Seattle in the early 1920s. By the 1930s, the Pentecostal mission reached Sulawesi. The Pentecostal Church's popularity and number of church buildings were growing rapidly in Java and Palu in the 1980s. Morris writes:

> Both Pentecostals and charismatics distinguish themselves from other Protestants by their belief that "the gifts of the Holy Spirit" as described by Paul in I Corinthians 12 are as accessible to Christians today as they were to the Apostles and early Christians. These gifts include the ability to speak in tongues, see visions, perform healings, prophesize, etc. (Morris 1991, 5)

It is logical that a church allowing for visions, spiritual healing, and other contacts with powerful unseen forces would be of interest to Central Sulawesi worshippers with their own history of shamanic communication. In the late 1980s, some charismatic Indonesian Pentecostal leaders were attracting independent followings in Palu with weekly all-night rituals that entailed fasting at private homes or outdoors in remote public spaces. Such "wild" (*liar*, Ind.) Christian activities, occurring beyond the blessings of any organized church, were sharply criticized by ministers in the Salvation Army and other "mainstream" churches of Palu.[3]

Invariably, ministers of churches arriving earlier in any area feel that their mission field is infringed upon by later sects. Salvation Army officers say that Seventh Day Adventists come to "steal sheep" (*mencuri domba*, Ind.). They accuse Adventists of unethically proselytizing with gifts in areas where the Salvation Army had been working hard for years. Indonesian regulations dating from the 1970s decree that churches should only enter areas that have no previous authorized religion, and wait for invitations from locals before they do so. In interior regions, however, often newer churches such as the Adventists or Pentecostals are called in as the result of community divisions, or sometimes because a marginal population has remained unconverted until a later decade than the mainstream church group. Such marginal communities are actively sought by new sects looking for congregations.

In the mid-1980s, a few Central Sulawesi areas still were being officially "opened" for missionization. Remaining "isolated or estranged ethnic groups" (*suku terasing*, Ind.) were identified through aerial surveys made with missionary planes. In other cases, communities feeling disadvantaged without an authorized religion themselves sought out missionaries. A Dutch Reformed minister who was called to a remote Da'a Kaili area commented somewhat cynically, "Well, now they learn from the government that they need a religion, and maybe they like to eat pork." The minister's implication was that the group sought Christian affiliation only under political pressures, in conjunction with a rejection of Muslim dietary restrictions.

First mission contacts of recent years look remarkably similar to those described in early twentieth century records, except for new "high-tech" approaches and the obligation to acknowledge competing sects. At the introductory public meeting held to establish Protestantism in the same Da'a Kaili village, the European missionary began by making light of the differences among the Christian sects. He suggested that the various churches were merely different "name brands" (*cap*, Ind.) for the same thing—that is, a path to worship the one true God. As with the early missionaries, Bible stories were visually illustrated, only now with 35-mm slides, a technology seen for the first time that evening by local people. In present times as in Kruyt's day, highlanders often are impressed by novel material goods and information. New Tribes missionaries have baffled their audiences by presenting maps of the "Holy Land" of Jerusalem to people who have never seen a map, or even traveled to the village that links a vehicle road to the base of their mountain range.

SIL missionaries enter Sulawesi on a different type of visa than most missionaries because they work through the Department of Education and Culture rather than the Department of Religion. They are admitted to Sulawesi on five-year contracts that require them to participate annually in linguistics instruction at universities. They are considered resident scholars as much as missionaries, and they are posted only to areas that already have Protestant affiliation. Unlike New Tribes missionaries, they are not assigned to "open" animist groups for initial exposure to Christianity.

Like Kruyt and Woodward, present-day SIL and New Tribes missionaries move into interior areas as families and, much like anthropologists, ask for local permission to live and study villagers' language and culture. Often they choose a location on the basis of its geographic suitability to their planned airplane landing strip or hydroelectric power needs. They then encourage locals of the targeted ethnic group to settle beside them. They offer income and material benefits to their neighbors and usually become involved in local medical and educational affairs.

New Tribes missionaries say that the first several years of each mission are spent on information gathering rather than preaching. In recalcitrant areas, New Tribes missionaries begin by living not within the homeland of the targeted group, but only at the base of the nearest road to that region. From there, they make contacts with traders going in and out of the proposed mission field and collect preliminary information. In some instances, years have passed before highlanders permitted New Tribes missionaries access into their home villages.

In the Wana region of northeast Central Sulawesi, two New Tribes men first hiked in twice to plan an airstrip. Once the airstrip was completed with hired local labor, the missionaries' wives, children, and supplies were flown in. After two more years, a primary school was opened. A hydroelectric pump installed in a small waterfall created electricity for the missionaries' private needs, which in 1988 included washing machines and desktop computers. Surplus electricity was sold for the considerable sum of Rp 10,000 per month to Wana who built homes near the airfield. The missionaries said that the Wana earned money to pay their electric bills by doing jobs for the missionaries, such as cutting grass on the airfield with machetes or selling cash crops such as coffee or dammar resin. By the late 1980s, there were four airstrips in the Wana region for the New Tribes' exclusive use, plus one built by the Seventh Day Adventists, who proselytized an adjacent group.

Some regions under recent missionization have responded more favorably to missionaries than others. The Lauje are said by New Tribes and Dutch Reformed missionaries to accept Christian conversion very easily, but the Wana and Saluan people in the northeastern peninsula are less yielding. The situation among the Wana was touchy enough in the late 1980s that after eight years of missionization, two visiting European language teachers were denied access to Wana settlements by their New Tribes hosts in Palu because "the locals keep running off." Dutch missionaries working in Poso confirmed these reports of fleeing Wana, and the one anthropologist who worked in the region also describes recent millenarian movements by Wana under government pressure to migrate down from the highlands (Atkinson 1979, 1989).

New Tribes missionaries claim that those Wana who have "entered religion" (*masuk agama*, Ind.) now trust the missionaries and no longer run from government officials. They argue that social changes like the use of soap could not be put into effect until conversion was accomplished because pre-Christian shamans forbade the use of soap. New Tribes missionaries question the effectiveness of other missionaries who do mainly community work ("good works") in lieu of vigorous religious proselytizing. Dutch Reformed and Mennonite missionaries, by contrast, argue that missionaries who exclusively seek conversions leave the Christian highlanders little better off than the so-called "isolated tribes" who "do not yet have a religion." They note that Christian highlanders often graduate school without being able to tell time, do simple arithmetic, or master intensive farming or husbandry skills. Like the New Order government, these missionaries advocate economic development and its associated view of modernity in conjunction with religious training.

To explain his perspective, Reverend Hans van der Kers said, "What good is it to talk to these people about heaven when they are ignorant, starving, and sick here on earth? Why convince people to pray because Jesus died for their sins when they continue to sin for lack of understanding of a better way?" In his view, there were already too many vacuous church services being conducted in Central Sulawesi, and local ministers all too often were tempted to take economic advantage of their powerful positions in the community.

By the 1980s, the Salvation Army was just one among many Protestant denominations in Central Sulawesi. Rival sects sometimes sought to cooperate and share resources, but more often they aimed to coopt each other's disciples. The New Order government, by chance or design, engaged in a divisive strategy that kept each sect relatively weak and rivalrous with the others. All the Protestant missions responded meekly in the face of nationalist and Muslim opposition to missionaries by applying themselves vigorously to the government's prescribed programs. In the next sections, I explore how the Salvation Army interfaced with governmental health care and domestic projects aimed at "development" and "leadership" in the Kulawi District.

Churches as Mediators of Development through Health Care

Take the example of philanthropy in the early nineteenth century: people appear who make it their business to involve themselves in other people's lives, health, nutrition, housing . . . there emerge certain personages, institutions, forms of knowledge: public hygiene, inspectors, social workers, psychologists. . . . It was in the name of medicine both that people came to inspect the layout of houses and, equally, that they classified individuals as insane, criminal, or sick.

Michel Foucault, Power/Knowledge

In light of Foucault's discussions of the state's paternalistic organization of populations to control security, health, and productivity (Foucault 1978, 141–147), anthropologists have explored how domestic arrangements and medical care have supported national development agendas, and conversely, how citizens have taken countermeasures to maintain personal control (E. Martin 1987; Anagnost 1988; Ginsburg 1989; Ong 1987, 1990a, 1990b; Scott 1998; Tsing 1993). This section examines New Order efforts to control the physical bodies of Tobaku highlanders—people for whom the well-being of the body reflects a cosmological status—as a case of how Christian institutions mediate between development programs and local opposition.

The New Order government, often funded by foreign aid, upgraded biomedical care for many distinctly secular reasons, such as to increase economic productivity. By contrast, Tobaku people consider physical disorders to be spiritual rather than economic problems, and they diagnose and treat them as such. The Salvation Army, which operates virtually all clinics in the Kulawi District highlands, affirmed and implemented the government's goals. Yet it also introduced rationales of Christian charity and salvation to secure patients' allegiance to itself. Using the indigenous rhetoric of spirituality and the modernist techniques of secular science, the Salvation Army acted to usurp most indigenous healing practices in the name of the Protestant God. Nevertheless, highlanders still utilize home remedies and ancestral ritual practices, which they sometimes view as more economical or effective than Salvation Army clinic care.

Health, like any measure of prosperity, indicates cosmological harmony in Central Sulawesi and other comparable Indonesian religions. Atkinson (1979, 1989) focuses on the Wana shaman who, like the Malay shaman (Laderman 1991), mediates with unseen forces to drive illness and other misfortunes from the community. Given the public eradication of shamans in the Kulawi District, their replacements are the Salvation Army staff who attend the sick—both officers who conduct prayer services and nurses who provide medications and health-related advice. Although Salvation Army officers are referred to in Uma as *tobalia*, the name for pre-Christian shamans, their roles in healing rituals are far less theatrical than the pre-Christian ones described by Kruyt (1938) and Atkinson (1987, 1989).

Tobaku people have become eclectic and pragmatic in combining traditional medicine (*pokuli'*, Uma; *obat tradisional*, Ind.) and clinic biomedicine (*obat klinik*, Ind.). Their basic understanding of these two systems is different than that of most Westerners, however. For many Indonesians, ancestral medicine is considered familiar, natural, reliable, and within the realm of local social control. Biomedicine, by contrast, often is viewed as mysterious, very strong, potentially dangerous, and outside of local comprehension and control (Klopfer 1991). Village healers are trusted elder relatives with whom communication is easy. Practitioners of biomedicine usually are strangers to whom it would be rude to pose questions. Most Tobaku individuals maintain that biomedical injections and pills are potent in curing some physical disorders, yet many find financial or spiritual reasons to choose indigenous curing techniques over clinic care.

Most Salvation Army clinic nurses are unmarried young women who dispense injections, pills, and advice with little ceremony. Nurses assigned to the highlands often have no ethnic or kinship ties to their region of duty. While this foreign status places them at a linguistic and cultural disadvantage, the Salvation Army implements this policy to avoid nurses who might too easily bow to the social pressures of elder relatives. Largely uninformed about local healing practices and social hierarchies, the nurses assigned are thought less likely to shirk their duties as biomedical practitioners and bill collectors.

The only Protestant rituals devoted to healing are family-sponsored statement of thanks (*pengucapan syukur*, Ind.) ceremonies where Salvation Army officers pray for an ill household member before a meat and rice meal. Prayers are raised and thanks given even in cases where the patient's recovery is not at all certain. These Protestant ceremonies functionally replace pre-Christian ritual bargains (*pohanga'*, Uma) where deities were offered sacrifices in the hope of propitiation and restored health.

To cope with minor health problems, most Tobaku adults are familiar with an assortment of home remedy medicines (*pokuli'*), protective charms (*ajima*), activity and food taboos (*palia*), and other prophylactic or curative behaviors. Elements of indigenous practice include blowing (*mpotuwui'*) or spitting (*mpoteliku*) on the patient's body in conjunction with reciting verbal formulae (*mogane'*). Ritual bathing (*mponiu*) of the patient, or the ritual washing of some affected body part with herbal water (*pangimulu*) while healing words are recited, is also often part of the treatment. Heirloom china or brass vessels associated with ancestors may be used especially for these treatments.

In cases of fevers, injuries, and swellings, muscles or limbs may be massaged (*mo'ura'*), often with an herbal element such as gingerroot (*kula'*). Rubbing is aimed toward the extremities to rid the body of evil substances. In cases of wounds, certain kinds of inflammations, internal pains, and skin eruptions, compresses or poultices are applied. Leaves, roots, bark, or some other human or animal secretions considered powerful are crushed and applied to the affected area with a cloth or leaf strapping (*rababa'*). Alternatively, a fresh leaf may be heated over a hearth fire and then placed on, or stroked over, the body (*raramu'*). The ubiquitous camphor balm, marketed as Rheumosone, is a first-line treatment for every type of muscle or stomachache. It is placed under the nostrils to ease respiratory problems and rubbed on insect bites or other small wounds. Healers also use forest products to produce teas or brewed drinks to cure some ailments. Only if such home remedies are unsuccessful do most Tobaku people turn to Salvation Army personnel.

The Salvation Army implements government-prescribed programs such as public clinics, family planning, and infant weighing.

Two Salvation Army nurses, Sister Meli and Major Gantuada, arrive after a long journey through the mountains at the Kantewu church, where many patients await their services, 1986.

The clinic at Kulawi was opened in 1949. The maternity hospital (now a general hospital) in Palu was opened in 1973, and the clinic in Towulu' was opened in 1981 (Salvation Army 1985, 9–10). The Salvation Army generally installs clinics in areas that have had no prior contact with biomedicine. When vehicular roads reach interior villages, such as in Winatu, the government introduces its own community health centers (*Pusat Kesehatan Masyarakat*, or *PUSKESMAS*) and the Salvation Army is requested to withdraw its staff.

Variations between Salvation Army and government clinics involve variability among government doctors and staff, some of whom withhold expensive treatments from their public practice in favor of an after-hours private practice. Government and Salvation Army medical teams collaborate on some projects, but generally government clinics are maintained only at larger population centers with road access.

At Kulawi District outposts, Salvation Army clinics are staffed by the equivalent of Western licensed practical nurses (*suster*, Ind.). More centrally located church and government clinics are staffed by registered nurses and paramedics (*mantri*), supervised part-time by a licensed doctor (*dokter*). Patients' complaints usually are treated symptomatically with pills or injections by nurses who do not formulate or record diagnoses. The most frequently prescribed medicines include vitamins, analgesics such as acetaminophen, antibiotics such as sulpha or tetracycline, and, in malarial areas, chloroquine. Other low-cost medications such as antihistamines and diuretics also are available.

What struck me as remarkable about Central Sulawesi biomedical practices was the numerous injections, the routine administration of three to five drug treatments simultaneously, and the brevity of antibiotic doses, usually only for three days. When these generic clinic treatments fail to result in swift improvement, Tobaku patients and their families consider the cosmological problems that might be causing sickness. Elders consider whether the ill have angered dead relatives (*sesa'*), showed disrespect to superiors (*wunto*), encountered malicious spirits (*kamaroa*), violated *adat* traditions (*silaka*), refused hospitality or showed pride (*solora*), lost their "shadow" souls (*kao'*), or suffered sorcery (*kadua*; Aragon 1992).

Despite the spectrum of causes that highlanders assign to sicknesses, there are essentially three lines of treatment that are followed, at times successively, by Tobaku individuals. First, there are home remedies for minor ailments considered to be normal (*biasa*, Uma and Ind.). Beyond their physiological effects, these home remedies have psychological value in mobilizing family concern and care. Generally these treatments do not aggravate the illness. Compared to Salvation Army clinic diagnostics and prescriptions, indigenous assessments and interventions are more attuned to the symptomatic variety and social factors of illness. Tobaku home remedies, however, generally are discouraged by Salvation Army personnel, who prefer purchased biomedical treatments such as pills, injections, ointments, and so forth. Only one time did I hear a European officer preach that some local remedies were valid and acceptable as long as the aid of pre-Christian deities was not solicited.

The second line of treatments are those sought at a Salvation Army clinic, if there is one accessible. Most highlanders are now familiar with pill-taking or injection procedures and consider them potentially effective. Often their desire to receive Salvation Army treatment will lead them to walk or carry patients for several days to reach a clinic. If the biomedicines seem to work quickly, the illness again is concluded to be an ordinary one without major cosmological significance.

If neither home remedies nor Salvation Army medications bring positive results and the ailment is grave, it is considered evidence of a cosmological transgression that must be rectified by ritual activities, such as "thanks to God" feasts or grave renovations. Salvation Army officers work to convince highlanders of Protestant interpretations of their transgressions, as well as the superiority of clinic medicines. In this fashion, they serve the government's and their own modernist goals, which include separating individuals from reliance on their own relatives in favor of increased church and state dependency. The alternate curing practices and "hidden transcripts" (Scott 1990) concerning illnesses that exist, however, indicate that the simplified forms of biomedicine and spiritual ministrations practiced by clinics coexist with indigenous healing routines and localized interpretations of divine repercussions. Here the New Order, with church personnel, has reoriented but not fully dominated the health care field.

Family Planning, Women's Roles, and Transmigration

Family planning and child nutrition are areas of health care where the Salvation Army implemented New Order projects specifically focused on women. President Suharto departed from President Sukarno's policies on birth control. Although Sukarno noted his country's population imbalance among the islands and favored transmigration, he, like the leaders of the People's Republic of China, envisioned

Indonesia's future world strength as residing within its massive population. By contrast, Suharto's policymakers perceived that Indonesia's planned economic advances might be undone through additional poverty created by unrestricted population growth (Suyono 1984, 1, cited in Robinson 1989, 21). Therefore, foreign aid was accepted by Suharto's government to support a large-scale Family Planning Program.

Indonesia's Family Planning Program (Keluarga Berencana, or KB) is administered to rural families on sparsely populated islands such as Sulawesi, as well as to urban families on overpopulated islands such as Java. Civil servants receive financial incentives to keep their families small. The government slogan, "Two is Enough" (*Dua Cukup*), which may seem reasonable in the overcrowded cities of Java, usually strikes Central Sulawesi highlanders as ridiculous. Most Tobaku adults have been born into families of eight to twelve children, and they assess family wealth in terms of the number of children they have to help farm the land. Nevertheless, motivated by official persuasion and maternal exhaustion, many Tobaku women have accepted birth control options offered through church clinics.

In the Kulawi highlands, family planning and mother-infant health programs have been administered by the Salvation Army with foreign aid funds. Birth control aids such as pills, injections, and intrauterine devices (IUDs) are given at little or no cost to married women who have four children or to those who wish to stagger their pregnancies. Women with grown children often are happy to participate. Elder women describing their difficult lives, many miscarriages, or stillborn babies sometimes rue that there was no birth control in their youth. Salvation Army officers and government leaders say that reducing the number of children per family will help parents be more responsible in paying their school fees, donating to the church, and purchasing better clothes for their families. In other words, with fewer children, highland families will conform to government and church visions of modern, productive Indonesian families.

Indonesian birth control initiatives can go awry, and national statistics about their successes may be deceiving. Tsing describes a case in Kalimantan where a man sought political advantage with the regional government by organizing a list of forty women "acceptors" (*akseptor*, Ind.) of birth control pills. The man collected the pills without intending to distribute them to the women, who were never contacted directly by the project. A few women asked for some pills as a health tonic but lost interest when they felt no noticeable effects (Tsing 1993, 104–109).

The narratives I heard about ineffectual birth control "safaris" (*safari*, Ind.) in Central Sulawesi involved misunderstood procedures for contraceptive use. Birth control pills sometimes were stored diligently beneath a couple's sleeping mat or hung above their sleeping area just the way local herbal medicines would be utilized. In general, highlanders do not precisely follow clinic pill dose prescriptions, which, Tsing suggests, may be viewed "as merely another form of government discipline to be politely ignored whenever possible" (Tsing 1993, 109).

Aside from any passive resistance by villagers pressured to cooperate with government projects, the Indonesian Family Planning Program has been long on supplies and short on information. By assuming the ignorant and ineducable nature of marginal ethnic groups, they likely have maintained or helped create it. The drollest family planning case described to me involved the distribution of condoms in a highland Kaili area. A family planning official gathered all the village men together for instruction. He opened a condom packet and rolled it back carefully over his thumb to demonstrate its sheathlike qualities. Months later, when the incidence of pregnancies in the village showed no sign of abating, the official returned to the village to investigate the problem. The village headman swore that the men had used condoms every time they had sex with their wives. "Yes, Father, we used the condoms every night just as you showed us—like this." The headman proudly thrust out his thumb, which he, as well as the other participating village men, had covered with fresh condoms every evening for the previous months. Whether these errors were committed though ignorance or resistance to the program I do not know, but the mission nurse who reported the case assumed the former.

To avoid such mishaps, the Indonesian government and cooperating medical personnel often have promoted "foolproof" devices such as the IUD in communities with little biomedical experience. Unfortunately for some women involved, these devices—including problematic models such as the Dalkon Shield, which were pulled from U.S. markets—were widely installed without discussion of possible side effects or follow-up care. Seemingly, the goal of "maximum acceptance" sometimes has taken priority over full consideration of women's long-term health and safety. Although many individual women and international groups have been pleased with the New Order's birth control programs, Indonesian communities have noted the intrusiveness or attempted "penetration" of their domestic life by the state and its birth control initiatives (Brenner 1998, 225–226).

Since 1980 in the Kulawi District, the Salvation Army has administered for the Indonesian government the "Under Age Five" Nutrition Program (Bawah Lima Tahun, or BALITA). Babies are weighed every month at designated villages by a nurse and female volunteer "cadres" (*kader*, Ind.) who encourage mothers to introduce more nutritional solid foods to increase their babies' weights. The weights of highland babies usually drop below national standards by their sixth month. At that point the mother's breast milk is considered nutritionally insufficient. Customarily only rice porridge, lacking in some essential protein and vitamins, is added to babies' diets.

By 1986, thirty-one village outposts conducted baby weighing under Salvation Army management. For a nominal enrollment fee of Rp 300 per month, children under four years old were given monthly health checks with free medications, plus food and vitamin samples. Most eligible Tobaku mothers living within a day's walk of the clinic were enrolled, but seasonal agricultural demands resulted in high absenteeism. From a biomedical point of view, the baby-weighing program has identified and assisted babies whose weights left them at risk for health complications.

Tobaku mothers, however, often consider the program somewhat demeaning and too time consuming. Women lose entire workdays as they travel to the clinic with their youngsters and wait in long lines for their turn at the weighing scales. The health education goals of the baby-weighing program are lost upon overworked mothers impatient with nurses' harangues to cook special foods for their babies. With impeccable logic, Tobaku adults note that they were fed only plain rice porridge as infants, and they survived. Some women resent church and state efforts to tell them how they should feed and raise their children, although others appreciate the assistance and enter contests (*lomba* BALITA) where mothers of weight-gaining babies receive prizes of baby clothes, soap, or towels from the Salvation Army.

The New Order made a minor industry of redefining the ideals of Indonesian womanhood. New Order media stated explicitly that women, formerly major economic contributors to the family in their roles as farmers, artisans, or merchants, now were judged to succeed or fail primarily in their roles as housewives (Blackwood 1995; Brenner 1998; Sullivan 1983; Wolf 1992). Through such an ideological transformation, a key element of highland women's self-esteem—their skills as farmers of ancestral land—becomes negated, and the new criteria for "modern" womanhood, housewifery, measure them sorely lacking as citizens.

A national leadership organization aimed to ameliorate the domestic deficiencies of Indonesian women is the Family Prosperity Guidance Association (Pembinaan Kesejahteraan Keluarga, or PKK). This government-controlled women's group promotes appropriate concepts of modern femininity and housewifery. The Salvation Army version of this group is called the Household Leadership Program (Pemimpinan Rumah Tangga, or PRT). The PRT was initiated in the Tobaku region during the 1960s to draw women away from their daily focus on farm fields and reorient them toward their "more modern" duties as Indonesian culinary and child-care specialists.

PRT meetings combine a women's church service with home economics lessons. The nationally standardized lessons emphasize a host of unfamiliar domestic activities such as needlepoint or cake making. By necessity any recipes of European or Javanese origin must be adapted to hearth-fire cooking facilities and available food supplies such as rice, sago, or cassava. Meetings, at which a small church collection is taken, are led by an officer-wife who has been taught foreign recipes and lessons about proper femininity in the Salvation Army officers' training program.

Some wives of village leaders, in their roles as beacons of modern Christian womanhood, attend the PRT meetings on a regular basis and find them entertaining. Other women find what is taught there to be folderol, superfluous to the harsh realities of their swidden-farming life. Like the missionized Hawaiian women who found the sight of European missionary wives ironing clothes to be peculiar and pitiable (Grimshaw 1989, 35–36), many Central Sulawesi highland women find the newly invented modes of nationally prescribed female housework to be costly and frivolous additions to their already encumbered work lives.

For women not naturally drawn to PRT activities, church leaders have devised economic means to enforce their participation. Fundraising events in church are conducted by the women's leadership organization for the benefit of their treasury. In one Tobaku village, the PRT group bought a set of large cooking pots, enamel cups, and plates sufficient to serve the entire village. These items are loaned free to all PRT members in good standing for use in household rituals such as engagements, marriages, or funerals. With the availability of utensils from the PRT organization, former practices of serving rice in disposable leaf packets and serving drinks in coconut-shell bowls have fallen by the wayside. Women who refuse to attend weekly PRT religious meetings are left without access to the kitchen equipment, which puts them at a disadvantage in mounting all major family ceremonies. Under the thumb of such economic forces, highland women are pressured by the church to accept their reeducation as proper wives and mothers.

In line with the Salvation Army Church's and government's aim of escalating and monetizing individuals' work routines, PRT programs also organize wage labor groups during busy farming seasons such as harvest or weeding. Through the PRT, small households may contract female labor for one day on a particular field. In Towulu', the sponsoring family must provide a daily wage, plus coffee and snacks, for weeding work, or rice and chicken for harvesting assistance. In 1988, the daily wage per woman was Rp 1,000, or about seventy-five cents. This source of labor has become important recently for the smaller families with few resident members capable of physical labor, and for salaried workers such as teachers or officers who cannot work regularly on their own fields. Although the church groups employ New Order rhetoric, calling the paid system "mutual cooperation" (*gotong royong*, Ind.), it weakens the extended family relations and generalized reciprocity that characterized wage-free highland farming of the past.

The Salvation Army also draws some exceptional individuals away from their village farming life toward higher education and urban citizenship. Tobaku parents recognize the potential value of school education for their children, although pupils often are kept out of school during peaks of planting, weeding, and harvesting. Some parents now make great personal sacrifices to send at least one of their children out of the highlands to secondary schools in Kulawi or Palu. These youths are boarded with migrant relatives who shelter them in exchange for household help. As few Tobaku families have sufficient urban connections to get their children hired in the civil service, Salvation Army careers as nurses, teachers, and officers are the most accessible professional jobs. As it happens, given the European tradition of female nurses and elementary school teachers, more Salvation Army jobs in Central Sulawesi are open to girls than to boys.

Nurse Captains Tampu and Ngale in uniform outside the Woodward General Hospital in Palu, 1986.

For a small entry fee to pay for uniforms and supplies, teenage girls may assume menial service positions by "entering a post" (*masuk pos*, Ind.) at the Salvation Army hospital in Palu. Their room and board is provided for six months, after which they are tested for basic hospital service skills. Those who fail are sent home to their villages. Those who pass continue for another six months, when they take exams prerequisite to nurse training. Nursing is a lucrative career by Tobaku standards, one that can send cash back into the highlands. In 1987, registered nurses in Palu were paid as high as Rp 200,000 (about US$175) per month. Approximately 70 percent of the two hundred nurses and aides working at the Palu Salvation Army hospital in the mid-1980s came from the Kulawi, Pipikoro, or Tobaku areas. The remaining 30 percent were from Christian Kaili, Javanese, Balinese, Minahasa, or Toraja ethnic groups.

Western missionaries report that highland girls require much basic training to adapt to the urban hospital conditions in Palu. Recruits initially leave faucet taps open so that the hospital water will flow continuously, like the mountain springs at home. New arrivals sometimes panic and jump out of windows when they find themselves alone in rooms where they do not know how to operate doorknobs. The Salvation Army has implemented novice-training programs to modify highlanders' insufficient notions of hospital etiquette and hygiene. After a few difficult years, most trainees meld into the "modern" world of Palu and thereafter return to their highland villages only for major events such as weddings and funerals.

As in much of Indonesian bureaucratic life, the true testing ground for Salvation Army advancement is Java. Officer candidates from Central Sulawesi are sent to the training college or study center (*pusat latihan*) outside of Jakarta for a two-year program, after which they graduate as ministers or nurses ranked as lieutenants. After two years of service, they usually are promoted to captain. After twenty years, they can hope to become majors and be assigned to the larger outposts. Usually, the highest rank that indigenous officers attain is that of major, but some few have become colonels, brigadiers, or commissioners. Officer candidates must enroll either as unmarried persons vowing to remain single throughout the two-year training period or as married couples without children. Any prior children must be boarded with relatives during the training course, which allows for no familial distractions. In 1989, nine of the thirty-two Indonesian candidates were selected from Central Sulawesi, although many were sent to Java a year early for remedial "practical fieldwork" before entering the formal officer program.

The movement of highland women out of their villages and into positions as Salvation Army nurses, teachers, and ministers poses a seeming contradiction to both missionary and New Order gender ideologies (Aragon 1999a). On the one hand, the girls are pulled away from their "backward" villages and families. On the other hand, they seemingly defy the newly idealized female role of wives and mothers through the fulfillment of prestigious careers created under church auspices. Needing the local women both as labor and as wives for indigenous male officers, the Salvation Army has had to resolve the contradiction of their status by encouraging the eventual marriage of all indigenous female staff to indigenous male officers, whose rank determines that of their wives. Such marriages were routinely arranged by European staff during the colonial era and still sometimes are. Thus women's devotion to their church-sponsored work and to God is nestled within their potential responsibility to their husbands. Any overt threat to the New Order's and the Salvation Army's housewife-first ideology is therein resolved.

Salvation Army staff training programs are one means by which individuals from backwater communities can be moved to central locations for personal "development." The Indonesian government's regional transmigration programs aim for a similar goal at the group level. Transmigration programs are state-imposed forms of "deterritorialization" (Baudrillard 1990, 119; Appadurai 1992, 192) that often pit the precedence claims of different ethnic or religious groups against

one another as they all are pressed to alter and standardize their subsistence and residence patterns. Although the Salvation Army is less
directly responsible for transmigration than just about any other aspect
of development in Central Sulawesi, they inevitably become involved
with transmigration villages holding missionized people.

In the late 1970s, a transmigration project was created in the
Palolo Valley as part of a government program called Residence for
Isolated Communities (Permukiman Masyarakat Terasing). Unlike the
better-known transmigration projects aimed to reduce populations on
Java and Bali, these regional programs are designed to move highlanders down from the mountain ranges of the Sulawesi interior. Each
family originally joining the Palolo Valley project was promised one
hectare of wet-rice land plus a small wooden house and five months of
food supplies. Most of the inhabitants of the project were recruited
from officially designated "isolated or estranged tribes" (*suku terasing*)
such as Da'a Kaili, but residents of all highland villages beyond the
reach of roads were encouraged to join. The project turned swidden
farmers into "more productive" wet-rice farmers as well as making
cheap labor available for timber concessions or plantations nearby.[4]

The Palolo Valley project attracted "volunteers" from a Tobaku
village that has far outgrown its surrounding swidden lands.
Approximately ten extended families agreed to move to the transmigration settlement upon its inception. By 1989, over eighty Uma-speaking families had moved to the project. Despite early problems with
promised supplies and participants who returned home, the remaining
Tobaku transmigrants reported a decade later that they would not consider returning to the more physically difficult conditions of their
mountainous homeland.

Even in the 1980s, however, there were recurrent incidents of
ethnic and religious tension in the project. Tobaku and other Uma
speakers were placed beside Kaili, Seko, Kulawi, and Toraja families.
Each ethnic group maintained a separate church or mosque with
exclusive social activities. Tobaku families looked to one early-migrat-

ing couple as their founding leaders, and these elders assumed social priority over more recent arrivals. Newly arriving Kaili families, however, often acted as if they merited deference in disputes because the land assumed by the Palolo Valley project was within the peripheries of precolonial Kaili kingdoms. In this case the Kaili transmigrants based their claims on a broader historical view of founders' cults, while the Tobaku migrants envisioned the project territory as more akin to a "wild" area, harnessed by the state, in which they were the founding occupants. The ethnic and historical tensions between the project's groups were aggravated by religious differences between Christians and Muslims who were unaccustomed to such close coresidence and competition for resources.

The Salvation Army provided medical services for the population of the Palolo Valley project until the late 1980s. At that point, government officials informed the Salvation Army that their medical administration was no longer required and that the government health system would assume control of the project clinic. Major Carron noted that the government often follows the same pattern: they allow the mission to do the expensive and hard work of setting up the first clinic in a region before requesting that the clinic be turned over to them. In turn, however, the government offered the mission a chance to build a clinic in a new, formerly unserved, area. Thus the Indonesian state conserves funds and attains development targets, while the mission spends funds to expand its "mission field" and ultimately its congregation and collection base.

Through its medical and other development-oriented activities, the Salvation Army is first an active fund-raiser and implementer of government programs and second a sometime competitor in those programs' administration. By drawing some highlanders, particularly women, into church and medical careers, the Salvation Army provides novel opportunities for villagers to move to "modern" urban environments such as Palu. Therefore, in the areas of development that the Indonesian government and foreign missions associate with modernity—permanent agricultural settlements, birth control, infant nutrition, trained housewives, wage labor, biomedicine, and higher education—the Salvation Army serves the government as well as itself.

Facets of economic development promoted by the churches on behalf of the government assume moral and religious significance. An elderly Tobaku woman once declined to treat my throbbing boil with an herbal compress because she feared "trouble with religion," that is, censure from church leaders. Injections from the church clinic become Protestant and "good," while grandmother's leaf compress and soothing words become pagan and "evil." Cooking a European- or Javanese-style cake at the women's group meeting becomes "virtuous," while collecting ferns on a Sunday afternoon for that night's meal becomes "sinful." Farming ancestral land for one's family becomes "dirty," while staying at home to do housework becomes "clean." Living in a city with a salaried job becomes "modern," while living near the swidden fields becomes "primitive." With the backing of the Protestant churches, the New Order government thus has increased its potential for delivering messages about "modern development" and assigning them a moral certitude—a certitude that has transnational as well as national support. Religious devotion and economic development have become quietly indexed to one another.

Political Authorities, Near and Far

In many important respects, the church, just as in the days of Kruyt's and Woodward's missions, *is* the government of the interior highlands, or at least the most familiar branch of it. Given the remoteness of the Tobaku region, much of what occurs with the government on a national level is of very distant concern to highlanders. In 1987, I was asked by Tina Kulu if Ronald Reagan was president of the United States. Before I had ceased being impressed by her knowledge of world politics—comparing it favorably to how few Americans would be able to name the president of Indonesia—she posed this follow-up question:

"And Father Suharto, is he president of . . . out there?" She nodded her head slowly toward the 7,000-foot-high mountains that separate the hamlets she knows from the coastal city of Palu.

This interchange startled me not because I was surprised by a rural Indonesian's knowledge about the United States. Millions of urban Indonesians watch Bill Cosby on television, listen to American pop musicians on tapes, and regularly view Hollywood-made action films. Rather, her words moved me because I realized just how distant Central Sulawesi highlanders feel, not only from the national capital in Jakarta, but from the provincial capital of Palu and the political nation as a whole. In such areas, Anderson's (1991 [1983]) vision of the nation as an "imagined community" is not yet even imagined, despite all the recent state policies promoting a uniform and productive citizenry.

The path of rapid development charted by New Order leaders was created without the participation, or often even the knowledge, of hundreds of ethnic minority groups in the hinterlands. Continuity in the way of life for most of these peoples hinges on the imminent elusion of, or partial control over, intruding development projects linked to global market forces. Significant efforts to expand logging, mining, tourism, and transmigration are recent in Central Sulawesi (Aragon 1997), and their rate of implementation will depend in part upon highlanders' ability to establish and consolidate village leadership that can negotiate effectively for local interests with provincial and national officials. The economic and political crisis that began in 1997, however, is likely to escalate the pursuit of natural resources that can be sold for foreign currencies, thereby further eliminating interior forests where minority groups such as the Tobaku live.

Local government in Central Sulawesi has been in a transitional period for the past few decades. While many descendants of the colonial aristocracy retained regional administrative positions, the Indonesian government also began to nominate younger, schooled men, individuals formally educated for their bureaucratic responsibilities. Often these two strands are combined, with descendants of former rulers or their affinal relatives being the ones selected for administrative training.[5] Village heads, under pressure from the regional government, struggle to collect taxes, get livestock registered and fenced outside of the villages, organize road maintenance crews, and enroll all children between seven and twelve in primary school so they will be able to read Indonesian as adults.

Only a few Tobaku thus far have become senior government or church officials in Palu or beyond. One prominent Tobaku leader, Bapak J. Ph. Tarro, headed the Regional Marriage Office (Kantor Wilayah Pencatatan Sipil) in the 1980s and served as a link and senior advisor to many Uma-speaking people who migrated to Palu. And one Salvation Army officer from Winatu, Commissioner Victor K. Tondi, became a territorial commander, which allowed him to travel abroad as far as Jerusalem. These local heroes are exceptional because most Tobaku never have access to the education and opportunities required for such superlocal positions. Many Tobaku inhabitants, especially older women, have never journeyed out of the mountains as far as Palu because they have had no cause to do so. Moreover, even those youth whose parents do make the effort to send them to high school in the lowlands often find that government jobs, largely controlled by Kaili, South Sulawesi, and Javanese Muslims, are not open to them without bribes or payments that their families can never afford.

Salvation Army officers in Central Sulawesi have performed bureaucratic functions for the government such as registering births, marriages, and deaths since the Dutch colonial regime. In the late 1980s, the most expensive of these processes was marriage registration, which cost about Rp 40,000, including the required photographs. Marriage documents were processed by local officers who carried them to the Kulawi marriage office. Formerly, villagers were expected to appear in Kulawi themselves, and so often did not register their marriages with the government. Most couples from the larger Tobaku villages now purchase the official government marriage authorizations; the couple and their parents aspire to a church wedding, and Salvation

Army officers refuse to perform marriage services without an official government certificate. In this way, again, the church provides the moral leverage to make government regulations enforceable.

The government's presence becomes most noticed in Tobaku when villagers are affected by policy changes or political elections. Campaign periods are tense times when rumors of violent crimes burgeon and talk of headhunting reemerges in transformed guise. Both army processions and police surveillance increased noticeably in Donggala Regency during the months prior to the national elections in April 1987. Foreign researchers and most missionaries were asked to relocate to the capital city of Palu or depart the country altogether. Restrictions were placed on public gatherings, and the Salvation Army was required to stop all medical and educational outreach activities between January and July 1987. Unusual cases of muggings and rapes were widely discussed, being explained as the actions of misanthropes "trying to perpetrate chaos" (*mau bikin kacau*, Ind).

Several highlanders insisted that the helicopters flying mysteriously at night over Palu prior to the elections were seeking victims, searching for heads needed for roads, buildings, and bridges. This connection between construction and headhunting has roots in an early Central Sulawesi practice where human heads were buried under the main posts of indigenous temples to make them strong (Kaudern 1925, vol.1). Despite the rampant rumors and reported increases in crime, 1987 and 1992 elections in the Kulawi District proceeded peacefully.

By the late 1980s, government officials seemingly feared, and acted to restrict, any direct political influence that missionaries might have over their congregations. Reverend Henrik Rinkes said he had been warned by local officials upon his arrival not to make trouble, that he better preach only within his assigned areas of jurisdiction. Reverend van der Kers similarly received a government order that prohibited his outspoken sermons from being broadcast on the radio along with sermons from the Indonesian ministers of his church.

In 1985, a letter was sent from the Department of Religion to all church leaders in Palu and to all religious leaders throughout Indonesia, requiring them to sign a document saying that they accepted the national philosophy of *Pancasila* as their "sole basis" (*azas tunggal*, Ind.) or "foundation" (*dasar*, Ind.) above sacred texts such as the Bible or Qur'an. While Central Sulawesi church leaders acquiesced and signed in order to stay in existence, the foreign missionaries strongly disapproved. They said that *Pancasila* had become merely a tool for the government to oversee the churches, and through them, the population. If all churches formally accepted *Pancasila* as their primary doctrine, there would then exist only the religion of the state. There would be no religious freedom at all.

In 1988, the government attempted to increase rural village legibility to visiting officials by sending embossed metal signs, resembling U.S. vehicle license plates, to every Central Sulawesi village official. The signs, intended for display outside one's residence, read "Village Head" (*Kepala Desa*), "Village Secretary" (*Sekretaris Desa*), and so forth. The sign received by the Salvation Army officer amused or offended everybody. It read "Imam." That the title sign for a Muslim priest had been distributed throughout the Christian highlands was considered indicative of the government's overall Muslim orientation. To add insult to injury, those Protestant ministers receiving the "Imam" signs were required to pay for them. They had no intention of posting them, however.

SIL missionaries complained of harassment from Muslim officials both in the local government and in universities to which they were assigned. Pilots of the Missionary Aviation Fellowship (MAF) and the New Tribes Mission also spoke of egregious difficulties in obtaining and maintaining their landing permits, especially in newly missionized areas. Aside from any animosity by Muslim officials that might actually have existed, keeping the missionaries insecure about their various permits undoubtedly ensured more ready cooperation with requests for development aid and acts of subservience such as bribes.

The MAF airfield that was opened at Kantewu in 1979, just prior to a SIL missionary family's arrival, was considered such a boon to economic development that another airfield site was planned for Tobaku, near Towulu'. Although my fieldwork notes from early 1986 mention a Salvation Army officer's prediction that the airfield would be finished by June of that year, I saw little progress by local volunteers to complete the landing field between 1986 and 1989. Salvation Army officers blamed this inertia on a lack of local leadership, but the foot-dragging also demonstrated some local resistance. Villagers were well aware of the changes, including increased visits from outsiders, that a more easy transportation link would bring to a people who have chosen to live in a relatively remote location for many centuries. When I returned to Towulu' in 1993, the landing field still did not meet the aviation requirements of the mission pilots, and no further progress had occurred by 1999.

Christians and Muslims, Ethnic Identity and Pancasila

Ethnic differences worldwide often are represented as religious differences, and vice versa. The first European definitions of ethnicity referred to people of different religions, specifically the heathens of Western Europe (Armstrong 1990; Abramson 1980; Royce 1982). Only more recent social science has defined ethnicity in terms of common ancestry, history, behavioral practices, or self-identity. Features of group identity such as religion, customs, rank, and common ancestry can be concordant or, in other cases, separated for alternate situational alliances (Kipp 1993). My interest here is to explore the recent path of Christian-Muslim relations in Central Sulawesi and consider how Indonesia's national philosophy of *Pancasila*, in its bid to be a civil religion, has affected ethnic and religious identifications.

Highlanders' proud and vocal association with Christian organizations of wealthy nations in Europe, Australia, and North America helps to counterbalance their minority self-image as isolated, impoverished, and technically "backward" swidden farmers. Christianity provides highland minorities in Indonesia with a legitimate and rival religious status vis à vis the Muslim majority. This situation parallels the adoption of Christianity among highland ethnic minorities in Burma and Thailand such as the Karen, who thereby elevate their status with respect to the Buddhist majority (Keyes 1993, 1996; Lehman 1979; Scott 1976, 238). Christianity serves as a focus for political unity among small-scale populations, aiding them in their negotiations with national majorities affiliated with other world religions.

The government's philosophy of *Pancasila* and its policy of promoting Indonesia as one "nation, people, race" (*bangsa*, Ind.) support recent efforts by some groups to dissociate the twin identities of religion and ethnicity (Kipp 1991a, 1993). Kipp writes that among the Karo Batak of Sumatra, who are 60–70 percent Christian, 10–15 percent Muslim, and 15–30 percent animist or Hindu, the colonial-era association of highland Batak ethnicity with Christianity and lowland Malay ethnicity with Islam has undergone a transformation resulting in the secularization of Karo ethnicity. Such secularization of ethnic identities is useful to a government striving to downplay ethnic-religious tensions among various population groups. The dissociation that Kipp describes for the Karo, however, has not occurred among the highlanders of western Central Sulawesi because they, unlike the Karo, are rather uniformly Christian and their regional "others" at the coast are uniformly Muslim. The Central Sulawesi type of coastal-interior religious and ethnic schism is common throughout the "outer islands" of the archipelago, creating a social geography of potential religious conflict.

The *Pancasila* philosophy (from Sanskrit *panca*, "five," and *sila*, "principle") was declared by President Sukarno on June 1, 1945, at the advent of Indonesia's independence. The five principles to guide the nation are:

1. belief in one supreme God;
2. just and civilized humanitarianism;
3. nationalism based on the unity of Indonesia;

4. representative democracy through consensus;
5. social justice.

Despite the tenets' beneficent ring, many observers of *Pancasila* training courses and official expositions point out that the ideology has been interpreted by government leaders primarily as justification for their current policies and actions. The principle of monotheism is invoked to intervene among less developed minorities, the principle of a "civilized" humanity is used to redefine local morality, the principle of unity is invoked to clamp down on movements for regional autonomy, and the principle of consensus is invoked to allow the economic interests of the central government to supersede those of the regions.

Pancasila, then, has been viewed variously by missionaries and scholars as a philosophical program by the government to eliminate communism, to create a civil religion, to protect non-Muslim religious minorities, to extirpate indigenous religions that do not easily support development, to meld and smooth over differences among Indonesian religions, to neutralize any influence that religious sects have to take issue with national platforms, or to support the dissociation of religious and ethnic identities (Kipp 1993; Liddle 1988; Purdy 1982). As a pleasantly vague doctrine requiring much interpretation, *Pancasila* has done all these things. Yet as Bowen (1986) notes among the Gayo of North Sumatra and Warren (1990) notes among the Balinese, well-organized community groups occasionally have been able to quote and interpret *Pancasila* to support their own economic and political goals in the face of central pressures.

Few individuals that I met in Central Sulawesi during the 1980s and early 1990s were willing to take the risks involved in publicly criticizing the New Order regime. One highland woman who was labeled "crazy" (*gila*, Ind.) by a local Salvation Army officer once spoke to me both earnestly and recklessly about the government inequities and corruption that affected her Protestant village. With a clever Indonesian pun about the national philosophy, *Pancasila*, she repeatedly concluded each complaint by saying, "These are not the Five Principles (*panca sila*). They are the Five Wrongs" (*panca salah*). The occasional hypocrisy surrounding implementations of the national philosophy has not gone unnoticed.

In a case more focused on *Pancasila*'s religious rather than economic and political dimensions, George (1996) ends his book on contemporary headhunting rituals with a South Sulawesi highlander's explanation for why he has *not* converted to a world religion. The highland man says:

> I have God inside of me. I am Muslim. I am Protestant. I am Catholic. I am Hindu. This is Pancasila. I have Pancasila inside of me. What is wrong if I am mappurondo [a follower of the local ritual tradition], too? (George 1996, 272)

Through such gambits of philosophical encompassment, this South Sulawesi highlander invokes *Pancasila* to justify his refusal to convert to any world religion endorsed by the government. If the government allows them equally, then why cannot he entertain them all and his own religious practice as well? This kind of politics of local tradition, although rarely reported in New Order Indonesia, essentially "turns the ideology of modernism against itself" (Comaroff 1994, 307).

The highlanders of the Kulawi District were converted to Protestantism in an era long before the ecumenism introduced by the *Pancasila* doctrine was legislated. Yet such concepts of spiritual envelopment and logical extrapolation are commonplace to them and are allied with their pragmatic appropriation of religious practices as both solutions to practical problems and as mechanisms of alliance with surrounding polities. As this book has implied throughout, religion has no consummate meaning, even as a body of doctrines and practices, apart from past and present relationships with ruling polities and neighboring social groups.

At present virtually all western Central Sulawesi highlanders are active members of one or another Protestant sect. The district of Kulawi has been estimated to be 90 percent Christian, with pockets of

Muslim traders in Gimpu, Kulawi, and Lindu (Acciaioli 1989). This local Christian-Muslim ratio is basically the reverse of the national one. The 1980 Indonesian census, the last one to specify religious affiliation, listed Muslims as 87.1 percent of the population, down from 95 percent in 1955 (Cohen 1992; Kipp 1993, 101). The apparent decline in Muslim affiliation, likely lost to increasing Christian conversions, may result in part from government efforts to reduce the political influence of Muslim groups. Christian increases in the Indonesian population between 1955 and the present occurred first as mass conversions, especially in Java, that happened after the coup and anti-communist backlash beginning in 1965, and second as Western missionaries, supported by the Suharto government, began to convert the unaffiliated, especially the isolated ethnic minorities. The national Muslim decline, in addition to the upswing of modernist Islam (Bowen 1993; Peacock 1978), likely contributes to burgeoning tensions between members of the two religions in many areas.

Indonesian conversions to Christianity during the late 1960s and 1970s led to angry protests in the Muslim strongholds of Aceh, Sumatra, and South Sulawesi. Although President Suharto publicly described the conflicts as misunderstandings and urged tolerance, he also agreed that followers of one legitimate religion should not proselytize members of another (Suharto 1991). Further Muslim concerns with both the methods of Christian proselytizing and the importation of foreign church funds led to two government decrees (No. 70 and No. 77) in 1978 that gave the Muslim-dominated Department of Religion the authorization to regulate Christian missionary activities and foreign funds (H-J Kim 1998).

During the 1980s, Central Sulawesi was represented to me by many outsiders as the tense and potentially explosive boundary between Christian North Sulawesi and Muslim South Sulawesi. Yet I often observed relations between Christians and Muslims operating remarkably smoothly, especially given the Muslim-Christian violence that occurred during the Kahar Muzakar rebellion and *Permesta* movement of the 1950s and 1960s. To give the New Order government some unbegrudging credit, the promotion of generic monotheism and nationalism under *Pancasila* seemingly encouraged locals to disavow any significant animosity to the other major religion in the region. In urban areas such as Palu, mixed marriages were not infrequent. Local ideals of tolerance and social harmony, as well as government propaganda concerning "Unity in Diversity" (*Bhinneka Tunggal Ika*, Sanskrit) and well-heeled security forces, all likely were contributors to a prolonged period of peace, if not democratic freedoms.

A process of supra-ethnic convergence of local Christianity and Islam also appeared during the 1980s. The longer I lived in Central Sulawesi, the more convinced I became that Christian and Muslim practices in Palu were conforming to each other. Christmas became, like the Muslim holiday of Lebaran, a weeklong visiting holiday where Christian and Muslim employees alike were invited to visit and eat at their superiors' homes. Christians who were invited to their Muslim coworkers' homes on Lebaran returned the invitations at Christmas, and vice versa. Common gifts such as jars of cookies, Western-style frosted layer cakes, or cases of imported soft drinks were exchanged both within and across religions at the major holidays.

As any visitor to Muslim regions of Indonesia knows, mosques of the past decades have used the miracle of electronic amplification to broadcast their five-times-daily calls to prayer throughout the surrounding community. In urban areas, these amplified chants in classical Arabic reverberate loudly in a manner that only the most hearing impaired could ignore. In the late 1980s, Christian churches similarly began to adopt the use of loudspeakers for their services. They then broadcast the ministers' words not only to their in-church congregations, but, like the mosques, also beyond the church walls to all those thinking they might sleep through the words of God.

Muslim services in Palu also began to include sermons comparable in format and length to those given in the Christian churches. One Protestant missionary wife claimed that local Muslim leaders were imi-

tating her husband's sermon topics and delivery style. Even within
Muslims' and Christians' minor discourses of rivalry, there was religious convergence. Christians disparaged goats as unclean Muslim
animals, just as Muslims decried pigs as unclean Christian livestock.

How are these changing local features of Christian-Muslim protocols, competitions, and accusations to be explained? I submit that
the New Order government not only played Muslim and non-Muslim
ethnic groups against each other in the pursuit of state regulatory
favors, but also spurred them to compete as moral vehicles for modernization. In Sumatra and Java, too, modernist Islam escalated during
the New Order and sought to eliminate ancestral ritual practices in
favor of more "modern" monotheistic ones (Bowen 1993, 327; Brenner
1998, 229–236). Christian and Muslim institutions similarly contended to pull villagers away from their ancestral and family orientations
toward compliance with a more remote state and God wielding more
awesome powers. These common goals of modernization, at least in
Central Sulawesi, made Christianity and Islam companions and peers
as well as erstwhile adversaries.

Despite the jealous competitions, only one public incident of
religious violence occurred in Palu during my three and a half years of
residence in Central Sulawesi. At the end of March 1988, close to
Easter, a fight broke out in the largest open-air market in Palu.
According to several local reports, a Christian Toraja policeman told
some Bugis vendors of Muslim religious materials to move their wares,
arranged on the ground for display, out of a crowded market passage-
way. The vendors entered into a verbal dispute with the policeman
about moving their merchandise, at which time the policeman moved
backward and accidentally stepped on a Qur'an. This sacrilegious act
angered the Muslim merchants to the point where a physical fight took
place, forcing the Christian policeman to flee for protection to a nearby police post. The following night, a Toraja church school was burned
down by an arsonist, and rocks were thrown in the windows of several
Chinese storefronts and the houses of certain Western missionaries.

The next day, the downtown stores of Palu were closed and an armed army unit patrolled the streets. By the day after that, however, all seemed back to normal, and no further outbursts occurred before my departure a year later.

This single 1980s incident of religious violence in Palu was an exception to the overriding peace that Central Sulawesi experienced under President Suharto's regime after the turmoil of the mid-1960s. Yet it also exposed underlying tensions similar to those that flared up, especially in Java, during the bloody transition between the Sukarno and Suharto regimes (Anderson 1990). The wealthy Chinese minority long have been potential targets of resentment by poverty-stricken "sons of the soil" (*bumi putra*, Ind.; cf. Siegel 1986, 232–254), and in Central Sulawesi many Chinese, like Westerners, are identified with Christian churches. These Christian churches, in turn, are associated with a number of ethnic minority groups, mostly interior highlanders. Thus a three-way association is made among Christians, Chinese, and ethnic minorities. That triumvirate, created under the shadow of colonial influence, again became the target of post-Suharto Muslim anger in 1999, an ire still searching for reconciliation—most desperately in East Timor. Even though many observers of the post-Suharto violence throughout Indonesia suspected the handiwork of provocateurs seeking an excuse to resume authoritarian military rule, the nature of the underlying religious acrimony still must be addressed.

The widespread Habibie regime conflicts between Muslims and Christians suggest that the dissociation of ethnic and religious identities described by Kipp (1993) for the Karo in Sumatra is far from complete in the archipelago and has not achieved the class or ethnic tension-neutralizing aims that the Suharto government might have intended. Rather, just as the Dutch employed a divide-and-rule strategy, separating Muslims from non-Muslims and each local *adat* law community from the others, so the Suharto government seemingly pursued a policy of internal fragmentation to bolster the apparent need for its military-dominated, authoritarian political structure. While the

Suharto government gave many ethnic groups of the nation, both Muslims and non-Muslims, a place at the table, its efforts to keep them in separate, centrally defined political spaces also promoted fractious jealousies.

As Woodward (1998, 5) notes, a fundamental doctrine of the Sunni Islam practiced by most Indonesians is that Allah determines the outcome of events, or fate (*takdir*, Ind.). Similarly, Javanese comprehend power and its loss through the external signs of prosperity and harmony (Anderson 1972). I have shown here that this principle of divine justice also pervades outer-island religions of Indonesia. Among all these groups, financial and social problems are seen as indicators of cosmological disharmony and divine dissatisfaction over political leadership. Thus Indonesian politics does not simply propel or regulate religions, domestic life, and ethnic relations, as New Order policies often suggested. Rather, culturally entrenched spiritual interpretations of economic and social events guide political assessments, which require stability and prosperity to be commendatory.

The swift decline of Indonesia's currency and finances in 1997 shook most every Indonesian's confidence in President Suharto's government, especially that of middle-class groups fed up with corruption and impatient for democratic reforms. The removal of Suharto's iron hand, in conjunction with destructive riots and further economic decline, unleashed a spate of formerly contained Muslim-Christian tensions. Although this book's research indicates that these tensions began with European policies for colonial control and missionization of ethnic minorities, they took on a new dimension when the New Order government promoted competition for modernization among religions and more thoroughly regulated the ways in which followers of Islam and Christianity could relate to one another. This shifted the interpretation of *Pancasila* from President Sukarno's loose prescription of monotheism and religious choice to a view that the relations among followers of different world religions must be carefully guarded by their communities and government (H-J Kim 1998).

Although Kim (1998) argues, without foreknowledge of the Christian-Muslim violence beginning in 1998, that New Order constraints on Christian proselytizing unfairly privileged Muslim over Christian views of religion and religious freedom, the more basic problem is the long-standing colonial and Indonesian government presumption to define religion per se, and to regulate religious manifestations and their interrelations. The New Order's deployment of rival religious institutions to foment economic development advanced the conditions under which blame for financial inequities could be placed on members of differing religious groups. In this way, President Sukarno's effort to protect non-Muslim groups through the general prescription to have "belief in God" (*ketuhanan*, Ind.) has gone awry. It has become transposed to an effort by individual ethnic groups to intensify those religious practices that display their efforts toward modern citizenship, and to defend themselves against other religious groups aiming to hinder or interfere with those practices.

∽ 9 ∽

Conclusions

Religions, even world religions, do not have an existence apart from congregations and the social flux in which those communities live. Although terms such as "syncretism" imply the existence of pure religious entities that only sometimes are "mixed," such pristine spiritual ideologies and practices are not common realities, at least not in the contemporary world. The events described here illustrate that even the defining criteria for what constitutes a religion or religious behavior are conceived differently by various cultural and political groups. This book, then, is an ethnography not just of particular peoples or their abstracted religions, but of the processes by which certain groups and their religious practices have been reformulated in relationship to each other during the twentieth century as their environmental and sociological milieus changed.

My argument in this book and elsewhere is not that Central Sulawesi people have made Protestantism, both doctrine and practices, whatever they wanted it to be. That is far from the case. The lives of Central Sulawesi people—their images of deity, their celebration of ritual, their priestly institutions, their daily work habits, their economic ideals, even their domestic habits—have changed immeasurably through missionization. Many of these changes clearly are not even "religious" in any terms that the missionaries would recognize, but, like the worldly asceticism of nineteenth-century Protestants described by Weber (1930, 1965), these matters become entrenched and unrecognized cultural habits tacitly attached to the formal tenets of religious

320

doctrine. Nevertheless, Central Sulawesi highlanders have had to make European Protestantism serve the practical religious needs of Asian rice-farming communities familiar with other spiritual and behavioral antecedents for communication with the unseen forces in the world. Herein lie the religious and behavioral tensions described in this research—tensions that are still being negotiated.

Central Sulawesi religion has shifted in concert with state polities and policies. Beginning with the region's conquest by the Dutch in the early 1900s up to the present, "religion" has been defined by government authorities in terms of "development," both social and economic. Conversely, implementation of state modernization programs has been presented to local populations through the rhetoric of religion and its associated moral ideals. This book has tracked the history of this Janus-faced relationship between Indonesian state development and religion in the peripheral Indonesian province of Central Sulawesi.

In its broadest view this study concludes that religious shifts or conversion occurs through processes of political marginalization that:

1. redefine the criteria of valid religion;
2. subvert local patterns of reciprocity associated with prior ritual patterns;
3. reclassify deity categories;
4. reformat ritual acts with introduced substitutions;
5. reroute transcendent verbal communications by congregation members and priests;
6. introduce new methods of healing authorized by the new deities;
7. index religious change to an idealized vision of economic development or "modernization";
8. legally subvert religious doctrines to political ones.

Such a concatenation of processes clearly never was preconceived as a cohesive method by missionaries or even understood while it occurred. Yet this set of operations, beyond biblical teachings, missionaries' plans, or governments' intentions, is what has most thoroughly shaped Tobaku Christianity and laid the foundation for future transformations.

This study also reveals the potential limits of these conversion processes. Even under colonial and authoritarian regimes, highlanders have remained connected to their ancestral homeland and ensconced in a pattern of subsistence and social relationships that retain a measurable autonomy from state control. The politically imposed world religion was appropriated locally with formal acceptance, much compliance, and also several largely unnoticed processes of potential diversion:

1. deities with new Christian names often retained ancient personas and ancestral laws;
2. vows and sacrifices remained viewed as efficacious rather than becoming largely symbolic;
3. Salvation Army officers assumed comparable ritual and economic roles to the pre-Christian shamans;
4. negotiations continue to occur over what practices are acceptable as "Christian";
5. some precolonial ritual practices declared unacceptable as Christian "religion" (*agama*) become permissible instead as just "ancestral custom" (*adat*);
6. Protestant ritual speech forms such as prayers, testimonials, and songs are employed as surrogates to execute precolonial bargains, oaths, and expiations;
7. church clinic biomedical treatments are supplemented with ancestral curing techniques, and their results are understood to be under similar constraints of divine retribution;
8. government and church perspectives on economic "modernization" and the omnipotence of the state philosophy undermine certain Christian gospel tenets.

Missionaries, as partial agents of states seeking new political hierarchies, could never deliver the "pure" transcendent and egalitarian

Christianity that they idealized both to themselves and their mission field populations. Having renounced their own European worlds to create more perfect Christian worlds abroad, missionaries were troubled by communities whose ancestral religion unambivalently pursued the benefits of life, not their ascetic rejection. As this book has argued, there is no empirical justification for excluding the pursuit of this-worldly benefits, as opposed to the otherworldly pursuit of an afterlife salvation, as part of legitimate religious ideology and practice (Reader and Tanabe 1998).

A general contribution of this book to religious studies lies in its detailed assessment of western Central Sulawesi peoples' ancestral traditions in light of Europeans' misunderstandings and reclassification of their cosmology and ritual behaviors. Highlanders who followed ancestral practices became "pagans" whose "lack of religion" warranted state intervention in all manner of social affairs. Although Europeans ostensibly sought to reproduce their moral values and proper "Christian" behaviors in Central Sulawesi villages, they simultaneously created the economic conditions whereby highlanders became subordinate to and marginalized from not only Europeans, but their lowland Muslim neighbors as well. This process of moving autonomous cultural and ritual centers into the role of subservient peripheries is what Tsing (1993) calls "marginalization" and what Kuipers (1998) terms "hierarchic inclusion." The present study demonstrates how the rhetoric of religion has been used to implement and justify this process as well as to evade or reinterpret it.

Conversion is not an event but a process (Kipp 1995; Hefner 1993a). This process, comprising various stages, is generational, and its supposed conclusion may be assessed diversely. Missionaries began the conversion process in Central Sulawesi with Dutch government assistance by subverting reciprocal trade and political relations that formerly existed among Muslim lowlanders and animist highlanders. The first missionaries in the highlands then reclassified all local spirits and deities to fit the Protestant Trinity. This relabeling process resulted in the official subversion of local deity categories, what might be called their "erasure" (Gal and Irvine 1995, 974; Kuipers 1998, 19). Yet the ill-fitting relabeling also resulted in the native categories' tacit semiotic perpetuation within the performative matrix of local Protestantism. Thus God represents the interests of the local deities of the land, becomes angry with humans for similar trespasses, and expects compa-rable exonerating communications, animal sacrifices, and retribution.

Just as European missionaries worked to replace local deities, they worked to reformat the rituals whereby deities were contacted or worshipped. The resultant ritual substitutions make Central Sulawesi church services and formal elements of their household services look like replicas of contemporary European church services. One primary point of departure, however, resides in the continued performative efficacy of animal sacrifices for Central Sulawesi highlanders. Whereas most contemporary Westerners view ritual meals as merely "symbolic" markers of their thanks to God, highlanders view animal sacrifices as intrinsic features that validate and functionally fulfill the ritual itself. Therefore, missionary and local Indonesian assessments of both Protestant theology and ritual often speak past each other given the potential "duality of patterning" or polysemy that can be attached to standardized religious pronouncements and ritual acts.

By introducing the gospel to Central Sulawesi, Europeans pre-sented their written words as "the Word," thereby attempting to down-grade the relative value of local oratory and its role as a medium for contacting deity. Many precolonial rites that showcased local ritual speech were eliminated. Yet some verbal gambits that relate to deities, such as vows, have perdured in conjunction with the missionaries' rerouting of local oratory toward rituals of thanks, prayers, and testi-monials about God's beneficence. Even local *raego'* songs that have been under almost a century of Dutch colonial and mission suppres-sion have reemerged in diverse forms that recall as well as reform ancestral cosmology and ritual practice. Thus the linguistic decline and marginalization described so poignantly by Kuipers (1998) for

Sumba both holds true and maintains its counterpoint in Central Sulawesi, where locals largely ignore the demands of the national Indonesian language and channel their spoken Uma language vows and oaths through the medium of Christian rituals.

The relationship of religions and states throughout history has concerned the issue of legitimization. Religions legitimate states by giving them otherworldly authority, while states legitimate religions by providing their constructions of the universe with an institutional basis in empirical reality (Berger 1969, 29–51). I have argued here that the Dutch regime used religion as a field resource and legitimizer for colonial policy, and that the post-independence Republic followed suit in many respects. After 1985, President Suharto even elevated the government's philosophy, or civil religion, above world religions, while continuing to use the institutions of world religions as vehicles to advance economic modernization programs.

The New Order government's regulation of the relationships among religious and ethnic groups harkens back to Dutch colonial efforts to weaken threatening Muslim movements and justify a regime that purported to prevent native groups from falling into violent chaos (Anderson 1990; Lev 1985). New Order development programs in Central Sulawesi similarly followed Dutch strategies to "modernize" the more remote areas through the services of religious missionaries. State rhetoric about economic development, often represented by massive government buildings, has had a parallel focus on the "internal" development of citizens, especially their domestic morality and religion.

In their efforts to champion the path of economic development, post-World War II religions have become their own fierce competitors. Both denominational friction among Christian sects and Muslim-Christian tensions have increased as the Indonesian government contracted religious institutions to advance development goals. President Suharto's regime became increasingly mired in defining both world religions and the proper relationships among adherents of Muslim and non-Muslim faiths. Government leaders, therefore, engage the emotional rhetoric of religion for development purposes in plural societies with significant potential peril for national harmony. When the New Order government legislated in 1985 that all religious institutions acknowledge the philosophy of *Pancasila* as their sole foundation (above the Qur'an, Bible, or other doctrinal source), the regime elevated itself politically above religious leaders, yet simultaneously lost the possible spiritual legitimization of religion—because legitimization from a subordinate element means much less.

Religion's intimate link with state development in Indonesia, although not unprecedented either in the history of conversions or revitalization movements, aggravates an underlying tension between idealistic or transcendent "world-rejecting" religions such as Christianity and Islam and the "goods-embracing" cult of economic development. The official doctrines of these world religions devalue "the manifest differences of custom, wealth, blood, and place that divide people, to propound transcendent truths that join everyone for all time" (O'Connor 2001, Notes, n. p.). In Southeast Asia, these religions did not fully support the Indic-influenced hierarchy of states, but rather became cultural allies of local communities seeking a more direct and effective route to spiritual forces. State efforts to anchor religion to development, therefore, ultimately highlight the material ambivalence in Christian and Muslim messages, which likely draws people back to their ancestral traditions for guidance in the actual conditions of misfortune or financial success. It is in these debates— whether the neglect of respect to ancestors can cause sickness or whether Protestant services can bring blessings—*and what the true blessings of life are*, that the fine points of Christianity's future in Southeast Asia will be resolved.

Notes

1. Before and After Religion

1. The "estranged ethnic group" label (*suku terasing*) is applied more often to highland Central Sulawesi groups such as the Da'a, Wana, and Lauje. For more background on the Da'a people, see Acciaioli (1985) and Barr (1988). On the Wana people, see Atkinson (1979, 1983, 1989, 1990). On the Lauje people, see Nourse (1984, 1989, 1999) and Li (1998).

2. Headhunting occurred in precolonial Central Sulawesi, as in many other regions of Southeast Asia, as a form of ritualized warfare and violence. Yet headhunting's former reality as an occasional method of attack is not an accurate measure of violence among contemporary Tobaku or other highland people who, as individuals as well as societies, are far less violent in either deed or imagery than most in the United States and other large states. Nevertheless, contemporary echoes and images of headhunting do exist and have prompted some insightful anthropological scholarship concerning contemporary Indonesian politics as well as historical regional tensions—for example, George (1996); Hoskins (1987c, 1996); Schiller (1997).

3. Similar questions about the "ownership" of Western-originated doctrines or disciplines such as anthropology or feminism have been raised by Asian and other non-Anglo scholars concerned with their exclusion from the construction of principles and policy agendas. See, for example, hooks (1990); C. S. Kim (1990); and Trinh (1989).

4. I once suggested (1991/1992) that the term "syncretism" be reserved for combinations of religious ideas and practices that are not just historically disparate, but arguably disjunctive. This usage follows the *Oxford English Dictionary* definition of "attempted union or reconciliation of diverse or opposite tenets or practices, esp. in philosophy or religion." Although this definition gives syncretism a crisper analytical margin, it still does not address the pervasive cultural and political forces that drive these unions, or "reconciliations."

2. Highland Places and Peoples

1. The Uma language is spoken all along the Lariang River. The SIL linguist Martens (1988ms) identifies four dialects of Uma: Winatu, Tole'e, Tobaku, and Kantewu/Southern. Tole'e now often is considered a derogatory term connoting "hillbillies," so villages using this dialect usually classify themselves as Pipikoro or Tobaku instead. People in the Winatu Valley classify themselves as Tobaku, although they share certain linguistic features with both Kantewu and Kulawi.

2. I noted that the rules of land-borrowing rights are complementary to marriage rules that locate first cousins (who have closely overlapping land rights) as too close to marry and second or more distant cousins (who have less overlapping land rights) as more appropriate mates.

3. The unusual aspect of Uma terminology is that despite the lineal terms separating uncle and aunt from father and mother in the first ascending generation, this type of distinction is not maintained in the zero generation, where ablineals (in this case, cousins) are classified with colineals (in this case, siblings), provided they are consanguines. A more detailed analysis of Tobaku kinship and an Uma terminology list is provided in Aragon 1992, 80–102.

4. The value of the Indonesian rupiah was about Rp 750 per US$1 in 1986, and dropped to about Rp 1,900 per US$1 from 1987 through 1989. By comparison, during the peak Indonesian financial crisis of late 1997 and 1998, the value of the rupiah plummeted to over Rp 16,000 per US$1.

3. Precolonial Polities, Exchange, and Early Colonial Contact

1. Tobaku people are said to include descendants from the old villages of Hungku, Ntipe, Tompi, Porelea, Wilowali, and Pangana (near Koja). The longest oral genealogies that I collected from founding families in Towulu' extended only four to seven generations back. They appear compressed and begin with an apical ancestress born in Lomo, near Siwongi, who married in Mangkau, near Towulu'. This key Tobaku ancestress, Bula Woo' (White Hair), symbolically unites the western and eastern Uma speakers because her older brother, Wulu Wingke (Hairy Forehead), is said to have migrated east to found Kantewu.

2. By contrast, Kaudern (1941, 106–107) writes that Bolapapu Village was burned down by Lindu warriors in the 1850s. Perhaps Lindu and Tobaku warriors joined forces on the expedition, or else the village may have been burned upon more than one occasion.

3. Exactly the same argument was made to me in the late 1980s by members of the New Tribes Mission working with "pagan" Wana of eastern Central Sulawesi.

4. Onward Christian Soldiers: The Salvation Army in Sulawesi

1. In a later publication, Brouwer more closely identifies Zuppinger as an "Indo-Swiss" man who previously had assisted a European Salvation Army officer in the Kalawara school for Javanese boys (M. Brouwer 1996, 49).

2. A Salvation Army "corps" in Sulawesi is a base of operation with a church supervised by an officer whose rank is at least that of captain. Corps are attached to divisional headquarters located in the district centers. Smaller "outposts" are branches of the corps that are served periodically by corps officers. Outposts may or may not have their own church, but they usually have a locally trained "sergeant" who coordinates services with more formally trained visiting officers.

3. One Tole'e Salvation Army officer reported that his father was leader of an eighty-man war party that fought southeast of Kantewu during the *Permesta* rebellion. The minister claimed that his father's warriors reverted to their former practices of headhunting and cut two enemy dead into small pieces, some of which were ritually eaten (*molula*, Uma). This report corroborates others concerning the Philippines and eastern Indonesia, where ideas and practices of headhunting are revived during periods of severe community stress (Drake 1989; Erb 1991; Forth 1991; Hoskins 1996; Pannel 1992; R. Rosaldo 1980; M. Rosaldo 1980; Tsing 1993, 85–91; Tsing 1996).

4. Kruyt apparently set a precedent for such conversion feasts in the Lake Poso region. In an isolated paragraph with no further discussion, he writes:

> When a village had decided to convert to Christianity, the great funeral feast, during which the death souls were promoted to become revered ancestors, was celebrated for the last time. On this occasion they were informed that the traditional decrees would no longer be followed because henceforth people would go "a new way." (Adriani and Kruyt 1968 [1950], 2:104)

5. Precolonial Cosmology and Christian Consequences

1. Kruyt's hypothesis that tribal warriors took enemy heads to capture the "soulstuff" concentrated in these trophies is criticized by numerous authors

who find it unsupported by all available ethnographic data (Downs 1956, 1977 [1955]; Needham 1976; McKinley 1976; Metcalf 1982; M. Rosaldo 1980; R. Rosaldo 1980, 1984). George (1996) and Hoskins (1996) provide good summaries and critiques of this literature plus ethnographically based analyses concerning how and why headhunting, related rituals, and imageries have perdured in the twentieth century.

2. Keesing's (1984) reconsideration of the Polynesian concept of *mana* demonstrates how complex and fluid Austronesian concepts can be made overly concrete by Western interpretations. Keesing argues from linguistic evidence that *mana* refers to a state of efficacy known retrospectively by outcomes, not a thing or a force contained by some people or beings.

3. The category of angry spirits of women who die in childbirth is very widespread in Southeast Asia (Sell 1955). In mainland societies they generally are described as a subset of so-called "green [unripe] deaths" (Lehman 1987, 577). Having died at an "unripe" age, the souls of women who perish during labor are considered justifiably vengeful.

4. Lienhardt (1982, 90) describes parallel translations of similar concepts from "breath" to "soul" by Catholic missionaries working among the Dinka of the Sudan.

6. Sacrificial Dialogues and Christian Ritual Qualifications

1. Experienced mothers sometimes choose to deliver on their own. Tina Doo described how she harvested rice right until the onset of labor for her third child. Then she excused herself, ostensibly to fetch something she had forgotten at her village house. She successfully gave birth alone at home and then cooked the prescribed postpartum rice porridge meal before resting.

2. Martens's Uma word list (1988ms) does not recognize an etymological relationship between the verb *mobali'*, meaning "to change, alter" and *tobalia*, "shaman, witchdoctor," which Martens transcribes without a glottal stop. Martens relates the term "*tobalia*" only to the verb form *mobalia*, which he defines as to "practice curative magic," overlooking the term's reference to pre-Christian harvest feasts (A. C. Kruyt 1938, 4:205–207). Thus Martens denies a possible semantic connection between indigenous curing, transformative rituals, and ritual leaders. While I defer in general to Martens' fluency in Uma and his ear for distinctive glottal stops, I find the possible relationships among the verb *bali'*, meaning "to change"; the noun *bali'*, meaning "enemy"; the noun *bali'mata*, meaning "sorcerer" or, literally, "changing eye" or "changing enemy"; and the forms *tobalia* (or perhaps

better *tobali'a*), meaning "shaman"; and *mobalia* (or *mobali'a*), meaning "curing rituals with spirit possession" or "harvest ritual," too outstanding to be ignored.

7. *The Powers of the Word*

1. Muslims consider the Qur'an to be the exact words that God spoke to Mohammed. Thus the Qur'an, written in classical Arabic, is in principle untranslatable, and Muslims are expected to learn to recite it in its original form. This is in striking contrast to the Bible, which Christians translate into thousands of national languages and local vernaculars in order to relay God's messages more effectively, if not precisely.

2. Transvestite ritual leaders, representing the symbolic union of complementary male and female spiritual powers, formerly were widespread in Sulawesi. Although Tobaku elders recollect a few transvestite males with extraordinary powers to speak to spirits, the area does not seem to have employed transvestite shamans to the extent of the Kaili kingdoms or the Bugis kingdoms of South Sulawesi.

3. Gauchet (1997), by contrast, emphasizes the social repercussions of the rise of all early states as the key source of this philosophical shift.

4. Kaudern (1929, 4:381–438) is the only colonial observer who carefully describes *raego'* dances. He provides, however, virtually no information about the melodies or lyrics of the *raego'* songs, which varied by ethnic region, local language, and ritual context. To follow scholarly convention I also refer to the regional song and dance genre as *raego'* (*moraego'* is the intransitive verb form). More precisely, "*raego'*" is the Pamona and Kantewu (or Pipikoro) dialect Uma term, "*rego'*" is the Kulawi Moma and Kaili term, and "*rago'*" is the Tobaku dialect Uma term.

5. I made translations into Indonesian and English with line-by-line English annotations for all six of the Uma-language *raego'* song texts transcribed by Esser. Unfortunately, Esser left behind no known documentation about melodies, dance forms, or other particulars germane to the 1940s performances he documents with Uma transcriptions. Therefore, most information about *raego'* melodies and their regional or contextual variations must be obtained from recent documentation (Aragon 1996c). I audiotaped performances between 1987 and 1993, and I videotaped two performances in 1993. Spurred by my reports, Philip Yampolsky made professional-quality audio recordings of songs sung in Uma at Onu Village (Smithsonian Folkways Recordings 1999).

6. See Kruyt (1938, 4:205–215) for one of the few descriptions of *raego' wunca* harvest festivities performed in the early colonial era prior to widespread Christian conversions.

7. A comprehensive overview of the closely related but mutually unintelligible Kaili-Pamona languages is to be found in Barr, Barr, and Salombe (1979). A more recent and accessible survey of Sulawesi languages is available in Noorduyn (1991).

8. What struck me about the archways erected on the sole vehicular road into the Kulawi District was their potential to increase automobile collisions. For much of its steep and winding course the one-lane road from Palu through Kulawi to Gimpu already was too narrow for vehicles going in opposite directions to bypass one another safely without going off the road. The gateways narrowed the roadway further at unexpected points, thereby increasing the jeopardy of road travel. Possibly because of complaints from religious leaders or local drivers, the gateways were removed sometime between 1989 and 1993.

8. Constructing a Godly New Order

1. The motives and interests of "states" as institutions of power can be disentangled from the motives and interests of "nations," described famously by Anderson (1991 [1983]) as "imagined communities" of persons who share historical traditions, schooling, and media, thereby perceiving common interests.

2. By contrast, Anderson (1990, 114) has described how the outcomes of general elections were manipulated with thermostatic precision. He notes that in three national elections, from 1971 to 1982, the Government Party GOLKAR (from Golongan Karya) consistently achieved between 62 and 64 percent of the total vote. GOLKAR actually is a professional organization of all Indonesian civil servants rather than a political party as commonly understood (Emmerson 1978).

3. Morris notes that higher-status Javanese are more attracted to staid Dutch Reformed church services, while poor or commoner Javanese are more attracted to the less hierarchical Pentecostal churches. My observations in Palu support Morris' analysis of such class differences.

4. Scott (1998, 11–52, 223–306) contrasts the local, personal, and ecological advantages of swidden and multicrop farming with states' economic and security interests in sedentary, monocrop agriculture.

5. For example, in the late 1980s, the Bupati of Donggala Regency (*kabupaten*) traced his genealogy to the royal family of Sigi, as did the Camat of the Sigi-Biromaru District (*kecamatan*). The Camat of Kulawi District was married into the maradika family of Kulawi descended from the earlier Dutch-appointed ruler (*magau*) named Djiloi.

Bibliography

Abendanon, E. C. 1917–1918. *Midden-Celebes expeditie: Geologische en geographische doorkruisingen van Midden-Celebes (1909–1910)* (Central Celebes expedition: Geological and geographical survey of Central Celebes). 4 vols. Leiden: E. J. Brill.

Abram, David. 1996. *The spell of the sensuous: Perception and language in a more-than-human world.* New York: Vintage.

Abramson, Harold J. 1980. Religion. In *Harvard encyclopedia of American ethnic groups*, 869–875. Cambridge, Mass.: Harvard University Press.

Acciaioli, Gregory L. 1985. Culture as art: From practice to spectacle in Indonesia. *Canberra Anthropology* 8(1, 2):148–172.

———. 1989. Searching for good fortune: The making of a Bugis shore community at Lake Lindu, Central Sulawesi. Ph.D. dissertation, Australian National University.

———. 1990. Introducing Central Sulawesi. In *Sulawesi: The Celebes*, ed. T. A. Volkman and I. Caldwell, 155. Berkeley and Singapore: Periplus Editions.

Ackerman, Susan E., and Raymond L. M. Lee. 1988. *Heaven in transition: Non-Muslim religious innovation and ethnic identity in Malaysia.* Honolulu: University of Hawai'i Press.

Adams, Kathleen M. 1993. The discourse of souls in Tana Toraja: Indigenous notions and Christian conceptions. *Ethnology* 32(1):55–68.

Adas, Michael. 1992. From avoidance to confrontation: Peasant protest in precolonial and colonial Southeast Asia. In *Colonialism and culture*, ed. N. B. Dirks, 89–126. Ann Arbor: University of Michigan Press.

Adriani, Nicolaus. 1915. Naschrift van Dr. N. Adriani (Postscript from Dr. N. Adriani). *Mededeelingen van wege het Nederlandsche Zendinggenootschap* 49:335–338.

———. 1919. Onderwijs, Geneeskunde, Bestuur en Godsdienst-prediking onder een animistische volk in Nederlandsch-Indie (Education, medicine, administration, and preaching the gospel amongst an animist people in the Netherlands Indies). *Koloniaal Tijdschrift* 1919. [Republished in *Verzamelde Geschristen*. 3 vols., 365–386. Haarlem, The Netherlands: F. Bohn.]

———. 1932. De Toradja's van Midden Celebes, wat zij zijn en wat zij kunnen worden (The Torajas of Central Sulawesi, what they are and what they could be). In *Verzamelde Geschriften*. 3 vols, 171–189. Haarlem, The Netherlands: F. Bohn.

———. 1933. *Bare'e-verhalen* (Bare'e stories). The Hague: Martinus Nijhoff.

Adriani, Nicolaus, and S. J. Esser. 1939. *Koelawische Taalstudiën*. Bandung, Indonesia: Nix & Co.

Adriani, Nicolaus, and Albertus C. Kruyt. 1912. *De Bare'e-sprekende Toradja's van Midden Celebes* (The Bare'e-speaking Torajas of Central Celebes). 3 vols., 1st ed. Batavia: Landsdrukkerij.

———. 1950. *De Bare'e-sprekende Toradja's van Midden Celebes* (The Bare'e-speaking Torajas of Central Celebes). 3 vols., 2d ed. Amsterdam: N. V. Noord-Hollandsche Uitgevers Maatschappij.

———. 1968 [1950]. *The East Toradja of Central Celebes*. 3 vols. (trans. of Adriani and Kruyt 1950), trans. Jenni Karding Moulton. New Haven, Conn.: Human Relations Area Files.

Ammerman, Nancy T. 1987. *Bible believers: Fundamentalists in the modern world*. New Brunswick, N.J.: Rutgers University Press.

———. 1990. *Baptist battles: Social change and regional conflict in the Southern Baptist Convention*. New Brunswick, N.J.: Rutgers University Press.

———. 1991. North American Protestant fundamentalism. In *Fundamentalisms observed*, vol.1, ed. M. E. Marty and R. S. Appleby, 1–65. Chicago: University of Chicago Press.

Anagnost, Ann. 1988. Family violence and magical violence: The woman as victim in China's one-child family policy. *Women and Language* 11(2):16–22.

Andaya, Leonard Y. 1981. The heritage of Arung Palakka: A history of South Sulawesi (Celebes) in the seventeenth century. *Verhandelingen van het Koninklijk Instituut voor Taal-, Land- en Volkenkunde*, no. 91. Den Haag, The Netherlands: Martinus Nijhoff.

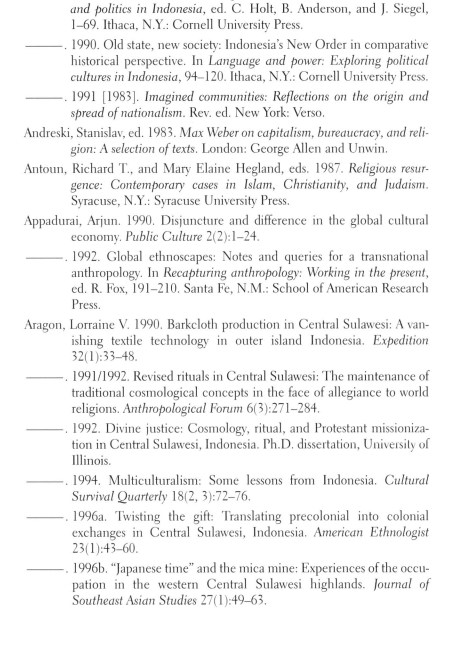

Anderson, Benedict. 1972. The idea of power in Javanese culture. In *Culture and politics in Indonesia*, ed. C. Holt, B. Anderson, and J. Siegel, 1–69. Ithaca, N.Y.: Cornell University Press.

———. 1990. Old state, new society: Indonesia's New Order in comparative historical perspective. In *Language and power: Exploring political cultures in Indonesia*, 94–120. Ithaca, N.Y.: Cornell University Press.

———. 1991 [1983]. *Imagined communities: Reflections on the origin and spread of nationalism*. Rev. ed. New York: Verso.

Andreski, Stanislav, ed. 1983. *Max Weber on capitalism, bureaucracy, and religion: A selection of texts*. London: George Allen and Unwin.

Antoun, Richard T., and Mary Elaine Hegland, eds. 1987. *Religious resurgence: Contemporary cases in Islam, Christianity, and Judaism*. Syracuse, N.Y.: Syracuse University Press.

Appadurai, Arjun. 1990. Disjuncture and difference in the global cultural economy. *Public Culture* 2(2):1–24.

———. 1992. Global ethnoscapes: Notes and queries for a transnational anthropology. In *Recapturing anthropology: Working in the present*, ed. R. Fox, 191–210. Santa Fe, N.M.: School of American Research Press.

Aragon, Lorraine V. 1990. Barkcloth production in Central Sulawesi: A vanishing textile technology in outer island Indonesia. *Expedition* 32(1):33–48.

———. 1991/1992. Revised rituals in Central Sulawesi: The maintenance of traditional cosmological concepts in the face of allegiance to world religions. *Anthropological Forum* 6(3):271–284.

———. 1992. Divine justice: Cosmology, ritual, and Protestant missionization in Central Sulawesi, Indonesia. Ph.D. dissertation, University of Illinois.

———. 1994. Multiculturalism: Some lessons from Indonesia. *Cultural Survival Quarterly* 18(2, 3):72–76.

———. 1996a. Twisting the gift: Translating precolonial into colonial exchanges in Central Sulawesi, Indonesia. *American Ethnologist* 23(1):43–60.

———. 1996b. "Japanese time" and the mica mine: Experiences of the occupation in the western Central Sulawesi highlands. *Journal of Southeast Asian Studies* 27(1):49–63.

———. 1996c. Suppressed and revised performances: *Raego'* songs of Central Sulawesi, Indonesia. *Ethnomusicology* 40(3):413–439.

———. 1996d. Reorganizing the cosmology: The reinterpretation of deities and religious practice by Protestants in Central Sulawesi. *Journal of Southeast Asian Studies* 27(2):350–373.

———. 1997. Distant processes: The global economy and outer island development in Indonesia. In *Life and death matters: Human rights and the environment at the end of the millennium,* ed. B. R. Johnston, 26–42. Walnut Creek, Calif.: AltaMira Press.

———. 1999a. Male gods and female careers: The Salvation Army and gender in Central Sulawesi. Paper presented at the annual meeting of the Association for Asian Studies, March 13, 1999, Boston, Mass.

———. 1999b. The currency of Indonesian textiles: Aesthetic politics in local, national, and transnational emblems. *Ethnos* 9(2): 151–169.

———. 2001. Expanding spiritual territories: Owners of the land, missionization, and migration in Central Sulawesi. In *Founders' cults and political hierarchy in Southeast Asia,* ed. N. Tannenbaum and C. Kammerer. New Haven, Conn.: Yale University Center for Southeast Asian Studies.

———. n.d. What species were Adam and Eve? Rethinking evolutionary science and creationist religion. Unpublished manuscript.

Armstrong, M. Jocelyn. 1990. Christianity and Maori ethnicity in the South Island of New Zealand. In *Christianity in Oceania: Ethnographic perspectives.* ASAO Monograph no.12, ed. J. Barker, 237–258. Lanham, Md.: University Press of America.

Asad, Talal. 1983. Anthropological conceptions of religion: Reflections on Geertz. *Man n.s.* 18(2):237–259.

———. 1996. Comments on conversion. In *Conversion to modernities: The globalization of Christianity,* ed. P. van der Veer, 263–273. New York and London: Routledge.

Atkinson, Jane Monnig. 1979. Paths of spirit familiars: A study of Wana shamanism. Ph.D. dissertation, Stanford University.

———. 1983. Religions in dialogue: The construction of an Indonesian minority religion. *American Ethnologist* 10(4):684–696.

———. 1987. The effectiveness of shamans in an Indonesian ritual. *American Anthropologist* 89(2):342–355.

———. 1989. *The art and politics of Wana shamanship.* Berkeley: University of California Press.

———. 1990. How gender makes a difference in Wana society. In *Power and difference: Gender in island Southeast Asia*, ed. J. Atkinson and S. Errington, 59–93. Stanford: Stanford University Press.

Atkinson, Jane Monnig, and Shelley Errington, eds. 1990. *Power and difference: Gender in island Southeast Asia*. Stanford: Stanford University Press.

Bala Keselamatan (Salvation Army). 1981. Doktrin Bala Keselamatan (Salvation Army doctrine). Bandung, Indonesia: Kantor Pusat Bala Keselamatan.

Barker, John. 1990a. Introduction: Ethnographic perspectives on Christianity in oceanic societies. In *Christianity in Oceania: Ethnographic perspectives*. ASAO Monograph no. 12, ed. J. Barker, 1–24. Lanham, Md.: University Press of America.

———. 1990b. *Christianity in Oceania: Ethnographic perspectives*. ASAO Monograph no. 12. Lanham, Md.: University Press of America.

Barker, John, ed. 1979. Papuans and Protestants: A sociological study of the London Missionary Society, Methodist and Anglican missions in Papua, 1870–1930. M.A. thesis, Victoria University of Wellington, New Zealand.

Barr, Donald, Sharon G. Barr, and C. Salombe. 1979. *Languages of Central Sulawesi: Checklist, preliminary classification, language maps, wordlists*. Ujung Pandang, Indonesia: Hasanuddin University Press.

Barr, Sharon G. 1988. Da'a kinship and marriage. In *Papers in western Austronesian linguistics* no. 4, ed. H. Steinhauer, 51–75. Canberra: Department of Linguistics, Research School of Pacific Studies, The Australian National University.

Baudrillard, Jean. 1990. *Cool memories*, trans. Christ Turner. New York: Verso.

Becker, A. L. 1989. Introduction. In *Writing on the tongue*, ed. A. L. Becker, 1–10. Michigan papers on South and Southeast Asia no.33. Ann Arbor: Center for South and Southeast Asian Studies, University of Michigan.

Beidelman, Thomas O. 1974. Social theory and the study of Christian missions in Africa. *Africa* 44:235–249.

———. 1982. *Colonial evangelism: A socio-historical study of an East African mission at the grassroots*. Bloomington: Indiana University Press.

———. 1994. Review of *Christianity in Oceania: Ethnographic perspectives*, ed. J. Barker. American Ethnologist 21(4):1016–1017.

Bell, Catherine. 1997. *Ritual: Perspectives and dimensions.* New York: Oxford University Press.

Bellah, Robert N. 1964. Religious evolution. *American Sociological Review* 29(3):354–374.

———. 1965. Epilogue: Religion and progress in modern Asia. In *Religion and progress in modern Asia,* ed. R. Bellah, 168–229. New York: Free Press.

———. 1970. *Beyond belief.* New York: Harper & Row.

Bellwood, Peter. 1997. *Prehistory of the Indo-Malaysian archipelago.* Rev. ed. Honolulu: University of Hawai'i Press.

Berger, Peter L. 1969. *The sacred canopy: Elements of a sociological theory of religion.* Garden City, N.Y.: Anchor Books.

Bernstein, Jay H. 1997. *Spirits captured in stone: Shamanism and traditional medicine among the Taman of Borneo.* Boulder, Colo.: Lynne Rienner Publishers.

Bhabha, Homi. 1985. Signs taken for wonders: Questions of ambivalence and authority under a tree outside Delhi, May 1817. In *"Race," Writing, and Difference,* ed. H. L. Gates, Jr., 163–184. Chicago: University of Chicago Press.

Bigalke, Terence. 1981. A social history of "Tana Toraja" 1870–1965. Ph.D. dissertation, University of Wisconsin, Madison.

Bird-David, Nurit. 1999. "Animism" revisited: Personhood, environment, and relational epistemology. *Current Anthropology* 40(Feb. Supp.): S67–S91.

Blackwell, H. Benjamin. 1949. *Doctrinal foundations. The Salvation Army yearbook 1949,* 14–17. London: Salvationist Publishing and Supplies, Ltd.

Blackwood, Evelyn. 1995. Senior women, model mothers, and dutiful wives: Managing gender contradictions in a Minangkabau village. In *Bewitching women, pious men: Gender and body politics in Southeast Asia,* ed. A. Ong and M. G. Peletz, 124–158. Berkeley: University of California Press.

Boas, Franz. 1911. Introduction. In *Handbook of American Indian languages,* part 1, ed. F. Boas, 1–80. Bureau of American Ethnology, bull. 40. Washington, D.C.: Government Printing Office.

Boonstra van Heerdt, R. 1914. De berglandschappen behoorende tot de onderafdeeling Paloe van Midden-Celebes (The mountain landscape belonging to the subdistrict Palu in Central Sulawesi). *Tijdschrift Koninklijk Nederlansche Aardr. General* 1914:618–644.

Borofsky, Robert. 1987. *Making history: Pukapukan and anthropological constructions of knowledge*. Cambridge: Cambridge University Press.

Bourdieu, Pierre. 1977. *Outline of a theory of practice*, trans. R. Nice. Cambridge: Cambridge University Press.

———. 1985. The social space and the genesis of groups. *Theory and Society* 14:723–744.

Boutilier, J. A., D. T. Hughes, and S. W. Tiffany, eds. 1978. *Mission, church, and sect in Oceania*. ASAO Monograph no.6. Lanham, Md.: University Press of America.

Bowen, John R. 1986. On the political construction of tradition: Gotong Royong in Indonesia. *Journal of Asian Studies* 45(3):545–561.

———. 1993. *Muslims through discourse: Religion and ritual in Gayo society*. Princeton, N.J.: Princeton University Press.

Brenner, Suzanne April. 1998. *The domestication of desire: Women, wealth, and modernity in Java*. Princeton, N.J.: Princeton University Press.

Brouwer, K. J. 1951. *Dr. A. C. Kruyt dienaar der Toradja's* (Dr. A. C. Kruyt, servant of the Torajas). Den Haag, The Netherlands: J. N. Voorhoeve.

Brouwer, Melattie. 1973a. Tanah Toradja: Tour of reconnaissance. *The War Cry* (Australia) (November 17):4, 8.

———. 1973b. Tanah Toradja: The pioneers. *The War Cry* (Australia) (November 24):4; continued on (December 1):4.

———. 1973c. Tanah Toradja: Migration. *The War Cry* (Australia) (December 8):4; continued on (December 15):4.

———. 1973/1974. Tanah Toradja: Antique and unique people. *The War Cry* (Australia) (December 29, 1973):5; continued on (January 5, 1974):4.

———. 1974a. Tanah Toradja: Education. *The War Cry* (Australia) (January 12):4; continued on (January 19):4.

———. 1974b. Tanah Toradja: Medical services. *The War Cry* (Australia) (January 26):4; continued on (February 2):4.

———. 1974c. Tanah Toradja: Farther inland. *The War Cry* (Australia) (February 9):4; continued on (February 16):4.

———. 1974d. Tanah Toradja: Training of officers. *The War Cry* (Australia) (February 23):4, March 2; continued on (March 9):3.

———. 1974e. Tanah Toradja: Goodwill and co-operation. *The War Cry* (Australia) (March 16):4.

———. 1974f. Tanah Toradja: Separated, but one in spirit. *The War Cry* (Australia) (April 6):4.

———. 1974g. Tanah Toradja: A new start—then civil war. *The War Cry* (Australia) (April 20); continued on (April 27).

———. 1974h. Tanah Toradja: Trigger to progress. *The War Cry* (Australia) (May 4):4; continued on (May 11).

———. 1974i. Tanah Toradja: Doors still wide open. *The War Cry* (Australia) (May 18):4.

———. 1996. *History of the Salvation Army in Indonesia, vol. 1: 1894–1949.* Hawthorn, Victoria, Australia: Citadel Press.

Brumann, Christoph. 1999. Writing for culture: Why a successful concept should not be discarded. *Current Anthropology* 40(Feb. Supp.):S1–S27.

Burghart, Richard. 1996. The purity of water at hospital and at home as a problem of intercultural understanding. *Medical Anthropological Quarterly* 10(1):63–74.

Caddy, Raymond. 1982. *Where the pepper grows: The story of Edward Rosenlund.* London: Salvationist Publishing and Supplies, Ltd.

Carpenter, Minnie Lindsay. 1957. *William Booth: Founder of the Salvation Army.* London: Wyvern Books.

Chadwick, H. 1967. *The early church.* Harmondsworth, England: Penguin.

Chung, Hyun Kyung. 1990. *Struggle to be in the sun again: Introducing Asian women's theology.* Mary Knoll, N.Y.: Orbis Books.

Clifford, James. 1982. *Person and myth: Maurice Leenhardt in the Melanesian world.* Berkeley: University of California Press.

———. 1988. *The predicament of culture: Twentieth century ethnography, literature, and art.* Cambridge, Mass.: Harvard University Press.

Clifford, James, and George E. Marcus, eds. 1986. *Writing culture: The poetics and politics of ethnography.* Berkeley: University of California Press.

Cohen, Margot. 1992. To Mecca with love. *Far Eastern Economic Review* 9(April):28–29.

Coleman, John. 1970. Civil religion. *Sociological Analysis* 31(2):67–77.

Comaroff, Jean. 1985. *Body of power, spirit of resistance.* Chicago: University of Chicago Press.

———. 1994. Defying disenchantment: Reflection on ritual, power, and history. In *Asian visions of authority: Religion and the modern states of*

East and Southeast Asia, ed. C. F. Keyes, L. Kendall, and H. Hardacre, 301–314. Honolulu: University of Hawai'i Press.

Comaroff, Jean, and John Comaroff. 1986. Christianity and colonialism in South Africa. *American Ethnologist* 13:1–20.

———. 1991. *Of revelation and revolution: Christianity, colonialism, and consciousness in South Africa.* Vol. 1. Chicago: University of Chicago Press.

———. 1993. Introduction. In *Modernity and its malcontents: Ritual and power in postcolonial Africa*, ed. J. Comaroff and J. Comaroff, xi–xxxvii. Chicago: University of Chicago Press.

Cooley, Frank L. 1962. *Ambonese* adat: *A general description.* New Haven, Conn.: Yale University Center for Southeast Asian Studies.

Coté, Joost J. P. 1979. The colonization and schooling of the To Pamona of Central Sulawesi, 1894 to 1924. M.A. thesis, Monash University, Australia.

Coville, Elizabeth. 1988. "A single word brings to life": The Maro ritual in Tana Toraja (Indonesia). Ph.D. dissertation, University of Chicago.

Cribb, Robert. 1998. Will Indonesia survive? Paper presented at the annual meeting of the Association for Asian Studies, March 28, 1998, Washington, D.C.

Cuisinier, Jeanne. 1951. *Sumangat: L'ame et son culte en Indochine et en Indonésie* (Sumangat: The soul and its cult in Indochina and Indonesia). Paris: Gallimard.

Descola, Philippe. 1992. Societies of nature and the nature of society. In *Conceptualizing society*, ed. A. Kuper, 107–126. London and New York: Routledge.

Diamond, Jared. 1999. *Guns, germs, and steel: The fates of human societies.* New York: W. W. Norton & Co.

Dirks, Nicholas. 1987. *The hollow crown: Ethnohistory of an Indian kingdom.* Cambridge: Cambridge University Press.

Dirks, Nicholas B., Geoff Eley, and Sherry B. Ortner, eds. 1994. Introduction. In *Culture/power/history: A reader in contemporary social theory.* Princeton, N.J.: Princeton University Press.

Downs, Richard E. 1956. *The religion of the Bare'e speaking Toradja of Central Celebes.* s'Gravenhage: Uitgeverij Excelsior.

———. 1977 [1955]. Head-hunting in Indonesia. In *Structural anthropology in the Netherlands*, ed. P. E. Josselin de Jong, 117–149. The Hague: Martinus Nijhoff.

Drake, Richard Allen. 1989. Construction sacrifice and kidnapping rumor panics in Borneo. *Oceania* 59:269–279.

Dumont, Louis. 1980. *Homo hierarchicus: The caste system and its implications*. Chicago: University of Chicago Press.

Durkheim, Émile. 1915. *The elementary forms of the religious life*, trans. J. W. Swain. New York: The Macmillan Company.

Eickelman, Dale F. 1992. Mass higher education and the religious imagination in contemporary Arab societies. *American Ethnologist* 19(4):643–655.

Emmerson, Donald K. 1978. The bureaucracy in political context: Weakness in strength. In *Political power and communications in Indonesia*, ed. K. D. Jackson and L. W. Pye, 82–136. Berkeley: University of California Press.

Encyclopedië van Nederlandsche-Indie (Encyclopedia of the Netherlands' Indies). 1917–1939. 's-Gravenhage: Martinus Nijhoff.

Endicott, Kirk Michael. 1970. *An analysis of Malay magic*. Oxford: Clarendon Press.

Erb, Maribeth. 1991. Construction sacrifice, rumors and kidnapping scares in Manggarai. *Oceania* 62(2):114–126.

Errington, Shelly. 1989. *Meaning and power in a Southeast Asian realm*. Princeton, N.J.: Princeton University Press.

———. 1990. Recasting sex, gender, and power: A theoretical and regional overview. In *Power and difference: Gender in island Southeast Asia*, ed. J. Atkinson and S. Errington, 1–58. Stanford: Stanford University Press.

———. 1994. What became authentic primitive art? *Cultural Anthropology* 9(2):201–226.

Esser, S. J. 1964. De Uma-taal (The Uma language). *Verhandelingen van het Koninklijk Instituut voor Taal-, Land- en Volkenkunde*, no. 43, ed. J. Noorduyn. The Hague: Martinus Nijhoff.

Evans-Pritchard, Edward E. 1937. The notion of witchcraft explains unfortunate events. In *Witchcraft, oracles and magic among the Azande*. Oxford: Clarendon Press.

Feld, Steven. 1990. *Sound and sentiment: Birds, weeping, poetics, and song in Kaluli expression*. 2d ed. Philadelphia: University of Pennsylvania Press.

Feld, Steven, and Keith H. Basso. 1996. Introduction. In *Senses of place*. Santa Fe, N.M.: School of American Research Press.

Forth, Gregory. 1991. Construction sacrifice and headhunting rumors in Central Flores (Eastern Indonesia): A comparative note. *Oceania* 61:257–266.

Foucault, Michel. 1978. *The history of sexuality, vol.1: An introduction*, trans. R. Hurley. New York: Pantheon Books.

———. 1980. *Power/knowledge: Selected interviews and other writings 1972–1977*, ed. C. Gordon. New York: Pantheon Books.

Fox, James J. 1971. Semantic parallelism in Rotinese ritual language. *Bijdragen tot de Taal-, Land- en Volkenkunde* 127:215–255.

———. 1974. Our ancestors spoke in pairs: Essays on the ritual languages of eastern Indonesia. In *Explorations in the ethnography of speaking*, ed. R. Bauman and J. Sherzer, 65–85. London: Cambridge University Press.

Fox, James J., ed. 1988. *To speak in pairs: Essays on the ritual languages of eastern Indonesia*. Cambridge: Cambridge University Press.

Frazer, James George. 1924 [1890]. *The golden bough: A study in magic and religion*. Abrdg. ed. New York: The Macmillan Company.

Friedman, Jonathan. 1994. On perilous ideas. *Current Anthropology* 35(2):173–174.

Gadamer, Hans-Georg. 1975. *Truth and method*, ed. G. Barden and J. Cumming. New York: Seabury Press.

Gal, Susan, and Judith Irvine. 1995. The boundaries of language and disciplines: How ideologies construct differences. *Social Research* 62(4):967–1001.

Garang, Phil. J. 1985. *Dunia Kulawi: Masyarakat, budaya dan gereja di Sulawesi Tengah* (The Kulawi world: Society, culture, and church in Central Sulawesi). Peninjau 1983, year 10, no.2. Jakarta: Departemen Penelitian dan Pengembangan Persekutuan Gereja-Gereja di Indonesia.

Gauchet, Marcel. 1997. *The disenchantment of the world: A political history of religion*, trans. O. Burge. Princeton, N.J.: Princeton University Press.

Geertz, Clifford. 1960. *The religion of Java*. Chicago: University of Chicago Press.

———. 1963. *Agricultural involution: The processes of ecological change in Indonesia*. Berkeley: University of California Press.

———. 1968. *Islam observed: Religious development in Morocco and Indonesia*. Chicago: University of Chicago Press.

———. 1973a. Religion as a cultural system. In *The interpretation of cultures*, 87–125. New York: Basic Books.

———. 1973b [1964]. "Internal conversion" in contemporary Bali. In *The interpretation of cultures*, 170–189. New York: Basic Books.

———. 1983 [1974]. "From the native's point of view": On the nature of anthropological understanding. In *The pleasures of anthropology*, ed. M. Freilich, 58–73. New York: The New American Library.

George, Kenneth Martin. 1989. The singing from the headwaters: Song and tradition in the headhunting rituals of an upland Sulawesi community. Ph.D dissertation, University of Michigan.

———. 1991. Headhunting, history, and exchange in upland Sulawesi. *Journal of Asian Studies* 50(3):536–564.

———. 1996. *Showing signs of violence: The cultural politics of a twentieth-century headhunting ritual*. Berkeley: University of California Press.

———. 1998. Designs on Indonesia's Muslim communities. *Journal of Asian Studies* 57(3):693–713.

Gerth, H. H., and C. Wright Mills, ed. and trans. 1958. *From Max Weber: Essays in sociology*. New York: Oxford Press.

Ginsburg, Faye D. 1989. *Contested lives: The abortion debate in an American community*. Berkeley: University of California Press.

Glucklich, Ariel. 1997. *The end of magic*. New York: Oxford University Press.

Gonda, J. 1973. *Sanskrit in Indonesia*. New Delhi: International Academy of Indian Culture.

Gouda, Frances. 1995. *Dutch culture overseas: Colonial practice in the Netherlands Indies, 1900–1942*. Amsterdam: Amsterdam University Press.

Grimshaw, Patricia. 1989. New England missionary wives, Hawaiian women and the cult of true womanhood. In *Family and gender in the Pacific: Domestic contradictions and the colonial impact*, ed. M. Jolly and M. Macintyre, 19–44. Cambridge: Cambridge University Press.

Grubauer, Albert. 1913. *Unter Kopfjägern in Central-Celebes; ethnologische Streifzüge in Südost- und Central-Celebes von Professor Albert Grubauer* (Among headhunters in Central Celebes; ethnological survey in Southeast and Central Celebes by Professor Albert Grubauer). Leipzig: R. Voigtlanders.

Guthrie, Stewart. 1993. *Faces in the clouds: A new theory of religion*. Oxford: Oxford University Press.

Habbema, J. 1904. Onderwijs politiek en economisch belang van onderwijs aan de bevolking van Nederlandsch-Indie (Educational policy and the economic importance of education for the population of the Netherlands Indies). *Indische Gids* 22.

Hannerz, U. 1987. The world in creolization. *Africa* 57:546–559.

Harries, Patrick. 1988. The roots of ethnicity: Discourse and the politics of language construction in South-East Africa. *African Affairs* 87(346):25–54.

Harris, William G. 1923. Kejali land and people: Unique and antique children of nature well worth winning for Jesus. *All the World* (May):85–89.

———. 1925. Nothing without God. *All the World* (March):114–117.

Harvey, Barbara Sillars. 1974. Tradition, Islam, and rebellion: South Sulawesi 1950–1965. Ph.D. dissertation, Cornell University.

———. 1977. *Permesta: Half-a-rebellion*. Ithaca: Cornell Modern Indonesia Project Monograph Series, no. 57.

Hatcher, M. 1932. Soul-hunting among head-hunters. *Salvation Army Yearbook*, 24–26. London: Salvationist Publishing and Supplies, Ltd.

Hefner, Robert W. 1987a. The political economy of Islamic conversion in modern East Java. In *Islam and the political economy of meaning: Comparative studies of Muslim discourse*, ed. W. R. Roff, 53–78. Berkeley: University of California Press.

———. 1987b. The politics of popular art: Tayuban dance and culture change in East Java. *Indonesia* 43:75–94.

———. 1993a. Introduction: World building and the rationality of conversion. In *Conversion to Christianity: Historical and anthropological perspectives on a great transformation*, ed. R. Hefner, 3–44. Berkeley: University of California Press.

———. 1993b. Of faith and commitment: Christian conversion in Muslim Java. In *Conversion to Christianity: Historical and anthropological perspectives on a great transformation*, ed. R. Hefner, 99–125. Berkeley: University of California Press.

Henley, David E. F. 1996. *Nationalism and regionalism in a colonial context: Minahasa in the Dutch East Indies*. Leiden: KITLV Press.

Herrenschmidt, Olivier. 1982. Sacrifice: Symbolic or effective? In *Between belief and transgression*, ed. M. Izard and P. Smith, 24–42. Chicago: University of Chicago Press.

Hick, John. 1989. *An interpretation of religion: Human responses to the transcendent*. New York: Yale University Press.

Hobsbawm, Eric, and Terence Ranger, eds. 1983. *The invention of tradition*. Cambridge: Cambridge University Press.

Hockett, Charles F. 1958. *A course in modern linguistics*. New York: Macmillan.

————. 1977. *The view from language: Selected essays, 1948–1974*. Athens: University of Georgia Press.

Hofman, Ph. H. C. 1908. De zending in de werkkring Kasigoentjoe in 1907 (The mission in the work district Kasiguntu in 1907). *Mededelingen van wege het Nedelandsch zending genootschap* 52:81–94.

Holmgren, Robert J., and Anita Spertus. 1989. *Early Indonesian textiles from three island cultures*. New York: The Metropolitan Museum of Art.

hooks, bell. 1990. *Yearning: Race, gender, and cultural politics*. Boston: South End Press.

Hoskins, Janet. 1987a. Entering the bitter house: Spirit worship and conversion in West Sumba. In *Indonesian religions in transition*, ed. R. Smith Kipp and S. Rodgers, 136–160. Tucson: University of Arizona Press.

————. 1987b. Complementarity in this world and the next: Gender and agency in Kodi mortuary ceremonies. In *Dealing with inequality: Analysing gender relations in Melanesia and beyond*, ed. M. Strathern, 174–206. Cambridge: Cambridge University Press.

————. 1987c. The headhunter as hero: Local traditions and their reinterpretation in national history. *American Ethnologist* 14(4):605–622.

————. 1989. On losing and getting a head: Warfare, exchange, and alliance in a changing Sumba, 1888–1988. *American Ethnologist* 16(3):419–440.

————. 1993. *The play of time: Kodi perspectives on calendars, history, and exchange*. Berkeley: University of California Press.

————. 1996. The heritage of headhunting: History, ideology, and violence on Sumba, 1890–1990. In *Headhunting and the social imagination in Southeast Asia*, ed. J. Hoskins, 216–248. Stanford: Stanford University Press.

Hubert, Henri, and Marcel Mauss. 1897/1898. Essai sur la nature et la fonction du sacrifice. *l'Année Sociologieque* 2:29–138.

Hughes-Freeland, Felicia. 1990. Tayuban: Culture on the edge. *Indonesia Circle* 52:36–43.

Hutchinson, Dale L. 1977. God, king, and cultus: Ancient near Eastern and Israelite concepts. B.A. thesis, Department of Religion, Alma College, Michigan.

Jay, Robert R. 1969. *Javanese villagers: Social relations in rural Modjokuto.* Cambridge, Mass.: MIT Press.

Johnson, Mark. 1993. *Moral imagination: Implications of cognitive science for ethics.* Chicago: University of Chicago Press.

Kammerer, Cornelia Ann. 1990. Customs and Christian conversion among Akha highlanders of Burma and Thailand. *American Ethnologist* 17(2):277–291.

Ten Kate, P. 1915. Het Moraego (The Raego). *Mededeelingen van wege het Nederlandsche Zendinggenootschap* 49:332–334.

Kathirithamby-Wells, J. 1990. Introduction: An overview. In *The Southeast Asian port and polity: Rise and demise,* ed. J. Kathirithamby-Wells and J. Villiers, 1–16. Singapore: Singapore University Press.

Kaudern, Walter. 1925–1944. *Ethnographical studies in Celebes. Results of the author's expedition to Celebes, 1917–1920.* 6 vols. Göteborg: Elanders Bokytryckeri Aktiebolag.

    1925: vol. 1, *Structures and settlements in Central Celebes.*

    1925: vol. 2, *Migrations of the Toradja in Central Celebes.*

    1927: vol. 3, *Musical instruments in Celebes.*

    1929: vol. 4, *Games and dances in Celebes.*

    1938: vol. 5, *Megalithic finds in Central Celebes.*

    1944: vol. 6, *Art in Central Celebes.*

———. 1941. The noble families or Maradika of Koelawi, Central Celebes. *Etnologiska Studier* 11(1940). Götcborg: Elanders Boktryckeri Aktiebolag.

Keane, Webb. 1995. Religious change and historical reflection in Anakalang, West Sumba, Indonesia. *Journal of Southeast Asian Studies* 26(2):289–306.

———. 1996. Materialism, missionaries, and modern subjects in colonial Indonesia. In *Conversion to modernities: The globalization of Christianity,* ed. P. van de Veer, 137–170. New York and London: Routledge.

———. 1997a. *Signs of recognition: Powers and hazards of representation in an Indonesian society.* Berkeley: University of California Press.

———. 1997b. From fetishism to sincerity: On agency, the speaking subject, and their historicity in the context of religious conversion. *Comparative Studies in Society and History* 39(4):674–693.

Keeler, Ward. 1987. *Javanese shadow plays, Javanese selves*. Princeton, N.J.: Princeton University Press.

———. 1990. Speaking of gender in Java. In *Power and difference: Gender in island Southeast Asia*, ed. J. Atkinson and S. Errington, 127–152. Stanford: Stanford University Press.

Keesing, Roger M. 1982. *Kwaio religion: The living and the dead in a Solomon Island society*. New York: Columbia University Press.

———. 1984. Rethinking *mana*. *Journal of Anthropological Research* 40(1)137–156.

Kenyon, Albert. 1952. *Leonard goes east*. London: Salvationist Publishing and Supplies, Ltd.

Keyes, Charles F. 1991. Christianity as an indigenous religion in Southeast Asia. *Social Compass* 38(2):177–185.

———. 1993. Why the Thai are not Christians: Buddhist and Christian conversion in Thailand. In *Conversion to Christianity: Historical and anthropological perspectives on a great transformation*, ed. R. Hefner, 259–283. Berkeley: University of California Press.

———. 1996. Being Protestant Christians in Southeast Asian worlds. *Journal of Southeast Asian Studies* 27(2):280–292.

Kim, Choong Soon. 1990. The role of the non-Western anthropologist reconsidered: Illusion versus reality. *Current Anthropology* 31(2):196–201.

Kim, Hyung-Jun. 1998. The changing interpretation of religious freedom in Indonesia. *Journal of Southeast Asian Studies* 29(2):357–373.

Kipp, Rita Smith. 1990. *The early years of a Dutch colonial mission: The Karo field*. Ann Arbor: University of Michigan Press.

———. 1991a. The secularization of an ethnic identity. Paper prepared for the annual meeting of the Association for Asian Studies, April 11–14, 1991, New Orleans, La.

———. 1991b. A practice approach to conversion as a change of identity. Paper prepared for the annual meeting of the American Anthropological Association, November 23, 1991, Chicago, Ill.

———. 1993. *Dissociated identities: Ethnicity, religion, and class in an Indonesian society*. Ann Arbor: University of Michigan Press.

———. 1995. Conversion by affiliation: The history of the Karo Batak Protestant Church. *American Ethnologist* 22(4):868–882.

Kipp, Rita Smith, and Susan Rodgers, eds. 1987. *Indonesian religions in transition*. Tucson: University of Arizona Press.

Kirsch, A. Thomas. 1973. *Feasting and social oscillation: Religion and society in upland Southeast Asia*. Data Paper no. 92. Ithaca, N.Y.: Cornell University Southeast Asia Program.

Klopfer, Lisa. 1991. Choosing health care in a West Sumatran village. Paper presented at the annual meeting of the American Anthropological Association, November 23, 1991, Chicago, Ill.

Koentjaraningrat. 1989. *Javanese culture*. Singapore: Oxford University Press.

Kotilainen, Eija-Maija. 1992. *"When the bones are left": A study of the material culture of Central Sulawesi*. The Finnish Anthropological Society Transactions, no. 31. Helsinki: The Finnish Anthropological Society.

Kruyt, Albertus C. 1898a. Verslag van de zending te Posso over 1896 (Report from the Christian mission at Poso during 1896). *Mededelingen van wege het Nedelandsch zending genootschap* 42:170–194.

———. 1898b. Verslag van de zending te Posso in 1897 (Report from the Christian mission at Poso in 1897). *Mededelingen van wege het Nedelandsch zending genootschap* 42:254–73.

———. 1900. De zending te Posso in 1899 (The Christian mission at Poso). *Mededelingen van wege het Nedelandsch zending genootschap* 44:341–356.

———. 1906. *Het animisme in den Indischen archipel*. 's-Gravenhage: Martinus Nijhoff.

———. 1907. De inlandsche staat en de zending (The native state and the mission). Address delivered to the Indisch Genootschap, October 23, 1906. *Verhandelingen van de Indisch Genootschap* 1907:70–109.

———. 1924. De betekenis van de natten rijstbouw voor de Posso'ers (The importance of wet-rice agriculture for the Poso people). *Koloniale Studieen* 8:31–53.

———. 1929. The influence of Western civilization on the inhabitants of Poso. In *The effect of Western influence on native civilizations in the Malay archipelago*, ed. B. J. O. Schrieke, 1–9. Batavia: G. Kolf.

———. 1935/1936. Zending en volkskracht (The mission and national character). *Mededelingen van wege het Nedelandsch zending genootschap*, vols. 79–80.

———. 1938. *De West Toradja's op Midden-Celebes* (The West Torajas of Central Celebes). 4 vols. Amsterdam: Uitgave van de N.V. Noord-Hollandsche Uitgevers-Maatschappij.

Kruyt, Jan. 1970. Het zendingsveld Poso: Geschiedenis van een konfrontatie (The mission field Poso: History of a confrontation). Kampen, The Netherlands: J. H. Kok, N.V.

Kuipers, Joel C. 1990a. *Power in performance: The creation of textual authority in Weyéwa ritual speech*. Philadelphia: University of Pennsylvania Press.

———. 1990b. Talking about troubles: Gender differences in Weyéwa ritual speech use. In *Power and difference: Gender in island Southeast Asia*, ed. J. Atkinson and S. Errington, 153–175. Stanford: Stanford University Press.

———. 1993. The society and its environment. In *Indonesia: A country study*, ed. W. H. Frederick and R. L Worden, 69–135. Washington, D.C.: Federal Research Division, Library of Congress.

———. 1998. *Language, identity, and marginality in Indonesia: The changing nature of ritual speech on the island of Sumba*. Cambridge: Cambridge University Press.

Laderman, Carol. 1991. *Taming the wind of desire: Psychology, medicine, and aesthetics in Malay shamanistic performance*. Berkeley: University of California Press.

Lansing, J. Stephen. 1991. *Priests and programmers: Technologies of power in the engineered landscape of Bali*. Princeton, N.J.: Princeton University Press.

Lawrence, Bruce. 1989. *Defenders of God: The fundamentalist revolt against the modern age*. San Francisco: Harper and Row.

Leach, Edmund R. 1954. *Political systems of highland Burma*. Cambridge, Mass.: Harvard University Press.

———. 1976. *Culture and communication: The logic by which symbols are connected*. Cambridge: Cambridge University Press.

Lebar, Frank M., ed. 1972. *Ethnic groups of insular Southeast Asia, vol. 1: Indonesia, Andaman Islands, and Madagascar*. New Haven, Conn.: Human Relations Area Files.

Lehman, F. K. 1963. *The structure of Chin society*. Urbana: University of Illinois Press.

———. 1979. Who are the Karen, and if so, why? Karen ethnohistory and a formal theory of ethnicity. In *Ethnic adaptation and identity*, ed. C. F. Keyes, 215–253. Philadelphia: Institute for the Study of Human Issues.

———. 1987. Burmese religion. In *The encyclopedia of religion*, ed. M. Eliade, 574–580. New York: Macmillan Publishing Co.

———. 2001. The relevance of the founders' cult for understanding the political systems of the peoples of northern South East Asia and its Chinese borderlands. In *Founders' cults and political hierarchy in Southeast Asia*, ed. N. Tannenbaum and C. Kammerer. New Haven, Conn.: Yale University Center for Southeast Asian Studies.

Lev, Daniel S. 1985. Colonial law and the genesis of the Indonesian state. *Indonesia* 40:57–74.

Li, Tania Murray. 1998. Working separately but eating together: Personhood, property, and power in conjugal relations. *American Ethnologist* 25(4):675–694.

Liddle, R. William. 1988. *Politics and culture in Indonesia*. Ann Arbor: University of Michigan Press.

Lienhardt, R. G. 1982. The Dinka and Catholicism. In *Religious organization and religious experience*, ed. J. Davis, 81–95. Association of Social Anthropologists Monograph no. 21. London: Academic Press.

MacGregor, Geddes. 1987. Soul: Christian concept. In *The encyclopedia of religion*, vol. 13, ed. M. Eliade, 455–460. New York: Macmillan Publishing Co.

Martens, Martha Ann. 1993. Uncovering the widow among the Uma. In *Ritual, belief, and kinship in Sulawesi*, ed. M. Gregoerson, 91–97. Dallas: International Museum of Texas, Summer Institute of Linguistics.

Martens, Michael P. 1988a. Phonology of Uma. In *Papers in western Austronesian linguistics*, no. 4, ed. H. Steinhauer, 153–165. Pacific Linguistics Series A, no. 79. Canberra: The Department of Linguistics, Australian National University.

———. 1988b. Notes on Uma verbs. In *Papers in western Austronesian linguistics*, no. 4, ed. H. Steinhauer, 167–237. Pacific Linguistics Series A, no. 79. Canberra: The Department of Linguistics, Australian National University.

———. 1988c. Focus and discourse in Uma. In *Papers in western Austronesian linguistics*, no. 4, ed. H. Steinhauer, 239–256. Pacific Linguistics Series A, no. 79. Canberra: The Department of Linguistics, Australian National University.

———. 1988d. Focus or ergativity? Pronoun sets in Uma. In *Papers in western Austronesian linguistics*, no. 4, ed. H. Steinhauer, 263–277. Pacific Linguistics Series A, no. 79. Canberra: The Department of Linguistics, Australian National University.

———. 1985ms. Dialects of Uma. Unpublished manuscript in files of the author.

———. 1988ms. Uma-Indonesian-English word list. Unpublished manuscript in files of the author.

Martens, Michael P., and Martha Martens. 1988. Some notes on the inelegant glottal: A problem in Uma phonology. In *Papers in western Austronesian linguistics*, no. 4, ed. H. Steinhauer, 279–281. Pacific Linguistics Series A, no. 79. Canberra: The Department of Linguistics, Australian National University.

Martin, David. 1994. Evangelical and charismatic Christianity in Latin America. In *Charismatic Christianity as a global culture*, ed. K. Poewe, 73–86. Columbia: University of South Carolina Press.

Martin, Emily. 1987. *The woman in the body: A cultural analysis of reproduction*. Boston: Beacon Press.

Marty, Martin E., and R. Scott Appleby, eds. 1991. *Fundamentalisms observed. The fundamentalisms project, vol.1*. Chicago: University of Chicago Press.

Masyhuda, Masyhuddin. 1977. *Monografi daerah Sulawesi Tengah* (Monograph on the Central Sulawesi region). 4 vols. Jakarta: Departemen Pendidikan dan Kebudayaan.

———. 1980/1981. *Tradisi megalit di Lembah Palu* (Megalithic traditions in the Palu Valley). Palu: Proyek Pengembangan Permuseuman Sulawesi Tengah, Departemen Pendidikan dan Kebudayaan.

———. 1988/1989. *Etnik dan logat di Sulawesi Tengah* (Ethnicity and dialects in Central Sulawesi). Palu: Departemen Pendidikan dan Kebudayaan.

Mattulada. 1991. Manusia dan kebudayaan Kaili di Sulawesi Tengah (Kaili people and culture in Central Sulawesi). *Anthropologi Indonesia* 48(15):110–182. Jakarta: Department of Anthropology, University of Indonesia.

Mauss, Marcel. 1967. *The gift*, trans. I. Cunnison. New York: W. W. Norton.

Mayr, Ernst. 1982. *The growth of biological thought: Diversity, evolution, and inheritance*. Cambridge, Mass.: Belknap Press of Harvard University Press.

———. 1991. *One long argument: Charles Darwin and the genesis of modern evolutionary thought*. Cambridge, Mass.: Harvard University Press.

McKinley, Robert. 1976. Human and proud of it! A structural treatment of headhunting rites and the social definition of enemies. In *Studies in*

Borneo societies: Social process and anthropologiccal explanation, ed. G. N. Appell, 92–126. DeKalb: Center for Southeast Asian Studies, Northern Illinois University.

McKinnon, Susan. 1989. Flags and half-moons: Tanimbarese textiles in an "engendered" system of valuables. In *To speak with cloth*, ed. M. Gittinger, 27–42. Los Angeles: UCLA Museum.

McNeill, J. T. 1933. Folk-paganism in the Penitentials. *Journal of Religion* 13:450–466.

Meijer, D. H. 1932. De Kentongan en de Veiligheid. *De Nederlandsch-Indische Politiegids* 16(4):104–108.

Metcalf, Peter. 1982. *A Borneo journey into death: Berawan eschatology from its rituals*. Philadelphia: University of Pennsylvania Press.

Middelkoop, Pieter. 1960. *Curse-retribution-enmity as data in natural religion, especially in Timor, confronted with the scripture*. Amsterdam: Jacob van Campen.

Milner, A. C. 1982. *Kerajaan: Malay political culture on the eve of colonial rule*. Tucson: Association for Asian Studies and University of Arizona Press.

Moerman, Michael. 1965. Ethnic identity in a complex civilization: Who are the Lue? *American Anthropologist* 67:1215–1230.

Molnar, Andrea K. 1990. Nitu: A symbolic analysis of an Austronesian spirit category. M.A. thesis, University of Alberta.

Moore, Hyatt, ed. 1984. *Pass the word: 50 years of Wycliffe Bible Translators*. Huntington Beach, Calif.: Wycliffe Bible Translators, Inc.

Morris, Leslie. 1991. Weeping, clapping and detachment among Javanese charismatic Christians. Paper presented at the annual meeting of the Association for Asian Studies, April 11–14, 1991, New Orleans, La.

———. 1996. Reading the Bible in a Javanese village. *Journal of Southeast Asian Studies* 27(2):374–386.

Mulder, Niels. 1978. *Mysticism and everyday life in contemporary Java*. Singapore: Singapore University Press.

Müller, F. Max. 1872. *Lectures of the science of religion*. New York: Charles Scribner and Company.

Murdock, George P. 1949. *Social structure*. New York: The Macmillan Co.

Mus, Paul. 1975 [1933]. *India seen from the east: Indian and indigenous cults in Champa*, ed. I. W. Mabbett and D. P. Chandler. Monash papers on Southeast Asia no.3. Monash, Australia: Monash University Centre of Southeast Asian Studies.

Neal, Harry Edward. 1961. *The hallelujah army*. Philadelphia: Chilton Company.

Needham, Rodney. 1976. Skulls and causality. *Man* 11(1):71–88.

Nieuwenhuijze, C. A. O. van. 1958. *Aspects of Islam in post-colonial Indonesia: Five essays*. The Hague: Van Hoeve.

Noorduyn, J. 1964. Ter inleiding (Introduction) In *De Uma-taal* (The Uma language), ed. J. Noorduyn, v–x.Verhandelingen van het Koninklijk Instituut voor Taal-, Land- en Volkenkunde no.43. The Hague: Martinus Nijhoff.

————. 1991. *A critical survey of studies on the languages of Sulawesi*. Koninklijk Instituut voor Taal-, Land- en Volkenkunde, bibliographical series no.18. Leiden: KITLV Press.

Nooy-Palm, C. H. M. 1975. Introduction to the Sa'dan Toraja people and their country. *Archipel* 10:53–92.

————. 1979. *The Sa'dan-Toraja: A study of their social life and religion, vol. 1: Organization, symbols and beliefs*. Verhandelingen van het Koninklijk Instituut voor Taal-, Land- en Volkenkunde no. 87. The Hague: Martinus Nijhoff.

Nourse, Jennifer Williams. 1984. Tomini. In *Muslim peoples: A world ethnographic survey*. 2d ed., ed. R. M. Weekes. Westport, Conn.: Greenwood Press.

————. 1989. We are the womb of the world: Birth spirits and the Lauje of Central Sulawesi. Ph.D. dissertation, University of Virginia.

————. 1999. *Conceiving spirits: Birth rituals and contested identities among Laujé of Indonesia*. Washington, D.C.: Smithsonian Institution Press.

O'Connor, Richard A. 1995. Agricultural change and ethnic succession in Southeast Asian states: A case for regional anthropology. *Journal of Asian Studies* 54(4):968–996.

————. 1996. Blessings and merit: Elementary forms and religious complexes in comparative and historical perspective. In *Merit and blessing in mainland Southeast Asia in comparative perspective*, ed. N. Tannenbaum and C. Kammerer, 212–230. New Haven, Conn.: Yale University Center for Southeast Asian Studies.

————. 2001. Founder cults in regional and historical perspective. In *Founders' cults and political hierarchy in Southeast Asia*, ed. N. Tannenbaum and C. Kammerer. New Haven, Conn.: Yale University Center for Southeast Asian Studies.

Ong, Aihwa. 1987. *Spirits of resistance and capitalist discipline: Factory women in Malaysia*. Albany: State University of New York Press.

———. 1990a. Japanese factories, Malay workers: Class and sexual metaphors in West Malaysia. In *Power and difference: Gender in island Southeast Asia*, ed. J. Atkinson and S. Errington, 385–422. Stanford: Stanford University Press.

———. 1990b. State versus Islam: Malay families, women's bodies, and the body politic in Malaysia. *American Ethnologist* 17(2):258–276.

Orr, William W. 1977. *Setan, ada atau tidak?* (trans. of: *Are demons for real?* 1970, Scripture Press Publications, Inc.), trans. M. Inggriani. Bandung: Penerbit Kalam Hidup.

Ortner, Sherry. 1984. Theory in anthropology since the sixties. *Comparative Studies in Society and History* 26(1):126–166.

———. 1989. *High religion: A cultural and political history of Sherpa Buddhism.* Princeton, N.J.: Princeton University Press.

Osborne, Peter. 1995. *The politics of time: Modernity and avant-garde.* London: Verso.

Pakan, Priyanti. 1977. Orang Toraja: Identitas, klasifikasi dan lokasi (Toraja people: Identification, classification and location). *Berita Antropologi* 9(32–33):21–49.

Pals, Daniel L. 1996. *Seven theories of religion.* New York: Oxford University Press.

Pannel, Sandra. 1992. Traveling to other worlds: Narratives of headhunting, appropriation and the Other in the eastern archipelago. *Oceania* 62:162–178.

Peacock, James L. 1968. *Rites of modernization: Symbolic and social aspects of Indonesian proletarian drama.* Chicago: University of Chicago Press.

———. 1978. *Muslim puritans: Reformist psychology in Southeast Asian Islam.* Berkeley: University of California Press.

Peacock, James L., and Ruell W. Tyson, Jr. 1989. *Pilgrims of paradox: Calvinism and experience among the primitive Baptists of the Blue Ridge.* Washington, D.C.: Smithsonian Institution Press.

Peel, John D. Y. 1968. *Aladura: A religious movement among the Yoruba.* London: Oxford University Press for the International African Institute.

———. 1984. Making history: The past in the Ijesha present. *Man* 19(1):111–132.

Pelras, Christian. 1985. Religion, tradition and the dynamics of Islamization in South Sulawesi. *Archipel* 29:108–135.

Pemberton, John. 1994. *On the subject of "Java."* Ithaca, N.Y.: Cornell University Press.

Perwakilan Departemen Pendidikan dan Kebudayaan. 1973. *Peningalan Nasional di Sulawesi Tengah* (National archaeological remains in Central Sulawesi). Palu: Team Prasurvey Kebudayaan Propinsi Sulawesi Tengah.

Pietz, William. 1985. The problem of the fetish, 1. *Res* 9:5–17.

Poewe, Karla, ed. 1994. *Charismatic Christianity as a global culture.* Columbia: University of South Carolina Press.

Price, Sally. 1989. *Primitive art in civilized places.* Chicago: Chicago University Press.

Purdy, Susan S. 1982. The civil religion thesis as it applies to a pluralistic society: Pancasila democracy in Indonesia (1945–1965). *Journal of International Affairs* 36:307–316.

Rafael, Vicente L. 1993. *Contracting colonialism: Translation and Christian conversion in Tagalog society under early Spanish rule.* Durham, N.C.: Duke University Press.

Ranger, Terence. 1987. An Africanist comment. Special issue: Frontiers of Christian evangelism. *American Ethnologist* 14(1):182–185.

———. 1993. The local and the global in southern African religious history. In *Conversion to Christianity: Historical and anthropological perspectives on a great transformation,* ed. R Hefner, 65–98. Berkeley: University of California Press.

Reader, Ian, and George J. Tanabe, Jr. 1998. *Practically religious: Worldly benefits and the common religion of Japan.* Honolulu: University of Hawai'i Press.

Redfield, Robert. 1956. *Peasant society and culture.* Chicago: University of Chicago Press.

Reynolds, Frank E. 1977. Civic religion and national community in Thailand. *Journal of Asian Studies* 36(2):267–282.

Robison, Richard. 1986. *Indonesia: The rise of capital.* North Sydney: Allen and Unwin.

Robinson, Kathryn May. 1989. Choosing contraception: Cultural change and the Indonesian family planning programme. In *Creating Indonesian cultures,* ed. P. Alexander, 21–38. Oceania Ethnographies no. 3. Sydney: Oceania Publications.

Rodgers Siregar, Susan. 1981. *Adat,* Islam, and Christianity in a Batak homeland. *Papers in International Studies, Southeast Asia Series,* no. 57. Athens, Ohio: Ohio University Center for International Studies.

Roff, William R. 1985. Islam obscured? Some reflections on studies of Islam and society in Southeast Asia. *Archipel* 29(1):7–34.

Roff, William R., ed. 1987. *Islam and the political economy of meaning: Comparative studies of Muslim discourse.* Berkeley: University of California Press.

Rosaldo, Michelle. 1980. *Knowledge and passion: Ilongot notions of self and social life.* Cambridge: Cambridge University Press.

Rosaldo, Renato. 1980. *Ilongot headhunting 1883–1974.* Stanford: Stanford University Press.

———. 1984. Grief and a headhunter's rage: On the cultural force of emotions. In *Text, play, and story: The construction and reconstruction of self and society,* ed. E. M. Bruner, 178–195. 1983 *Proceedings of the American Ethnological Society,* ed. S. Plattner. Washington, D.C.: American Ethnological Society.

Roseman, Marina. 1990. Head, heart, odor, and shadow: The structure of the self, the emotional world, and ritual performance among Senoi Temiar. *Ethos* 18(3):227–249.

Rosenlund, Edvard. 1933. Understanding native customs and languages. *The Officers' Review* (July).

Royce, Anya Peterson. 1982. *Ethnic identity: Strategies of diversity.* Bloomington: Indiana University Press.

Russell, Susan D. 1989. Ritual persistence and the ancestral cult among the Ibaloi of the Luzon highlands. In *Changing lives, changing rites: Ritual and social dynamics in Philippine and Indonesian uplands,* ed. S. D. Russell and C. E. Cunningham, 17–43. Michigan Studies of South and Southeast Asia no.1. Ann Arbor: University of Michigan Center for South and Southeast Asian Studies.

Sahlins, Marshall. 1981. *Historical metaphors and mythical realities: Structure in the early history of the Sandwich Islands kingdom.* Ann Arbor: University of Michigan Press.

———. 1985. *Islands of history.* Chicago: Chicago University Press.

———. 1994. Cosmologies of capitalism: The trans-Pacific sector of "The World System." In *Culture/power/history. A reader in contemporary social theory,* ed. N. Dirks, G. Eley, and S. Ortner, 412–457. Princeton, N.J.: Princeton University Press.

Said, Edward W. 1978. *Orientalism.* New York: Pantheon Books.

Salvation Army. 1915. Progress in Celebes. *All the World* (June):303–306.

———. 1919. Pioneering in Mid-Celebes. *All the World* (February):65–68.

———. 1922. Salvation amid semi-barbarism. *The War Cry* (July 15):10.

———. 1924a. A modern Queen Esther. *All the World* (April):55–58.

——. 1924b. Among the wild men of Celebes. *The War Cry* (July 26):5.

——. 1925a. Chats with missionary officers. *The Officer* (January):39–88.

——. 1925b. The first training garrison in Celebes. *All the World* (May):176–177.

——. 1949. A pioneer in Celebes. *The Warrior* (September):98–99.

——. 1976a. What is the Salvation Army? *The Salvation Army yearbook 1976*, 35. London: Salvationist Publishing and Supplies, Ltd.

——. 1976b. Salvationist doctrines. *The Salvation Army yearbook 1976*, 240. London: Salvationist Publishing and Supplies, Ltd.

——. 1985. *Disposition of forces: Indonesia territory*. Bandung, Indonesia: Kantor Pusat Bala Keselamatan (Salvation Army Territorial Headquarters).

Sandall, Robert. 1948. From mission to army. *Salvation Army yearbook 1948*, 17–18. London: Salvationist Publishing and Supplies, Ltd.

Sarasin, Paul, and Fritz Sarasin. 1905. *Reisen in Celebes aus geführt in den Jahren 1893–1896 und 1902–1903* (Travels in Celebes carried out in the years 1893–1896 and 1902–1903). 2 vols. Weisbaden: Kreidel.

Saunders, George R., ed. 1988. *Culture and Christianity: The dialectics of transformation*. New York: Greenwood Press.

Saussure, Ferdinand de. 1974. *Course in general linguistics*. Glasgow: Fontana.

Schärer, Hans. 1938. *Das Menschenopfer bei den Katinganern* (The human sacrifice by the Katinga). Tijdschrift van den Indische Taal-, Land- en Volkenkunde van het Bataviaasch Genootschap van Kunsten en Wetenschappen, Jakarta, vol. 78.

——. 1940. *Die Bedeutung des Menschenopfers im Dajakischen Totenkult* (The significance of the human offerings in the Dayak death cult). Mitteilungsblatt der deutchen Gesellschaft für Völkerkunde no. 10, Hamburg.

——. 1963. *Ngaju religion: The conception of God among a South Borneo people*. The Hague: Martinus Nijhoff.

Scheper-Hughes, Nancy, and Margaret Lock. 1987. The mindful body: A prolegomenon to future work in medical anthropology. *Medical Anthropology Quarterly* 1(n.s.):6–41.

Schiller, Anne. 1997. *Small sacrifices: Religious change and cultural identity among the Ngaju of Indonesia*. New York: Oxford University Press.

Schneider, Jane, and Shirley Lindenbaum. 1987. Frontiers of Christian evangelism: Essays in honor of Joyce Riegelhaupt. Special issue: Frontiers of Christian evangelism. *American Ethnologist* 14(1):1–8.

Schrauwers, Albert. 1998. Returning to the "Origin": Church and state in the ethnographies of the "To Pamona." In *Southeast Asian identities: Culture and the politics of representation in Indonesia, Malaysia, Singapore, and Thailand*, ed. J. S. Kahn, 203–226. Singapore: Institute of Southeast Asian Studies.

Schulte Nordholt. 1971. *The political system of the Atoni of Timor*. The Hague: Martinus Nijhoff.

Scott, James C. 1976. *The moral economy of the peasant: Subsistence and rebellion in Southeast Asia*. New Haven, Conn.: Yale University Press.

———. 1985. *Weapons of the weak: Everyday forms of peasant resistance*. New Haven, Conn.: Yale University Press.

———. 1990. *Domination and the arts of resistance: Hidden transcripts*. New Haven, Conn.: Yale University Press.

———. 1998. *Seeing like a state: How certain schemes to improve the human condition have failed*. New Haven, Conn.: Yale University Press.

Sears, Laurie. 1993. The contingency of autonomous history. In *Autonomous histories, particular truths: Essays in honor of John R. W. Smail*, ed. L. Sears, 3–35. University of Wisconsin Center for Southeast Asian Studies Monograph no. 11. Madison: University of Wisconsin-Madison Center for Southeast Asian Studies.

Sell, Hans Joachim. 1955. *Der schlimme Tod bei den Völkern Indonesiens* (Bad death among the Indonesian peoples). 's-Gravenhage: Mouton & Co.

Shaw, Rosalind, and Charles Stewart. 1994. Introduction: Problematizing syncretism. In *Syncretism/anti-syncretism: The politics of religious synthesis*, ed. C. Stewart and R. Shaw, 1–26. London: Routledge.

Siegel, James T. 1986. *Solo in the New Order: Language and hierarchy in an Indonesian city*. Princeton, N.J.: Princeton University Press.

———. 1997. *Fetish, recognition, revolution*. Princeton, N.J.: Princeton University Press.

Skeat, Walter William. 1901. *Malay magic: An introduction to the folklore and popular religion of the Malay Peninsular* [sic]. London: Macmillan and Co.

Slobin, Mark. 1983. Rethinking 'revival' of American ethnic music. *New York Folklore* 9(3–4):37–44.

Smith, Wilfred Cantwell. 1978. *The meaning and end of religion*. San Francisco: Harper & Row.

Smith, William Robertson. 1889. *Lectures on the religion of the Semites*. New York: Appleton.

Smithsonian Folkways Recordings. 1999. Sulawesi: Music for celebrations, funerals, and work. *Music of Indonesia*, vol.18. Recorded by P. Yampolsky. SFW CD 40444. Washington, DC: Smithsonian Institution.

Soelarto, B., and S. Ilmi Albiladiyah. n.d. *Adat istiadat dan kesenian orang Kulawi di Sulawesi Tengah* (Traditions and art of the Kulawi people in Central Sulawesi). Jakarta: Proyek Pengembangan Media Kebudayaan, Departemen Pendidikan dan Kebudayaan.

Sperber, Dan. 1996. *Explaining culture: A naturalistic approach*. Oxford: Blackwell.

Steedly, Mary Margaret. 1993. *Hanging without a rope: Narrative experience in colonial and postcolonial Karoland*. Princeton, N.J.: Princeton University Press.

———. 1996. The importance of proper names: Language and "national" identity in colonial Karoland. *American Ethnologist* 23(3):447–475.

Stoler, Ann Laura. 1985. *Capitalism and confrontation in Sumatra's plantation belt*. New Haven, Conn.: Yale University Press.

———. 1989a. Making empire respectable: The politics of race and sexual morality in 20th-century colonial cultures. *American Ethnologist* 16(4):634–660.

———. 1989b. Rethinking colonial categories: European communities and the boundaries of rule. *Comparative Studies in Society and History* 31:134–161.

———. 1992. "In cold blood": Hierarchies of credibility and the politics of colonial narratives. *Representations* 37:151–189.

Strathern, Andrew. 1971. *The rope of Moka*. Cambridge: Cambridge University Press.

Suharto. 1991. Pidato Sambutan Pejabat Presiden Republik Indonesia, Soeharto, Pada Pembukaan Musyawarah Antar Agama Pada Tanggal 30 Nopember 1967 di Jakarta. In *Toleransi dan Kemerdekaan Beragama Dalam Islam Sebagai Dasar Menuju Dialog dan Kerukunan Antar Agama*, ed. U. Hasyim, 393–397. Surabaya: PT. Bina Ilmu.

Sullivan, Norma. 1983. Indonesian women in development: State theory and urban Kampung practice. In *Women's work and womens' roles:*

Economics and everyday life in Indonesia, Malaysia, and Singapore, ed. L. Manderson, 147–171. Canberra: Australian National University.

Suryakusuma, Julia I. 1996. The state and sexuality in New Order Indonesia. In *Fantasizing the feminine in Indonesia,* ed. L. Sears, 92–119. Durham, N.C.: Duke University Press.

Suyono, H. 1984. Indonesia's integrated program facing family planning needs of the future. Unpublished manuscript.

Tambiah, Stanley J. 1968. The magical power of words. *Man* 3(2):175–208.

———. 1991. *Magic, science, religion, and the scope of rationality.* Cambridge: Cambridge University Press.

Tannenbaum, Nicola. 1995. *Who can compete against the world? Power-protection and Buddhism in Shan worldview.* Monograph and Occasional Paper Series no. 51. Ann Arbor, Mich.: Association for Asian Studies.

Tarro, Ph. Gideon. 1982. *Ceritera rakyat Towulu* (Towulu' folktales). Unpublished manuscript, 9 pages, dated September 30. In possession of the author.

Taylor, Paul Michael. 1988. From *mantra* to *mantaráa*: Opacity and transparency in the language of Tobelo magic and medicine (Halmahera Island, Indonesia). *Social Science and Medicine* 27(5):425–436.

Taylor, Robert. 1985. The Summer Institute of Linguistics/Wycliffe Bible Translators in anthropological perspective. In *Missionaries and anthropologists, part II. Studies in Third World societies,* no. 26, ed. F. A. Salamone, 93–116. Williamsburg, Va.: Department of Anthropology, College of William and Mary.

Thomas, Keith. 1971. *Religion and the decline of magic: Studies in popular beliefs in sixteenth and seventeenth century England.* London: Weidenfeld and Nicolson.

Thomas, Nicholas. 1991. *Entangled objects: Exchange, material culture, and colonialism in the Pacific.* Cambridge, Mass.: Harvard University Press.

Thune, Carl F. 1990. Fathers, aliens, and brothers: Building a social world in Loboda Village church services. In *Christianity in Oceania: Ethnographic perspectives.* ASAO Monograph no. 12, ed. J. Barker, 101–125. Lanham, Md.: University Press of America.

Toer, Pramoedya Ananta. 1996. *This earth of mankind (Bumi manusia),* trans. M. Lane. New York: Penguin Books.

Tolen, Rachel J. 1991. Colonizing and transforming the criminal tribesman: The Salvation Army in British India. *American Ethnologist* 18(1):106–125.

Traube, Elizabeth G. 1986. *Cosmology and social life: Ritual exchange among the Mambai of East Timor.* Chicago: University of Chicago Press.

Trinh T. Minh-ha. 1989. *Woman, native, other: Writing postcoloniality and feminism.* Bloomington: Indiana University Press.

Tsing, Anna Lowenhaupt. 1987. A rhetoric of centers in a religion of the periphery. In *Indonesian religions in transition,* ed. R. Smith Kipp and S. Rodgers, 187–210. Tucson: University of Arizona Press.

———. 1990. Gender and performance in Meratus dispute settlement. In *Power and difference: Gender in island Southeast Asia,* ed. J. Atkinson and S. Errington, 95–125. Stanford: Stanford University Press.

———. 1993. *In the realm of the diamond queen: Marginality in an out-of-the-way place.* Princeton, N.J.: Princeton University Press.

———. 1996. Telling violence in the Meratus mountains. In *Headhunting and the social imagination in Southeast Asia,* ed. J. Hoskins, 184–215. Stanford: Stanford University Press.

Turner, Bryan S., ed. 1990. *Theories of modernity and postmodernity.* London: Sage Publications.

Tylor, E. B. 1903 [1871]. *Primitive culture: Researches into the development of mythology, philosophy, religion, language, art, and custom.* 2 vols., 4th rev. ed. London: John Murray.

Unsworth, Isaac. 1922. A nation born in a day: The coming of the Salvation Army to Celebes. *The War Cry* (February 4):10.

Valeri, Valerio. 1985. *Kingship and sacrifice: Ritual and society in ancient Hawaii.* Chicago: University of Chicago Press.

van de Werken, Colonel. 1924. In the land of the head hunters: Woman officer's intrepid journey to carry the message of a saviour's love. *The War Cry* (April 19):4.

van den Berg, Johannes. 1956. *Constrained by Jesus' love: An inquiry into the motives of the missionary awakening in Great Britain in the period between 1698 and 1815.* Kampen, The Netherlands: J. H. Kok.

van der Kroef, Justus M. 1970. Messianic movements in the Celebes, Sumatra and Borneo. In *Millennial dreams in action,* ed. S. Thrupp, 80–121. New York: Schocken Books.

van der Veer, Pieter. 1996. Introduction. In *Conversion to modernities: The globalization of Christianity,* ed. P. van der Veer, 1–21. New York and London: Routledge.

Van Esterik, Penny. 1982. *Women of Southeast Asia*. Northern Illinois University Series on Southeast Asia, Occasional Paper no. 9. DeKalb: Northern Illinois University.

van Leur, J. C. 1967. *Indonesian trade and society*. The Hague: W. Van Hoeve.

van Roorden, Peter. 1996. Nineteenth-century representations of missionary conversion and the transformation of Western Christianity. In *Conversion to modernities: The globalization of Christianity*, ed. P. van de Veer, 65–87. New York and London: Routledge.

De Vogel, H. 1909. Unpublished letter from Assistant Resident H. De Vogel to A. C. Kruyt, dated October 11. The Kruyt Archives, Hendrik Kraemer Instituut, Oegstgeest, The Netherlands.

Volkman, Toby Alice. 1980. The pig has eaten the vegetables: Ritual and change in Tana Toraja. Ph.D. dissertation, Cornell University.

———. 1985. *Feasts of honor: Ritual and change in the Toraja highlands*. Illinois Studies in Anthropology no. 16. Urbana: University of Illinois Press.

———. 1987. Mortuary tourism in Tana Toraja. In *Indonesian religions in transition*, ed. R. Smith Kipp and S. Rodgers, 161–167. Tucson: University of Arizona Press.

———. 1990. Visions and revisions: Toraja culture and the tourist gaze. *American Ethnologist* 17(1):91–110.

Wallace, Anthony F. C. 1966. *Religion: An anthropological view*. New York: Random House.

Warren, Carol. 1990. Rhetoric and resistance: Popular political culture in Bali. *Anthropological Forum* 6(2):191–205.

Waterson, Helen Roxana. 1981. The economic and social position of women in Tana Toraja. Ph.D. dissertation, Cambridge University, England.

Weber, Max. 1930. *The Protestant ethic and the spirit of capitalism*, trans. T. Parsons. London: Allen and Unwin.

———. 1958. *The religion of India*, trans. and ed. H. H. Gerth and D. Martindale. New York: The Free Press.

———. 1965. *The sociology of religion*, trans. E. Fischoff. Boston: Beacon Press.

Wehr, Hans. 1976. *Arabic-English dictionary*. 3d ed., ed. J. M. Cowan. Ithaca, N.Y.: Spoken Language Service, Inc.

Weiner, Annette B. 1985. Inalienable wealth. *American Ethnologist* 12(2):210–227.

Weinstock, Joseph A. 1981. Kaharingan: Borneo's "oldest religion" becomes Indonesia's newest religion. *Borneo Research Bulletin* 13(1):47–48.

———. 1987. Kaharingan: Life and death in southern Borneo. In *Indonesian religions in transition*, ed. R. Smith Kipp and S. Rodgers, 71–97. Tucson: University of Arizona Press.

Wessing, Robert. 1999. A reverberating voice: Some slit-drums of Indonesia. In *Structuralism's transformations: Order and revision in Indonesian and Malaysian societies*, ed. L. V. Aragon and S. D. Russell, 115–140. Tempe: Arizona State University Program for Southeast Asian Studies.

Wheatley, Paul. 1983. *Nagára and commandery: Origins of Southeast Asian urban traditions*. Chicago: Chicago University Press.

Whittier, Herbert, L. 1977. Changing concepts of *adat* and cosmology among the Kenyah Dayak of Borneo: The shaman as a structural mechanic. Paper presented at the 26th Midwest Conference on Asian Affairs, October 14–15, 1977, DeKalb, Ill.

———. 1978. Concepts of adat and cosmology among the Kenyah Dayak of Borneo: Coping with the changing socio-cultural milieu. *The Sarawak Museum Journal* 26(47):103–113.

Wiener, Margaret J. 1995. *Visible and invisible realms. Power, magic, and colonial conquest in Bali*. Chicago: University of Chicago Press.

Willis, Avery T., Jr. 1977. *Indonesian revival: Why two million came to Christ*. South Pasadena, Calif.: William Carey Library.

Winstedt, Richard. 1982 [1951]. *The Malay magician*. Kuala Lumpur: Oxford University Press.

Wolf, Diane. 1992. *Factory daughters: Gender, household dynamics, and rural industrialization in Java*. Berkeley: University of California Press.

Wolff, John U. 1972. *A dictionary of Cebuano Visayan*. Ithaca, N.Y.: Cornell University Press.

Wolters, Oliver W. 1970. *The fall of Srivijaya in Malay history*. Ithaca, N.Y.: Cornell University Press.

Woodward, Leonard H. 1933. Army building in Celebes. *The Officers' Review* (January):11–16.

Woodward, Mark R. 1989. *Islam in Java: Normative piety and mysticism in the Sultanate of Yogyakarta*. Tucson: The University of Arizona Press.

———. 1998. Indonesia—February 1998: Financial, political, and spiritual crisis. *Antara Kita* 53 (March):2–19.

Wycliffe Bible Translators. 1987. *Kareba Lompe' to na'uki Lukas pai' tutura pobago suro Pue' Yesus* (The Good News written by Luke and the story of the Acts of the messengers of Lord Jesus). South Holland, Ill.: World Home Bible League.

———. 1996. *Buku Tomoroli' Pojanci to To'u: Kareba Lompe' hi rala basa Uma hante Buku Rona'* (Holy Bible New Testament: The Good News in Uma language with songs). Jakarta: Lembag Alkitab Indonesia.

Yampolsky, Philip. 1995. Forces for change in the regional performing arts of Indonesia. *Bijdragen tot de Taal-, Land-, en Volkenkunde* 151(4):700–725.

Yunus, H. Ahmad, and Zohra Mahmud. 1986/1987. *Adat istiadat daerah Sulawesi Tengah* (Traditions of the Central Sulawesi region). Jakarta: Proyek Penelitian dan Pencatatan Kebudayaan Daerah, Departemen Pendidikan dan Kebudayaan.

Zehner, Edwin. 1996. Thai Protestants and local supernaturalism: Changing configurations. *Journal of Southeast Asian Studies* 27(2):293–319.

Index

Abendanon, E.C., 112

Acculturation, 8–9

Adat: boundary with religion, 15–16, 158–163, 184, 191–192, 263, 270; etymology of term, 158; performances of, 269–273; violation of, 292. *See also* Religion; Rituals

Adriani, Nicolaus: arrival in Sulawesi, 102; death of, 110; on Islam, 90–91; linguistic studies of, 102–103, 106, 137, 176, 205; on social structure, 73; on songs, 257–258. *See also* Kruyt

Afterlife, 166–167, 171, 181, 196–197. *See also* Heaven; Hell

Agama: before and after, 14–15; compared to *adat*, 158–163, 263; official list of, 281. See also *Adat*; Religion; World religions

Agriculture: burning fields, 211; choosing land, 210–211, 328n. 2; cosmology of, 55–56, 188, 192, 196, 221–223; dry season, 211; farming cycle, 62; harvest, 205–209; during Japanese occupation, 143–144; and missionization, 108–110, 154–155; permanent, 23, 57, 60, 74, 332n. 4; planting, 211–213; rituals of, 205–213, 236–239, 259; shifting, 55–57, 59–60, 62–65, 332n. 4; in transmigration projects, 303; wage labor in, 299; and women, 78–79, 299. *See also* Foods; Land; Rituals

Ambon, conflict in, 2

Ancestors: authority of, 240, 270–271, 326, 328n. 1; in Bible, 180; compared with missionaries, 31; knowledge of, 184; naming of, 175; relations with, 6, 170, 193, 221–225, 248, 273, 292; spirits of, 168–175; views about, 28, 30. *See also* Spirits

Angels, 22, 195

Animals: anoa, 86; birds, 199, 242, 259; buffalo, 192, 209–210, 216, 222, 271; cats, 188; cattle, 192–193, 216, 222, 249; chickens, 206, 208–214, 225, 231, 234–235; fish, 197; goats, 316; horses, 191, 227–228, 250–251; pigs, 118, 209, 211, 216–217, 219, 222–225, 232–235, 316; prawns, 183; in rice gardens, 226; rodents, 221, 234, 242; stories about, 188; taboo names for, 128. *See also* Food; Sacrifices

Animism: in Central Sulawesi cosmology, 28–29; definitions of, 28, 164; Kruyt's writings on, 110, 164–167; Sulawesi Christianity as, 33, 36

Anthropology, recent trends in, 42, 327n. 3

Arabic, 158, 172, 174, 240, 260, 315, 331n. 1

Financial crisis, beginning in 1997, 2, 278, 306, 318, 328n. 4

Fishing: use of poison for, 197; on Sundays, 227

Foods: for babies, 296–297; of coastal peoples, 49–50, 315; of foreigners, 298; of interior peoples, 50, 59–60, 62–65, 206–207, 212–213, 227, 298; as offerings, 259, 273; for officers, 230; praying over, 246; religious meanings of, 203, 212, 231, 234–236, 284; utensils for, 298; women's and men's rights over, 80; for workers, 299. *See also* Agriculture; Animals; Taboos

Forests, 50, 60–63. *See also* Agriculture; Environment

Founders: missionaries as, 31, 89, 104; origins of cults, 56, 87–89; and ownership, 169; precedence of, 199, 303–304; as precolonial leaders, 73–75, 90–91; of rice gardens, 31. *See also* Spirits

Frazer, Sir James George, 17–18

Fundamentalism, 39, 45. *See also* Fanaticism; Islam

Funerals. *See* Death

Geertz, Clifford, 18, 39

Gender: in dances and songs, 254–255, 265, 268–269; of deities, 173; and the Indonesian state, 276, 279, 293–302; and inheritance, 67; during Japanese occupation, 142; and land rights, 61; missionaries' changes to, 80–81, 299–302; of shamans, 331n. 2; and speech, 241–242; symbols of, 215; and travel, 49, 307; women's and men's roles, 77–82, 212–213, 220. *See also* Kinship; Women

Gifts: ethnographer's, 51, 195; highland and lowland, 96–99; at holidays, 315;

missionaries' use of, 129–134; religion as, 16; as religious offerings, 97; and stratification, 99. *See also* Trade

Globalization: concept of, 8; institutions of, 21; and missionization, 5, 44, 305; process in Sulawesi, 306; and religions, 40; and trade with Indonesia, 41. *See also* Economic development

God(s): anger of, 183–184, 197, 238; expectations of, 170, 227; omniscience of, 195; petitions to, 244; portrayal of, 169–170, 173; praise for, 253; reclassification of, 30, 158, 167–175, 238–239, 323–324; of rice, 173, 208; will of, 21, 186–193, 197. *See also* Spirits

GOLKAR (Golongan Karya), 152, 332n. 2. *See also* Indonesian government; New Order

Gospel. *See* Bible

Govaars, Gerrit, 117–118

Government. *See* Indonesian government; State

Grubauer, Albert, 112

Habibie, President B.J., 2, 317

Harris, William, 125–126, 137

Headhunting: 34, 91, 113, 124, 189, 327n. 2, 329n. 3, 329–330n. 1; missionary views of, 127, 164; rumors of, 308. *See also* Violence; War

Headmen. *See* Leaders, village headmen

Health: state regulation of, 287–288; 293–302. *See also* Illnesses

Heaven, 128, 183. *See also* Afterlife

Hell, 30, 128, 183, 254. *See also* Afterlife

Hierarchy. *See* Status

Hinduism: in India, 88; in Indonesia, 33, 281, 311

History, construction of, 84

Holy Spirit, 165, 174. *See also* Spirits

Westerners' introduction of, 130, 132, 286. *See also* Capitalism

Monotheism: as government aim, 22, 263, 271, 276; and *Pancasila*, 152, 281, 311–312, 318–319

Morality, as tied to concrete events, 36

Music: American pop, 306; Christian pop, 183, 269; at death, 219–220; flute, 136; hymns, 30–31, 204, 206, 247, 269; precolonial songs, 207, 269; revivals of, 262; as ritual petition, 242; of Salvation Army, 13, 116–117, 124, 136; temple drums, 75. See also *Raego'*

Muslims: conflict with Christians, 1, 150–151, 275, 303–304, 314, 317–319, 325–326; district leadership by, 266–267; as favored group, 309; government fear of, 24, 275, 281; historic connections with Christians, 221; homelands of, 24; as majority, 1, 22, 282; marrying Christians, 252; mission schools for, 105–106; population of, 4, 282, 311, 313–314; religious services of, 315–316; rivalry with Christians, 140–141, 192, 310–319; scholarly views of, 44–45; separation from highlanders, 116, 323. *See also* Islam

Names: for babies, 216; of deities, 169, 173–175, 238–239, 323–324; of ethnic groups, 47–48; European changes to, 32, 70, 72, 136, 139; taboo, 174–175; Tobaku terms, 70–72, 136, 244

Nationalism: development of, 140, 332n. 1; limits of, 305–310; New Order goals for, 3, 34, 244, 273, 275, 311–312, 316. *See also* State

Nature, position of humans in, 18. *See also* Environment

Nelwan, Philippus, 122

Netherlands, 100–101

Netherlands Bible Society, 102. *See also* Adriani

Netherlands East Indies. *See* Dutch colonial government

Netherlands Missionary Society (Nederlands Zendelinggenootschap), 101

New Order: bureaucracy of, 159; and churches, 275–277, 282, 287, 319; criticism of, 312–313, 319; dates of, 14; development during, 275–280, 287–305, 325; elections of, 152, 308, 332n. 2; goals for nationalism, 244, 315–319; goals for women, 276, 293–297; health care during, 287–305. *See also Pancasila*; Suharto

New Tribes Mission, 33, 107, 185, 279–280, 282, 285–287, 309, 329n. 3

Nobles. *See* Leaders

North Carolina, 9, 41

North Sulawesi, 105–106, 140, 149, 183, 266. *See also* Manado; Minahasa

Oaths. *See* Promises

Orthodoxy: accepted, 26; debates over, 35–37; as untenable idea, 16, 45–46, 320

Overseas Missionary Fellowship, 282

Owner deities, xii, 30, 62, 87–88, 169–170, 173, 197; addressed in song, 259; bargains with, 154–155, 209–211, 238; link to kinship, 97; missionary views of, 127; retribution by, 222–223; of rice, 173, 208. *See also* Spirits

Ownership, concepts of, 157, 168–173, 327n. 3

Paganism: and the Bible, 190; colonial terms for, 52–53; consequences of,

ranking of, 117, 301–302, 307; relations with congregations, 198–201, 236–239; and trade, 140–141, 227; during wars, 147–148, 150
Sanskrit, 74, 260, 263, 311, 315
Sarasin, Paul and Fritz, 112
Satan: 125–128, 167, 172–173, 175; Western views of, 182. *See also* God(s); Spirits
Schools: curriculum, 106–107, 138; government aims for, 307; highlanders' aims for, 299; Kruyt's early control of, 103; loss of texts by, 153; and missionization, 40, 101–106; for nurses, 299–301; for officers, 139, 301–302; of Salvation Army, 121–122, 136–140, 147; teachers for, 106, 134, 138–140, 183
Science, and animism, 29. *See also* Evolution
Settlements: founding of, 89; patterns of, 105, 141; rearrangement of, 23, 48, 57–59, 105, 141, 302–305; support for officers in, 232–233. *See also* Founders
Seventh Day Adventist Church, 283–284, 286
Shamans: compared to officers, 22, 28, 205–208, 221, 225, 229–234; compared to Pentecostals, 283; conversion of, 153–155, 248; missionary views of, 127; names for, 255, 330–331n. 2; precolonial role of, 75, 196, 229, 288–289; rituals led by, 209–215, 255; transvestite, 271, 331n. 2. *See also* Rituals
Shinto religion, 40
SIL. *See* Summer Institute of Linguistics
Sin, 186–187, 191, 194, 200; ancestral wrongs as, 222–225; committed for others, 227; disavowal of, 250; of idleness, 257. *See also* Punishments

Slavery: among highlanders, 73–74, 76–77, 93–95; by Japanese, 142–149. *See also* Status; War
Songs. *See* Music; *Raego'*
Sorcery, 183, 187, 196–197, 223, 249
Souls: Protestant concepts of, 157, 163, 174, 330n. 4; Sulawesi concepts of, 163–167, 330n. 2. *See also* Spirits
Southeast Asia: ethnicity in, 52, 311; gender in, 77; religion in, 56, 88, 311; stratification in, 75, 98–99. *See also* Buddhism; Founders
South Sulawesi: ancestral religions in, 281, 313, 331n. 2; churches from, 283; clothing of, 64; conflict in, 2, 314; ethnicity in, 52; government officials from, 307; kingdoms of, 90–93, 172; rebellion from, 149; trade with, 91. *See also* Bugis; Toraja
Speech. *See* Language
Spirits: ancestral, 6, 87, 106, 149, 168–173, 225, 229, 238; breath, 163, 165–166, 174, 330n. 4; dangerous, 71, 147, 168–173, 183, 214–215, 220, 292, 330n. 3; missionaries' views of, 126–128, 329–330n. 1; owner deities, xii, 30, 62, 87, 127, 168–170, 173, 238, 259; semangat, 165–166, 330n. 2; shadow, 163, 165–167, 171, 181, 292. *See also* God(s); Satan; Souls
Spiritual, problems with concept, 17
State: control over domestic life, 287–288; development of, 16, 332n. 1; and religion, 325, 331n. 3; separation from church, 5. *See also* Indonesian government; Nationalism
Status: in Dutch colonial period, 73, 95; in New Order government, 31; among Tobaku, 73–77; village hierarchies, 32. *See also* Founders; Gender; Leaders; Wealth
Subsistence. *See* Agriculture; Foods

Woodward, Maggie, 122–123, 147–148
World religions: alteration of, 7;
    boundary with *adat*, 160–163, 270;
    characteristics of, 40, 158, 325–326;
    in competition, 314–319, 325; and

ethnic minorities, 310–311; as state
    requirement, 5, 281, 311–313, 325.
    See also *Adat*; Religion
Wycliffe Bible Society. *See* Summer
    Institute of Linguistics

About the Author

Lorraine V. Aragon has conducted research on Central Sulawesi, Indonesia, since 1984. She earned an M.A. from the University of Pennsylvania, and a Ph.D. in anthropology from the University of Illinois in 1992. She is coauthor (with Paul Taylor) of *Beyond the Java Sea: Art of Indonesia's Outer Islands* (1991), and coeditor (with Susan D. Russell) of *Structuralism's Transformations: Order and Revision in Indonesian and Malaysian Societies* (1999). Her research articles are published in *American Ethnologist, Ethnomusicology, Ethnos,* and *Journal of Southeast Asian Studies.* Lorraine Aragon currently is Visiting Associate Professor in the Department of Anthropology at East Carolina University in Greenville, North Carolina.